COURTNEY KING DYE

An autobiography

Courtney's Quest

Courtney's Quest 2014 © Copyright Courtney King Dye

Publisher: Words In The Works LLC
info@wordsintheworks.com

ISBN 978-0-9910364-4-8

Cover Photo: Judith M. Bosco
www.judybosco.smugmug.com

Cover Design & Photo Editing: Nina Marie Rambo
www.ninamariephotography.com

This book is dedicated to the countless people—both those I know and the many I've never met—who have been unfailing in their support, who have carried me toward my goals and been there for me through the toughest times with unrelenting love.

Foreword

Originally I hired a ghost writer because, although I can write, I wasn't confident in my ability to put everything together to create a cohesive, flowing book. As we got underway though, I realized that no one, no matter how good of a writer, can write my story but me and to expect someone else to do so was unfair. Not only do I feel that my own voice is the only way to properly convey the intensity of emotions, but once we started working and I was reading through the story of my life, many unimportant but amusing snippets occurred to me. It dawned on me that when I put myself in the moment, details I'd never have thought to discuss in an interview revealed themselves and perhaps they'd give the story character, allow the reader to experience *with* me instead of read *about* me. Once I started writing solo, it was an immense amount of fun. I'm almost sad it's done.

I hope you enjoy reading it a fraction of how much I enjoyed writing it.

Some names have been changed to respect people's privacy. There is also a glossary at the end of the book for those readers unfamiliar with horse terminology.

Prologue

It's 1:30 a.m. Friday, April 26, 2012 and I'm lying in bed. I tell myself that if I pretend the right side of my body works properly, maybe it will. If I simply forget about the effects of my brain injury, perhaps my body will forget, too. Mind over matter.

So I try to nonchalantly roll onto my left side. My shoulders turn an inch but the right side of my body is like dead weight. Like half of a cadaver. Every single morning my body confirms its inability to function normally and every single morning I'm surprised. That a miracle hasn't taken place. That overnight my brain hasn't figured out how to heal itself.

Sometimes I have dreams that I forgot my cane, without which reality necessitates a person hold onto me. I'm loping up long pavilion steps and my sister and husband are standing at the top cheering me on. The steps become bigger and my strides easily match them, the wind blows my hair and the sun peeks through the clouds. It's like one of those ridiculously cheesy movies with two lovers running towards each other in slow motion, except I'm not running towards anyone. I'm just running.

I reach over for the glass containing Xyrem, the one sleeping aid the doctors have found that works on me. The drug boys dump in girls' drinks to make them unable to fight off sex. The date-rape drug. It's made a horrendous flavor in order to prevent this misuse but it's worth it. I need sleep.

Today I ride in the Houston CPDI, my first Para Dressage show and a qualifier for the Paralympic Selection Trials. People comment that it must be so frustrating, depressing, infuriating to ride at my current level—walk only—when three and a half years ago, I rode in the able-bodied Olympics. I never even think about it. I have different struggles now but they absorb my focus as much as canter pirouettes or one-time flying changes used to. Work on what you can control.

Waiting for the drug to kick in, I ride the pattern of the test I do tomorrow. As I do the night before every show while waiting for sleep.

At 6:45, I swing my legs off the bed and push myself into a sitting position. As my right heel presses to the ground, my leg begins bouncing up and down like a person does when they're nervous or impatient. Doctors call it clonus due to the spasticity caused by my injury, but I refer to it as Thumper as that's the sound it makes. When it subsides, I pick up my cane and carefully walk to the bathroom thinking of the two things I'm currently working on: shoulders back and butt in.

I pause in front of the mirror and smile at my reflection. The right side of my mouth lags, doesn't rise as much as the left. My left eye scrunches properly and, although my right eye is clearly trying, the cheek simply won't rise enough to finish the task. Jason, my husband, comes in and says, That's getting better. My reflection nods in reply. Small steps.

I look into one eye and then the other and my brow furls. I *will* return to the Grand Prix ring, do a second Olympics. Maybe I'll surprise the equestrian world and have a sudden miraculous recovery. In the meantime, Para provides an excellent way to appease my competitive heart in what my body can do now.

My show clothes are strategically placed in the closet at shoulder level to allow their retrieval. Righty, my right hand, pulls them off the shelf as the more I use him, the more my brain will remember how to communicate with him, and Lefty throws them on the bed as Righty still lacks the ability to release. I sit on the bed to pull on my sports bra and shirt and lie down to do my underwear and breeches as my lack of balance prevents upright dressing.

◆ ◆ ◆

We're staying in the Solana senior living home and as Jason, Koryn—my working student in the barn who's also become an ideal personal helper—and I make our way to the elevator, an elderly gentleman stops me and comments on how cool my cane is. I act shocked that he can see it because it has a camouflage design. He leans in, conspiratorially looks around, slides the handle from his cane and shows me it's a flask. Impressed, I ask him where he got it and he says he made it, he makes all sorts. He has time. He smiles a toothless grin, gives a salute and shuffles away.

Time. Something I've never had enough of and now that I have it, I'm afraid of having too much. I'm very thankful that I have a great many other things within which I can invest myself. I teach riders. Am writing a book. Write monthly columns for a dressage magazine, am a mentor for an online journaling program. Ride. Paint and make clay sculptures. Do lots and lots of therapy. And more therapy. I'm never bored.

I *will* get better.

◆ ◆ ◆

We pull into the showgrounds and the scenery that's as familiar to me as the backs of my hands appears: several twenty by sixty meter riding arenas on brilliant beige footing surrounded by booths for the judges. Flowers and bushes decorate the perimeters and small paths of footing lead from one arena to the next.

When we walk into our aisle, Sydney Collier is peering into the stall of our shared mount, crutches supporting her five foot frame and her pink hair adding a bit of color to the otherwise bland horse show. She's fourteen and was born with Wyburn-Mason Syndrome, had a stroke during brain surgery followed by several more strokes. She was left with bilateral hemiparesis and is blind in her right eye.

In the week that I've known her, she's never made a complaint about her circumstances, revealed an iota of resentment. She bubbled over with joy when she told me about the therapy dog she's getting and cracked up as she told an anecdote of one of her frequent falls—the time she broke her collarbone. She's dear and sweet and joyful. Pure pleasure to be around. She instills the feeling of a good mood that settles on you for no particular reason.

Months ago I asked a woman why seeing me always makes people cry, and she said that witnessing the joy with which I still view life despite my hardships is extremely touching. Now I understand. Seeing the joy with which Sydney views life humbles me. Inspires me. Solidifies my need to take advantage of this wonderful life.

She's never had the chance to experience life outside of being handicapped whereas in my thirty-four years, I've ridden in the Olympics, danced on table tops, gone sky diving, jumped into water from fifty feet. I've lived life to the fullest so it makes sense that I can be content, but there are some things she'll never be able to do. Instead of wasting her time complaining about the unfairness of what life has dealt her, she chooses to be happy. Proves that we all have that choice.

◆ ◆ ◆

When it's time to get on, Koryn climbs onto the mounting platform with me and hands my right leg over the saddle to Jason who places it in the stirrup while Lendon, my trainer of seventeen years, holds the horse's head.

Koryn leads me into the stadium and my natural instinct to focus only on me and the horse prevents me from looking around. But when she lets me go and I walk up the centerline to start my test, it feels like I've returned home. There's been a storm outside and I'm battered, perhaps I was captured and beaten, but I'm home.

COURTNEY KING DYE

Horses to me are like
pepper to salt

Horses go with me
like blame goes with fault

Me guiding a horse is like
fate guiding love

Me on a horse is like
feathers on a dove

Always people are asking me,
"What's so special about horses, Courtney?"

This poem should explain
to me horses are not lame

They will always be in my life,
a constant companion like husband and wife

Journal of poems 1990-1993, thirteen to sixteen years old, untitled.

COURTNEY KING DYE

A Brief History

Mom and Dad were the perfect farm parents. Dad went to work and Mom took care of the four kids, cleaned and cooked big dinners every night. We had a plethora of pets. Our house pets included cats, bunnies, dogs, hamsters, mice, rats, canaries. We added animals from the wild to our domestic menagerie: a bat named Dracula, a squirrel named Sammy, a raccoon named Roxy, a crow named Isaac, a wolf named Josh, snakes, turtles, salamanders and toads. Our barns were filled with cows, pigs, chickens, goats, sheep, geese. And horses.

When I was seven, my parents divorced. Dad got the two boys, Gib and Gray, and Mom got the two girls, Greta and me. Dad's mentality of everything must fit in the box and Mom's mentality of box, circle, diamond, blob—whatever you make—stopped balancing each other out and our perfect farm life ended: the huge summer parties playing pin-the-tail on the donkey and having three-legged and wheelbarrow races, looking for silver dollars in the man-made beach, catching blue gills in the pond, looking for hidden treasures in the enormous stack of hay bales, driving Abby—my Shetland pony—around the field. When all the animals were sold, I realized I couldn't live without horses.

I started saving money to buy a horse of my own immediately. My five dollar allowance was a healthy start and I made sure to be able to keep the entire amount by never missing the school bus as Mom charged a dollar to give us a ride—her incentive for us to get up, dressed and be at the end of our five-hundred foot driveway on time without her help. To supplement my allowance, I found that if I stood at the end of the drive, which was gravel, and sold the rocks I picked up, people would stop and buy them. I also sold peanut butter—smashed peanuts mixed with butter—and dog treats which were hoof trimmings smeared in molasses and baked.

When I was nine, my mom moved us to Harbor Springs, Michigan, and my horse fund was able to grow exponentially. Our neighbor hired me as a mother's helper and my mom paid me fifteen cents a package to shrink wrap the artwork she was selling. I also got paid to mow our huge yard and clean the birdcages.

Dad gave me a packet of five riding lessons at a local stable, Black Forest Hall, for Christmas—his compromise for the HORSE that was always the only thing on my list. Upon completion, I told Mom with absolute certainty, I'm going to ride in the Olympics.

Abby, 1982, five years old

· 1 ·

My dad stands in front of the stove cooking eggs, hair still wet from the shower. I'm eleven years old, visiting him in Saginaw, Michigan, for the weekend and the pause after my plea seems eternal. Finally he rubs a hand through his moustache and slowly shakes his head. No, Courtney, I will not buy you a horse. You've been obsessed with horses forever. You need to be well-balanced, play team sports, have a group of friends.

But, Dad, if you bought me a horse, I wouldn't have to work at the barn so much and I promise that then I'll be more well-balanced! Please, Dad!

He leaves the stove and comes to stand in front of me, hands on hips. His top lip disappears under his moustache which it does when he's angry. No. It's what is best for you, Courtney. I'm not *not* buying you a horse to be mean. I love horses, I owned and trained them for years, but this obsession you have with them is too much. He walks back to his cooking.

The trembling in my lip travels to my chin and my forehead crumples in agonized frustration.

He serves the eggs and stays obtusely silent while he eats. I push my plate away and his fork pauses but he doesn't look at me. I wonder if it would help if I screamed. Pounded my fists on the table. Threw myself on the floor. What can I do to make him understand? This is no little-girl fantasy; I don't *want* a horse, I *need* a horse.

When he's finished, he asks if I'm ready to go, lip still hidden under moustache. I grab my suitcase in a huff and pointedly stomp out to his Cadillac. I miss the old blue van he used to drive when I was a kid. I miss the old dad. He would have bought me a horse but he's changed.

For the four hour drive to Harbor Springs, I listen to the whirr of car wheels and when he pulls up in front of my house, I sit still and stare at my knees, waiting for him to say something. He doesn't. He just gets out of the car, grabs my bag and opens my door. As I get out, he tries to hug me, but I recoil and run inside. I know he won't follow me because he and Mom will *not* see each other. I don't understand: how can you love someone and then hate them?

· · ·

My alarm goes off at five o'clock the next morning as it does every school day. After ten minutes, I convince my body to move and reach for the closest pair of jeans in the pile of clothes that carpet my floor. One in front of the other, my feet plod downstairs under protest, I put a granola bar in my pocket and begin the two and a half mile walk to the barn. After a half mile, the hill that continues all the way to the barn door begins and my brain goes back to sleep.

At long last, a gravel drive leads me between two large paddocks, the horses within which amble over to greet me, and as I enter the barn aisle the horses lean over their stall doors and nicker eagerly for breakfast. Their expectant faces, the aroma of hay, grain and shavings, the sounds of them munching on hay and moving around their stalls breathes life into me, awakens both my body and soul enough to join the living.

I go straight to Spring's stall to luxuriate in the feeling of her warm breath on my neck and imagine that she was my very own horse, that my dad gives her to me for my birthday tied in a big red ribbon. As she impatiently lips my hair, my imagination takes me all the way to the Olympics, but eventually she gives a shove to remind me that she's starving. After acquiescing to her demands and feeding, I give the necessary medications and muck stalls. The work not only earns my time in the saddle, it provides sustenance like a good bowl of porridge, fortifying me for the coming day.

The school bus picks me up at 7:50 and as I sit in class, my pen covers my folder with horses of every shape and size: fat ones, skinny ones, spooking ones, old sway-backed ones, ones lying down, galloping, prancing. As always, my school day is spent fantasizing about the future as well as an alternative present.

When the bell finally rings to dismiss us, I leap out of my chair and run to the school bus which will deposit me back at Black Forest for my lesson. As I wait my turn to get on, though, my stomach drops and I stop dead. Other kids give me dirty looks as they go around me while I frantically dig through my backpack in search of my breeches. As if they may have been hiding during my six classes. Upon confirming my horrible memory lapse, I try to think of any alternative to walking home to get them: could I borrow some? No one is even close to my size. Could I ride in jeans? My boots won't fit over them. Ride in my underwear?

I trudge the half mile home in spitting rain and after changing into almost clean breeches, begin the pointless task of begging my mom to give me a ride. She moved to Harbor Springs for the precise reason that we

7th grade

could walk to everything and wouldn't need a ride from her, so I know the chance is round about zero. She looks at me unsympathetically and takes a deep drag from her cigarette. Her long thin hand which matches her long thin body, elegantly holds the disgusting stick of nicotine. Pumpkin, you can't look to me to rescue you, she says. I glare at her and shout the obvious: It's raining! She glances at me, shrugs and continues working on her watercolor, short, mouse-brown hair bouncing with the movement.

I clamp my fists, give her my dirtiest stare—which she ignores—put on my raincoat and slam the door behind me. I don't even bother to wipe the tears from my cheeks. If someone pulled up and offered me a ride, stranger or not, I'd take it. She's not busy, she could take me if she wanted to, but *noooo*. She claims that her continual refusal to help us is to make us independent, is for our own good, but I'm certain it's just an excuse to be selfish. Most parents would never allow their nine, ten or eleven-year-old child to walk all this way alone.

When I was nine, she declared she was finished raising children. She makes it clear that she loves us, both by physical affection and constantly telling us how special we are—that we're extremely smart or talented, gifted in creativity as well as book smarts. But she loves us as one loves a friend, as if we're separate from her, not protecting, nurturing, guiding as a mother should.

When I get to the barn, the scent of hay soothes me and I feel more at home than I do in my own house. My instructor, Lou, walks out of the tack room as I'm returning to the solace of Spring's warm breath, closing my eyes and savoring the sensation.

You're too late for a lesson, he tells me. My eyes snap open to meet his and words tumble out of my mouth in an unorganized fashion trying to explain. When he makes no response, my head falls and tears join the raindrops on my coat. You can still ride, of course, he adds with a chuckle, putting his arm around me and giving a shake. Without looking up, I feign laughter, playfully push him away and reach for Spring's halter, but he puts a hand on my wrist and says, No, ma'am, you're riding Sox. I freeze.

Hey, if you're afraid of a bucking horse, you need to ride a bucking horse. He shrugs, turns and walks away.

I stare at his retreating form hoping he'll turn around and say he's kidding. When he goes through the tack room door, my gaze turns wistfully to Spring before my feet take me to Sox's stall. I slowly groom him, stroke his head, promise he'll get a ton of carrots if he doesn't buck me off.

When we go from trot to canter, he risks not deserving his carrots. My stomach clenches, my muscles become paralyzed and my face feels like it entered an incinerator as his butt goes toward the ceiling and his hind legs take flight toward the wall. Anger at my fear overcomes these reactions which my mind knows full well will only aid in his desire to dismiss me. My muscles return to life—although my face still feels like it's in an incinerator—and I hold his head up so he can't do a nose-between-toes bronco, try to be like a cattail and stay rooted while my body absorbs his motion.

When Sox eventually gives up and canters on, Lou hollers from the doorway to do trot to canter transitions until he doesn't buck at all. He's done with work, he doesn't have to help me, but he goes beyond the call of duty with my training. I bring my shoulders back and put my heels down more, raise my eyes to where they should be instead of focusing on his neck, try to look my best to earn his overtime. After twenty minutes of transitions, I get a trot to canter with no bucking. Good job, kiddo, Lou calls and walks away.

As Sox and I walk around to cool out, I think on what I learned: by riding a bucking horse, I was able to conquer my fear instead of always avoiding it. My heart fills with gratitude to Lou for forcing me to face it head-on. He says I'm his diamond in the rough, and I'm absolutely certain that although I'm coal now, he'll create a diamond.

When I dismount, I hug Sox and savor the feeling of his sweaty warmth on my cheek, the special odor of hot horse. He gets his ton of carrots and I genuinely look forward to the next time he's my mount.

Spring, 1989

• 2 •

The next year is spent adding to my horse fund however I can and worshipping Lou for the knowledge he's giving me. He takes me to a couple small competitions and even convinces my dad to lease Spring for me for the summer. I feel like I'm crawling toward the Olympics, but half way through my eighth grade year, he tells me he's quitting. I understand his leaving—we're in Podunk, Michigan—but I was improving because of him and my education will leave with him. Harbor Springs is no longer the path to my dream. A boarding school is my best option since no one will adopt me.

Dad's vehemence against my *obsession* with horses will doubtless prevent him from paying for a school for me to ride so although I know it's pointless, I go to Mom.

Sweetie, I can't afford to send you, but I think it would be great. If you really want it, I'm sure you'll find a way, she says, puts out her cigarette and looks back down at her painting.

After staring at the back of her head waiting for I don't know what, I hopelessly mope into the kitchen and collapse in a chair. Greta walks in and opens the fridge but when she hears my sniffling, she closes it, kneels in front of me and takes my hands. What happened, Court?

I look into her big brown eyes, tearing up because I'm crying even though she doesn't know why. Her appearance is the exact opposite of mine: small and curvy. She says she prayed every night she wouldn't be tall like Mom.

I tell her of the impossibility of my desire and we commiserate about how tough we have it—how Dad is so consumed with being *normal* and following the guidelines prescribed by society and Mom doesn't even follow the guidelines of normal parenting. When we return to my present dilemma, she offers a potential solution: a full scholarship to a boarding school.

I apply to four academies and weeks later, get a response from the Andrews School for Girls in Willoughby, Ohio. They won't give me a full scholarship but they'll give me one for seven thousand dollars.

After reading and rereading the letter several times in the hopes that it may change, I go to my mom again. Her face lights up.

You applied? she says with a big smile. See, Sugar Pie, I told you you'd figure out a way!

But, mom, they said no.

They'll give you seven thousand dollars! I don't have the eight thousand remainder, but I'll find a way.

My disappointment turns to elation. Eight thousand dollars is an enormous struggle for her and I deeply appreciate the way of thinking she's always shown me by word and action but which I haven't always agreed with: act now and you'll figure the rest out later because you have no choice.

◆ ◆ ◆

As she drives me down to my new school, my mom seems as excited as I am. When we pull in the driveway which is flanked by large fields and elegant colonial-style buildings, she takes my hand and I look at her with new tenderness. Her lessons are often weird—like when each of us was two years old, she blew out a match and burnt our hand saying HOT, so like Pavlov's dog we'd relate hearing that word to causing pain: the pond is hot, the outlet is hot. But she always makes us believe in ourselves by believing in us. I wouldn't have had the guts to attempt this plunge without her forcing my independence.

As I walk into my assigned room, my roommate, Molly, is crouching on the floor muttering to an open suitcase. Brimming with excitement, I introduce myself and she looks around, states her name, and then continues her conversation with the bag. I glance at my mom, who begins an uninterrupted soliloquy to Molly's back while I unpack.

Five days later, I'm woken by a continuous drip coming from the bed above me and turn on my bed lamp to see that the drips have left a yellow mark on my white comforter. I throw off the covers and leap out of bed, stare at the stream coming from Molly's mattress and bounce between anger and confusion. She sits up and looks from me to her urine, assessing the situation. She says she uses these plastic under-sheets...

I demand to know why she *chose* the top bunk? The plastic sheets may keep the mattress dry but what about the person beneath her? If bed-wetting is enough of a problem to necessitate *using* plastic sheets, why would she think of taking the top bunk?

◆ ◆ ◆

As the weeks pass by, there are none of the late night giggling sessions I'd imagined, no commiserating or sharing clothes and ideas, and Molly continues to prefer conversations with inanimate objects over me. Despite this disappointment, I revel in making friends at the barn with whom I can converse about horses. We muck stalls together, eat, live, go to school, to dances, the mall. Our lives are a continuous stream of silliness interrupted by the seriousness we each apply to our daily lessons.

After four months of appreciating the phenomenon of sharing a passion with girls my own age, however, I become frustrated. I enjoy our lessons as one does bowling or waterskiing, but they consist of taking turns jumping a course to the repetitive comments of good or do it again. No instruction. I could deal with the social and scholastic disappointments if my riding were improving but it's not.

Since I've been here, I've shared my many woes with my mom and she's always been sympathetic, comforts me as many moms would when their child is sick. But when I tell her I've decided not to return to Andrews for my sophomore year because it's not my path to the Olympics, she says, Pumpkin, you have the grass is greener on the other side syndrome. You don't think any place you live is the *path to your dreams*.

I dispute this and point out that I've only experienced Harbor and Andrews, but then it dawns on me that I've been approaching the problem completely the wrong way: how can I accomplish my dreams without a horse? I tell her that I want to live with Dad and when she expresses her surprise, explain my rationale: if I live with Dad, he'll get to know me and love me. If he loves me, he'll buy me a horse. She's dubious that he'll take me but supports the idea.

The next evening, I call my dad, tell him that I'm frustrated that I can do no work and still get A's. That socially this school is a letdown: my roommate peed on me and the two friends I made are graduating. I want to live with him. He says to let him talk to his wife, Pam, and he'll call me back. When he does, he says they're happy to have me. If I don't ride. I'm prepared for this stipulation, know they want me to do other things and be a regular kid. I often point out that getting up early on the weekends prevents other teenage mischief but this rationale doesn't alter his viewpoint. I tell him I'm ecstatic.

• 3 •

My dad's house sits in a perfectly manicured lawn surrounded by other perfectly manicured lawns. It's white and two stories with a basketball hoop in the driveway. Looks like it was taken out of *Better Homes and Gardens*.

Pam's son is away at college so I have his room and Dad carries my two big suitcases up the stairs in front of me. Well, I'll leave you to unpack, he says and squeezes my arm. When he walks out, I take in my surroundings. The carefully made bed. The neatly organized desk with a stapler, a paperweight and spare paper organized around its perimeter. I'm afraid that when I unpack, I'll mess something up.

I wander down the hallway to Gib's room. The wallpaper is green with ducks lining the top, the bedspreads are a subtle brown camouflage, a deer head protrudes from the wall next to a poster of a turkey with a bullseye on it. A bone collection decorates his dresser. It's total Gib but there's no teenage boy messiness. I'm a slob. But I can't be.

YO! I hear grunting loudly from the first floor followed by the stomping of an angry giant coming up the stairs two at a time. I smile and continue studying the rock with a fossilized bug I'm holding. Hey, little sis, what's up? he squeaks, converting his deep, gruff voice into a sound resembling a mouse.

Each of my siblings has an established role in the family and his is the clown. Gray's the smart one as when he was six years old, he took apart toasters and put them back together again. Greta's the normal one because she always has a boyfriend, a group of friends, plays sports, was the homecoming queen. I'm mislabeled the rebel for not doing what people—namely my dad—want. They don't understand that I don't do things *because* I'm told not to, but if I want to do something and am told not to, I'll do it despite anyone's misgivings.

Living with Gib is different from living with Greta; there's no emotional cleansing, but he provides support of another kind. He's the perfect example to follow for my goal of being a normal kid. When we start school, he introduces me to my first friend and I integrate myself in her group, gets me into the high school sorority that sisters his fraternity, and despite being atrocious at it, I cheerlead for his football team.

♦ ♦ ♦

One day, I'm sitting in the kitchen struggling with biology and my dad and Pam sit down with me. I think, *this can't be good*, lay my pencil on the table and look at them.

We'd like you to go to catechism and be confirmed Catholic, Dad says. Gib did, and we think you should, too. Dad used to be Presbyterian but Pam is Catholic, so when they got married, Dad was confirmed Catholic.

They're caught off guard by my enthusiastic acceptance of the request. Religion is something I've always wanted to understand. We went to church when I was young but as soon as my parents divorced, we stopped going because my mom's not religious. Most of the animals on the farm had Bible names: Obadiah and Hezekiah the pigs, Naomi the cat, Joshua the wolf, Isaac the crow, Mary, Abe, Judy and Joseph the horses. I want to know who these people were and why they're so important.

So once a week, I sit at a big round table with fourteen other people studying to become Catholic, but each class reduces my eagerness to continue. At the end of the fifteenth one, the teacher asks if there are any questions and I raise my hand. Why aren't we supposed to eat meat on Fridays?

She says, It's the day Jesus died. To show him we love him.

Why? Did he not eat meat on Fridays? Tell his disciples not to?

It's a sacrifice to honor his sacrifice, she says, gives me a don't be a smartass look and asks the class if there are any other questions.

I don't know whether the *teacher* doesn't know or if the reason is arbitrary, but I'm no closer to understanding Catholicism. I still have no idea who Obadiah or Hezekiah were.

On the ride home, I tell Dad I don't want to be confirmed. He coils his top lip in and asks why. I relate what just happened and he gives a similar explanation.

Why?

The rest of our car ride is in silence.

I go to the final two classes but vehemently tell Dad and Pam that I won't be confirmed. I guess they figure that in front of a crowd, I will, because they make me go to the ceremony anyway.

◆ ◆ ◆

I stand with the rest of the class in front of the congregation.

A gray-haired man with black rimmed spectacles calls each of our names to confirm our presence. Then he approaches the first student. Are you ready and willing to be confirmed? Upon acceptance, he dips his thumb in prism oil and makes the sign of the cross on her forehead. He then says, Receive the gift of the Holy Spirit.

He goes through the ritual with eight students and then comes to me. Are you ready and willing to be confirmed?

No.

He looks at me with his thumb in the oil, thinks I didn't hear him right.

Are you ready and willing to be confirmed? he repeats louder.

No.

He looks at me a moment and then continues on. I bring my chest up and look solidly ahead while he goes through the process with the remaining students. At the end, everyone goes down to be embraced and congratulated by their families and I walk out to Dad's Cadillac. The only sound in our twenty minute ride home is an occasional huff.

After seven months, I have a group of friends, played volleyball and basketball, was as much of a regular kid as I could be. I want to do everything Dad thinks I should, show him that I *can* be well-balanced—that not being so is a choice—but I can't pretend to believe in something I don't.

I thought the only explanation for him not supporting my riding was that he didn't know me and therefore couldn't love me, so I was sure that by living here I could win his affection. But what I didn't realize is that he already loves his daughter. He loves *her*, the idea he has of who I should be and he's trying his best to mold me into her. He thinks I'd be much better off if I were this person, is convinced that the road I want to take is filled with disappointment, that I'll regret everything I gave up when I wake up and realize life is full of other options. I know he wants what's best for me, but he wants what *he* thinks is best for me and places no value on my thoughts or feelings because I'm only sixteen.

I need to get out of here. I have no next plan, I just know it's not here.

• 4 •

The day after school gets out, I take the Greyhound bus to Harbor Springs and Greta picks me up. Golf courses line the drive home and as always, I imagine galloping through them and jumping the decorative hedges and logs. This is the sort of freedom I need in life: to focus all my energy on leaping my chosen hurdle. The necessity to go to school snuffs out this freedom and severely limits my path options. It's like a leadline that keeps me in tight circles if I run. An unnecessary impediment.

I walk around my house. Everything's unchanged: the potpourri scent of the carpeting, the spider plants clinging to life above the TV, the sunken middle cushion on the flowered sofa. My room is unchanged, too. Clothes strewn about from my frenzied packing. My snake's aquarium abandoned on the floor. Breyer horse models on the shelf lining the perimeter of my room. Nothing will change in my life either. My riding education is at a standstill.

I lie on the bed and begin to fantasize, imagine what I could do with no school. Turn on my right side. Then on the left. Fantasies are supposed to be joyful but the sensation this creates must be similar to that of a paralyzed person fantasizing about walking: it elicits only agony.

Suddenly, the pounding in my head screeches to a halt. What if I graduated this year? Then I'd be free. I'll take double the classes, do two years in one.

I set my chin and before I unpack, my most purposeful strides carry me to the school.

Well, the principal says peering at my transcript, Your grades are good. And you've taken many of the classes our juniors do. He ponders me a moment and then gets up and walks out. I wait. Ten minutes. Fifteen. Twenty. Finally he comes back in, sits down and looks between me and my transcript. He blows out his nose but doesn't say anything.

It feels like leaden snakes are squirming around in my stomach and my nostrils begin to tingle threatening tears. He looks in my eyes. Do you think you can do two college courses? I nod and the snakes freeze. And keep your grades up? I continue nodding and a smile begins to join the brewing tears. He raises his eyebrows. OK then, he says, welcome to the class of 1995.

Instead of walking home, my feet carry me straight to the barn while I fantasize about what next year will bring. Now the fantasy elicits jubilation and I barely feel my feet touch the ground.

• • •

The dirt aisle mixed with spilled shavings is raked crosswise back and forth as we were taught, the warm, clean, dirty smell wafting into my expanded nostrils. The first stall I go to is Spring's. Her butt is to the door but she ambles over to me, her big doe eyes searching to see if I have any treats. She lips my hand to make sure and I lean down to feel her warm breath on my cheek, breathe in that coveted scent of chewed hay. She lips my hair, loses interest and turns away.

I walk down the aisle and into the tack room, savor the aroma of a mixture of newly cleaned leather and horse sweat from the used saddle pads. Into the feed room next door and drink in the scent of molasses and sweet feed.

When I was away, I knew I missed the feel of the massive power beneath me, the soft muzzle breathing on me, the expectant eyes, but I didn't know till now that I missed the scent, the essence of a horse.

I actually enjoy my walk home.

◆ ◆ ◆

I spend several days composing a letter aimed at persuading my father that since I'll graduate a year early, I have a year to be a working student for a big-time rider before returning to college. Several weeks later, I get his response. It's fine to take that year, I'd earned it. He'd happily pay for school after that year if I don't ride. He wasn't going to pay for me to go to the barn every day, he wants me to have the whole college experience.

It's a pill I have no choice but to swallow. What he says is true: riding is an unstable income, exceptionally few make it big and it's dangerous, so I know that getting an education is imperative. But the fact that he doesn't give me a hard time about next year fills me with relief and excitement.

I need to save as much money as possible to prepare, so for the summer I get a night job at Cravings, the ice cream store where Greta works, and do chores at the barn during the day to earn both my riding as well as some pay. When school starts, I continue to work off my riding in the mornings and on weekends and I babysit as much as possible in the evenings. Other than clothes—which I continue to outgrow and Greta is smaller than I am—the only thing I consistently spend money on are toiletries such as shampoo, soap and tampons because my mom stipulated that when we turned thirteen, they became our responsibility.

◆ ◆ ◆

I tentatively accept a working student position in California. It sounds perfect. I'd get paid a small salary, be given a place to live and a horse to show. But in April, I come across an ad in a 1988 *Chronicle of the Horse* magazine that Lendon Gray, who was a member of the Olympic dressage team twice, is looking for a working student at her stable in Bedford, New York.

I constantly read about her in magazines. She's winning everything—and on a pony, no less, which is nearly unheard of. She's the only Olympian who placed an ad.

I take the magazine home and for days, the idea keeps nagging at me. I already have a job. But this may be my only chance. The ad is from nearly seven years ago so chances are slim that she's still looking. But if I don't try, I'll never know. This is my education and I'll leave no stone unturned.

With little hope, I dial the number.

Hullo, says a gruff monotone. Yes, she'll take a working student. There's no pay but I'd be given a place to stay. I'd work six or sometimes seven days a week. I'm not guaranteed the opportunity to even ride consistently much less compete.

The California situation sounds much better in every way, but something about the conversation with Lendon—her blatant honesty, her refusal to sugarcoat, no bullshit—makes me feel strongly that I should go to her. My gut demands it. I figure my money will last three to four months, then I'll go to California.

I'm nervous, but I'm excited. I'm scared to go, but I'm scared to stay. I take it.

◆ ◆ ◆

On my final night at home, I panic. What if I run out of money? Where would I go? Mom's selling the house and will live with a friend. I have five hundred dollars. After buying a train ticket, that will leave about three hundred. What if that's not enough? What then?

For several hours, I toss and turn, try to convince myself that everything will be all right. When one door closes, another one opens. I've known my path isn't straight and narrow and I'm prepared to jump from boulder to boulder as long as I'm traveling in the right direction.

This is the end of my dream chasing and the beginning of chasing my dream.

Journal

I love change and new situations but I hate to lose the past. I hate what can never be again. Sometimes I think about the date and time and how this time will never reoccur; this exact moment can never be replayed. We live each moment, and then it's gone. I love the past because it's full, it's certain. The future is empty, like a blank, white wall, waiting to be painted. And you just look at it, wondering where to start. Or sometimes you look at it and wonder where you'll finish.

• 5 •

Journal
I'm on my way to New York... on the train this very moment. So far I've only had one
sweep of emotion. It's to be expected though, right? I'm seventeen, moving to someplace
I've never seen and people I've never met to an ass-hard job with essentially no money.
But I do believe there's a reason for everything and this was meant to happen.

The train pulls into my station—Stamford, Connecticut—and the butterflies threaten to fly right out of my stomach. I peer around looking for someone resembling the photographs—maybe in white breeches and a tailcoat with a visible aura. When the crowd disperses and no one has approached, I sit on a bench and wait. Shuffle the contents of my backpack. Organize my hair. Read the train schedule. Read it again.

After forty-five minutes, I find a payphone. Stare at it and then walk back to my bench. After ten more, I return. Stare at it again. Then I resolutely pick it up and dial. The butterflies begin to ram into my stomach lining in a desperate attempt to get out.

Hullo.

Lendon, it's Courtney King, the working student you hired? I say in a voice an octave higher than normal. I'm at the train station.

Oh shoot, sorry, I completely forgot! I'll send Peter right over.

Twenty-five minutes later, a rusty brown Buick pulls up and a man steps out who I know is Peter because of the breeches he's wearing. He's about twenty-five, tall and good-looking. Which makes me aware of my non-good-lookingness.

As usual with new people, I'm consumed by awkwardness. I put one leg under the other trying to look cool. Tap my knee in rhythm although there's no music. Purposely look out the other window. When he eventually tells me about days at Sunnyfield, curiosity overcomes my anxiety and my butterflies relax into a calm flutter.

We go around a curve and the trees that have lined our journey suddenly give way to reveal rolling hills dotted with grazing horses and enveloping a huge riding arena. Four light yellow barns sitting amongst the acres and acres of paddocks complete the image of perfection and a sign saying Sunnyfield Farm announces we've reached my destination. All remaining nervousness floats away like pollen in the wind as I breathe in the mixture of horses, fresh fields and clover, close my eyes and savor it. All the years of trying to find my dream, this is it.

The driveway makes a steep decline facing the long side of the arena which is littered with women on horses. Some walking around and chatting, some elegantly moving sideways, some lengthening the strides. The one closest to me is doing a canter pirouette. It makes my skin tingle.

Peter opens my car door and grins at me. Come on, I'll introduce you to your roomie. We walk across the parking lot—my eyes never leaving the riding arena—to a barn shaped like an L, peek into a stall and Peter says, This is Meredith. She comes out, looks me over and smiles.

I'll show you our lovely room, she say and rolls her eyes. She's medium height and skinny. Her pale bordering on sallow face is surrounded by black hair and she wears a too-big T-shirt tucked only into the front of her breeches.

We walk silently on a paved road around the L barn, by a large manure pile and a ways further to a big indoor arena. This place is huge, fifty-three stalls. I'm sure I'll get lost.

A door for humans attaches to the arena and leads to a hallway decorated with framed magazine covers of Lendon. Meredith pauses while I stare at them in awe and then leads me to a stairwell with a dirty cement floor and rickety wooden steps. At the top, a large living room carpeted in yellow shag boasts a stained brown sofa and opens to a kitchen with food-smeared countertops and dishes surrounding the sink. The whole place suits my sloppy nature perfectly.

Then she opens a door and, commenting on its beauty, says it's our bedroom. There are two single beds, a dresser with the drawers open and clothes hanging out, and posters of heavy metal bands cover the walls. The smell of smoke is suffocating.

She plops down on her bed, lights a cigarette and asks if I have a horse. When I reply in the negative and ask if she does, she says, Yup, Nine Inch Nails. Call him Nails.

She tells me we share the apartment with two Mexican guys, Lupe and Conce, including the bathroom. But they cook, she adds as if it's their one redeeming quality. She pointedly exhales making her lips flap and says she better get back down to the barn before she gets in trouble. After taking a final drag of her cigarette, she reaches under the bed and pulls out a jar of water filled with butts to which she adds hers.

When she's gone, I look out the window at the horses speckling the property and my chest contracts, squeezing my pounding heart. Peter calls up to see if I'm ready to start the day and after one last look, my feet carry my body down the stairs while my brain remains on its cloud of ecstasy.

He pauses at the indoor to introduce me to Lendon who's riding a small gray horse. He says the horse is Last Scene, barn name "Scenic", and is her renowned Grand Prix almost pony. Without shoes he's fourteen-two hands, the official maximum height of a pony. With shoes, he's too tall.

Lendon has shortish dark hair and big glasses. She's cantering down the long side directly toward us looking straight ahead—in our direction but not at us—and doesn't appear to be moving at all. She's completely absorbing the motion of the canter, something I'm always aiming and failing, to achieve. Then I see she's actually doing one-tempi flying changes—the horse is changing his leading leg in the canter every stride as if he is skipping—and you can't see her doing anything.

The aim of dressage is to make it look like the horse is doing the movements of his own accord, to make the aids invisible. The best compliment a rider can be given is that it looked as if they were doing nothing. I knew it was possible but I've never seen it in person. Finally, I've found the place where the grass is green.

Journal
You know those dreams you have that are just so great it never really occurs to you that it's possible although you never consider it impossible either? Well, I'm basically living a dream I established more than ten years ago.

· 6 ·

Journal
I'm looking out on the beautiful farm, breathing in the hot air, still heavy from the thunder and rain, paddocks with open gates and a puddle in the ring large enough to house a family of geese. Tingles emerge inside my throat and travel the innards of my ears and out my nostrils.

I spend the first two weeks learning the barn chores and figuring out how to get from place to place. My riding entails walking horses to warm them up for Lendon or taking them for hacks through woods and watching her unfathomable ability to silently, invisibly communicate.

One day, she tells me to warm the horse up at trot and canter for her. I've heard her screaming, *I'm not a traffic cop!* several times when riders aren't looking where they're going and cut people off, so I'm very aware of keeping my eyes up.

Peter, follow, she hollers. Follow!

Pause.

Walk to me, Peter.

Pause.

Peter, walk to me!

Peter, are you listening to me? she screams and stands up.

There are eight people in the ring and even though only one is scheduled for a lesson, she teaches everyone, so I look around wondering if Peter is hard of hearing. But Peter's not here; they're all women. She's looking directly at me with her hands on her hips. I turn beet red and walk over to her. Sorry! I say. She just stares at me, makes me feel an inch tall. I guess I'm Peter.

Your first goal is to be a part of the horse, she tells me. Until you can be part of the horse and do *nothing*, you can't ask him to do *something*. She says the mistake many people make when trying to do nothing is to stay still. To stay still is doing nothing relative to the ground; to be still relative to the horse requires a great deal of movement. Your joints need to be pliable to absorb the motion. When your horse walks, his head goes forward and back, so in order for your hand to be still relative to the horse, your elbow must open and close. When his back moves, so should your seat.

This explains that illusive ability to do nothing and becomes my primary goal. Every afternoon I take Scenic for a hack in addition to the schooling Lendon does with him in the morning. The hack is for him—the hills help him build muscles without work, the trails relax him and he enjoys it—but I take advantage of this time to work on my ability to do nothing, to be part of him. If he turns to look at something, it's especially good practice because in order for there to be no change in pressure on his mouth, one hand has to be pulled forward to let his head turn and the other has to come back to take up the slack and maintain pressure.

◆ ◆ ◆

After a month I begin to get a Sunnyfield rhythm: be in the barn by 6:45, sweep the tack room, Lendon calls at 7, feed, scoop the next meal, give medications, turn out the first group of horses and weave in the basic work of laundry, sweeping, doing what clients ask, rotating the turn out and scooping meals to accommodate Lendon's schedule which includes grooming, warming up and hacking specified horses at specified times. Then medications, feed and scoop again.

One chore that comes every three weeks and is universally dreaded is unloading the hay delivery. Conce, Lupe and I develop a system: Conce throws the bales off the truck, I put them on a conveyor belt that carries them up to the loft where Lupe stacks them. One day, a light sprinkle that's been cooling us in the sun suddenly turns into a downpour. We abandon the hay and scramble to get the horses in from the steeply hilled fields which once wet, become very slippery.

We each make a mad dash to vacate the six fields and when all the horses are safely in their stalls, I look out at the storm and recollect: when I was young—maybe six, seven, eight—I'd take a dozen stuffed animals (dogs, horses, elephants) and hug them to me, pull a comforter over us and pretend it was storming outside. I was protecting them, our bond was protecting us all. As many kids daydream of being a rock star or an astronaut, this was my fantasy. To give security and therefore to get it. Now the barn provides this same feeling; it joins us in offering mutual security.

When the storm clears and the sun emerges, it strikes me that two worlds exist in this one farm, each rewarding me with a long desired wish. As much as the shelter provided by the farm makes me feel secure, it also makes me feel free. It's become clear and sunny and birds are chirping—like a fairytale, almost not real.

I need to ask Lendon a question so, basking in the glow of the sun on the newly cleansed earth, I walk to the outdoor arena where she's riding. A six foot blonde woman is standing by the fence speaking to her with a French accent, her belly bulging with pregnancy. He looks fabulous, she says. Donkey ears or no, this horse has it! Isn't he lovely? she says to me indicating Jester, the four-year-old Dutch Warmblood gelding she bought for Lendon, but it's more of a statement than a question. I'm Francine, she continues pronouncing the "a" like "audacious".

You own Mozart, too, right? I ask. She confirms and tells me she's been in the Adirondacks for the summer so she hasn't seen either horse in several months. Her gaze drifts back to Jester. My flying mule is growing up!

Lendon's looking for another one for you, right?

Not anymore. My husband says that for every horse I have, he gets a baby, so I think two is it. This is number one, she says pointing to her belly and smiling.

She looks right in my eyes as she says this, looks at me as if I matter. She has the twinkliest light blue eyes I've ever seen and is dressed impeccably, all in white. She doesn't seem to care if she gets dirty but she doesn't have a spot on her. I think she must buy new clothes every day—obviously, money is no issue. Board here is two thousand dollars a month so everyone here must be wealthy.

I never could have managed the cost of keeping a horse. Although I thought my dad was horribly mean for not buying me a horse all through my youth, I now know it was the best thing he could have done for me. Not having a horse actually gives me the freedom to chase my dreams.

◆ ◆ ◆

As I'm scooping dinner that evening, my head heavy with the realization of the good fortune I so resented, Meredith stomps in red in the face and ranting. I'm so sick of Lendon screaming at me! she spouts. Who does she think she is? Then she stands up tall, pulls her shoulders back and says, This morning I screamed right back at her, really put her in her place. It feels like she respects me now. She pauses and looks at me. You ought to try it sometime instead of being such a brownnoser.

But I'd seen the interchange. *Bullshit. Lendon decided you don't want to learn and gave up on you. She sees that I'll do anything to learn—I know I'm dirt, or coal—so she doesn't scream at me. Maybe you should try* that *instead of thinking you know something.*

Over the weeks, Meredith continues to have bouts with Lendon and repetitively backtalks. Eventually she leaves and I'm glad. She may be cool, but I don't want to be like her, don't want to be *with* her. Peter leaves too, so now I'm the only Peter.

I, on the other hand, need to find a way to stay. I don't want to go to California but my savings are well and truly gone—tonight will be my eighth night eating Raisin Bran for dinner. Babysitting and dogsitting aren't enough. Luckily I inherited some of my mom's artistic talent so I begin to commission horse paintings and design watches for a company one of Lendon's clients owns to supplement my meager income. At least it's enough to stay.

Journal
After all my discontent, I'm so glad I found my happiness, right inside of me. Coming here was such a good decision.

· 7 ·

Journal
The darkness comes earlier every day, and dawn takes longer to open her eyes. She must be sleepy. Tired of spreading the sunshine for everyone to enjoy. Tired of smiling for long breezeless days. Her heat is being slowly overcome by an intrusive chill and her bright flowers are beginning to feel the effects of the visits from one Jack Frost. It gets more and more difficult to peek her nose over the horizon each day, and she allows herself to fall back into the sea with less and less struggle. If you catch her just as she retires, if you catch the last glimpse before she's completely consumed by the Earth, you'll swear you can see her give a sad wink, promising she's not giving up. Promising to be back.

I spend the winter convincing my body to be part of the horse, teaching it to follow, and Lendon gradually increases the difficulty of the movements I ask of my horses. I never have lessons but I always try to ride when not many other people are hoping she'll give me attention, which she usually does.

I know Lendon teaches Lee at eight o'clock every morning and very few people normally ride that early, so I generally ride Roccoco then. He's a sixteen-two hand, jet black, nineteen-year-old Grand Prix gelding. He has a pudgy barrel on stick-like legs and I call him my burnt marshmallow.

He and Paiute, an Arabian who does endurance trail riding with his owner, Alex Rukeyser, are the first horses who are "mine". They're owned by other people but I always ride them when their owners can't. I'm their person.

One morning as I'm cantering around thinking of following with my left arm as much as my right and keeping my right leg as far back as my left, Lendon bellows, Diagonal, flying change, Peter!

I obediently go across the diagonal and do a single flying change.

Four-tempis! she shouts.

Flying changes are like jumping. When all his legs are in the air, the horse switches from one lead to the other. When doing tempis, which are changes every four, three, two or every stride, it's instinctual to *ask* for the change when you want to do it—ask for the change on four if you want to do fours.

I learned and am trying to teach my body, that you have to ask the stride before you want the change. And not only do you have to ask the stride before, you have to ask at a particular moment in that stride. There are three beats to every stride: the outside hind, then the diagonal pair of inside hind and outside front, then the inside front. You have to ask when the inside front leaves the ground, the final beat before all four legs are in the air and the change happens.

The first line, I do fives. The second line, I do two twos, a five, a three and another five.

It's hard to count to four isn't it? Lendon says with a chuckle.

I try once again and succeed. Then she asks for threes and when I get those, twos.

Now that my body has learned to do nothing, it's time to teach it how to speak. The language of dressage is as complex as Japanese and nearly as foreign. We first learn how to say words. Then our vocabulary expands and we learn phrases. Lendon speaks in complete sentences.

I love the mental aspect of the sport, it challenges my mind more than school ever has. Although maybe that's just because I care more.

Journal
Oh, I love this life. It's freezing cold, I'm utterly exhausted, work long days, live in filth. Man, it's heaven.

◆ ◆ ◆

Despite being happy and having confirmed that this is the life I want, I need to go back to school.

I know I'm fortunate to have a parent pay and not riding is a necessary sacrifice, so I apply and get into the University of Michigan.

Although I don't let it diminish my enjoyment of the education that makes my heart beat, the knowledge that my time here is limited is a continuous weight.

Journal
I hate squirming under the thumb of my father's checkbook. I feel like I'm living in the footprints of someone else.

• 8 •

Journal
What amazing creatures these are. So big. So sweet. And curious and confused and subordinate and rebellious. They love and they worry and they anticipate. Lukas worries so much. He worries about his work. He worries that he's not good enough, that I won't love him. I don't spend enough time telling him I do love him. Jester doesn't need to be told he's wonderful; he just needs to be entertained and bonded with and shown he's appreciated.

The appearance of spring, the warm April sun and cool air, somewhat alleviate the weight caused by my awareness that my time here is limited and are a welcome change from the winter of layering blankets on the horses, breaking ice out of the buckets and trying to maintain some circulation when bouncing back and forth between sweating and freezing. My ability to follow, to let my body be part of the horse, is becoming instinctual so I don't have to think about it and can just absorb the sunshine and enjoy being here.

I take Jester, who's become my horse in terms of hacking and basic work, for a hack through the woods and when I'm ambling past the ring where Lendon's giving a demonstration, she bellows, Come and show that horse off!

His movement is enormous. When he goes well, I can't imagine anything closer to riding a cloud, but he has somewhat of a delinquent brain so I know this will be interesting. I pick up my reins and as we walk by the group of onlookers, I can see the whites of his eyes. I barely put my leg on and he jumps into a massive floating trot, soft as butter in my hands. I can hear the comments of the crowd: Wow, that's incredible. What level is he? Is that his natural trot? Lendon always tells me that great dressage is being on the brink of out of control, and that's how I feel. On the cusp of my presence becoming inconsequential, his energy at the max and his movement challenging the boundaries of what his skin can contain.

Now this is a horse with a tremendous amount of talent. Courtney, don't just keep trotting around and around in circles, canter! Now, you'll rarely see a canter of this quality in a four-year-old, Lendon hollers to the people. I can feel the incredible swing of his back, the strain of his muscles yet the easy swing of his movement.

Lendon calls to take him through the caveletti, poles on the ground spaced evenly for the horse's stride. Two times we go through them and my mind is conscious only of the perfection and harmony of this ride. All my muscles relax and I allow my body to melt into his back as we change direction and come to the poles a third time. As we head toward them, a pony in the far field wheels and gallops off and Jester's head pops straight up to look at the commotion. I'm not quick enough to correct him and we meet the first pole wrong; he jumps the first two, trips over the third and then bucks. My still smiling face finds itself directly in the wet sand.

As I lie there slightly dazed, Lendon calls for the horse to be caught and begins teasing me sharply about choking under the spotlight. She pauses for a second realizing I'm not getting up. I don't know why I'm not getting up. I can hear the people joking and calling things to me.

Give her the horse. Get on, Courtney, she says abruptly. That was barely even a buck, J, she says turning to smile affectionately at the gelding who seems somewhat dazed at his success in finally getting me on the ground.

My arm is broken, I say.

Why do you think that? she demands unbelievingly but crawls beneath me so her lap is a pillow.

I heard a snap, crackle, pop, I say. Shit! I broke my arm! I start to cry, not from pain but from anger. I was so stupid! I knew I didn't have him set up right, I should have circled away!

Then I hear sirens. Two ambulances, a fire truck and two police cars file into the ring and with them comes the crowd from the barn.

Guess Bedford's pretty slow today, eh? I say to Lendon. She begins to get up and Lupe takes her spot as my pillow. She explains what happened to the man who's apparently in charge. She thinks she broke her arm, I hear her say.

He looks in my eyes, ask me some questions: the date. I don't know the date. I see his expression change and my eyes turn to Lendon. Hey, Lendon, what's the date today? I ask with a wry smile. She laughs and shrugs.

Horse people never know the date, I explain to the man. I'm fine. It's just my arm.

You hit your head, he says.

No I didn't, I say.

You may not remember. I begin to try to shift my weight up so I can look him in the face. Don't move, he warns as he kneels next to me. You may have injured your neck. We're going to put a neck brace on just in case, he says as gently as if he were breaking the news of a brain tumor.

My neck is fine.

It's just a precaution. They strap in my neck so I can only look at the faces above me, but I can still feel the commotion of all the little workers busying themselves with trying to find something wrong with me.

It's just my arm, I protest weakly under my breath.

Look at her legs, Bob, someone whispers.

Bob turns to Lendon, Have you seen her move her legs at all?

She says her arm is the only thing that hurts, Lendon answers shortly.

I'm sorry, but we're going to have to cut the boot off. Her leg looks very distorted.

That's it. I worked a whole summer saving up for these boots. A hundred-fifty dollars is a lot of babysitting for a fourteen-year-old.

My legs are fine, I say summoning up all my sternness.

I'm sorry, Courtney, Bob begins. Immediately, I pop both my legs out perfectly straight.

It's *just* my arm.

A few of the technicians laugh. Looks like she wants to keep the boots, Bob, one of them says. Finally their attention turns to my arm.

I wish they wouldn't all stand there and watch, I say feeling the presence of the whole barn looming around me.

They're just concerned, Lendon replies.

We're going to have to cut your sweatshirt so we can see what's going on, one of the technicians says. The cold metal and cool air on my arm are a relieving sensation from the tight burning on the inside. Tears stream down my face but I bite my lip to keep from crying.

I look around as far as the brace allows, can see the crowd from the barn moving in for a better look and all the excited technicians hovering over me waiting to see the treasured injury. I know we're a long way from the poles because we're close to the fence on the other side.

My gaze finally returns to Lupe. His eyes are glazed over with tears and his lower lip sticks out with the heaviness of his frown. His hands are gently trying to flatten the curls to my head. As I look at him, it all seems so silly to me. Here I am, in the mud, in the middle of a beautiful day with four-hundred people swarming around me. It seems so stupid that although it's only my arm that's broken, I can't even get up. And if I don't think about it and just lie here, it doesn't really hurt that much.

They wake me from my thoughts by telling me they're going to put my arm in a brace for the ride to the hospital. I think, no problem, then I won't have to clamp the muscles to hold it steady. But as they pry it into position I for the first time experience what I consider pain. I force a sigh, blink away the tears and say to Lupe, Better than a leg, huh? I can't afford new boots.

Well, the worst part's over. Good job, kid, Bob says. Now we're just going to lift you into the ambulance and you'll be all set. They bring over a long body-shaped board and lay it on the ground next to me.

I think if you just help me, I can get in, I say, strangely conscious that I don't want them to have to pick me up.

We've got to keep your back straight, just in case, he says with a smile. So tell me how that son of a bitch got you off. I tell him briefly what happened and suddenly it seems absolutely hilarious to me. Lendon regains her light attitude and begins teasing and telling stories of our past. She tells about some of my dealings with barn prima donnas, the time one particularly pristine client tried to get out of cleaning up her horse's manure by telling me she'd puke if she did. Lendon loved my response of, Well, then you'll have to clean that up too. Although at the time the loss of two-thousand dollars a month for board sort of overshadowed the humor. She explains to the emergency crew that my wild hair is the effect of me never brushing it and says, as she's told me many times, that I'm the only eighteen-year-old girl who's never used a blow dryer or a curling iron.

It's comforting to hear Lendon tell her stories. It's something she does when she's happy.

During this whole time my body's being turned and manipulated every which way, somewhat carelessly in the humor of the moment. I don't say anything. It almost makes me feel better that they aren't treating me as if I were a piece of cracked porcelain that may shatter from the smallest touch.

The cord designed to strap me onto the board is being twisted around and around with no apparent correct attachment. Finally the technician calls Bob to his attention. This isn't long enough, I can't get it attached here. Bob reaches over and begins pulling on the cord, tightening it in places and then pulling on it again, but he can't get it attached.

It's caught on my boob, I say.

What?

It's caught on my boob, I repeat as I twist my torso.

Everyone laughs. Leave it to Courtney to say it like it is, Lendon says.

◆ ◆ ◆

In the emergency room, many doctors try to twist my arm into the right position for the necessary x-rays. I brace and writhe and give every effort to remain still but the doctors seem exasperated that they can't get the arm in the right position. Lendon watches each of their attempts with cold condescending eyes. Most of the time I feel the doctor is more aware of her than of me and for once I'm grateful for her overwhelming powers of intimidation. This stare has diminished me to tears many times and I think about the five working students who've come and gone since I've been here. People generally don't stay at Lendon's for long because they're scared of her. Lying in my hospital bed, I realize that this stare, this critical surveillance we as students find so intimidating, is aimed at protecting the horses just as it's now used to protect me. For some reason people become very careful under her scrutiny.

Finally a doctor enters the room who doesn't reach for my arm. I'm sorry you had to go through that, he says and shifts uneasily under Lendon's stare. Your elbow is dislocated, which is why we couldn't get your arm in the right position for the x-rays. His eyes dart to Lendon then quickly back to me. We'll have to get a specialist down here to put it back in the socket since we can't see what else is wrong. It shouldn't be too long.

While we wait, I busy myself with imagining what the inside of my arm looks like with the long bone on the outside of the joint. All those tendons and ligaments must be stretched at very odd angles. The image my mind creates is interesting and makes the injury less scary. I don't have any tears left anyway and my eyes are uncomfortably dry.

After a while the specialist comes in complaining to his nurse that he shouldn't have to do ER. And for a workman's comp case. He takes my arm without acknowledging that it belongs to a person, they give me a healthy dose of valium and he pops it back into socket. Now I experience pain.

He shakes his head and finally looks at me. I look back at him. I hope everything works out, kid, he says and walks out.

After more x-rays are taken and another long wait, our first doctor comes in to give us the news. He says I shattered one of the three small bones in my elbow. It will require surgery to remove the pieces. He says I should act on this as soon as possible to ensure his estimated sixty to seventy percent recovery.

They secure my arm in a temporary cast and after Lendon has filled out some paperwork, I'm allowed to go home. On the way, Lendon says with a wan smile, Guess we know what the 'snap, crackle, pop' was.

◆ ◆ ◆

Two days later, Lendon takes me in for the surgery. One of her clients, Lynne, has connections with one of the best surgeons in New York, Andrew Bazos, and arranges for me to go to him.

I'm not scared. It seems unreal, distant. They say I should be in and out in around four hours, then I'll spend the weekend with Lynne recuperating before returning to the farm. When we fill out our paperwork, I write workman's comp on the billing and Lendon says not to worry about a thing.

My name is called and I'm taken to a room where they draw blood. To take my mind off the needle, the lady asks what happened and I tell my story once again. At the mention of Lendon Gray, the woman's face lights up; she's a big fan and her daughter has taken lessons with Lendon. Small world. I tell Lendon who it was, but unfortunately it's hard for her to recall all of the ten thousand students of her past. I tell her she better never forget me. She says I'm her family and she couldn't forget me if she wanted to.

◆ ◆ ◆

I think I open my eyes before I'm awake and now I'm sure I feel real pain. I have no breath and try to suck air as tears surge out of my half closed eyes. There are tubes coming out my nose and I'm in a room I've never seen before.

A woman comes over and says I'm in recovery, I've been asleep a long time. The surgery had gone fine. I'm confused. When was the surgery? When had they put me to sleep? I can't even feel my arm...my whole body feels broken. I look around. She says my friends can't come in here but I can go out soon.

When I open my eyes again, I'm in a different room. I don't remember when I was moved but I slowly become aware that someone's stroking my hair. I look up and see Lupe's big brown eyes traveling from my bandaged arm up to my eyes. When he sees they're open, his mouth drops a little bit and he says as lightly as he can, Good morning sunshine. It hurts again and my face tightens against the pain.

The next time I open my eyes, someone's still petting my head but it feels different. I try to focus. It's Lendon. I've never seen her look like this; her face is soft and she seems to be studying my hair... organizing it. She smiles when she sees my eyes. Tells me she sent Lupe home despite his protests to check on the barn. The nurses said I had to stay for the night. I try to tell her to go home, too, but I'm not sure I get it out.

I wake again in a large bed in a single room. It's dark and Lendon's sitting in a chair. She leans over to see if I'm awake. Tells me it's two in the morning and she has to go, she'll talk to me the next day. She stands above me and strokes my head. Then she turns and walks slowly out of the room.

◆　◆　◆

Dr. Bazos refuses to charge us for the eighteen-thousand dollar operation. Lendon won't say how the rest of the bills got paid but I know it wasn't covered by workman's comp. They tell me I'm looking at four to six weeks of doing nothing, six to eight months of physical therapy, seventy to eighty percent recovery, and most probably future wrist problems. This, they tell me, is very good and I'm lucky I had an excellent surgeon.

I spend a week recovering at Lynne's house before returning to the farm to be showered in gifts and sympathies. I'm on a horse in four days doing light hacks, and within two weeks I'm really riding and doing most barn work. Letting the horse's neck reach to the ground, which we do to stretch their backs, invites my arm to stretch as well, and because when the horse pulls down I *want* to let the arm follow, my arm doesn't resist so it's better than therapy. Before, when riding that arm was my problem arm; it was rigid. After, it somehow follows better so one of Lendon's favorite stories becomes telling how she fixed my left arm, and she constantly threatens students to use a similar method.

• 9 •

By mid-May, I'm well enough to enter my first real dressage show and Alex lets me take Paiute to Millbrook Dressage. Lendon is showing seven horses so I'm busy helping Lupe take care of them which keeps my mind off showing.

As I clean the manure stains off Paiute, who's gray and loves to use his manure as a pillow, I go through the pattern of the test over and over in my mind: First Level Test 1. Many riders at the lower levels have their patterns called—someone tells them where to go which gives the rider one less thing to think about—but Lendon forbids this. It's not allowed at the international levels, so why should we do it at the lower levels? I've seen her ride ten different tests in a day and she memorizes every one.

But despite my efforts to ingrain the pattern into my memory, when I enter the show ring it's gone. I'm so concerned about where to go next that I don't ride the *horse*, don't get nearly the quality of movement I do when I'm home. Accurate, yes, quality, no.

Lendon finishes a test at the same time I do and joins me for the walk back to the barn. She asks how it went and I explain what happened. She's silent. I look at her and wait. Say, How do you do it?

Well, twenty-five years. It takes practice, like anything, she answers.

Although she says it as just a fact, an honest answer not said to make me feel better, it does. This is the beginning. It alleviates my disappointment in the past and excites me for the future.

Then I ask how hers was. She was showing Mia, a mare I warm up for her who's extremely strong in the contact.

I just smiled and pretended she was soft as butter. My arms kill, she says with a chuckle.

I get a 62% and sixth place. She gets a 75% and high point of the show. 60-65% is good, 65-70% is very good and above 70% is excellent. 75% or over is very rare. I guess the judge was convinced that Mia was soft.

• • •

In July, I get to show Paiute First Level again but I also get to show Rekel Fourth Level. Beyond being daunted by the higher level, I've only ridden Rekel four times and he has a tendency to be naughty, so my goal is to not get last place.

I've spent the last two months memorizing and rememorizing Paiute's tests. I diagrammed an arena on a piece of paper with all the letters at their proper spots, and almost every evening, I drew the test pattern with my finger over and over again, so this time when I show Paiute I'm determined to know the pattern so well that I can ride *him*. But I'm not so confident with Rekel. Since we entered so late, I've only had a few days to memorize the tests.

I succeed in adding quality to accuracy in Paiute's test and he wins. To my surprise, the same thing happens with Rekel. In only a few days, I've memorized the test so well that I don't have to think where I'm going. He gets fourth place.

I knew showing would be enjoyable, but it's also useful; it highlights things to improve and tells you what would make them better. The riders are given their test sheet back which shows the score the judge gave each individual movement and comments on why they gave that score. Scores range from zero through ten and we're told *Halt: 5, not square*. Then we go home and our job is to figure out how to get the horse to halt with his legs square like the legs of a table.

Paiute

◆ ◆ ◆

Although my showing is done, opportunities I wouldn't have even fantasized about continue. Lendon's doing a demonstration at the 1996 Atlanta Olympics and she chooses me to be Scenic's groom. I get to eat lunch in the same room as Steffen Peters and Guenter Seidel. Robert Dover and Michelle Gibson. I get to see my idols, Isabell Werth and Klaus Balkenhol, win gold with the German team.

I still take my hacks on Scenic around the venue, which since I mastered following are always done bareback in a halter and lead rope. Girl bareback on white pony must be a sight to see at the Olympics. Lendon's demos are divine. If Scenic were eight inches taller, I'm sure he'd be competing.

On our way home, I bring up a topic that's been on my mind about my latest roommate, Renee.

Lendon?

Yeah.

Renee's been complaining about everything.

I know.

She's even complaining to the clients.

I know.

Silence.

Doesn't it bother you? Her posture is absolutely perfect, as it always is.

Yes. I'm going to clean house when we get back. Kick out all the sour apples.

Workers?

Workers and clients. Unhappiness breeds unhappiness.

Even though Lupe, one other groom and I will be left with an immense amount of work if she fires all the complainers, nothing could make me happier. She can easily replace the problematic clients because the farm is an hour from Manhattan and many city dwellers with money crave the rolling countryside the farm offers. She has a waiting list, so every client she kicks out will be replaced by another.

When we get home, she sends out a letter explaining the alteration. She says:

As most of you know, I have decided to make some changes and return to the way I used to run the stable. I hope that these changes will make all of us involved, both human and equine, happier and more productive.

There is a complete turnover in working students. All current working students will be leaving by August 23, which is Courtney's last day. Courtney will be sorely missed, but we hope she will return during her Christmas vacation from the University of Michigan. Courtney demonstrated unusual maturity and resilience during her year here and I am very proud to send her out into the equestrian world as my student.

This letter fills me with pride that she thinks highly of me but it also fills me with despair at leaving, at being replaced, at giving up what I've worked so hard to get.

Although intrinsic sadness and a dread of leaving cloak my last two weeks, the reduction in staff leaves my work days even longer than they were so there's no time to sulk. Instead I just immerse myself in my heaven and am cognizant of the poignancy of all I've learned. I found the sport through a love of horses and can think of no way to be closer to them. Good dressage is like being a centaur: your mind and the horse's body are one. Invisible communication, absolute harmony, power. It's not only riding, it's a complete relationship. And I'm happy here. This is the path

I've been searching for and I'm about to leave it.

• 10 •

Four years at the University of Michigan. 1996 to 2000. I can do it. The clients give me many gifts, tears, and see-you-soons. Lupe promises to call and write. Lendon says she hopes I come back next summer and Francine says she'll buy me a ticket to come back for Christmas.

Journal
Here's my Wish List:
Do really well in school.
Have fun.
Get along with Dad and Pam. Somehow, miraculously prove to them I'm not an evil, manipulative rebel.
Make friends.
Stop worrying about not having enough friends.
Become a normal, everyday kid who doesn't analyze herself to death.
Get over my ridiculous awkwardness.

I call Lendon about once every two weeks. She feels distant in our phone calls and it saddens me that I'm just a part of her past. Just one of her ten zillion past working students. Lupe tells me she said I was her absolute favorite working student, but I don't know if that makes being gone easier or harder.

I miss...I miss everything about life at the farm: Lendon's moods, my stench at the end of the day and the luxurious sensation of the water eliminating it. Lupe and my wagers on new roommates: how long do you think this one will last? I like school, like learning and making friends, the atmosphere of education both academic and social. I have fun here, but there's a difference between being entertained and being happy. My happiness remains in New York.

Although I try to force it to focus on school, horses occupy every neuron of my brain. In the warm days of early fall, I can almost smell the scent of hot sweaty horse, the bath they get after work. As the days become crisp, I can't help but imagine the gentle puffs of steam that would escape their nostrils.

Creative Writing University of Michigan

"Within My Womb, There is a Horse"

How long has it been

46

since the day has offered me a smile?

The clouds threaten to smother the land
and seem to have already done in the sun

The thermometer flirts with zero
and the heater, as always, "will be fixed next week."

Voila First Edition lies open on my lap
mocking me with meaningless words

Phone calls and knocks at my door
parties and homework and questions and plans

And a soap opera star, I play the part
of someone who actually cares

I invent claims of trivial stress and fatigue
but my heart is stampeded by a million wild horses

Their hooves mutilate my worries
for anything else

Palpate me and you'll find a dead foal, kicking and screaming

◆ ◆ ◆

College is a place kids are meant to find themselves, but I'm losing myself. Last year I knew who I was. I *liked* who I was. Now I have no clue. It's as if the person I was is stuck inside the shell of this person at U of M, beating at her from the inside and trying to escape. And I don't know which one I am: the one trying to contain her, to teach her to submit and do well in less-than-natural circumstances, or the one trying to escape.

The thing that does seem to go with the normal college experience—or at least college-aged experience—is being misunderstood.

Journal
They say I'm feisty and rebellious and do what I want. I'm stubborn and hard-headed and proud and independent. I always take the difficult route instead of accepting help with restrictions. I don't respect authority and never let anyone tell me not do/try something.

But I'm not rebellious to authority. I'm indifferent to it. Why should I care what you tell me to do? I do nothing to spite anyone, I do it without regard to them. I do exactly as

I'm told by the people I respect. If Lendon or Lou told me to take up dogsled racing, I would because they know me, like me, respect me, know what I want and who I am. You respect them because they share your passion, Courtney, they say. Yes, I do and what is wrong with that? Who better to understand me than someone who shares my core?

They say I always have to struggle and that part is true. I've never known a time when I wasn't struggling for something Dad didn't want me to do and Mom couldn't help me with.

◆ ◆ ◆

It's especially hard to convince my heart to accept being here because riding doesn't even require a degree. My brain says, Yes, but I want to learn, to have an education. My heart replies, We need to take classes *and* ride. Brain: But Dad's paying. Heart: Who cares?

My heart is winning the battle. Is giving up riding really a worthwhile sacrifice? Foregoing my education in something I *know* I'll use in order to be educated in something I hope not to?

Julia who lives down the hall, wants to be an actress and that doesn't require a degree either so we often commiserate, console ourselves with the theory that the people who are happy and content at school are the ones without a passion…without a known goal. We simply know too much about our ultimate desires to be content swimming in this fishbowl checking out the bait of possibilities. Knowing that doesn't change anything though. Nothing here matters to me.

Creative Writing, University of Michigan

"It's All Greek to Me"

The keg sweats and little liquid beads race
each other into the barrel
tempting teens cold promises of refreshment

Two hundred freshman women cling
to the liquid socializer, like staples to a magnet
and one eighteen-year-old stumbling hormone
plays with the power of the tap

The room, barren of furniture,
is itself a smoke-filled lung
toying with the toxins by allowing
periodic breaths of fresh air

Standing in separated observation, the scene

Is just the fuzz on the TV screen
A constant hum of idle talk, commotion
Creating whirlwinds of meaningless jabber

Pi Phi or Alpha Delts,
Makes no difference
It's all just Greek to me

◆ ◆ ◆

What disturbs me about the prospect of not continuing school (besides the fear of ending up broke and lost) is the possibility of destroying the first seed of an actual relationship with Pam and Dad. It's nice having them like me and approve of what I'm doing, but if the fabric of our relationship consists of me being in a sorority and a typical college student, it's not a relationship at all.

However, there's the possibility that these little details of life are the first stitches in a big solid rug and I don't want to risk inhibiting such a creation. I take much of the blame for them misunderstanding me because I usually spring huge changes on them. While I may have been contemplating things for a long time, they never hear any of my thoughts before my decision.

So I make a pact with myself: I'm going to keep them informed of what I'm feeling, let them know my thoughts so even if they don't like the ultimate decisions, at least they know nothing was made off the cuff.

◆ ◆ ◆

I write them letters and call once a week. I try. But after spending Christmas break at Lendon's, I know this will be my only year at U of M. I got to ride a great deal of horses including a six-year-old superstar Dutch stallion, Idocus, who just came in. I warmed him up every day and fell in love. I promised myself that I'd notify Dad and Pam of my feelings when they began, but the thought and the decision came simultaneously.

I call Dad. Small talk, How was your Christmas, Good, how was yours. Dad, we need to talk.

What's up? he asks.

Can we talk face to face?

He drives the hour and a half to Ann Arbor the next day and takes me to dinner. After some uncomfortable small talk and starting on our entrees, I blurt out, Dad, I need to go back to Lendon's. As usual, completely shocking him.

His top lip disappears and he stops chewing, but he doesn't say anything.

I'm sorry but I can't stay here. I thought I could do four years but I can't. I just can't.

Why can't you do horses as an avocation rather than a vocation? he asks without releasing his lip. The horse business is a tough business.

I know.

The horses can wait, he says.

Dad, if you convince me to give up on my dream, I'm going to hold it against you and against myself. I tell him I have every intention of going to school part time in New York and to eventually get my degree.

He mutters something under his breath, looks away and throws his napkin on the table. I glare at him and before I know what I'm doing, get up and storm out, march all the way back to the dorm. He keeps trying to mold me into the girl he wants me to be but I'll never fit his mold. I don't know exactly who I am but I know it's not her.

◆ ◆ ◆

Creative Writing , University of Michigan

"Unreachable Dreams"

A solution to a problem that
doesn't exist,
groping and grasping and getting pissed

I've been here so long
in this dingy old town
eight months and a day
all tying me down

My dreams they all call
me, scream my name,
back to the world with
minimal fame

to enjoy the leisure
of collegely life
how much I would give to relinquish
this strife

Forever searching for that one
right way
right here right now, I can
never stay

So strangled in darkness and blinded
by light
I maintain with vigor the age old
fight

Equine images invade
my dreams
So vivid I can smell
them, it sometimes seems

A bounding leap
an Olympic debut
then sent back to college, a nightmare
come true

Stroking stroking to the sandy shore
and cast away yet once more

When will I reach that beach of my dreams?
Keep on trying, however futile it
Seems

My friends think leaving school takes immense courage——the guts few people have. But they're wrong. I'm not strong enough or courageous enough to stay in school. Asking me to function without horses is like asking me to breathe without lungs: it's not possible. I have little choice.

Journal

"Ode to LFG"

Ah, Lendon, here it is what can I say?
I've thought about you every day.
You've given me so much, taken me in.
I can't help but wonder how I've been
Deserving of all the chances you've given,
Making possible the goals for which I have striven.
So many pictures, so many poems
Attempted for you, but too bad for your home.
I get worried sometimes about the future to come,
How everyone thinks I'll become a bum
I think of how hard it's gonna be
School, job and barn, 100% to all three,

51

But I think of last year and how it was
Two grooms and me, clients bitching at us
And yet I was happy and never had doubt,
It was perfect for me, it was what I was about
And when it came time for me to leave
It made me so sad I couldn't believe,
The thought of the others taking my place
Depressed me so much I hid my face
My little Scenic carrying somebody else
My wonderful Lendon screaming "Sit up or else"
My barn being run by more capable hands
Memories of me left only in strands
Now my only feelings are gratitude
For not being forgotten or even subdued,
I think the group is now quite great
And I just can't wait to integrate
With all of them and my ponies too
But most of all, of course, with you

· 11 ·

Essay

The scent of the breath. The independent vulnerability. The subdued strength, controlled power. The perk of ears, the look of curious eyes. The twist of a begging neck. The pounding of hooves against the stall door at feeding time. The friendly nicker. The smell of fresh shavings. Hay. Sweaty horse. Fly spray. These all produce feelings of home, much like a home-cooked meal produces for others.

I walk into the indoor arena where Lendon's teaching. I didn't have enough money for a plane ticket but one was sent to me "from Lendon and the clients". She spots me out of the corner of her eye and reveals just a hint of a smile.

Well, Judy, she barks to her pupil, I can fix your arm like I did Courtney's if you refuse to fix it yourself!

Hearing these words is like popping a bottle of champagne; they mean my party has begun and initiate the celebration of my re-emergence into the place for which my heart has been yearning. This is my Lendon: harsh front, loving soul.

She turns and walks towards me with a business-like stride and when she reaches me, we look at each other for a moment. Her hair is shorter. She's gotten a new sweater.

I see you've learned to brush your hair at college, she says, her face cracking into a full-blown grin. We hold each other in a hug for several moments.

So, if we break another bone, we get to keep you? she teases.

I don't need a broken bone to be convinced, I say. Her face grows serious.

You've been missed, she says. Welcome home.

Francine welcomes me like I'm her own child. Those twinkly eyes have become even twinklier. It's always clear with her that she respects who I am and supports who I want to become. It's a relief to be able to be myself and be loved for it.

◆ ◆ ◆

Journal

Mary's forty-eight. Andree's thirty-eight, and another working student is in her fifties. They all grew up with a love for horses but logically got schooled for something else to make a profession. Michelle's a lawyer, Andree an artist. And they all, in their older age, weren't content and left their jobs because they realized they weren't happy without riding. They regret not having followed their heart or their dreams when they were young. I don't want to make that mistake. When I get old and realize a career in horses was stupid, I'll have tried. It will have been my mistake.

The riding continues as if I never left, as if U of M was a bad dream. I get a feeling when I'm schooling a shoulder-in down the long side and Lendon's schooling a pirouette, just as I pass her, I feel so proud. This is it, I'm doing it...my dream.

Lendon shows her happiness to have me back by giving me a lot of attention. Working students never have lessons but I know if I ride in front of her she'll give me guidance. Eventually I begin to feel sorry for the clients I ride with because I feel I'm taking half their lesson, so I try to not ride with the same client every day. But it's almost impossible because I ride so much.

Courtney, she tells me one day, You should feel like you can do anything at any moment: extension, halt, shoulder-in. They should all be ready. Then she continues on with her lesson.

I experiment with this. I trot down the long side with no plan then decide to halt. To my surprise, it takes me four strides to prepare to halt. I have to get him *ready* to be ready to halt. Then I trot down the long side focusing on making every stride ready to halt, but instead of halting, I ask for an extension. It's a slightly better extension than I normally get.

I understand now. The balance of the trot, the carry and push, are the same whether you're preparing to extend or to halt and the goal is to have that trot all the time; you're always preparing for something.

◆ ◆ ◆

Although my heart and mind are exactly where they want to be, my body isn't happy; the inside of my right knee is purple and green from bruising. For the first month, I assumed it was simply an effect of a lack of riding but after six weeks, my body should be fit. So when Lendon gets exasperated that I refuse to use my right leg, I explain why I can't. In typical Lendon fashion, she considers every technical reason why. Am I flapping my knees? No. Why the right and not the left? She says she's stumped.

I guess you just have to ride better, she says with a grin and turns back to her lesson.

I lament to Francine about it and Martha, who's some type of sports therapist, overhears. She says, Courtney, will you ride my horse a couple of times if I work on you? Let me figure out that knee?

I don't want someone to *work* on me, don't think there's the slightest chance of her helping my knee, but she actually thinks me riding her horse is helpful. No one has ever offered me something in return for riding, so I happily reply in the affirmative.

She walks with me to the mounting block and tells me she's been having trouble with the leg yields. He leads drastically with the shoulder, she can't get him to move sideways parallel to the wall to save her life.

I do a bit of warm up and notice immediately that he's dead to the leg, lazy and unresponsive. How's a horse going to respond to one leg if he won't respond to two? So I begin with transitions between walk and trot. When I ask him to trot, I squeeze my legs lightly, give him a chance to respond and if he doesn't or is half-hearted, I give him a double barrel kick. He leaps away and I pat him. Then we walk again and do the same thing. It only takes two times for him to learn to respond to the light aid.

Then I begin the leg yield: turn right down the centerline and ask him to move sideways off my right leg. As expected, his shoulder goes toward the track much quicker than his haunches. I simply walk and make him just move his haunches over to the left by keeping the left rein and pressing with the right leg. I need to give him one serious kick with the right leg to make him take it seriously and move his haunches left, but I've already made him sensitive to the leg so after one time he's got it. The next time we don't need to come to walk at all because he responds well in the trot.

Then I have Martha get on and try. It's perfect and she says it's easy. She's ecstatic that I fixed the problem and I'm ecstatic that I'm actually a trainer. I helped her. I knew how to resolve an issue and was able to make it easier for her to ride.

After I put him away, we go to my bedroom to do the work she insists she owes me. When I take off my pants and lie on the bed, she asks about the large scar at the top of my thigh. I explain that when I was here over Christmas, Lupe was teaching me how to cook and I spilled boiling oil on my leg. She's been feeling around my leg while I've been talking and asks if I rode.

Of course I did! I had two weeks of break, two weeks to ride, so I just bandaged it up.

Did it hurt? she asks.

Well, yeah, I say, rolling my eyes.

She says that my muscle there had flipped over to protect the burn and in my months of not riding, the burn had healed but the muscle remained flipped. The bruising comes from the muscle being flipped but trying to behave normally and she has to manually flip it the other way.

More tears come out when she works on me than when I broke my arm but after two weeks, the bruising is gone.

◆ ◆ ◆

Now my mind, heart, and body are all in bliss, but mid-way through summer my bliss is interrupted by the memory that I have other duties to attend to: college. I tell Lendon I want to enroll part time in SUNY Purchase, an extension of the State University of New York, but I need to get another job. She says, Just enroll, it'll be paid for. She doesn't tell me where the money will come from but my gut says it's Francine.

After I start school, I don't know how I would have done it without the amazing help. I start work in the barn at four in the morning three days a week in order to be done in time to make a class at two. To earn money to live, I babysit and work weekends at Flanagan's, a bar in Mt. Kisco. I get more commissions for horse paintings. How could I possibly do another job?

Journal
But I have to go for the dream or I'll always wonder what could have happened. If in fifteen years I'm sitting on a New York street corner with fingerless gloves and a shopping cart of cans and old journals hoping my black-toothed smile will finagle a buck out of some pitiful sympathizer, at least I'll have tried.

◆ ◆ ◆

But despite my excessive efforts to earn money, by November I'm four hundred dollars in debt. I'm slowly dragging a broom across the cement floor one day, more moving the dirt than sweeping it, when Francine walks in and hands Mozart to me to groom after she's finished riding. She pats him and says, This one wants a different job.

My lips smile back but my eyes remain flat.

Hey, what's up? she asks.

Hmmm? Nothing, I say.

She furrows her eyebrows. Come on kid, I can tell there's something.

You're dragging your feet, you look tired.

Well, I worked at the bar till two this morning, I explain.

She pinches my cheek and walks away. Then she comes back and gives me five hundred dollars.

You work too hard, she tells me in a matter-of-fact, non-sympathetic way.

When I protest and assure her I'm fine, she says she knows I work to pay for living and she wants me to do well in school which I can't if I'm exhausted. Use this, she says.

But you do enough, Francine.

She tells me to absolutely not feel guilty about letting her pay for school; she feels good about it so I should too. No strings. It's not a loan and she doesn't expect anything in return. She just wants me to go to school and get good marks.

What an incredibly generous person. I often use the term wonderful but this woman is truly full of wonder.

· 12 ·

Journal

I was on this young horse and he hadn't been turned out in a few days so I was just galloping around the ring. I had my big jacket and hat on because it was freezing, and the sun was shining through the windows into the indoor. At first I closed my eyes and just felt the sunlight playing on my face and the horse beneath me so glad to be allowed his head, although still in control (How do they let us do this shit to them?). I opened my eyes as we came around the corner and saw my shadow galloping beside me. So pleasant, so free, so happy. And that's me. I love what I do.

For all the struggle it's taken to go to school, by the end of the first semester I'm severely disappointed. I'd gone in prepared to work hard, determined to get A's for Francine, but getting A's takes no effort at all. The school is completely uninspiring. Yes, I want a degree, but I want to be educated, to be capable of conversing about something other than horses.

However my bigger goal of being educated in riding, the reason for my very existence, is definitely being achieved. In January, Lendon decides I should pursue the 1998 North American Young Rider Championships, or NAYRC, which takes place in August, so I spend the winter learning pirouettes and becoming more capable of four and three-tempi changes which are required in the tests.

The NAYRC is like a mini Olympics. Of course it's at a much lower level, but it's our only chance to compete as a team. It includes all the current Olympic disciplines—dressage, jumping and eventing—and teams of four in each discipline are selected from each of the eight regions in the U.S. and sent to Parker, Colorado, to compete. Every Young Rider, riders under the age of twenty-one, wants to go. I need to get high enough scores at two qualifying competitions to make the team.

Lendon appropriates four horses to do the job. Abaluga is Francine's new fourteen-year-old Grand Prix gelding and is immensely talented, but it's nearly impossible to get his forehead away from your own much less get him to put his face on the vertical where we want it. He can move like an Olympic horse but he's extremely unpredictable. Lukas, who's owned by Lisa Hess, Lendon thought would never go past Third Level, two levels below Young Riders, but his heart has overcome his physical limitations. Looking into his eyes feels like looking into the eyes of a devoted dog: your best friend who would be quick to jump off a cliff if he thought you wanted him to. Weston, owned by Sally Bailey, is the most viable candidate of these three: black, beautiful and well trained to the right level. Comfortable and easy, like putting on your slippers. But he has soundness issues. And Lendon's letting me show her own show mount, Scenic. She says no promises that his owner will let me take him to Parker but he's one more horse under my butt to give me experience.

◆ ◆ ◆

To compete in the Young Riders division, I need a shadbelly, or tailcoat. They're six hundred dollars and I'm anxious about finding a way to make the money, but when I finish riding Jester one day, Francine puts her arm around me and says, We have to go get you a shadbelly. She responds to my incredulous silence by enveloping me in a full-body hug. It feels like she's directly hugging my heart. As always, she's wearing white and has remained impeccable. I'm aware of the layer of dirt that covers my layer of sweat. And my stench.

We walk in the tack store door and the scent of new leather fills my nostrils. All the grooming supplies, the breeches, boots for people and horses. All perfectly clean. A lady says, Can I help you?

We need to be outfitted for Young Riders, Francine says with her arm around me.

Shall we start with a top hat? the clerk asks with a smile.

Sure. Francine replies then looks at me and asks, Do you want black or navy?

I stare at her in disbelief.

She shrugs, her eyes go back to the clerk and she says, Navy.

She outfits me head to toe, literally, down to the invisible undies. I feel like Pretty Woman: here, try this. How's that? Stock tie, white gloves, two pairs of two hundred dollar breeches, top hat, hair bow, boots. She easily spends three thousand dollars, everything top of the line, specially fitted. The cashier says, It's a treat to see someone get to do what everyone dreams of, and Francine replies, You should see her ride, that's the real treat.

I have to ride fully outfitted to make sure everything feels OK and all the clients come like it's a filming of a movie star. They believe in me like they believe the sun will come up in the morning. I *pray* I don't let them down.

◆ ◆ ◆

In April, we take Abaluga, Lukas and Weston to a non-qualifying show as practice. We don't take Scenic because he does enough showing and I have the others to practice on. Plus the owners pay for the other horses' entries but Lendon pays for Scenic's.

I'm happy with each horse in a different way. Even though Abaluga isn't exactly round, it's not an embarrassing test, although people must see his extraordinary movement and think I can't ride. He gets a 59.487%. Lukas has the opposite problem of Abaluga; instead of putting his head up toward the rafters, he puts it down and goes like a snowplow. He also gets a 59.487%. Weston is perfect as usual. Not fancy enough to get super high scores, but everything flows and is easy. 61.316%.

Journal
I'm really just waiting to wake up. I feel like crying. The horse show, the outfit.

◆ ◆ ◆

My first qualifier is Westchester Fairfield in May. Weston is lame so I have to scratch him and Abaluga is convinced there are monsters in the plants surrounding the arena. In dressage, we want the horse to go round like a ball but he goes like an upside down banana and gets 53.675%. This test *is* embarrassing. No one watching could possibly know how difficult he is; even Lendon can't get him round consistently. They must just think I'm an awful rider.

Luckily Lukas provides some redemption. He's a trooper. His increased strength combined with the fact that I'm learning to ride his head up better improves the score a great deal: 65.527%. I can picture his heart growing like the Grinch's as we go through the test. I couldn't be prouder of him.

Scenic is the super star we all expected, but I make some mistakes. 65.965%. Of all the horses, I'm the most disappointed in his test because it was my fault. He would have done the test perfectly if I'd ridden. I think I ride Lukas better because he needs me to, but a good and well-trained horse still needs the rider to ride well. I need to ride every horse, every stride and not take anything for granted.

◆ ◆ ◆

The next show, Dressage at Saratoga, is two weeks later, and I bring Chopin, Bese, Jester, Lukas, and Abaluga. Scenic's owner said no one can show him but Lendon and Lendon respects and obeys her like no one else because she gave her her first opportunities.

Abaluga decides the plants are safe and I'm learning to tap into his extravagant movement at times, but his head carriage is still sporadic. He's not a banana often but it does make appearances. Despite this, I'm thrilled with the test; it had some ugly moments but some great ones as well and gets a 63%. The team will be selected based on an average of the scores, though, so he's out of contention for NAYRC.

Lukas is once again an absolute champion. Even though he hasn't progressed as much as Abaluga, he's as steady as the Sunday paper and gets a 65.1%. If it were physically possible for him, he'd be more probable to achieve 100% than any other horse.

I enter fifteen classes, win eleven of them, get three seconds and a third.

Journal
All the clients think I'm so great, I'm just worried they'll find out I'm not.

· 13 ·

To everyone's surprise, I make the team with Lukas, Mr. Consistency. Lisa has paid for all the qualifying shows but she can't shoulder the unexpected expense of Colorado, so Lendon organizes a fundraiser: a silent auction at the farm during a picnic lunch where Lukas and I will do a demo. The clients are generous both in donating items to be sold and purchasing them. They also make Lendon's idea of a "journal list", to which I'll email updates as they occur, highly lucrative.

As I sit down at a picnic table with my hotdog after our demo, one of the clients says, Bring home the gold!

Although I know it's meant as a remark of encouragement, a show of support, it makes my stomach clench. Makes me feel nauseous.

I promise her I'll try, but truly I know it's not in my capacity to win even if Lukas and I give the best test we can. Lukas has a heart of gold, but his physical limitations won't allow him to compete with the fancy, talented horses who are known to qualify. Lendon says some have the quality of Idocus. Lukas's walk is lateral—it has two beats instead of four like he's pacing—the pirouettes are nearly impossible despite his will and undying effort, and he wants to go with his nose down like a snowplow.

I don't want to discourage myself (or especially him) by setting a goal of doing something I know we can't achieve. Of course I always *ride* for the gold—what's the point of showing if you're not going to try for the best?— but I don't want to mislead anyone that I might actually get it. These will be the best young riders in the country and it's a lot just to be going. Plus, if I go just wanting to win, I have to want everyone else to do badly, and I *don't* want them to do badly. I just want to do well.

I'm afraid I'm going to let everyone down after all their amazing support.

Journal

I was so overwhelmed by the enthusiasm and generosity of everyone…so much so that any compliment broke my heart because I'm already anticipating my failure. Now, two days later, I'm looking back at all that confidence people have in me and how the hard work and time spent doing this has earned me all that trust, and I think it's pretty cool. Now I just have to stop being a baby and do the best I can. (I know Lukas will just bust trying to do well!) And, as Lendon says, I know my limitations and I know my horse's limitations, and I just have to do with them what I can.

◆ ◆ ◆

My teammates and I arrange to ship our horses from New York to Colorado together on August 1st but they all plan to fly. The fundraiser made my trip possible but I still need to cut as many financial corners as I can, so in order to save the cost of a plane ticket, I tell them I'll ride with the horses and look after them. It will be forty hours traveling directly toward my dream.

Sunnyfield is the final pickup, so I load Lukas with the other horses and the two drivers and I stand in the trailer looking at them. I wonder why they aren't getting ready to close the doors; with Lendon, departure is always a hustle. They both look at me and I realize they must be waiting for me so I leap out, grab my bag, pillow, and blanket and go up to the cab. But they're still with the horses.

I peek in. Everything OK? I ask.

We thought you were ridin' with the horses?

Yup, I'm ready.

They glance at each other. We thought you could lie on this rug we use to make sure the horses don't slip when they walk up the ramp and lean up against this side.

I look back and forth between them, waiting for one of them to laugh at the joke on the dorky teen. Nothing.

I thought I could ride with you?

When they gave permission for a groom to ride with the horses, they literally meant *with the horses*. No more than two are allowed in the cab, he says.

Lendon gives me an old sleeping bag and some expendable pillows and they close me in with the horses. It will still be forty hours directly toward my dream, but I guess this part of my journey won't be more comfortable than the rest.

◆ ◆ ◆

When it gets dark, I ask them to turn off the lights because I want to sleep, but they say they can't because the headlights from the cars outside would be disruptive for the horses. I squeeze my eyes closed, begging for sleep, but a pssstt sound and urine smell forces me to open them and I see the last bit of urine dripping from Lukas's sheath. The shavings part and let the yellow river wind onto my sleeping bag.

Only twenty six hours to go. In horse urine.

Sleep finally rescues me accompanied by a dream.

Fundraising Journal

Lying in a torn up trench (the rug used for loading the horses on the trailer), mortar is flying in my face (the shavings). There's constant machine gun fire (the steady rattling of the trailer) and bombs explode once in a while (a horse kicking). Also there are tanks (passing motorcycles) and frequent diving planes (passing semis). As I gradually become conscious, I think I'm wounded and bleeding from my mouth, but really I'm just asleep and drooling.

◆ ◆ ◆

When we finally arrive at the competition site in Colorado, I could go trick or treating as a pile of sawdust. Lukas anointed me and my belongings with a partially digested bran mash and Lendon won't be happy about the state of her blankets. But she *will* be happy that I was able to fit in a good amount of homework.

My teammates, Alison, Kristen and Tara, help me unload the horses and put them in their stalls. They feel sorry for me, feel badly that my trip was so horrendous. I tell them I'm sorry I smell but I was happy to do it.

You have to be able to deal with some unpleasantries if you want to be in this business, right? I say with a smile.

That's why I don't want to be in this business, Kristin says.

Really? I ask, astonished. You don't want to be a trainer?

Nope, I'll be rich and buy my horses, she tells me with complete confidence.

She's the daughter my father wanted me to be. After talking to many people, I seem to be the only one who wants a career in horses. I assumed everyone here would be like me, live and breathe horses, but they all own their own horses. Tara says she needs balance in her life, a phrase I'm all too familiar with.

I do worry about being so one-track minded. There are so many hundreds of other things I want to learn how to do: play the piano, write with my left hand, become fluent in other languages. I want to travel and see things and I know this career makes adventure-seeking impossible. But the truth of it is, I would easily give up every ounce of travel and evenings with friends for the life I have now.

. . .

Fundraising Journal
I'm so glad Lendon arrived. Another astounding difference between my experience and that of the other girls here has now peaked. I'm so grateful – more for this than for all the physical opportunities she's given me – for the attitude she displays… a complete security and professionalism… an ability and belief to stay out of the gossip, a constant supporter of learning experiences outside of herself. These girls were shocked at the prospect of taking a lesson with another trainer, much less of bringing one to their facility, for the welfare of their trainer's ego. They were flabbergasted at the thought of exterior horse work—especially teaching or riding. I thank my lucky stars (and Lendon, too) that her attitude is beyond politics and insecurity and that her beliefs are too pure to be corrupted by a world that I'm seeing the sick side of. What I'm trying to say (not very coherently) is that I'm simply so glad that my environment has been one to produce confidence, acceptance, genuineness, and ability to not have to put others down to make oneself look big.

The fact that I don't fit in doesn't bother me very much; the kids are nice. What has unexpectedly been hard is that it feels very different competing for a team rather than just for myself. I generally simply don't have nerves, but they come on strong now. Normally it's only me I can disappoint or let down. Now there are three others.

When I get on Lukas, though, my nervousness disappears. All that's in my mind is the same as when I'm at home: make him look the best I can. In the Preliminary Test, which is just to let us practice and doesn't count toward the medals, I ride him with his head above the ideal vertical to avoid his desire to put his chin on his chest. The deductions for this along with our normal weaknesses earn a 59.4%.

Despite the low score, when I come out of the show ring several strangers come up to tell me they really liked my test, that it was *fun to watch*. I'm not sure how true this is because there are so many good riders and horses here, but at least people don't think I'm out of my league.

I continue the safe route of riding him above the vertical for the Team Test and get a 62% and eleventh place. The test was much like my qualifiers which got 65%'s, but because I rode him above the bit, they couldn't reward me as much for movements well done. As a team, we place fifth.

Before the Individual Test, Lendon says, You know if you ride him safely above the bit as you have been, you're going to get a 61 or 62%. Take a chance. If you go for it, you may get a 64 or 65% or it may backfire and you'll get last. But why go for mediocre?

As usual, she's right and, as usual, I take her advice. The first part of my test feels lovely. He's solidly into the bit, I feel pressure pushing to my hands, his back rising under my seat, the ideal powerful ball. Then he comes a bit above the vertical and I make him come a bit too low, his chin goes to his knees and stays there. It's awful. I knowingly took the chance and it backfired. I'm so disappointed in myself that I corrected him too much; I should have known better. I let everyone down. *I* did, not Lukas and I, me.

Lendon walks down the aisle as I'm slowly grooming Lukas.

Courtney. I look at her and my tears erupt. Courtney, I couldn't be more proud of you if you'd won. You did a great job, you rode him the best anyone could.

But, I start.

No buts, she says. You took a horse no one thought would go past Third Level, and you're going to show him Intermediare I. Be proud.

The clients rescue me and fly me home, and to my great relief, no one seems to care that I got last. I'm ashamed, but they just seem to be relieved to have me back in the barn, behind the scenes to make sure things get done.

• 14 •

Soon after I'm settled, my dad calls and says he wants to come for a visit. Not surprisingly, I'm quite nervous. He tells me not to change anything around, just to let him see my life.

I have a full day—nine horses to ride and four lessons to teach—so I'm panicked that he'll be bored out of his mind as even people who *ride* normally can't stand watching dressage for ten hours. I'm afraid his disapproval of how I want to spend my life will deepen as he sits in agony watching horse after horse. But to my surprise, he seems to utterly enjoy himself and the farmer who fathered me in my early years appears. He picks up poop, pulls down the stirrup, holds the reins, walks the horses back to the barn when I'm finished. The shell of propriety that's separated us for as long as I can remember completely disappears.

Perhaps his checkbook was not only stifling me but controlling him as well, encasing him in the desperate need to be responsible for my life, assigning the blame to himself for any mistakes I make.

When he leaves, my hope to have a real relationship is rekindled.

• • •

Lendon begins to ride less and teach me more. Her knees are killing her, Jester's trot is bouncy and she says she doesn't get along well with him, so she and Francine agree that Jester will become a horse for me. When I'm scheduled to warm a horse up for her, which is normally about five times a day, she teaches me on them instead of getting on herself. Even Idocus and Jamboree, who Alex Rukeyser bought for Lendon as an Olympic hopeful.

With Jambo, the main focus is on the quality of his movement—the magnitude of his collected trot and extended canter—and the focus with Idocus is on getting him ready for Grand Prix. Not only does this entail increasing the difficulty of the lower-level movements he's been doing for years—half-passes: trotting or cantering sideways; extensions: elongating the strides without quickening them; and pirouettes: cantering a tiny circle as if their hind legs are on a dinner plate—we need to introduce him to the new movements—one-tempi flying changes: skipping; piaffe: trotting in place; passage: a slow elevated trot like a trot in slow motion. I've done most of the Grand Prix movements on Scenic, but he knows them. Idocus is just learning so Lendon is teaching him through me; I'm like the doll attached to her marionette strings.

One day we're learning piaffe, one of the most difficult movements of the Grand Prix for most horses. I've always wondered how a person could possibly teach a horse to stay in one place but move his legs as if he's trotting. To teach a dog sit, you can push his butt down as you say *sit* until he understands the word, but with horses that's not possible. There are no words, only body-language, and you can't *show* the horse the correct response.

For weeks I've been doing regular trot to tiny trot (almost walk but don't) and then trot forward again. Lendon told me this was to teach him to maintain the rhythm and build the strength necessary for piaffe. They're called half-steps.

When we try actual piaffe, which is more on the spot, though, she recognizes a big failure in my training. She told me to bring both my legs back to teach him that legs back means shorten the trot but don't stop the rhythm, so I've been doing this, but I automatically squeezed when I brought my legs back.

Don't squeeze, Courtney! she tells me. He has to learn to piaffe on his own. If he stops, touch him with the whip, but you're not to help him. Bringing your legs back is just a cue, like a garage door button: you press it and he piaffes.

Idocus doesn't understand. I was pressing and now I'm not, so to him that means stop. I'm not confident or skilled enough to use the whip at the right time, so finally Lendon says to let her get on.

From the walk, she brings her legs back to ask for piaffe. He piaffes, but then she takes her legs away and he stops. She smacks him with the whip and he pins his ears and gallops forward. She pats him and explains that although she didn't want him to gallop, he had the forward response she wanted so she praised him.

Then she goes to sitting trot and does transitions: big trot, small trot, big trot, small trot—the half-steps we've been practicing—but she just moves her leg with no change in pressure. If he loses activity or sensitivity in the small trot, she gives him a little smack with the whip to tell him becoming sluggish is not an option; he must maintain the half-steps until she tells him otherwise.

She goes back into forward trot, turns perpendicular to the long side of the arena and draws her legs back, slowly shortening the stride to piaffe across the centerline as it is in the test. She takes her legs off, he stops and she whacks him. He understands this time. She does the same thing once again—trots and then takes her legs away while piaffing across the centerline—but this time he doesn't break stride. Lendon makes a huge fuss over him and you can see his pride as he struts around the ring, blows air and looks for his admirers who are in the corner watching.

Then she has me get on again and try one more time. I collect his regular trot then bring my legs back thinking garage door button. Boom, piaffe. Idocus is a quick study. All he had to do was understand.

Lendon says, Now be aware that this horse has immense talent, a great deal of natural rhythm and strength. It won't always be this easy.

She moves on to her next lesson, but I'm riveted. It's like in the movies where numbers and calculations are shown in rapid succession going through a math genius's mind. I'm digesting the many meanings and results of this concept. This is how you teach true dressage. Making what they do in nature look as if it's their idea when you ask for it. Piaffe, which horses do instinctually when excited, from a cue. I'm not only learning how to ride, I'm learning how to train.

Essay

Dressage is the ultimate feeling of harmony. A fifteen hundred pound mass of conditioned muscle listens to the ounce of my ring finger, the slightest shift of my weight, the movement of a leg. They don't listen because they have to. It amazes me that they do what we want at all; they could easily kill us if they wanted to. They listen to us because they want to. They do it because it's their desire to please us. I think of it as a business partnership: the human is the CEO but the horse is a partner, not a servant.

· 15 ·

Journal

I'm amazed at my status now. Everything happens so quickly. Everyone thinks I'm so good and it doesn't matter to them if Lendon rides a horse or I do. I'm entrusted with a three million dollar stallion and someone gave me a hundred dollar tip the other day. But the thing is, I want to be a good rider so badly. Not just people thinking I'm good.

Although I spend the whole winter being Idocus's rider, his owner, Chris McCarthy, wants Lendon to show him. It makes sense; she wants a big-name rider for her stallion, someone who can make him the superstar he is so he becomes a big name. I'm a nameless little girl, a nobody. I feel honored to even ride him. Even though she's been teaching us the Grand Prix movements, Lendon will show him Prix St. Georges and Intermediare I because he's not yet confirmed at Grand Prix.

I get to ride him in clinics, symposiums and demos that Lendon puts on or pays for, though, and in the spring, I ride him and three other horses in a symposium with Mike Poulin, Lendon's own trainer and a member of the 1992 Bronze Medal Olympic Team. He takes away my stirrups and puts me on a lunge line so I don't need to control the horse.

Now, pat your head and rub your tummy, he says.

I do.

Now pat your belly and rub your head.

Now circle your ankles, one clockwise and the other counter-clockwise.

Switch, he says.

Ok, now, windmill your arms the opposite way of your ankles.

He pulls the horse to a stop and says to the audience, This is to test coordination, to separate each part of your body which is a skill needed in dressage. It appears silly but it's extremely difficult. If this girl sticks with it she'll go international and blow them all out of the water.

Tears sting my eyes. Hope envelopes me. All my hard work is paying off and if I keep working like this, I may achieve my Olympic aspiration. I spend all my time on hacks after this symposium on every quiet horse practicing this separation of aids. I wedge my whip between my thigh and the saddle and put my reins around it so I don't need to hold the horse and raise and lower one arm while doing big circles with the other. Make circles with my ankles while bending and straightening alternating elbows. Transfer my weight from one seat bone to the other while making circles opposite ways with each wrist.

I have this well mastered by the time I ride Idocus with Conrad Schumacher, a famous German trainer, the following month, but he's only interested in the Grand Prix movements. I show him that Idocus can do nine of the fifteen one-time changes required in the Grand Prix. He sets up poles on the ground making a twenty meter square to canter within and has me go forward on the straight sides and collect to the length of stride of a pirouette for each corner. When Idocus does this with ease, he makes it a fifteen meter square. Then ten.

Ok, now we piaffe, he says.

He has me walk along the wall and ask for piaffe. To his amazement, Idocus doesn't hesitate: walk, piaffe. I walk again and look at him. He says I've done a very good job, tells me I'm skilled and gifted and have a ton of feel. He wants to start buying and selling good horses, and if I come to Germany, he wants me to ride them.

I'm dumbfounded. Further confirmation that my hard work is paying off.

◆ ◆ ◆

Although I can't show Idocus, I show five other horses regularly plus a few here and there. Lendon teaches me precise test riding—to go exactly from one letter to another, to ask for transitions the stride before a letter to ensure it happens right *at* the letter. It's becoming easy to memorize my tests so well I can ride the horse within the pattern. And I think schooling a Grand Prix horse makes me ride the younger ones better. If your horse takes three strides to go from trot to canter, how is he going to be quick enough to do one-time changes? Now I ride every horse, at whatever level they are, to prepare for Grand Prix.

In May, I enter fourteen classes in every level from Second to Intermediare I at the WFDA show in Port Jervis, New York, and Jester's Fourth Level Test Three is my final test of the weekend. I can tell he's simply not in the mood to show the moment I start grooming him; he won't move over when I ask him to and when I give him a little fwack, he pins his ears, swishes his tail, and steps *into* me. Francine's nickname for him, the flying mule, isn't only due to his ears. In the class, he actually *kicks* the judge's table.

I'm mortified. Francine was watching and I think she must be going to take him away from me, but she says she knows it's not going to be all blues all the time and she doesn't care. The only thing she cares about, the only reason for Jester, is getting *me* to the top.

I never thought about it before: he was a horse for Lendon but now he's a horse for me. She pays all these enormous bills *for me*. I look down and smile, but she wraps her arms around me and says, We're in this together, kid, OK? And 63% shows there was a lot of good stuff when you almost killed the judge.

This knowledge doesn't gratify me, doesn't confirm that my hard work is paying off, it makes me feel I have a partner. Like on a basketball team, I owe it to her to play well. I walk down the aisle proudly getting used to the weight of this responsibility, and a girl says, Hi Courtney! I say hi. I don't know who she is but I don't think anything of it because I have a Swiss cheese memory when it comes to people. Then she says, Wait, I just have to tell you, you're like the best rider I've ever seen. All of us at the University of Massachusetts agree. You're incredible and an inspiration to us, she says with her hand on her heart.

This show is huge and prestigious and full of top riders, and she noticed *me*. My awkwardness appears and I drop my eyes, smile, and say thank you but my heart is bursting out of my chest. Confirmation from strangers.

I end up with ten wins, two seconds, a third and a fourth.

• • •

One effect of this success is that people notice me. Until now, my focus on my horses, which prevents friendly chatting, and the averting of my eyes, which is an effect of my awkwardness—I don't want to appear that I assume people know me—haven't been noticed. Now people are beginning to recognize me, so by not saying hi, I'm inadvertently being rude.

I try to reduce this rising perception by chatting with the second and third place riders in awards ceremonies. I can't alter my focus when I'm riding without risking what I've worked so hard for, but I can try to be chattier when I'm not in competition mode. This effort just comes off as gloating.

Of course it comes down to the horses and I'm incredibly lucky to ride good ones, but I believe the many not so good ones help me just as much. Everything is easy for an Idocus, but I have to find clever ways to get the Quarter Horses, the Saddlebreds, the Arabians and the Icelandic, whose natural conformations aren't helpful, to do good dressage. I ride mares, stallions, geldings, ponies and monstrosities, three-year-olds and twenty-one-year-olds. Lendon has shown me by example to ride any horse; every horse can teach me. If someone asked me to ride their cow, to *show* their cow, I wouldn't hesitate. My education is endless.

Although riding so many horses has fire-started my progress, Lendon can tell I'm exhausted and wants me to quit my job at the bar.

She calls me into her office one day and says, I'm going to pay you for the students you teach and horses you ride exclusively.

And that's that. I'm dismissed.

I'm getting *paid* to ride. Not only does this provide immense relief, it provokes the thrill of my graduation to professionalism.

• 16 •

Journal
When Mr. Responsibility eases himself, ever so comfortably on your deceivingly wide shoulders, and mingled reminders of have-tos, haven't-dones, should-dos and forgot-tos bounce uselessly around in your heavy head, do what you dare not do: open your mouth and breathe.

This alleviation of the need to have a night job allows the freedom to do just that: breathe. Allie—another working student—and I take occasional jaunts to New York City by train and find a bar specializing in P-Funk music, to which we love to dance. She's 6'1 compared to my measly 5'10 and is gorgeous. Walking through Grand Central one evening, a group of guys blatantly check her out as she walks by and she swings her hips a bit more to encourage them. One guy says, What magazine cover did *you* walk off of?

I enjoy the attention she brings to us and find that my awkwardness disappears when I know I won't see people again. These evenings of teenage-freedom leave me feeling refreshed.

◆ ◆ ◆

The one person's attention I fruitlessly crave is Lendon's. After years of feeling her eyes were always on me, that the only person who seemed nearly as committed to my education as I am was her, now she completely ignores me. I feel I could come in riding backwards and she wouldn't notice. Being paid is great but my education is far more important; it's why I'm here. Instead of enjoying my successes and being there for me more, she acts like she's done with me. She's made me successful and now it's time for the next project.

She has a new star pupil she's working on, Hanna, and I feel like an old has-been. In an article, she said that Hanna's one of the two best she's ever taught and has what it takes to make an Olympic team. I've never gotten a compliment like that. I produce little inspiration in her.

But what aggravates me even more than the unevenness of riding attention is how unfairly she treats our barn work. If there's an extra lesson to be taught, she'll *ask* Hanna if she has time, but she'll *tell* me I have two extra horses and an extra lesson. If I tell her I've worked until 6:30 every night, she flies off the handle.

Journal
I've always defended Lendon to the death when other people complain. She makes bitchy little comments and is snapping at everyone and suddenly it gets me seriously upset. I don't know if it's because I've finally gained some self esteem or the opposite. I've completely lost my confidence, but I've got to get back to that pure mentality. She's the boss. She's my mentor, and I just have to shut up and take it and learn.

◆ ◆ ◆

Despite being frustrated by Lendon not teaching me, I'm still improving by seeing and hearing. I still have light bulb moments from things she says to other people and from watching her work things out. I begin to improve the horses I ride—their knowledge, their responsiveness, suppleness, the swing and athleticism of their movement. It feels good to feel unified with the horse when I ride. I'm no longer just sitting on the horse, I'm riding.

I'm capable of teaching horses new movements on my own and one day, I'm introducing Bese to flying changes. To do an acceptable flying change, the horse needs to change clean—their front and hind legs should change leads in the same stride. Often when they're learning, they'll change their hind legs a stride after their front legs. Occasionally they'll change late in front. It's almost impossible, even for an experienced rider, to feel if a change is good.

Lendon's sitting in her corner teaching Hanna, and I stand Bese in front of her. Push him more forward, Hanna! she screeches.

Lendon? I say.

Yes, Courtney. Hanna, forward! If you want him to carry himself, you need some power into your reins!

What, Courtney? she glances at me then looks back at Hanna.

Could you watch some flying changes and tell me if they're good?

Yes.

I canter across the short diagonal and do a flying change.

Hanna, that's too forward, I love it.

Did you see? I ask.

Sorry, I didn't. Hanna, balance him!

I grit my teeth and go back to work, red with anger and tears streaming.

At the end of the day, I walk into her office—again, all the magazine covers hanging on the walls humble me—and tell her she's been ignoring me the past few months.

No I haven't.

You don't even watch when I ask you to anymore. I use today as an example. The tears are already spouting as they do every conversation with Lendon lately. I'm such a wimp.

You're doing fine on your own, she says monotone looking at me with a stern gaze. She never gets emotional. Then she says she's thinking of switching my Bese for Hanna's Lambada for a couple weeks so I can put some pressure on Lambada for her. I certainly don't mind riding Lambada but I can't stand the thought of somebody else on Bese. No one else has been on him since the first day he came and bucked Marjaleena, a day working student, off. He's sensitive with big doe eyes, certainly doesn't *mean* to be naughty, but he has to be comfortable or he panics. It would spoil all the trust I've worked so hard to earn.

I don't have it in me to fight her. How can I fight the very one who let me fly?

I turn and walk out. She doesn't stop me. I almost, not quite but almost, can foresee our partnership ending.

The very next day, Lendon tells Marjaleena she's going to let Hanna have Marjaleena's Zimry. This makes my skin boil. Marjaleena has done all the training on that horse and he loves her. The only reason Lendon wants to give him to Hanna is so she can show him in the Juniors because she's under eighteen. She's going to take the opportunity away from Marjaleena who's been here three times longer than Hanna, works her ass off and is *very* valuable and reliable. I've been here three and a half years and I still don't expect as much as Hanna gets.

I used to love giving Hanna lessons but now I won't be able to help having negative feelings. I just have to keep reminding myself that there's no contract saying Lendon will be fair. They are, after all, her clients and her horses. I just have to try to help the other girls myself. They deserve it.

Journal

It's really amazing how much confidence I've lost in the last year or so. I used to think: I'm so lucky, I have so many strengths and talents and friends and supporters. Now I think I'm a loser—not only a loser, a sore loser at that.

· 17 ·

Journal

Sometimes I just want to live life. I want to have a normal job and be able to take vacations. I get so frustrated. Wow! I just had an insight into how lost I'd feel if I didn't ride and train horses. Lost. No purpose. I guess that's how most people my age feel... It's like looking into a wilderness. Who knows where life will lead. No direction. No plan or goal. No wide scheme of things to cast a light on an inevitably variable future.

Although Allie left, my teenage urge to go out has been ignited, as well as the need to do something other than ride, so I find a local bar that has live music and spend many evenings on their dance floor. I'm completely at ease bantering with people when I know I won't see them again. I can't seem to get it through my thick skull that when I'm myself and don't worry about what people think, I'm likeable, but no one likes an awkward imbecile.

One night, I'm sitting at the bar and a thick arm reaches around me waving for the bartender's attention. The bartender lifts his chin acknowledging him and continues shaking the shaker he's working on. It's busy and loud and I'm happy. I look around and the face belonging to the arm says hi. His voice is soft like velvet but I can easily hear it amidst the noise.

I'm Mike, he says looking in my eyes as if no one else is here.

Courtney, I tell him, pushing my red headband back.

Who are you with? he asks.

I'm by myself, I tell him.

He tips his head and half smiles, wondering if it's a joke. Really? Why?

My friends are all fifty-year-old clients, I say with a smile. I don't have anyone to go out with. He chuckles and steps closer.

The bartender asks him what he wants and he says a Sam Adams, what do I want?

My beer is about three quarters gone. I shrug and raise my eyebrows at him, tell him I'll have the same and turn to face him.

He asks what I do and I tell him I ride horses. Do you have a race coming up? he asks.

I laugh and tell him, No, I do dressage.

He smiles and shrugs, indicating he has no idea what that is. It's the fancy prancy stuff, I tell him.

He's 6'4", thin but not skinny. Big Roman nose which suits him. He's Egyptian/Lebanese and is dark-complected. Good-looking. He tells me he traveled the world for three years and now works on Wall Street.

His friend comes up and tells him his drink is getting warm. Then he eyes me and says, Ah, I see. Mike looks somewhat abashed and admits he didn't need a drink when he came to the bar; he just wanted to talk to me.

We're ready to go. Finish up, get her number and let's hit the road!

Mike drove his four friends so he has to take them home. I give him my number and he says a long goodbye, never releasing my eyes from his own. When his friends tell him to get a move on, he gives my hand a final squeeze and leaves.

An hour later, he comes back saying he couldn't stop thinking about the girl with the red headband.

◆ ◆ ◆

He calls the next day and we plan a date at a little Mexican restaurant he knows. In the bar I'm the life of the party, the dancing queen, but now that I care what he thinks, I worry that the awkward imbecile will appear. I lament this possibility the whole week before he picks me up on Friday. The butterflies in my stomach have fangs and talons.

But when we sit down, we immediately fall into comfortable chatter. I worried that I'd have nothing to say but on the contrary, I feel I could talk to him forever. He's intelligent, caring. Gets my odd sense of humor and matches it.

Are you in school? he asks.

This question brings down my happy mood.

I say yes, but class started last week and I didn't even register till today. I just have too much going on. I look down.

Like going out with jerks like me? he teases.

I smile a weak smile. No. I have school, working at the barn, riding a million horses, painting. I need these nights out to keep me grounded.

He waits.

School is my only link to my dad and step-mom, I continue. It's not fair to them if I don't take it seriously. They've finally decided to help me financially.

He takes my hand.

I shouldn't treat them with disrespect. I just wish they could see from my perspective, respect *my* dreams and happiness.

He leans across the table and slowly kisses each cheek, squeezing the tears out of my eyes.

I'm sorry, what a first date! I say.

He smiles. It's great. I get to know you; you let me in. You're strong but sensitive, funny but serious, tender but strong. I feel like I've known you my whole life, he says.

I don't even know me, how can you? I say with a smile and sink into the comforting embrace of his eyes.

He kisses my lips. Next time, will you wear your red headband? My happy mood is rekindled.

Journal
Sometimes I wish I could just be one of those blissful people. I have an ever-growing respect for them. I used to feel sorry for them because they didn't have any huge aspirations, something to work toward and strive for. Now I'm jealous of them for that freedom, that content with what simply is.

• 18 •

As the days pass by, Mike and I begin to talk on the phone every day and one morning I invite him to come to my apartment for dinner. I'm actually going to attempt to cook. I tell Greta and she says it means he's going to stay the night.

No it doesn't, that's ridiculous! I tell her.

Well, *you* may not think so, but I guarantee *he* does, she says.

The rest of the day, I worry about it, and when he arrives, I give him a quick kiss but break away from the long, drawn out embrace that's our usual hello. He tries to hug me as I stir the pasta but I bustle away saying I need to set the table.

When we finally sit down, he puts his hand on mine and looks at me. I stare into my spaghetti. I can't bear to look him in the eye. He asks what's up and I take my hand away, sit back. Eventually I sigh and look in his eyes, tell him what Greta said.

He's embarrassed and slightly offended. I apologize and he says, Baby, I'm not that kind of guy. Yeah, I'd like to go bed with you, but I'm here for your personality not your body.

I love the way he says baby; his lips just brush each other for the *B*, makes it soft, sensual. We hang out, joke and laugh, fool around and talk seriously. He's sweet and cool and fun and philosophical and honest and real, has intelligent input and doesn't mind disagreeing with me. He loves storms and cooks and is close to his family.

He sends me flowers the next day.

When it rains it pours: Mike's the perfect boyfriend and my riding dreams become reality when Lendon tells me I'm going to show Idocus and Jamboree this season. I'll do Prix St. Georges and Intermediare I on Jambo but I'll show Idocus in both our first Grand Prix. I've done the St. Georges and I1 several times on other horses and there's space between the movements to prepare, but the Grand Prix, which is the same test required in the Olympics, is one difficult movement after another with no time in between.

I memorize and begin working on the test as soon as Lendon tells me. I learned years ago that it's one thing to do a movement by itself but another altogether to sandwich it between the other movements of the test, so although I never do the whole test, I school pieces of it every day. I do several movements in the order they are in the test and teach myself to anticipate and avoid the possible problems.

Our first show is at the beginning of April and I'm excited but slightly more nervous. I hate expectations. Idocus is awesome and everyone will expect us to do well. Chris doesn't want me to show him—when she finds out she's going to be *pissed*—so I feel like I have to do well or else she'll blame Lendon and Lendon will get in trouble when she's trying to do something wonderful for me. The reason Lendon takes such liberties with him is because Chris owes her so much money.

As has become my habit, right before I put the bridle on I ride the test on him in my mind. Every step. If I'm riding the same test on two different horses, I imagine it on each horse anticipating their particular issues. In my mind, I always make it perfect.

When I get on, I leave my nerves in the barn and focus only on the test and the horse. It doesn't ever enter my mind that I'm doing my first Grand Prix. The things that are new like piaffe, passage and one-tempis, I'm so concerned about getting at all, I never think about making them good. Making the one-tempis and passage expressive, keeping the piaffe on the spot. But I do it all with no mistakes. Like my first show, accurate, yes, quality, no.

Now that we're finished, I think of what we just did: *our first Grand Prix*. People are watching Idocus as we strut by and I'm aware of just how striking he is—his walk always makes me feel like a queen. I lean down and stroke his silky neck, impressed yet again with its muscular hardness, the softness of his coat.

It's really not bad for our first time but I'm absorbed in thinking of what can be better. But this is it, there's no test above this one. We have our whole lives to work on it. My thoughts are interrupted by Lendon walking up on a horse.

How'd it go? she asks.

He was very good but I could have been better.

How? she asks.

Simple things like I needed more right leg in the right half pass, but also I was so concerned about getting the movements, I didn't go for quality. I rode flat passage, crept forward in the piaffe. I know he can do better but I'm not brave enough, not clever enough, to be certain it will work.

We'll work on it, she says.

I hope we will.

We get a 63% and win. Chris is here and seems happy.

Mike takes me out for a celebratory dinner that night and we get champagne and toast to my first Grand Prix. My heart couldn't be happier; I have two great men in my life, one with four legs and one with two.

◆ ◆ ◆

In addition to getting to show Idocus, I become Lendon's body in demonstrations. She's a great speaker and used to wear a mike while riding, but now I ride and she talks. The week after the show, we demonstrate the complete development of a horse from the lowest level to Grand Prix.

We begin with First Level changes of lead through trot. Then Second Level changes of lead through walk. Then Third Level single flying changes. Then we reduce the number of strides in a sequence as we move up the levels, all the while making his frame more collected, finishing with the one-tempis from Grand Prix. We take his normal Training Level trot and gradually increase the collection until it's Grand Prix passage. She has me show that I have absolutely no leg in piaffe by taking my legs all the way away.

During these demos, Lendon and I are partners working seamlessly together. That's how I want our relationship to be, but when we're not doing demos, she still ignores me. As my riding has improved, demand for me has grown and in addition to riding more horses than I comfortably can, I'm expected to fulfill the regular obligations of a working student—doing laundry, cleaning and organizing.

Becoming a trainer is a big step toward my Olympic dream, I just wish I had the time to enjoy it. Mike helps with that. Even when I'm not working, I'm worrying and he's a good distraction. Like going out used to, he provides regular escapes from my anxiety. We say he helps me to stop and smell the roses and I help him to be proactive.

◆ ◆ ◆

Journal
Now that I have a Grand Prix horse, my sponsors are throwing stuff at me. The drawback to my immense happiness is pressure. I'm now supposed to do super well, and what if I don't? I don't want to let any of them down.

At my next show, Windy Hollow, I win every class on the four horses I take from Training Level to Grand Prix and get the high score of the show with 79%. My sponsors are happy. Albion gives me a saddle for Idocus as well as a bridle and anything else I want. He gets another 63% because we make a couple of mistakes, but I'm beginning to feel confident enough to ask for quality. I get more expressive passage and all three piaffes are more on the spot.

Lendon hasn't *helped* me, but she's challenged my work with occasional barks of, More! or, Not good enough, and tests me in the piaffe with, Are you helping him?

As the following show, Westchester Fairfield, approaches, none of my horses are going well. Idocus has Lyme disease, Jamboree's ankle is swollen, Jester has me at my wit's end struggling to do the pirouettes and I have to scratch Lambada because he's lame. Overall the show's a disappointment.

I begin to realize that you can be the best rider, the hardest worker, even have a great horse and a sponsor, and still not make an Olympic team. Not only does your horse have to stay sound, he has to wake up on the right side of the stall the morning of the Selection Trials and all the stars have to be in alignment. Only four people make the team every four years and it's simply not realistic to think that I'll be one of them.

Like going for the gold at Young Riders, I'm going to *go* for the Olympics, but I'm not going to base my worth on it or mislead myself that it's only up to me. In running, you either run fast or you don't—it's completely up to you—but in riding you're only half of the whole and the owner plays a part too. My realistic goal is to ride as well as an Olympic rider. Going to the Games, I leave to luck.

The reduction in self-imposed pressure makes me ride more relaxed and I think my horses appreciate it because my scores take a dramatic upturn. Idocus gets consistent 67%'s and Jambo gets consistent 69's. Jester can get anything from a 53 to a 70%. My one disappointment is the Festival of Champions, the nation's invitational for the top twelve international level competitors. Jamboree's scared of a persistent butterfly in his Intermediare and gets a 57%, and Idocus and I have several abnormal mistakes and our usual 67% drops to a 65%.

I don't know if it's an effect of this improved relaxation or that more people are making an effort to watch me ride, but my reputation for being rude has amplified into I'm a bitch. People who know I'm not a bitch point out that when I ride, I frown, look grumpy. I say, That's my default face, that's how my face is when I relax. They suggest smiling but I tell them the last thing I'm going to think about is my expression. Some peoples' cheeks are tighter so when their face falls, it looks like a mild grin, but I'd rather get a 70% and be considered a bitch than focus on smiling, look friendly and get a 65%.

Nevertheless it bothers me.

Journal
I always want to remain humble...but with confidence. Man, looking back, growing up is hard and only in retrospect can you appreciate the struggle. I really had some problems, not that they're all solved but a lot of them are dissipating.

• 19 •

I complain to Mike about the effect of my default face and he tells me I look beautiful when I ride. I say, Beauty's in the eye of the beholder.

Well, my vision is twenty/twenty, he says. You're like...like the light that guides me to my destiny. Pause. He thinks a moment and then says, I just hope you're not a bug light!

We buckle over in laughter. One of the many great things about Mike is that he can make me laugh about anything.

• • •

Despite Mike making me feel better by making light of the situation, the reputation continues to bother me. I'm not a bitch. So when Mr. Schumacher comes to do another clinic, I ask him about it. He guffaws. This is not a popularity contest, it's a contest of scores, he says. Simple as that, subject closed, and we begin my lesson.

In the Grand Prix test, you turn right down the centerline, do a right pirouette, continue down the centerline and do a flying change, then do left pirouette. Mr. Schumacher makes us keep doing this sequence over and over: right pirouette, change, left pirouette, change, right, change, left, change, again and again. None are good enough. Idocus doesn't sit on his haunches enough or he turns too quickly, or his head is too high or too low. They're getting worse. I never talk back to a trainer, but I say, Mr. Schumacher, I think he needs a break. He's tired.

No! He must say yes, ma'am! Keep going!

I feel awful, I feel mean. Mr. Schumacher responds to my tears by saying, He's strong! He's not tired; he can and he will!

I continue until he's satisfied that the pirouette in each direction was good.

The next show is Ox Ridge and Idocus gets all eights and one nine on his pirouettes in his three classes. I never would have pressured him on my own but it proved invaluable. I still can't tell when I'm being fair or just a pushover. At the next two shows his eights and nines continue.

◆　◆　◆

I take seven horses to the 2000 Regional Championships and get Champion or Reserve at every level except Second which I don't enter, and Idocus continues his streak of pirouette success. The announcer deems me the "Tiger Woods of dressage" for so many wins at such a young age.

Even though I realize that Lendon deserves the majority of credit, she shows no interest in me now and Mr. Schumacher's one insight made major improvement. I've been daydreaming for months about going to Germany with him, but this convinces me to make it a reality. I wait till Lendon's working in her office and tell her about the amazing result of one lesson, say I think it's time to go to Mr. Schumacher.

I expect she'll support the idea because she's always so enthusiastic about external learning, but I feel the gravity as soon as I tell her. She just looks at me. I crumble under her stare and tell her my riding hasn't improved for several months, I think it's time for different insights. You think it's time, too, right? I ask. She continues staring me down. Tells me the reason my riding isn't improving is because I'm too tired and I *ride* tired.

It's true. With everything that's been added on, nothing's been subtracted. I never considered this place may not grow with me, but I've grown and it's stayed the same. If I want to continue to learn, I must go. The green grass here has gotten eaten down to the nub.

It hurts so much to realize my relationship with Lendon isn't personal. I thought I was special to her but I'm not. I'm just another working student who happens to have lasted longer.

I tell her I don't want to erase the past six years, that she'll always be my mentor and I want to be able to turn to her. That she was a big part of my growing up and I have a lot of admiration for her in a lot of ways. She finally looks down, lets out a sigh, and when she raises her eyes to me again, her stare has softened to a gaze.

Jester, Jamboree and Idocus, she says. I doubt the Kallands would let you take Bese, and Lisa's having too much fun on Lukas.

This is the Lendon I anticipated talking to, supporting my quest to improve. I hadn't thought of what horses I'd take, Jester of course, but Jambo and Idocus, too? Even though I've been riding them, they're meant for her, but it's clear she now thinks of them as for me. Planning the trip with Lendon eases the pain of leaving; as I have in the past, I'll leave but this will be my home.

She asks when I'm thinking of going and I tell her maybe November to

April so I'll be back for show season. You talk to the owners, she says and looks back down at her papers. I'm dismissed.

I nearly skip outside. My winter of 2000-2001 will be spent in Germany. I think of how Mr. Schumacher made me ride in the three days of his clinic and imagine riding like that for five months. He believes in me and brings out the best in my riding. I'll learn and get better and experience a whole different country. Then I think back about what Lendon said: *you ride tired.* But she's the one who makes my workload impossible to manage. Perhaps she thinks my social life drains me when it really refreshes me, relaxes me. No matter, my excitement to go to Germany overrides the need to analyze.

◆ ◆ ◆

That evening, I joyfully tell Mike the news. He says he's happy for me but I feel tension, a reserve in his happiness, so I ask what's up. He looks away and takes my hands. After a moment, he looks back at me. Says he's afraid of losing me, he's in love with me.

How can you love me when I don't know if I love you? I think love is only truly possible if it's reciprocated.

But you've never been in love, right? Maybe you just don't recognize it, he teases.

That's true, I say. But you have. I think there's one true love. Maybe you're mistaking something else for love.

Journal
Although I admonish Mike for making serious comments, I really kind of like it.

◆ ◆ ◆

Francine's excited about sending Jester. You're on your way, kid! she tells me. Alex does whatever Lendon thinks is best, so she's happy to send Jamboree.

Chris says she might send her young horse with me but she wants a big name to show Idocus, so if Lendon isn't interested, she's going to send him to Anky van Grunsven, a several time Dutch Olympian and one of the biggest names in dressage. This is no surprise. Chris has only seen me ride him once at the show. He really works for me, he loves me, but I'm not stupid. I know I can't compare to Anky.

A week later, she calls again. Listen, I have a proposition for you, she says. She wants me to take Idocus plus she has two good young stallions in Holland she'd like me to ride. She says as long as I keep doing well with Idocus, he'll stay with me and after we're done in Germany, she may send him to Anky.

I call Mr. Schumacher and tell him the fabulous news, does he have five stalls? He says no but he can stable me at a farm less than a mile away. How's Idocus doing? I tell him we're working on a musical freestyle for the Dressage at Devon horseshow. Lendon made one in her basement years ago by recording one cassette to another and although she doesn't remember the choreography, she helped me make some up. The piaffe/passage music is great, but I'm having so much difficulty with riding the *horse*. It took me a long time to learn to ride the horse within the test, add staying with the music and I'm sunk. I totally lose the push to the bit. Mr. Schumacher says, Ah, we must fix that. With you I feel I can fix anything; you have such gifts.

• 20 •

Journal
I've been un-heard-of-ly lucky to be riding horses of this quality at my young age.

Looking forward to going to Germany is like looking forward to Christmas: the anticipation itself is enjoyment. Lendon still ignores me other than barking an occasional comment, but it doesn't matter. My days are packed with riding, teaching and stable work, and as has often happened in the past, thrill overcomes my fatigue.

My final show before I leave is Devon, the most prestigious dressage show in the U.S., at the end of September. The show grounds are unique in that they're like a quaint little village; there are restaurants and beer gardens, grandstands and real buildings instead of the usual tents. A million viewers wander the vendors' paths. It's smack dab in the middle of Devon, Pennsylvania, and the feeling is that of a party. The vitality is invigorating.

Dad and Pam come to watch and instead of the nerves I felt before Dad's visit, only joyful anticipation makes an appearance. Friday night, they take me to dinner and meet Mike. They don't give me a hard time about going to Germany in the least. Dad wants to hear everything, about my plans, dilemmas, concerns, excitement, anxiety. He's fascinated by my world and clearly wants to be a part of it.

Although we're all early-to-bedders, I don't get back to my hotel room until 11:30 because of the city bustle in a small town, and I have to get up pre-asscrack of dawn to take care of my horses and be ready to take Jambo in the show ring at 8:17. But when my alarm goes off at 4:15, the exhaustion I'd been expecting to feel is accompanied by contentment, satisfaction. After my dad's decade-and-a-half-long effort to keep the door shut in order to prevent me from entering this world, it's as if he's seen through the window that I've entered it anyway and has decided to join me. And surprisingly, he fits in perfectly.

In the warm-up, the intense atmosphere of the showgrounds adds just the right amount of tension to make Jambo move even fancier. He has more power, more cadence and swing, yet gives me 100% of his focus. When we go in the show ring, for once I pay attention to my surroundings, see the full grandstand and people lining the fences to watch. I think, *this is a horse show and boy I'm going to show this horse off.* But unfortunately Jambo notices his surroundings, too. The atmosphere in the show ring creates too much tension and his mind goes. Our test is riddled with mistakes and continual spooks, gets a 60.500% and we don't place.

Idy's doing the Freestyle which is held at night under lights, and his time is 9:42. I'm exhausted from so little sleep, so after I feed dinner at 4:30, I go back to the hotel to take a two hour nap. But I set my alarm for a.m. instead of p.m. and wake up at 8:00, a full hour past when I should have. That gives me an hour and twelve minutes to get to the show grounds, clean him, braid him, put on my show clothes and tack him up before I get on to warm up 9:12.

I race to the showgrounds, run flat out to his stall and throw his halter on without the usual mushy hello. I tie him to the wall and he lays his ears flat back and does his Loch Ness monster face clearly not appreciating my negligence. A barn neighbor sees my panic and without asking her to, she grabs a brush and starts grooming him while I braid. Tacks him up while I listen to my music one last time. I thank her but don't learn her name.

He warms up like Jambo—the amplified energy making him move better than ever—but as we enter the show ring, I'm anxious he'll have the same reaction as Jambo here, too. But he struts in under the bright lights illuminating his many admirers and grows about a hand. He's always loved admirers and his pride, his desire to show off, makes him move with more energy and power, but his confidence doesn't waver.

The crowd is dead quiet as is considerate for our ride but when it's over, the applause erupts like thunder. Idy admires his admirers and saunters out. The feeling that wells up in me isn't pride but gratitude. My wonderful horse, a horse *for me.*

We get second with a 68.3% and the winner gets a 68.7%. Of the five judges, three had me in first, one had me second and one in ninth. When the announcer introduces me to accept my ribbon, he says, The crowd favorite, Courtney King! and cheering erupts again.

I look around at the million faces, so many I can't find my father. Now I feel a sense of pride. In training you never think of then versus now, so it hits me: I taught Idy all this. He didn't know these movements before I rode him. There can be no greater unity.

When I get back to the barn, I give Idy the loving my hello lacked and thank him for being such a fabulous partner, tell him that for how much *I* taught *him,* he taught *me* immeasurably more. But he's more interested in the multitude of apples I'm giving him. My friendly nameless neighbor is nowhere to be seen. She was like a fairy godmother.

My Dad, Pam and Mike are meeting me in the vendor's village and on my way there, a little girl walks toward me and says, Can I have your autograph? I move out of the way and stop, excited to see this famous rider. But I don't see anyone and when I turn around, she's holding a pen and paper in front of me. With a shaky hand I sign her prize list.

When I find my dad, his eyes tear up and he gives me the firmest, longest hug I can remember. I'm proud of you Court, he says. You were the people's winner.

• 21 •

When I get home, I delve back into my impossible schedule of clients and horses plus barn work. My high from the show and excitement about Germany carries me through two weeks, but then it begins to wear on me and I wake up every morning thinking about when the day will end, when I'll be able to climb back under my comforter and nestle into Mike.

Lendon's attitude toward me sucks any remaining energy. Although I appreciated her support of the idea to go, she acts like I'm already gone. Like she wants me to be gone. Although it certainly doesn't cause more physical labor, the worry about it, thinking about it, drains me. It's eating me up and one afternoon, I go to her office to talk to her about it.

What? she says without looking up.

I was just wondering if everything's all right? I say.

Yes, why? she asks, looking up but not sitting up.

Well, I don't know, you just…. I just…

Spit it out, Courtney.

I can't hold the tears in any longer. Lendon never wants to talk. I like reaching into my belly and that of my loved one and pulling out all our entrails. I want to know what she's thinking, if she's upset with me, what she's *feeling*.

Am I doing everything ok? I say.

Yes, Courtney, you're doing fine, she says irritably.

Are you upset with me?

No, I'm just busy, she says. She looks at me and waits. I look at my feet. Is there anything else? she asks.

I don't answer, just mope out. She hurts… hurts me. Of all people, my parents included, she's made me who I am. How can she not care anymore? She's never yelled at me but now if she looks at me funny, I cry.

I need to toughen up. If she doesn't care about me as a person, we still need to have a healthy professional relationship.

A few days later, she gives me a list of chores: clean the bathroom, laundry, rake the indoor. She gives Hanna no chores. I just show her my schedule:

7:45 Doc
8:30 Jester
9 Nancy
9:30 Jeanne
10 Julian
10:30 Denise
11 Fifi
11:30 Donna
12 Bubu
12:45 Music
1:30 Theresa
2 Idocus
3 Robert
3:45 Jambo
4:30 Jester

I finally stick up for myself. Say I don't think I'll get the laundry done.

She says, Are you willing to do anything to contribute to this barn?

Actually, Lendon, I thought my training was a contribution to your program.

So I do the work to pay you?

I don't understand what you mean.

Never mind, she says, throws her hands in the air and walks away.

I'm proud of myself. Not only did I stick up for myself, I didn't cry. We need to work this out if I'm coming back. I cannot continue to ride and teach so much if she wants me to do so much barn work as well. Period.

◆　◆　◆

Lendon does ease up on the work demands and stops giving me lists, so I'm left with only teaching my five or six lessons and riding my nine, ten or eleven horses. I thought getting rid of the chores would solve the problem but my days are still packed and long. I find myself thinking *only three more horses*, instead of looking forward to each one.

Finally fatigue completely overcomes thrill. Despite my desire, I'm questioning if I can *handle* this life; I'm *only* riding and teaching and I'm exhausted. This is the life I've always wanted and I'm not sure I can do it. It used to be that the day-to-day stresses didn't affect me, didn't upset me, I just dealt with them. Now, for no real reason I break down.

Journal
Sometimes I don't even realize what's bothering me. I'm not actively worrying about my horses, but it just weighs on me. I literally feel heavy.

◆ ◆ ◆

I spend my day off watching TV. I can't remember when I ever did that. The story of a young Olympic figure skater is on and it makes me think: when a dream is accomplished, what's life afterward? Perhaps when your life revolves around such a singular thing, nothing's left—everything else is neglected and then lost. What did they give up to go to the Olympics? What else do they have? Although I've changed my goal to simply being as good as an Olympic rider, the same sacrifices are necessary and maybe they aren't worth it to me.

I have nothing to cry about but a good cry would feel good now. A relief.

◆ ◆ ◆

I go to Francine's for dinner which I do every week. Get lost in their conversations, enamored with their sophistication, drunk on their wine. A guest says, What do you think, Courtney?

They're talking about a senator who of course I've never heard of because I've never heard of any senators. I look down and say, I don't know. Sometimes I feel like everyone's looking at me thinking, *Why the hell can't she say something worthwhile?* Knowledge is something I'm giving up to be the best in my sport.

The conversation moves on but when I look up, Francine's looking at me. She gives me a radiant smile. I give a half smile back and shake my head. She shrugs and keeps smiling. Then she gets up, walks over to me and puts her face by my ear, hands on my shoulders. She says, Like me, everything you do, you do a hundred percent. You're going to be the best rider and you have little time for anything else. I love you, kid. Then she walks back to her seat.

Journal

I wonder, how do you become less insecure? When you realize your own insecurities, you feel even worse about yourself and your self esteem falls farther. And I know that one of the least attractive qualities a person can have is to be unsure of themselves. It's a horrible cycle; knowing you're insecure makes you less secure.

◆ 22 ◆

Journal

I'm feeling burnt out with the horses and with Lendon. I never get a break. Damn is life complicated. I can do anything I want. I just have to piece together a little confidence. Confidence is crucial and it's ebbing out of me. Time to move on and stop taking life so seriously.

I continue to plow through life at the barn, count the number of days till my departure. When I'll only have five horses. And a groom. Since my horses will be at another farm, Mr. Schumacher will give me two hours of his time a day so I need to be able to ride back-to-back and can't spend half my time tacking up and untacking. I'll have plenty of time to spare. It'll be like a vacation.

Ten days before I leave, I'm walking between barns and see Lendon teaching another working student on Lukas. I put him on the schedule for a day off because the chiropractor worked on him yesterday and it's standard procedure to give horses a day off after being adjusted. My cheeks begin to burn and I march out to Lendon, demand, Why is she on Lukas?

She looks at me and growls, Well, if you don't care enough to fit him into your schedule, I'll have someone else ride him.

She probably expects me to just meekly walk away because in all my years, I've never complained or talked back.

The chiropractor *said* to give him the day off! I tell her.

He should not have the day off. You're just too busy and have better horses so you don't care about him, she says and turns back to her lesson.

I'm the only one who *does* care! I retort, raising my voice.

She just shoos me away like I'm annoying her.

When I come back from Germany, I won't be coming back here! My voice has crescendoed into a full-blown shout.

I march back to the barn to get my next horse. She thinks I'm being *lazy*. She should know better than that; no one works harder than I do. Except maybe her. Idocus is my next horse and I know I won't ride him well so I take him for a hack. I never get to hack anymore. I'm more useful training so the other working students hack my horses for me.

On my walk, I begin to regret my tirade. It was unprofessional, immature. Everyone could hear it. Lendon doesn't deserve that. I regret it but am too stubborn to go back to her. I hack all my horses.

◆ ◆ ◆

That night, Mike holds me and holds me, lets my tears soak his tee shirt. He tells me how much he loves me and makes me laugh through the tears. It's the perfect opportunity for him to tell me to give up riding, but he doesn't. I tell him I love him and I know I do. I expect this knowledge to make things easier. We're in love. That should be a good thing, but it makes me want to get away from him even more.

Journal
I run from relationships. I run from "love" because I'm scared. I like the beginning where it's curiosity and not ties and no worries. I'm young and I want to have experiences. This

85

shouldn't be so complicated. It's so fucked-up that people can be so incredibly aware of their own destructive thought processes and yet be so utterly powerless to alter them.

◆ ◆ ◆

I send a group email to the clients sending their horses with me explaining the situation. I say I'll continue the same as before until I go, and if they choose to send their horse with me, I'll find a facility to rent stalls when I return.

Francine says of course she'll send Jester. Alex responds that Lendon told her she wants to ride Jambo herself. My heart stops. My chest feels like a wet washcloth being rung. She was giving him up *for me*. How can someone so generous be so uncaring? Alex says it breaks her heart to take him from me but Lendon's just been too good to her.

That makes two of us.

She wants to ride Idocus, too, but Chris wants him to breed in Holland because he's a Dutch Warmblood, so she'll send him with me. This joyful news is mingled with guilt.

I send Lendon an email apologizing for my embarrassing tirade, expressing my gratitude and begging her to stay in touch. No response. I feel like I should walk away from her with nothing, just how I came. Show her that she means more to me than just a trainer. That I don't mind starting over. I know no one else could have given me my knowledge and I'll always have that.

Maybe she senses my recent angst—the battle between my passion to ride and the desire to have another type of life. School? Classes of interest? Travel? Photography? Learning to write with my left hand, playing the piano?

Journal
For the first time in my life, I don't KNOW what I want to do.

◆ ◆ ◆

I spend my final days at the farm basically unchanged. I still teach the same people and ride the same horses. Even Jamboree. And I pack for Idocus and Jester: boots, blankets, tack, supplements, enough feed to make the switch to German feed gradual. I gather everyone's email addresses to send them journals like I did for Young Riders.

Lendon isn't mean to me, she simply refuses to acknowledge me. Francine throws me a going away party and I celebrate, I'm happy, but I keep looking at the door, waiting for Lendon to come in. She doesn't. I'm not sure that bridge can be repaired.

The final thing I want to do before leaving is make sure the horses know what's going on, so a client recommends a horse communicator. It's done over the phone: I send her photos of the horses, call at an appointed time and picture each horse in my mind. She'll tell them what's going on but she'll also listen. My appointment is a half hour—fifteen minutes for each horse.

I picture Jester first. Ahh, she says. There's water next to him that leaks. He's sensitive to mildew.

He's by the wash stall! I say, amazed.

You sit too much on your left seat bone and your right toes scrunch. Your right hand is too tight. The dark haired woman who always yells makes him nervous. He likes the chestnut horse across from him, doesn't like the pinto next to him. He likes it when you call him Big J... she goes on and on. After twenty minutes, she says we better move on to the next horse.

Hmmm...hmmm...hmmm. I'm not getting anything from him. Hmm...hmmm. Nothing. Wait, here we go. He likes to put his ears back, he's learned this gets more respect from humans. He's like a seventeen-year-old Harley Davidson type. He thinks he looks good in dressage but he's talented at jumping. He's very sexually provocative, proud of his anatomy. Silence. Hmmm. Hmmm. I guess that's it.

I crack up. It's their personalities exactly. Jester would love being listened to and would say *and another thing*, and Idocus's reaction would be *this strange voice in my head doesn't belong here* and shun it. And Jester would focus on what others do whereas Idy would only focus on himself.

I want to know what Jambo's thinking.

⋅ 23 ⋅

The day of my departure, it rains. Maybe like if it rains on your wedding day, it's a good omen. Idy and Jester travel in the cargo section of the plane while I travel in the passenger section. I should sleep but I can't; I'm thinking of everything I packed, going through the list over and over again, checking to see if I forgot anything. The fact that I couldn't do anything about it now doesn't prevent me from worrying.

When we arrive, I wait impatiently while the perishables are unloaded and when it's finally the horses' turn, the pallets they're in are lowered onto wheeled platforms. I'm told we'll just go through customs and be on our way.

There are a couple other pallets of horses accompanied by grooms and we file into a large warehouse. Not a word is spoken to us and the people rolling the platforms leave. One of the grooms sits in a corner and lights a cigarette, and after a half hour, I ask him if he thinks they've forgotten us. He shrugs and says, Dis is Amsterdam, sometimes we wait ten minutes, sometimes we wait ten hours. Dey won't forget us.

After three hours, the customs man comes, checks Jester's, Idy's and my passports and we're released. I spend the four hour drive to Mr. Schumacher's farm absorbing the scenery, appreciating the fact that I'm in a different country, that horses are actually creating an adventure instead of preventing one. It's so different from the U.S.; little villages are connected by miles and miles of countryside, planted fields and windmills decorate the surroundings instead of strip malls and dilapidated shacks or enormous mansions, there are no sky scrapers or Dunkin' Donuts. No McDonald's.

We pull into a farm that looks newer than the others and the driver says we're at Kirschborn, the stable where my horses will live. A Dutch girl named Saskia shows me to my stalls and gives me a tour. Unlike Sunnyfield, one farm isn't made of many little barns. Everything's under one roof. The aisles are wide, the stalls are large and there's a big, comfortable viewing area with sofas. I ask her where the paddocks for turnout are and she says, No turnout. Idy will be broken hearted. He loves showing the world how fast he can go, how high he can buck.

After I get the horses settled and unpack their belongings, Saskia takes me to Mr. Schumacher's official training facility which is called Neuhof. The couple minutes drive between the farms is like going through a time warp; Neuhof looks like it's been here for centuries. It's made almost completely out of stone and appears to be at one with the surrounding foliage. It doesn't look like it was built around the trees or that the trees were planted around it but like they formed together.

Many separate buildings surround a courtyard, in the middle of which sits a large cement receptacle for the manure housing two cows. When I ask Saskia the reason for the cows, she answers as if it should be obvious, They stomp down the manure. Then she goes on to explain that when the manure pile is full after a year or so, the cows are butchered for Mr. Schumacher's restaurant and replaced. I'm impressed with the German efficiency and in answer to my question about his restaurant, she tells me he owns one of the best restaurants in Germany, points and says, It's right down that path. There's a bakery, too if you want bread or sweets.

Inside the barn, the aisles are narrow and the stalls are small. Although the feeling the barn evokes of going back in time is quaint and very welcoming to visit, I'm glad my horses are at Kirschborn where there's ample space to move.

Then Saskia leads me to a newer section where my room, one of many self-sustaining apartments for international students, is. When she leaves, I stand in the middle finally fully realizing my state of being. My mind has been completely absorbed in the anxiety of planning, the drama surrounding my departure and the excitement of escaping it. Now here I stand, smack in the middle of a fantasy that a year ago seemed as far-fetched as winning the lottery, and the only thing left to be organized is the apartment in which I stand.

Although filling the drawers with the contents of my suitcases is a brief temptation to complete this organization, curiosity quickly overcomes it. After one final look around, emptying my lungs of the last six months' drama and filling them with the cool, refreshing air of change—of a new country—I go to the riding arena. I feel as if I've reached an island after being shipwrecked and gasping for air on a stormy sea for days, weeks, months.

Ellen Bontje is the head trainer for Mr. Schumacher and is one of the current top riders. She's quite impressive, but I'm starting to realize with a mixture of relief and disappointment, that no matter how many Olympics or World Games one has under their belt, at home, training is training and there are mistakes and ugly moments.

I also meet some of the students and learn that Mr. Schumacher is the coach of the British Olympic team. As impressive as that is, what I appreciate more is that everyone speaks English. They show me the car I rented, a Twingo, as it was already delivered and Emma says in her posh English accent, How very humiliating. I reply with a shrug and a smile that at least it's wheels and independence.

◆ ◆ ◆

The next day, Chris's three-year-old stallions arrive, bomb off the trailer wild and studdy—brilliant all puffed up. They get the first day off but the second day, after lunging to make sure they're safe, I get on. For young horses, they're both remarkably well-behaved. Pyrete is small, black, and intelligent. He gives the impression of feistiness but doesn't put a foot wrong. Poppstarr is tall, bay, sensitive and gives a very good feel in the reins. I can hardly believe my good fortune.

The next day when I'm riding Pyrete, another horse comes into the arena and Pyrete screams and charges toward him. I lean back putting all my body weight into stopping him but he easily outmatches my strength. He's determined to breed to the other horse who isn't even a mare. He rears up, the other horse leaps away and I jump off thinking I'll have more control on the ground. He rears again and I hold on with the rein still riding style between my pinky and ring finger, the other horse leaves and Mr. Schumacher bellows, Lunge him!

So I put the lunge line on and let him out on a circle, but as he pulls the line loop by loop out of my right hand, something keeps getting caught on the line. When I look down, my pinky's sticking out at a right angle. As Pyrete continues bucking around at the end of the line, I hold up my hand to Mr. Schumacher and say, Something's wrong.

Ah, shit, he says. Go to the emergency room! and leaves.

Now that the need for immediate reactions ceases, my brain has a chance to notice the pain. I give Pyrete to my groom, get in my little Twingo and immediately the pain becomes nearly unnoticeable again as my brain is faced with another problem: the Twingo's a stick shift. After contemplating my dilemma for a moment, I slide the seat forward, steer with my left knee and change gears with my left hand. I have no idea where an emergency room is, though—I've been here four days—so I go to Neuhof and into the common room where the riders and workers are eating lunch and ask if someone can help me.

Anya, a working student, says, Let me see. I hold up the hand and she says, It's just out of socket; put it on the bench and I'll stomp it back into place. I agree that it's just out of socket so I consider it but Elsa says, Nonsense, I'll take you to the emergency room, and gives Anya a dirty look.

When my name is called in the ER, I try to lighten the mood by saying, Who needs a pinky anyway? Just take it off.

Take off? No, no, the doctor says without so much as a grin.

The x-ray shows that not only is it not out of socket, it's not the pinky; the bone in my hand is broken. Now I cry. Four days and my trip to Germany is ruined. He tells me I need surgery, a plate needs to be put over the bone to hold it together. My first thought at this news is at least health care is free here, but then he tells me I'll have to stay in the hospital for three weeks. In the U.S., I'd probably be sent home the same day, and unlike when I broke my arm, they don't let me go home first. I'm taken directly to the hospital.

Self-pity overwhelms me. Not only is my reason for being here taken away, I'm all alone. In an unknown country. There's no Lendon stroking my hair, telling me stories, comforting and distracting me. Watching over me. No Mike to absorb my tears and make me laugh. No one.

I get my surgery the next day and waking from it is just as confusing as when they did my arm. But instead of becoming aware of the pain and then remembering my injury, the first thing I become cognizant of is that I'm trapped in a blanket of misery. The fog slowly clears and only after realizing the reason for this agony does my body begin to recognize the secondary pain in my hand.

Then my three week stay begins. I have no way to call Mike—whoever said no news is good news obviously wasn't the one who was trapped in an avalanche and didn't call home—all the nurses disdain me for not speaking German and all I hear is, Ka ka ka, ka ka ka. It's the perfect time to learn German as I'd intended to do in my spare time here, but I decide I'll punish all of Germany by refusing to. In the first week, I read the six books I brought and then I begin mastering my long desired ability to write with my left hand. I don't get any visitors because no one knows me. Even Mr.

Schumacher doesn't visit.

When I'm finally released and call Chris, she informs me that Pyrete had only been breeding for the five weeks before coming. No riding. No wonder he had breeding on his mind. Saskia rides the young stallions for me and Pyrete sends her to the hospital, too. Then we can't find a rider for him. He needs exercise and there are no paddocks so he's turned out in the indoor. Six-foot doors at one end are open at the top and Pyrete jumps them, landing in the parking lot. Somehow he's uninjured and I tell Chris that at least we found a career for him.

When Saskia (who didn't break anything) comes home, she continues riding him and he sends her to the hospital yet again. I tell Chris no one is willing to ride him, to send him to a stable specializing in young stallions. She refuses so my groom just lunges him every day.

Mr. Schumacher's working students ride Jester and Idy for me while I can't ride, but Idy injures his deep digital flexor tendon. Six to eight week recovery.

Mike says I'm too stubborn to stay injured and I hope Idy is, too.

◆ ◆ ◆

When Mike's visit comes, I'm more relieved than excited. I sink into his arms at the airport, don't hug him but savor the feeling of his strong arms around me. We spend ten days immersed in our love for each other. Eat at Mr. Schumacher's restaurant and cook in my little kitchen. Explore all the paths. Pull a comforter over our heads and escape into Mike-and-Courtney-land. Mike learns to groom a horse and I laugh at his meticulousness; with only my left hand, I groom two horses in the time it takes him to do one side of one. The horse's leg gets tired it takes him so long to pick a hoof.

He tells me he needs to come before my horses. Never in two million years would I have thought I'd put a man before my riding but now I think it's unwise and unhealthy to put as foremost importance something that can't reciprocate your love, something so uncontrollable. So I assure him he does. When the time comes for him to leave, we pray he'll get bumped off his flight.

The first couple days after his departure I feel a dreadful longing for his presence, but then the comfort incited by the depth of his feelings for me is replaced by anxiety. Doubt. Confusion. He insists he's lucky to have me but I know he's way too good for me. He attributes me with qualities I lack. He says I'm so strong but I'm not, I'm weak. Thinks I'm so passionate but I feel like a stone. So smart but I can't keep up my end of a conversation on U.S. politics. He's completely sure of his love for me, says he's had me in mind forever but never thought he'd really meet me.

I can't believe that he's in love with me. That I'm still uncertain about

my feelings for him. I believe there's one true love, and although I love him, I don't know that he's my true love. And for how sure he is, I don't know that I'm his. I'm more confused than I was at home.

Maybe if I could figure out what I want to do with my life, I'd be one step closer to figuring out what I want to do with him. I'm lost. Do I even want to ride? Continue to base my whole existence on horses? I've had the notion and toyed with the fantasy of walking away from riding altogether for a long time, but there was always a glimmer of aspiration and excitement. And love. Now I feel nothing. I was *so* passionate, for *so* long, since I was tiny, and here I am, exactly where I wanted to be in all my fantasies and I want to give it all up, escape. I can't do the one thing I'm here for but I can't just go have fun either because I have clients to respect, expectations to live up to... obligations I feel very personal about.

I've always thought it's stupid for people to be unhappy in their situation because life is so open. If you don't like something, change it. Do something new. Without school to attach you, life is totally open, all decisions. Grown-up problems were so simple to me when I was young but I'm losing my idealism very rapidly.

Journal
I have my whole future out in front of me. Amazing how much time people spend doing what they don't want to do. Life is such a gift so full of choices! And yet here I sit in front of my washing machine in downtown Frankfurt...how can I feel so limited and restricted?

• 24 •

Seven weeks after my arrival, I'm allowed to ride. Although I'm poignantly aware that this progression lacks the soul-deep joy that should accompany it, I have hopes that my passion will be reignited. That simply sitting in the saddle and becoming absorbed in the daily mental challenges of training will light the fire in my gut, the one that drove me through years of struggles and then fizzled out.

I start to take lessons immediately and one day, Mr. Schumacher says he wants to get on Jester. As I hand him the reins, an unexpected thrill goes through me with the excitement of seeing him work through things the way I saw Lendon work through things. Mr. Schumacher's a genius.

He mounts in his khakis, loafers and puffy down jacket—looks like the Stay Puft Marshmallow Man. He begins to trot and it's not quite sitting but not quite rising. He looks like a beginner. I can't see him do anything, I just want him to get off. When he finally does, he tells me to get back on and much to my surprise, Jester feels the best he ever has. He's light off the leg, goes sideways easily and powers off his hind end in the extensions. I'm mystified. He must have done *something*, but I have no idea what. He *is* a genius.

Three days later, I tell him Jester's really tired and I should hack him. With Idy laid up and Poppstarr not being able to do much because he's a baby, Jester has worked hard in lessons every day. He says, So what? Some days I'm tired and I still have to work. So does he.

I'm apprehensive but it's stupid to disagree with a trainer if you want to learn, so I get on. Of all things, we work on extensions. Initially I think *poor J*, but they're awesome, he's not the sluggish I expected in the least. He reaches with his front legs and pushes with his hind. Like pirouettes with Idy, Mr. Schumacher's showing me I'm too sympathetic. If I push just that bit more, it makes a world of difference.

This piece of knowledge is like a match being set against wood and starts the flicker of passion I'd hoped for. Progression is the wood that keeps the fire burning and I've been stagnant for so long, the flames died, they had nothing to eat. The past couple years Lendon challenged what I already knew but no longer added new bits of information. This is the reason I came to Germany, to get new insights, and I lost sight of that excitement in my immense disappointment.

◆ ◆ ◆

But days after the flicker of passion is ignited, it's snuffed out, my ability to progress eliminated. Jester pops a splint and is laid up. Then Poppstarr tears his cornea and can't be ridden. With Idy's tendon injury and Pyrete being deemed *unrideable and dangerous* by Mr. Schumacher, I have zero out of four horses. I send my groom home and Mr. Schumacher says, I've never seen someone with such bad luck. The rain certainly wasn't a good omen.

Francine gives me strict instructions to get a dog. I tell her I'm afraid the dog will meet definite doom due to my hex and she says to get it at the pound because then it was doomed anyway. But the pound refuses to let me adopt because, from what I understand, they're worried I'm going to fight the dog. Of course my German is basically nonexistent so all I'm sure of is they won't let me have a dog.

Germany has been a slap in the face. The tidal wave I've been on for the past six years has just hit the shore and as I look around, that other world is like a mystical island, full of palm trees and white sand, bathed in the glow of pure sunshine. Women in hula skirts are beckoning me over. I feel like taking the first flight to Rome, then to some islands and then to Switzerland, Belgium to visit Francine's sister. Just to live, go, move. No love, no horses, no responsibility. Find myself. What a stupid concept. I've been trying for years now to find myself but a decade ago I would have thought *I am me, what's to find?* I wish I had the wisdom of my childhood.

Horses have been the singular force in my life since I was seven years old but now I'm no longer convinced I even want them to be part of it much less the main part. Only two things keep me from abandoning riding altogether. The main one is Francine; she's put so much into me and this horse. The second one is Idy. He's my dream horse, what if I give him up and the dream comes back?

Maybe I'll to go to school full time when I get home. No horses. No Mike. Just school. Alone. Become who I am, who I want to be. I shouldn't *not* do that because I'm afraid to lose what I have but at the same time, there's a lot to let go of.

I need to know that something's concrete, something's solid. So I call Lendon. She's been kept up to date on all my trials and tribulations because I put her on my email list, but we haven't really spoken since the day I regret most in my life. Initially she's a little cold and I'm a little awkward. I ask about Jambo. Lukas. Doc. Bese. Gradually she warms up and I relax. I ask her to come for a visit. No, I can't, Courtney. Please? We'll see.

I begin to call her regularly and although she doesn't seem to look forward to my calls, it comforts me hear her voice.

Journal
Is this my choice? To be unhappy and grow tired of the very thing that drove me through years of challenge? My ten-year-old self would be appalled at how wishy-washy her twenty-three-year-old self has become.

• • •

Two and a half months after landing on German soil, I can sit on Idy's back. My passion for riding remains a smoldering log, but my body and mind luxuriate in sitting astride his back. It's like stepping into a warm bath. He's an old friend, a comfort like Lendon and when I sit on him I forget about everything except the feeling of massive power coming from the magical being underneath me. Like I felt when I was nine years old.

Of course, he's ring sour. After the life he had—turnout, gallops, breeding and hacks—he must be frustrated after doing nothing but hand-walking for two months. I tack walk him in the parking lot weather permitting and wander where we can—the closest thing to a hack I can provide. When he begins to work, he gets happy again and my enjoyment of the learning process is stimulated. The flame isn't ignited but it feels good to have a purpose in my days, for my mind to be absorbed in reality instead of pondering the many possibilities.

The first couple weeks I'm disappointed because he's so hard in the hand, not sensitive to the bit—usually he's so soft, he feels like a second cousin to margarine—but Mr. Schumacher says, That's good, you need to take hold, he needs to *take* the bit. When I'm able to do more with him, I understand what Mr. Schumacher means. Now when I half-halt I can feel, as Lendon describes, his hind legs in my hand. When I stop following for that moment, his hind end still pushes and takes more weight. When he wouldn't put pressure on the bit, his hind end would stop pushing.

I believe in not questioning what your trainer tells you to do unless it borders on abuse. You go to a trainer because they know more than you and you often have to go through a lot of shit to get to a good point. So when Mr. Schumacher tells me to not reward Idy, I don't.

But eventually Idy becomes frustrated and stops trying. At home, I'd always pet and vocally praise him and maybe if he weren't used to that, he wouldn't expect it, but I think it's difficult for horses to understand such a drastic change. To him it must seem like all of a sudden he can do no right. I used to say *yes that's right* and *no that's wrong*. Now I tell him no that's wrong and never say anything's right. He's upset by this. Mr. Schumacher says his work looks good but I know it's not my Idy.

So for once I decide to ignore what my trainer says. In private, I make a big fuss and tell him what a star he is, and in our lessons, I pat him despite being admonished for it. Idy appreciates the appreciation and begins to try again. This is one big difference in training versus clinics; in clinics Mr. Schumacher never told me to reward my horses but he never told me not to.

◆ ◆ ◆

By mid-February, Idy's strong enough to school the Grand Prix work. He didn't forget anything, all the movements are still solid and Chris asks me to take him to the Zwolle stallion show March 3-7. I'm surprised how this excites me.

But then she tells me I'll be leaving him with his new rider at the show. Anky won't take him and she won't tell me who will, but she wants to leave him in Holland to breed. Another big name will take him and pay his expenses, which I know is important to her since she hasn't paid me a dime for three horses and I don't know if she ever paid Lendon.

And Jester's being sent home. The vet says the pop in the splint bone is pushing against the suspensory ligament so he wants to surgically remove the growth on the bone. Surgery itself is dangerous and even if it went well, it would require a three to four month lay-up, but Francine doesn't trust this vet who we don't know and decides to bring him home to get our vet's opinion.

So both of my reasons for staying in horses are gone.

I call Mike. He says it's a catalyst, he'll quit his job and we'll go traveling. Wandering.

I send an email to my journal list:

I have to admit that my humor is finally wavering. I'm going traveling. Horseless in

Germany, who'd have thought. But it's an opportunity I never thought I'd have and admittedly one I've longed for... just to travel, to see things, to be lost for a while. It's hard, it's sad, I'm not too proud to deny my tears, but everything happens for a reason... I guess the gods just had to knock me around a bit... what's wrong with this girl... can't she take a hint?! Ok, finally I got it. So, a month... just traveling... no horses. Freaky.

Then I call Lendon. Update her and beg her to come to the show. You have a trainer, she says. But I want *you*, I say, and she relents. Although I know it's not her way to talk about her feelings, I feel that she's forgiven me for the immature and obnoxious behavior I displayed. I have my mentor back.

• • •

Although it's cloaked in misery, I'm still excited for the show. I'll do the Grand Prix and the Freestyle. I've been doing all the movements but have been conservative on the quality—how much bounce in the passage, sitting in the pirouettes, push in the extensions—protecting his injury. But now he's strong enough, it's time. Mr. Schumacher says, Get the guy!

Mr. Schumacher wants me to use the double—the bridle with two bits—every day since we have to show in it. Most horses are better in the double bridle but Idy detests it. He has a small and sensitive mouth so putting more metal in it is offensive. At home I found the most success if I only rode him in the snaffle, which has one bit, except when we showed because having admirers made his need to show off overcome his defensiveness.

I tell Mr. Schumacher this because normally he's wonderful about varying the system, but because he hasn't seen Idy's reactions firsthand, he trusts his previous decades of experience more than my single experience.

Although I disregarded his advice on patting Idy, that was because of Idy's feelings and, as Lendon always said, a student knows their horse's personality better than the trainer, but Mr. Schumacher knows training better so I willingly take his advice. He's shown me twice that I'm too sympathetic. Maybe I shouldn't *not* ride Idy in the double just because he doesn't like it.

As we get into serious work, Mr. Schumacher insists that Idy looks good but I'm not happy with the work—there's no power, push or umph. He does everything but it's boring. So I ask Mr. Schumacher to get on. This time I watch very carefully, try to catch any glimpse of how his incomprehensible style communicates with the horse. He says Idy feels very good, too—supple and powerful. I say, What do I know? I want perfect. He replies, We are working on that.

Then I get back on and, although I utterly failed to see him do anything and Idy didn't look particularly special in the work he did, he magically feels better—takes the bits evenly, lowers his haunches more and trots with a bit more push and power. Maybe *Mr. Schumacher* doesn't even know what he does, it's just instinctual.

As I did at home, we work all the pieces of the test, but as the show gets closer, we do the whole thing. Mr. Schumacher says, Ja, this was a good test... a few things to work on, but we still have a week almost don't forget. Now I have a plan and we ride the test two more times before you go.

Ok, good, I say, and what about the freestyle?

Oh, shit. That is a different subject.

I just look at him and wait for him to continue. He leaves. Ok then. Only the top five make it to the freestyle so let's go for number six?

◆ ◆ ◆

I get many responses to my previous email and finally send a group email to explain my thoughts:

Many of you have asked me what my plans will be for when I come home. I wish I could tell you. I don't have the information I need to decide that yet. I could be any number of places. I want to be in school full time again. Maybe ride and teach part time. This trip has taught me more than I care to know but one of those things is the necessity of balance in one's life. I sacrificed my whole childhood for these goals, neglected people that loved me, let amazing friends slip through my fingers. I wouldn't go back and do it differently; I'm amazed and humbled by how my life has progressed, but I think to be happy and successful... to be able to remain honest and uncorrupt, one needs balance. Just imagine if these horses were the only thing in my life, if I didn't have a great boyfriend and love to go out dancing... I think I would have become a statistic. I think that anything one relies wholly upon for happiness and livelihood corrupts them. But I'm young and naive and blonde to boot, so all my philosophical jabber should probably be ignored. In other words, I'm checking my options... any suggestions, ideas, reciprocated philosophical jabber would be welcomed and appreciated.

◆ ◆ ◆

We're scheduled to leave for the show on Tuesday, but on Sunday I get a call that Idy has to go to the show ASAP because Zwolle is in Holland and there's danger of the borders being closed due to foot and mouth disease going around. I can't go because I need to get Jester on his flight at five a.m. Tuesday, so I put Idy on a trailer with a note: *to whom it may concern, please feed him and walk him if you have time.* Normally this would terrify me, I'd be hysterical, but it seems like par for the course. I can't believe how ridiculously ill-prepared I am for my first show in Europe.

When Jester's on the trailer ready to go, the truck driver finds his battery's dead. I ask him if he has jumper cables. Nein, he says. How about a flashlight? I ask. Dis truck is brand new, is his defense. We end up pulling the horse van forward with the farm's tiny tractor and a two foot rope giving the truck enough momentum to start, a method that can be used with a manual. Perhaps it's better to send him off when I'm irritated so it's not so sad.

Journal
Well, it seems that I'm coming to the last chapter of my "Deutschland dramas" saga... and true to my record here, I'm doing it with all the possible complications and tribulations the gods can deal out. Truly by this point, if we were still in those days of superstitions and gods, I'd have been burned at the stake long ago.

◆ 25 ◆

On the drive to Zwolle, my irritation becomes less and less and finally disappears. The young horses are going to a trainer in Holland tomorrow so I have no more horses in Germany. No horses anywhere.

It's sad. But it's liberating.

I feel both.

I feel neither.

I want to cry but I can't. My emotions are tired. I feel nothing. Empty.

When I get to Zwolle, Idy's stall is empty. He's gone. When my brain digests what my eyes are seeing and the information travels to my heart, my emotions are jumpstarted and I panic like a mother who misplaced her child. I race down the aisle and see him sauntering away at the end of a girl's leadline.

Courtney? an accented voice behind me says. I whip around. It's a young blonde girl and she introduces herself as Marlies van Baalen, she'll be Idy's new rider. She says it must be so hard to lose such a great horse, she's so sorry for me. She tells me not to worry, they've been looking after him. Katja's taking him for a walk and I can come to their stalls to wait for him if I want.

I hesitate, look around. Realize I have nowhere else to go. She's looking at me, her expression sympathetic and comforting. The numbness returns and I follow her to their stalls.

Her mother is Coby van Baalen, a Dutch Olympian, and they each have one horse. But there are two grooms plus the one walking Idy. The horses are sparkling clean and seem happy. Their stalls have name plates with ivy borders. There's a bowl of sugar on a table and two bags of carrots. I imagined Idy going to a dank, dark place and the only time he'd ever leave his stall would be to work. But he'll get the spoiling he deserves. If Idy has to go someplace, I'm glad it's to them.

◆ ◆ ◆

I school Idy for the remaining three days before the show begins certain that I'll embarrass my country. Marlies and her crew never come over, respect giving me my final time alone with Idy. In the Grand Prix test, the winner gets 69%. I get 64.7%. Fourth place. I'm in the Freestyle.

I ride through my choreography in the test without thinking. My body reacts but my mind is non-responsive. When I come out of the ring, Lendon's beaming and we stand together to watch the highlights on the TV screen while they calculate my score. The piaffes are on the spot. He looks up to the bit. The passage has swing and power. I watch removed, as if it's not me. The score comes out at 70.0% for third place and Lendon's amused at my surprise, acts as if my success was expected.

I feed Idy his dinner and stand looking at him through the bars. He occasionally looks up at me wondering why I'm there. I want to explain what's happening to him; he won't understand—tomorrow the van Baalens will put him on a trailer and he won't know why I'm not there. The first few days he'll look for me, but then he'll have new people. I take a deep breath and walk away.

Journal
Goodbye international competition. Goodbye plummeting toward the top.

• 26 •

Journal
Isn't life funny? Sometimes I look at my hands and realize that, at some point, they'll be dead. They'll no longer move. And sometimes I look at them and think...LIFE! How many options! How many chances and choices! It's amazing, and do I live my life in retrospect? Do I say, "I will have wanted this or that?" Does it matter? Yes, it does. You have to do what makes you happy. For each day and for the next fifty years.

Mike meets me at Neuhof, I get my stuff, and we go. Spend the rest of March and the beginning of April traveling—drive through Switzerland, down the west coast of Italy, Sicily to Tunisia and back up the east coast. We see the Cinque Terre, Florence, Rome, Naples, Palermo. Go to the island volcano of Stromboli, Naples, Bologna and Venice.

We find a stray puppy outside of Rome who reminds me of my childhood wolf, the best dog ever. He's big and white and we keep him, name him Qui Vicino which we think means nearby and use it often (is there a bathroom nearby?) but we're really not sure. We call him Quiver for short.

Mike and Quiver

As we travel, I appreciate Mike more but of course with that comes the fear of losing him. He swears his love for me will never end but I can't make myself believe him. I convince myself that he's looking at other girls, that he'll realize someone else is better. I get upset and don't tell him why. I'm paranoid about giving him my heart. I need time. It's so damn scary. So damn complicated and so damn irritating that I make it complicated.

My worries are my worst enemy. Because I keep questioning his love, it's testing it and I give him a reason to not love me. Am I weak to run away from my problems with him or am I weak to stay with him for fear of being without him?

But the question is, how am I supposed to have a good relationship with him if I don't have a good one with myself? I don't respect myself. As a matter of fact, I detest myself, loathe my wishy-washiness. One day, I'm convinced I want to marry Mike and the next I want to break up with him.

The one thing I'm certain of is that I'll go to school full time when I get home. Even if I get my passion for riding back, which with my current fickleness may happen, I need something to fall back on. What if I lose the passion again? Get hurt? Don't succeed?

Where to go to school and how are the only questions. I could go out west, somewhere new, or I could stay in New York where I know. Mike is understandably concerned about where he fits in. So am I. Do I want to be with him? Do I want to be alone? Wherever I go, I'll just ride a bit on the side to make money. I can't continue to ride full time and learn anything else. My brain is exhausted.

As the trip comes to an end, I miss the States. I look forward to rejoining all the wonderful people from the riding world who care about me. Having dinner with Mike's mom and giving our families their gifts. Going out with Mike's friends and visiting Sunnyfield. Visiting my sister, my Grammy. To getting a Dunkin' Donuts coffee, seeing a movie, shopping and cooking a nice dinner.

Quiver's plane ticket costs more than Mike's and mine combined, but he's worth it. I love him more than I did my wolf. And that's a lot.

• 27 •

I return home at the beginning of April and although my dad has come to appreciate my world and takes pride in its accomplishments, he's overjoyed at my uncertainty. Says he'd be happy to pay for school even if I ride.

I get brochures from schools out west and look them over as if they're real considerations, but I know they're not. The slow leak in my pool of passion may have completely drained the reservoir, but riding remains my best way to make money so I need to stay near Sunnyfield where I know people, where they know me.

Lendon's in her office when I go to see her. She looks up and when she sees me, her expression softens. She sets down her pen and smiles. Well, did you get it out of your system? I nod and hand her a small, blue, ceramic horse from Italy. She sets it down, walks over and hugs me. So, wanna ride? she asks.

I tell her I do but I may not fit into my breeches because my diminished work load hasn't diminished my appetite.

• • •

Jester's spent the month resting but our vet says he'll be fine and I gradually bring him back to work. The summer's spent like previous summers: riding, teaching and showing. Jester does well at Prix St. Georges, but mid way through the season his popped splint becomes a problem again. The vet says he'll be sound but won't hold up to upper level work which defeats Francine's purpose of keeping him for me. So we sell him as a lower-level horse and I just ride and show the horses she has for herself.

This should feel like a deep loss but I'm almost relieved. To not have to let Francine down, to not have to tell her after all she's done for me *thanks, but I changed my mind.* I'm pleased that I still enjoy riding—sitting on a horse's back and spending that hour lost in conversation, listening and making sure I'm understood—but my drive to get to the top remains like tumbleweed in the desert. It used to have roots, was grounded in the earth, but now it's dead.

I mourn the loss of these roots—the dream that's guided me through the vast majority of my twenty-three years—and with this comes mourning the loss of Idocus. I didn't know how much it hurt. I thought I was numb from the beating Germany gave me, that perhaps in some way losing him provided relief too, but I'd just tucked away the pain. He was the final step of reaching my international dreams and I lost him. Once I have a good, hard, soul-wrenching cry about it, I feel much better, more like myself than I have in months. It provides a sense of closure, like having a final, grown-up conversation with a boyfriend you love but the relationship can't be maintained.

◆ ◆ ◆

Feeling that I've made peace with the closing of a chapter allows me to put all my focus into opening the next one: school. I apply and am accepted to Columbia University in Manhattan, and as September approaches, Mike, Quiver and I move into an apartment in the Bronx. Forty-five minutes of walk plus subway ride get me to school and a forty-five minute drive deposits me at Sunnyfield.

At orientation, I'm reminded of my awkwardness. Despite my yearning to talk to people, to make friends, I can't force myself to make conversation. I'm afraid that anything I say will come out stupid and if I catch someone looking at me, I look away. I know that if I were them, I'd think I was a snob but as I've discovered with Mike, knowing the problem lies in me doesn't help to fix it. I decide I'll make friends in classes, but when they begin I don't see how I can when I don't live in the dorm; it's all listening to the teacher.

Although I utterly fail at my social intent, the education provides the inspiration I craved. I swear my Ancient Greece teacher puts on his toga at night. That my Comparative Religions teacher spends her evenings studying ancient scrolls. They're as passionate about their subjects as I was about riding. Their excitement excites me.

◆ ◆ ◆

One day when I get home from the barn, Mike is gone but his computer's on. I shower, make a cup of cocoa and nestle up in my cushy leather chair to study. I open my economics book to the correct chapter and look at the pages. Keep looking but can't focus. Then I look at his computer. It's open to his emails. I look at the economics pages again. Back at the computer. Finally, I huff, shove myself up and walk to his computer telling myself I'll just prove to myself how ridiculous I'm being. Yes, it bugs me that he's on it all the time but surely he has nothing to hide.

I look at the open email. It's from his ex-girlfriend, the one he loved. I close it and scroll through the other emails. They've been conversing for two weeks. I read them, fingers shaking, face hot but no tears. My jaw drops. Apparently they met up last week.

When Mike comes home, I'm sitting in my chair with my economics book lying open and ignored on my lap.

Hey, Babe, he says and comes over intending to kiss me.

I look him straight in the eye and finally tears of anger spill out.

He reaches to wipe them away and I slap his hand.

I know, I tell him. I read your emails. You saw Kim and didn't tell me!

Nothing happened! I feel nothing for her! I didn't tell you because I knew it would upset you!

You've been talking to her for two weeks. You didn't think I'd care?

I knew you would, that's the problem! I love you, Court, why don't you believe that?

You don't hide things from people you love! Get out!

He tries to take my hand and I snap it away. Out!

In the following months, I break up with him several times and always beg him to come back. Finally he refuses. Riding the subway to school, I can't believe people go on with their lives. A girl with a blue mohawk chats with another girl who has her nose and lip pierced. She snaps her gum. A guy talking on his cell phone laughs loudly and talks with his hands, which is pointless. A guy in a suit spills coffee on himself and gets very upset. They go on with their lives but mine is ended. It was my fault. I shit on his love and made him stop loving me.

Slowly I begin to realize that his refusal to come back was the only way to break up. It was a good thing. I love him, love the person who he is, but I'm realizing that's different from in love. I believe there's one true love for each person and I couldn't believe he loved me because I knew he wasn't mine. I may not find *the one* till I'm forty, but now I've learned. I won't make this mistake again. Although I know it's good that we broke up, I can't forgive myself for what I put this wonderful person through. I still love him.

• 28 •

Although Mike cutting the cord I used like the string of a yoyo to toss him away then pull him in again, releases my heart from the horrifying confusion of my feelings, it also leaves me with a problem: I need someone to cover half the rent. So my only friend from school, Kerry, moves in. After a couple months of cohabitating with her, I realize I'm never going to fit in at school because of the age and life experience difference.

I want to meet people, to go out and have fun, dance. I've gotten a taste of being carefree and I like it. I try to go to bars in Manhattan alone but am disappointed in the results; no guy is like Mike—they're interested in my body not my personality—and when I talk to girls, they think I'm hitting on them. So I join match.com which is mainly used as a dating site but offers a service for those who want to meet friends.

In February, a guy from New Zealand, Jason Dye, emails me. He asks why I joined match. I reply that my fifty-year-old clients don't want to go out partying till two a.m. and the nineteen-year-olds from school don't have IDs. Why did he? His company transferred him here and he wants to meet people outside of his industry.

After several emails and talks on the phone, we make a date at a little Italian restaurant in Soho. Instead of the anxiety I felt as my first date with Mike approached, only excitement appears. This is the start. I'm going to make up for the many years of childhood I lost.

Our date is at 7:30 and at 7:45, I'm speeding down the Henry Hudson Parkway. I hustle into the restaurant and scan the faces at the tables. He's sitting in the corner looking at me: blonde, blue eyes, tall. Handsome. I apologize for my tardiness to which he replies, No worries.

The chatter comes so easily we order our second bottle of wine before dinner. When Mike looked at me, it felt like he was trying to crawl inside my soul, and when the guys at the bars look at me, it feels like they see just the shell and whether I have a soul or not is inconsequential. But when Jason looks at me, it feels like he's inviting my soul to come out and play. He's the type of guy I can be a kid with, escape the intensity that's blanketed every aspect of my life.

He's seven years older than I am and a logistics manager for an ocean freight company. He'd accepted a transfer to L.A. but at the last minute they changed it to Carteret, New Jersey.

I tell him I love to dance. He says he hates to dance. So I invite him to a Zydeco concert, a Cajun style music I love to dance to, in the Bronx the following night. It will probably be mostly eighty-year-olds, I tell him. He shrugs and asks what time he should pick me up. When the dinner is finished, we walk out the door, stop and turn to face each other.

He points behind him and says, I'm parked that way.

I point behind me and tell him I'm parked that way.

He steps closer. I step closer. His lips just brush mine, linger there, and then are gone.

• • •

At the Zydeco concert, I can see why he hates to dance. Because he can't. I tell him to pick someone out and mimic them, pretend he's making fun of them. He mimics the seventy-year-old man next to us, then a younger woman, then another guy, then me. This is absolutely not a cool place, but he clearly enjoys himself, works up a sweat dancing.

The third time we see each other, he tells me a client gave him tickets to the opening ceremony of the Salt Lake City Olympics that weekend and asks if I want to go. The ceremony is only one evening, but we go for three days. Rent snowmobiles, sit in bars, play pool, pretend to shop and don't buy anything.

Whereas Mike was very affectionate and always had to be touching me, Jason never does. The only time our skin touches is in bed. We give each other a hard time—incessantly tease and bring attention to each other's faults. My, your hands are skinny, I'll tell him. Did you miss puberty or did you have a breast reduction? he'll say. Did you go to a special school for your special needs? Teasing certainly suits my humor but there are no compliments to back it up. I conclude that he simply doesn't like me.

So it's a surprise when he calls the day after we get home. We begin to see each other almost every evening, and for Valentine's Day, he brings a bag from CVS with chocolates for me and a toy clown for Quiv, which Quivvy repetitively dismantles. He meticulously detaches each button, the nose, the eyes, the hat with his enormous jaws before pulling out every bit of stuffing. Each time he finishes his task, Jason duct tapes it back together. After the fourth time, I find it on my rocking chair with a note:

To Quiver—my nemesis
You underestimate the ability and skill of a world renowned clown surgeon who with a few bandages and precise internal re-stuffing has made this clown as good as—no, better than—new.
Know this: we fear you not White Peril!
He he he ha ha ha (evil laugh)
Signed:
Butt-Crack
(Brothers United Together Today- Clowns Revolt Against Clown Killers)

◆ ◆ ◆

Jason eliminates my self-imposed pressure and reduces my tendency to overanalyze everything. He thinks when we die, we just go in the ground and are eaten by worms whereas I consider every possibility: perhaps, as cells make up a body, Earth is just a miniscule part of a greater being. Or maybe we're like chess pieces in a game between gods. Perhaps we live many lives and each life is a chapter in our whole story. With each life we're meant to learn, to grow, so the wisest individuals have lived the most lives, and when we finally learn the ultimate lesson, we enter a space of eternal happiness.

With Jason, I don't need to think of explanations. I don't need to be sure of anything. I can just be. My soul is slowly coming out to play.

105

◆ ◆ ◆

After Jason and I have been dating five weeks, Kerry and I are called into the dean's office. Some papers we wrote on Yeats were strikingly similar and they accuse us of cheating. They show us the papers. I'm astounded. They're almost identical except she changed a few words and phrases. How could she possibly think the teacher wouldn't notice?

She moves out that night and I stand in our bedroom, barren of her belongings. What am I going to do? I can't afford this apartment alone and no one wants to share a one-bedroom.

Jason says, I don't want to freak you out or anything, but what if I moved in?

I'm freaked out. What I love about our relationship is that there's no aspect of seriousness at all, and this would make it serious. But I need a roommate.

But I want to see other people, I tell him.

He shrugs and says, Just don't bring them here. He's not happy with his living arrangement so he'd move either way.

After a pause, he hugs me. Reminds me that I need a roommate.

I nestle into him. I want my organs to be crushed into each other, the act of breathing to become a challenge. For how much I want to be free, I crave the physical security of strong arms holding me together. Squeeze, I tell him. Hug me like you mean it.

I agree to a trial period.

◆ ◆ ◆

When he moves in, at first it's easy, as our whole relationship has been. I like who I am with him. He makes me feel beautiful. Smart. Funny. Because he's willing to point out my faults, I know he's telling me the truth. He blows confidence into my deflated ego.

The problem is, I don't see anyone else. Although I love all our time together, the last thing I wanted was to be in a committed relationship. I want to be silly, wild, reckless. Free. See a different guy every night.

After a month, my instinct to panic and run away from what I perceive as seriousness sets in. I tell him that living together makes it awkward to see other people. I still want to see him but I want to see other people, too.

If he'd told me that, I wouldn't hesitate to get up and leave. After having a temper tantrum. If you don't *know* if you want me, you obviously don't. But he's so mature, so secure. He doesn't get mad, says he doesn't understand why we need to see other people but if I need to get it out of my system, we can try.

We spend the night snuggling on the couch.

Journal

My problem is that I want everything. All at once. I need to decide what I really want. I want a boyfriend but I want to be free. I want to walk away and go to school and have a career. Work in a restaurant. Live alone in Paris. Paris is a perfect place to lose myself and then find myself. I want to move to Chicago to be with my sister. I want Jason but I don't want to be constricted.

It takes him two days to find an apartment and he moves out. My need for a roommate remains however, and I have no more options of people I know. So I place an ad. The first response is from a thirty-two-year-old Egyptian man and initially I think no way. But as the week my ad will run draws to a close with no more responses, Jason helps me hang a curtain between our beds and Ahmed moves in.

Soon after he moves out, Jason writes me a poem entitled *Eleven Weeks:*

A planned encounter, an enchanted evening, a soft kiss goodnight, a giggle.
The second liaison, a cheeky question,
An instant answer, dancing and laughing, a kiss in the rain.
A special night, flowers, wine and a ribbon wrapped bone, dancing together alone, falling asleep on the couch felt so right.
On a plane to the snow, cards and fun, on a stranger's bed, two strangers connected.
Riding snowmobiles together, enjoying the scenery, a playfight in soft powder, sunshine, laughter, photos, a perfect day.
Spending time together, learning about our pasts, open and honest, special.
Circumstances beyond our control, the trial period, the decision was ours, the decision was right. Living together, learning to hug, sleeping together, stealing a kiss in the dark.
Waking together, hugs in the morning, late for work, who cares.
Making love, looking in to each other, becoming one, making love.
Analyzing us, creating doubt, it's been eleven weeks, just be happy.
Eleven weeks, our relationship is but a germinating seed, waiting to sprout, to grow, to bloom.
Give it that chance.
Give it that chance.

◆ ◆ ◆

It takes three months to get the carefree-need out of my system. I've dated and danced but Jason's always the person I want to see. I ask him to move back in, tell him I'm ready to be committed.

As the months pass, a unified life forms. We develop standard meals to cook: chili, bruschetta, steak and spuds. Have Kahlua-o'clock every evening and discover a mutual love of poker. Simply have fun. I'm happy in the unique lack of complexity.

But then he begins to send me little emails from work: *thinking of you, can't wait to see you*, leaves me notes on the kitchen counter: *love you, xxx*. He says he knows he wants to spend his life with me but is fine that I don't. Once again, panic consumes me. Although I'm extremely happy with him right now, I fully believe that what allows that happiness is the elimination of considering our future. But he's considering it and the last thing I want to take a chance of doing is shitting on his love.

Right before school starts, he invites me to go to New Zealand with him for my Christmas break and my overactive brain which has been slowly awakening jumps into overdrive. Not only would that mean two weeks away from my horses, but it feels like if I go, I've got to be serious about *us*. He certainly doesn't pressure me, but I feel pressure.

◆ 29 ◆

I'm riding Lambada one day and it strikes me that it's odd that I *care* about two weeks of not riding him. I'm doing this to make money, right?

It's as if someone's shaken me awake from a deep slumber and I open my eyes completely surprised by my state of being. A change has crept up on me while I've been preoccupied with other things: making money was my initial incentive to ride, but now I'm riding to ride—I *want* to become really, really good. My passion has been reignited.

I lost my passion to burnout—non-stop work and horses—and I vow to not let that happen again. I'll make a point to take a solid ten-day vacation once a year and regular three-day excursions. Have activities that have nothing to do with horses. I may or may not be in the Olympics but I *will* be happy, not base all my happiness on one such uncontrollable thing. I remove every horse related decoration from my house and separate my life into two clear parts: the horse-life and the non-horse-life.

School provides me with this desired unrelated activity and when it begins, I pack as many classes as possible into Monday and Wednesday so I can spend the other days at the barn. I often study at four a.m. because my brain is more alert then than in the evenings. Which I want to save for Jason anyway.

The vow to take vacations eliminates half my concern about going to New Zealand—leaving my horses—but my anxiety about being serious remains. I tell Jason that I know I want to go but I'm not sure about *us*. He says, Court, you make everything so complicated. It's a trip, it's not going to change our relationship. We'll go have fun, no worries.

I buy a ticket and my first ten-day trip turns into two weeks.

◆ ◆ ◆

We spend a week in the Bay of Islands with his family and two best friends—D.P. and Buttcheeks—and their wives and kids. The feeling in their house is the more the merrier. We go on daily fishing excursions: net the bait in the morning, fish in the afternoon and eat it for dinner. Play bocce ball with his parents. Wander the miniscule town. As with my siblings, each evening is spent over a card table and of all places, New Zealand introduces me to Michigan Rummy.

The second week, we fly into Christchurch, rent a campervan and travel the South Island. Our first stop is Queenstown, the adventure capital of the world, and before we go downtown, we book ourselves to go tandem-skydiving the next day.

We wander into a pub late in the evening and sit at the bar. The boisterous table behind us attracts our attention; they're playing a drinking game that resembles duck-duck-goose. A little guy with reddish dread-locks walks around the table, touches each person's head and says something incomprehensible. When he gets to a certain person, they scramble up and chase him, but the chase is dramatically slow-motion and all the people sitting down chug their beers until the goose finally catches the dread-locked guy who sits down and does a shot. Their antics amuse us till one a.m., but our skydiving is at eight so we climb back in the campervan to buckle down for the night.

When we pull into the skydiving site the next morning, we're met by none other than the dread-locked guy who, other than some bloodshot eyes, looks no worse for the wear. He gives us jumpsuits to put on: a big powder pink one for Jason—which makes him look like the Easter bunny—and a smaller blue one for me.

A rusty blue truck pulls up and he instructs us to get in. The driver is a nine-year-old boy sitting on a book and he drives us to a yellow plane caked with manure parked in a sheep field. I'm attached to Mr. Dreads, who's a good six inches shorter than I am, and as we ascend, the pilot veers so close to cliffs it's an adventure in itself. I'm a little scared, I tell Mr. Dreads to which he replies, You should be, you're about to jump from fifteen thousand feet. The door opens and he tells me to jump. I tell my body to but like a horse refusing a fence, it won't. Suddenly my body is catapulted out the door and in sheer terror, I scream as I've never screamed before. Then I realize I can barely hear my screaming and become entertained trying to scream so loudly I can hear it. The rest of my forty-five second free-fall is spent joyously attempting to outmatch the noise of the wind and when we land, I beg Jason to do it again.

We drive up the west coast through the Canterbury plains and camp out wherever the views are good. Attach a hose to the sink nozzle and shower on the edge of a lake which appears undiscovered by the human race. Unlike my vacation with Mike, I never find my mind searching for complications. It's too busy experiencing.

I've had dreams about Mike for months. In them, he's always mean—callous and resentful—and I'm always apologizing. He's cruel even to my deepest pleas. But when we get home from New Zealand, I have a dream that he embraces me, tells me he could never hate me, hugs me tight and kisses my hair. I don't know if it's because my relationship with Jason is good, but I finally forgive myself for the torture I put Mike through.

Me, Jason and Mr. Dreads

• 30 •

When we get home, I schedule my spring semester the same way as the fall, but as the months drag on, Jason and I begin to discuss a move. We both hate living in the City—the smell, the parking dilemma, the endless concrete—wouldn't it be nice to live in the country? Maybe somewhere closer to the barn?

By summer, we decide to do it and rent a house in Sherman, Connecticut, which is an hour and a half from school but only twenty minutes from the barn. It's small, yellow and cozy, enveloped in trees with a gravel drive and a mailbox. And it has a yard, which will make Quivvy ecstatic.

Candlewood Lake is nearby so Jason buys a boat. He misses being near the water and although being in driving distance to a lake is a shabby substitute for being in walking distance to the ocean as he was in New Zealand, at least it's something.

My four a.m. starts continue during the summer, but now they're to finish my riding early enough to be home by one and spend the afternoon on the boat with Jason. Quivvy perches on the bow looking like a hood ornament, which attracts endless attention from other boats, and Jason and I play Texas Hold 'em, drink sangria, and munch on almonds. Afternoons on the boat feel like mini vacations and energize me, fill my lungs with fresh air.

But as the summer ease dwindles away and fall approaches, I'm faced with a quandary. I want to graduate this year, 2004, and in order to do so I need to take five classes each semester. But I have seven horses in full training. My best horses are a five-year-old Arabian cross and a four-year-old Friesian who aren't the most talented mounts, but that doesn't make me love it any less. I don't want to give up any horses. So the solution I come up with is: you can sleep when you're dead.

◆　◆　◆

When graduation day finally arrives, Jason has a party at our house. I still have no school friends but my whole family and all my barn friends come. We mingle in our ample yard, play bocce ball and horseshoes, and my brother puts a sticker on my forehead that says *I are a graduate and I no plenty.* My dad tings his glass and everyone turns to him.

We're here to celebrate Courtney's graduation from Columbia University, he says. We all know Courtney is a motivated and strong-willed individual. An example of these personality traits is the route she took to get her college degree. Let me tell you the story.

He tells about my year with Lendon, my freshman year at the University of Michigan and how he felt when I told him I was going back to Lendon.

But Courtney's mind was made up, he says, and it soon became clear to me that no amount of talk would change that. Our relationship was strained for a while because I thought she was making a mistake. Obviously, I was wrong because here we are, seven years later, and Courtney is a rising star in the dressage arena and holds a degree from one of the finest universities in the country. She kept her commitment to me and she kept her commitment to herself. You can imagine the discipline, the effort and the determination it took to tackle and accomplish these two pursuits simultaneously. Courtney, I'm so proud of you. Congratulations!

He has tears in his eyes and so do I. The party continues but I stay close to him, can feel the pride emanating off his skin. I've never been so touched in my life.

◆　◆　◆

Two days later, before my family has all flown home or I've come down off my cloud, Lendon calls. Do you want a nice young horse?

Of course I do! I say.

She tells me that someone named Richard Malloch owns a super young horse and wants to change trainers. He wants to see the horse go all the way.

I meet him at Abruzzi for lunch and like him immediately because he orders a beer. I was nervous but he makes me feel completely at ease.

He tells me he bought Roby II as a four-year-old. He'd done extremely well in the Young Horse competitions in Europe and needs a new rider here. When I tell him I'd love to be that rider, he says that if our relationship progresses in a positive direction, then in six months or so he'd be interested in buying me another top caliber horse, one more trained.

He asks me to email him a list of my short and long term goals. So I do:

Short Term Goals: 1-2 years
Be competitive at Grand Prix
Compete in the Pan Am Games
Be competitive in Europe: Aachen, Frankfurt, etc.
Overall goal to achieve recognition as a solid top-class competitor.
Ideal situation:
Have one solid Grand Prix horse, perhaps not Olympic quality, but very competitive right away
Have two horses competitive in the small tour (one extremely special, one good enough- this could be Lambada or someone else)
Roby and hopefully one more very good young one

Midterm Goals: 3-4 years
Make the Olympic Team
Ideal situation:
Have two possible contenders for the Olympics (if the solid Grand Prix horse wasn't good enough, sell and replace, the super small tour horse should now be solid Grand Prix)
Still have at least two special small tour horses: (Roby + another)
Keep the quality young horses coming in (hopefully other sponsors will have been attracted).

Long Term Goals
Continue being a presence in the top international sphere; be prime for the following two Olympic Games.
Consistently have a minimum of two top Grand Prix horses, two or three small tour horses and young ones at home

I know many sports psychologists disagree, but I don't try to make my goals realistic. I think what's the point in asking yourself to strive for something you know is attainable? Apparently Richard agrees because he says that hopefully Roby can help me achieve those goals.

Journal

A fantastical moment that has appeared in so many of my daydreams actually happened. Richard is his name. (I wonder how familiar and important that name will become in my future.) He's providing me with one very talented horse, possibly two. The one he has is a young horse, Roby, and he'll come to me on August 1st. Richard said that if everything goes well and if our relationship progresses in a positive direction, then in six months or so he'd be interested in buying me another top-caliber horse that's trained. It's truly amazing. I feel so deeply thankful, humbled and amazed.

When Roby comes, he surpasses my expectations; he's an extraordinary mover. And beautiful. Elegant and tall. But as we begin work, I find he's quite lazy and weak behind. Rich tells me he had rhino, herpes myelitis, so badly he could barely stand up as it affected his nervous system which explains his weakness. But he's cured and training should reestablish the strength.

◆　◆　◆

Days after he comes, Lendon calls again. She says that after the Olympics (which Idy and Marlies made), the von Baalens' lease is up and Chris is anxious to bring Idy back. No names were mentioned in their conversation but she'd love to see me and Idy reunited. Am I interested?

I point out that that's a sillier question than if I want a nice young horse. She says she'll suggest it to Chris.

Lendon amazes me. She's introduced me to every single equestrian opportunity I've had thus far: Francine, Rich, Young Riders. Idy initially and now she's trying to again. She's like my fairy godmother.

Later that evening, I'm on the phone with Rich and tell him about the conversation. He calls an hour later and says, I don't know if it would help or not, but I'd offer to cover Idocus's expenses and she could still breed him. Just a thought.

I tell him that if I know Chris, that's exactly what she'd want and thank him profusely. Well, we have a start on your goals, he says.

◆　◆　◆

When I tell Jason the incredible news that night, he doesn't seem as enthused as I expected. He knows how much I love that horse. He says, Don't get your hopes up, honey. It was an idea and may not happen. I tell him I won't be excited until I hear his hooves clopping down the aisle.

Then I find out what's really on his mind. He says he was offered a job managing his branch office in Melbourne, Australia. He'd make more money, get work experience and be closer to the friends and family he misses. He hates the lifestyle here.

I tell him he should take it.

It wouldn't be worth risking our relationship, though, he says.

He takes my hands and looks in my eyes. I look back in his. Then at our joined hands. Take a deep breath and say I'd certainly try to have a long distance relationship but admit it would be really hard. I live in the boonies and have absolutely no friends in the vicinity. And I know me, I want to have fun and in my industry there's no one young to hang out with. I try to meet girls at bars but they snub me, assume I'm a lesbian. I'm embarrassed to say this but my only way to go out is to date. Even when I signed up on match.com to meet friends I only got guys wanting dates. I don't want a new boyfriend but my only way to go out is to date.

He's shocked. It never occurred to him that I might feel the need to date. He says, When I'm committed, that just isn't a possibility. I believe him but tell him I can't picture myself sitting alone in my house for two years. I know it's not going to happen.

He says, If I asked you to marry me, would you say yes?

No, I reply.

He says he'll think about it.

* * *

After Lendon tells Chris about Rich's offer, Chris calls me and we arrange a meeting at my house. Chris, Rich, Jason and me. Rich says he'll incur the cost of Idy's transportation back to New York and make yearly contributions to his ongoing expenses. I'll cover the rest. During the following weeks a lease agreement is made, but I stick to my decision to not get excited until I hear his hooves clopping down the aisle.

When they leave, Jason takes my hands and sits me down on the couch.

I turned down the job offer, he says.

I look down and squeeze his hands. I'm glad, I tell him. When I look up, his eyes and arms embrace me.

◆ 31 ◆

In early winter, Idy comes home. As a stallion, he's required to spend a month in quarantine and the day he arrives there, I hang over the stall door and gaze at him while he sniffs at the wall for scents of his neighbors. When he finally glances at me, I think I see a flicker of recognition but he's immediately distracted by an incoming horse. Although he doesn't further acknowledge me, I have to believe he knows me. That face is too intelligent not to.

I put him at one of the few quarantine places that allows riding, but the footing is so horrendous I just hand walk him. Twice I find him with no water and three times with no blanket. When he's finally released, I breathe a sigh of relief. Finally I hear his hooves clopping down the aisle and can be excited.

The day after he comes to Sunnyfield, I take him for a hack and realize how much I missed his walk—the long, easy, powerful, purposeful swing. All the muscles in his back elongating and contracting. I'm sure that other horses technically have the same walk, but Idy's feels different. The shape of his barrel? The broadness of his back? I've ridden countless horses but none who I've felt were made for me like Idy.

The following day, I ride him in the indoor. He swishes his tail and pins his ears when I ask him to go forward, bloats against my leg and pretzels his body. I'm surprised at how pissy he is, but I'd be cranky too after a month in that place. After I do some walk, trot, canter, I take him for another hack.

Every day he gets a little less curmudgeonly but he doesn't return to my happy willing Idy. After a while I try to put the double bridle on him thinking maybe that's what he's used to. But he refuses to open his mouth, won't let the bits in at all. Even when I put sugar in my hand behind the bits, he obstinately refuses. Absolutely not. He's always hated the double but this is ridiculous. I relent and ride him in the snaffle.

I spend the winter making friends with him again. He's amazingly human; a good friend respects you and demands respect, so he doesn't get lovey-dovey treatment to make him think I'm swell. I praise him when he tries and discipline him when he doesn't. And I hack him every day in addition to his work as I know he loves to wander, see the sights. As with people, work and pleasure must have a balance. Pleasure makes the work better. By spring, he works willingly and begrudgingly accepts the double bridle.

The whole season, I go to shows with other horses but never take him because he's far from ready. He sees me load other horses on the trailer and leave him. The grooms call and tell me that Idocus is *pissed*; he paces the stall, rears up, pins his ears and pretends he'll bite anyone who comes near him. This is news I relish. If there's one thing I know about Idy, it's that he has to want.

I also don't show Roby as he's learning his flying changes for Third Level and I won't show him until they're confirmed. His hind end remains weak, but his ability to lengthen his strides and go sideways is phenomenal.

◆ ◆ ◆

One afternoon on the boat, Jason's lying down absorbing the rays and I'm just looking out at the sights. Jason squints up at me and says, What's on your mind?

Hm? I say.

You never do nothing, something has to be up, he says.

I smile and look at the book lying on my belly.

Well, I have two great horses, and I need help.

You have Lendon.

She gives a comment here and there, but I need serious *training*, I tell him.

He gets up on one elbow and says, So what are you going to do?

I've been thinking; Wellington, Florida, is the ultimate winter locale for big trainers as it's the home of big shows. I should go there, I say and wait for his rebuttal.

OK, he replies.

But it would be for three months. I don't want to risk our relationship.

He lies back down and closes his eyes. You wouldn't be risking anything. I'm not like you; it'll be fine. Besides, Florida will be a nice place to visit in the winter.

• 32 •

After much searching, I decide to go to Hans Beicker. He was born in Austria and has competed in two World Cups and a World Equestrian Games. He's always trained his own horses from a young age so I know he'll help me bring Roby along correctly.

Francine wants to send her new young horse, Wyoming, with me, too. He was supposed to eventually be for her but as he just turned four, I ride him. He's extremely talented but right from the beginning, showed he was opinionated. His response when he doesn't want to do something is to rear, which in my opinion is the worst thing a horse can do. If I want him to walk by a field but he wants to visit his friends, he'll rear. If I want to trot and he doesn't, he'll rear. The only time he's amenable is when we have him jump, but he's a talented dressage horse.

Francine knows he's never going to be a horse for her, so she wants to sell him and Florida is the place to do that. You should find someone to buy him for you, she tells me and it's not a suggestion, it's a command. I know Wyoming's very talented, but I'm not confident in judging the effect of his attitude so I don't know if I even want to pursue the unlikely task of finding someone to buy him for me.

I was already scheduled to take him to Hilltop Farm where Scott Hassler's hosting a clinic with Olympian Steffen Peters, who's my American hero, and I'm confident that Steffen will tell me how much his attitude will matter.

After our session, I explain the situation to him and say that I'll probably have to support him even if I'm able to find a buyer. Even though he didn't rear today because of the excitement of someplace new, it's there. I don't want to lose him but I don't know if I want to sink every penny I have into him either. Would you?

He puts a hand on Wyoming's haunches, thinks a moment and says, Yes, I think I would. He's a good horse. Horses are always a risk, but I think this one's worth it.

Scott was watching and on the way out of the arena, I tell him Steffen gave Wyoming the thumbs up. Now all I have to do is find a buyer, I say.

Scott says, I think I can help you with that.

He calls two weeks later and says he works with the owners of Harmony Sporthorses and they want him to keep his eye out for talented, deserving individuals to support. He says I meet that criteria and gives me the owner's number. Says her name is Leslie Malone.

After several days I reach her.

She says they'll buy the horse and give him to me. They'll pay half of his expenses and I'll cover the rest, and if I decide to sell him, I'll pay them back. But he'll be mine—my very own horse.

I sit in his stall expecting a huge change in how I feel about him. I wait, think... wait, think... Funny, there's no change. I call all the horses I ride regularly *my* horses, but I thought it was just because it's an easier way to indicate them. I guess I really do feel they're mine.

◆ ◆ ◆

The Malones didn't know they were giving me a birthday present but that's what it is. For my twenty-eighth birthday, I get the horse that's been at the top of my list since I was seven. My horse life couldn't ask for a better gift, and although Jason can't match the impact of this present, he ensures that the non-horse part of my life celebrates large as well by giving me a trip to Jamaica.

As we fly over crystal clear water and endless stretches of white beaches hand in hand, I'm convinced we've entered Paradise, but as soon as we're shown to our cabana, a melancholy mood settles over me. I don't know why, nothing's consciously bothering me but I'm constantly on the verge of tears.

On the second morning, I'm lying awake in bed, curled on my side and suddenly it hits me. My stomach clenches. Then it crumbles into a million shards.

I'm wasting his time.

Almost four years of wasted time. I'm preventing him from finding the person he's going to settle down with. Because I'm selfish.

Jason rolls over and strokes my back. What's wrong?

We should break up, I tell him.

What?

You're older, all your friends are married. You're ready to settle down, and I'm never going to marry you.

117

Court, I'm not asking you to marry me.

But I know you want to.

I don't care. I'd rather be with you now even if it will end.

I look at him.

Honey, we're enjoying each other. There's no reason to break up. Stop looking for reasons, OK?

He's right, there's no reason. Why do I insist on complicating things, anxiously anticipate what the future holds? I'm happy. He's happy. We may die tomorrow. Why can't I be the way he is and just enjoy the now? I know I should—have known for years I should—but like so many other tarnishes on my personality, knowing doesn't equal doing.

My melancholia disappears and the rest of our vacation is spent patroning an in-pool bar, lying on the beach and snorkeling. Enjoying each moment for what it is.

◆　◆　◆

When we get home, my first priority is tackling Wy's rearing problem head on. I hire a gentle cowboy—a western trainer specializing in helping to fix problems—named Kenny Harlow, tell him I'm usually able to avoid the situations that provoke him but I can't train him by avoiding confrontation forever. I need to teach him not to rear when he wants to and eventually eliminate him even considering it.

He listens carefully, nods and saunters out to his truck. Comes back with a full cheek bridle and slips it on. He tells me he's going to teach Wyoming to put his head down in response to upward pressure on the bit. A horse can't rear if their head is on the ground.

He puts a hand on Wy's poll between his ears and presses down. He doesn't push hard, just an annoying amount of pressure that stays there. Wy knows he can get away from the pressure if he puts his head down so that's what he does. After a few times of applying pressure, Kenny just has to lay a hand between Wy's ears and his head drops to the mat.

Then at the same time he's putting pressure on the poll, he pulls directly up on the bit. When Wy's head drops down, the pressure is released from both his poll and the bit. Soon Kenny only pulls up on the bit with no poll pressure and Wy's head plummets. He has me do it and after a few successful times, we tack him up and take him in the ring.

We need to convince him at a standstill that the same rules apply under a rider as in the grooming stall, so Kenny pulls up on the bit and presses down on Wy's poll. But Wy only puts his head part way down. The pressure simply doesn't go away—doesn't increase, just remains—until his nose touches the dirt. After showing him this one time, his head drops to the ground from only pulling up on the rein.

To my surprise he has the same reaction at the walk. After fifteen minutes, if I pull straight up on the rein at walk, trot or canter, Wyoming slams on the brakes and puts his nose in the dirt.

I always thought I had a good understanding of how a horse thinks, but this is horse psychology I can't fathom. I would never have thought pulling the bit *up* could make him put his head *down*.

· 33 ·

On January 1, 2006, Wyoming, Roby, Idy, Noah, Timber, Tsunami and I move to Wellington for three months. Wy, Roby and Idy are stabled in Hans's barn for full training and the others stay twenty-five minutes away in White Fences as I don't need training with them and it's less expensive. I bring one groom, Elias, so someone can be where I'm not in the mornings and afternoons and help me in the middle of the day.

Somehow it doesn't feel like I'm leaving Jason, I don't even contemplate missing him. No matter where he is, he'll be with me. Now I know how he felt when he was offered the transfer.

Within days of my arrival, Hans and his wife, Sophie, invite me to a party the barn is hosting. I sit on a barstool, awkward with people I know I'll see again as usual, but eventually the combination of alcohol and their friendly banter loosens me up.

Sophie compliments Tracey on her shoes and Tracey says, I got these Jimmy Choos for only eight hundred dollars.

Sophie responds, I got these Manalo Blahniks for only seven hundred fifty.

Then someone else says, Sophie wins the cute-shoe award.

I giggle and stick my foot out to display my red, backless, sneaker-shoe and say, What about mine? I got these Aldos for only thirty-nine dollars.

Sophie and Tracey give me straight-faced stares. Then they just look back at each other and continue their conversation as if I hadn't said anything. I feel like crawling in a hole and burying myself. I was trying to be funny but they're not amused. Like a teenager sitting alone at lunch, I feel like a loser.

· · ·

My routine is that I ride the horses in White Fences in the morning, take my lessons with Hans in the afternoon, then go back to check on and hand-walk the horses in White Fences. The cool clique is cold to me, say hi and no more. I'm sad because if they liked me, I could finally have friends to go out with. One of the grooms tells me they think I'm a snob because I never hang out.

I'm always in a hurry running to the other barn, I protest.

Well, *I* know that, she says.

Regardless of my social dilemmas, I'm learning a lot from Hans. He's teaching me to *make* the horse's movement. Lendon taught me how to allow the horse's most expressive natural gait to come out, but he takes it to a whole new level. How to make the trot even better. The collected trot has to have the power of an extension and the cadence of passage. Idocus shows me that this is possible.

I'm signed up to ride him in a Steffen Peters clinic and am excited to get Steffen's help, to ride an advanced horse with him with the same demand for perfection he had with Wyoming. But when Sophie gets wind of it, she calls me. Says, If you're not happy with the training here and want to ride with someone else, you should just go somewhere else.

This comes as a total shock because Lendon always encouraged me to ride with whoever I could, said I could learn bits and pieces from everyone and even if they're awful, I could learn what I *don't* want to do. I say I'm so sorry, I'm very happy with the training, I just didn't think it would be a problem. I explain that I already paid for these sessions but promise I won't do any more after this.

In the clinic, Steffen gets on Idy and makes him lower his haunches in the piaffe more than I thought possible. I'm always amazed by his riding: hands so low and quiet, he appears so mild but his body must be incredibly strong, his timing impeccable. He works on the same thing Hans is having me work on: *make* the passage, make it more forward and then more collected. Be able to not just do the movement but manipulate the gait.

◆　◆　◆

Although I'm getting myself more and more hated at Hans's barn, I make a friend who lives near me and keeps the fun aspect of my life, Jennifer Baumert. In the summers we do the same shows so I casually know her. I rent a room in White Fences and she and her husband Dave rent a house just down the street, so I make an evening ritual of inviting myself over and am always welcomed.

As we get to know each other, she tells me that initially my visits surprised her. She was a victim of misinterpreting my default face and mistaking my oblivion for aloofness. She says she said hi to me many times and I completely ignored her.

She's come to Wellington for many years so I get her opinion on what shows to do. I tell her I want to start Idy in an Open show and then do CDI's. The tests are the same in both, but Open shows are only recognized nationally and may have as few as one judge while CDI's are recognized worldwide and have five judges. CDI's are more demanding of quality and harder to get high scores.

She recommends beginning with the Florida Dressage Classic, so I enter an Intermediare II, which is the level below Grand Prix, and a Grand Prix. Around the outside of the competition ring, I feel my chest rise; I'm proud to show this magnificent creature. As we enter the show ring, though, it feels like Idy has a slow-leak. He does everything but he's ho-humming through the test and gives no effort. Several times, especially in the piaffe, I have to give him discreet taps with the whip to convince him to keep moving his feet. He gets 67% in the Intermediare II and 65% in the Grand Prix.

Our first CDI, the Palm Beach Derby, is three weeks later at the beginning of March. Most CDI's require "tours", which include two specific classes. The Small Tour is the Prix St. Georges and Intermediare I and the Grand Prix level, or Big Tour, has two choices: the Grand Prix test is required for each but the rider can enter either the Grand Prix for the Special or the Grand Prix for the Kur. The top fifteen in each Grand Prix do the next test the following day. The Special requires the same movements as the Grand Prix but in a different pattern, and the Kur is a musical freestyle that the rider choreographs to show all the Grand Prix movements in the order they choose. In bigger shows, like the Olympics, all three tests are done.

I choose the Special and foresee no problem as the movements are identical to the Grand Prix, but as soon as I begin practicing pieces of it in order, I find that Idy loathes it. One movement is walk to piaffe across the centerline and each time I try it, he stops and backs up or twists around and falls directly sideways. Although the passage to canter transition in the Grand Prix test is fine, he highly resents where it is in the Special.

When we get to the show and begin the Grand Prix test, he deflates like a popped helium balloon. My Idy disappears. I don't know this horse. He kind of sort of piaffes, shuffles his feet without picking them up. Whips aren't allowed in CDI's so I can't remind him, can't do anything but sit here and pray. His passage is flat as a pancake and he slowly and laboriously does his pirouettes—movements that are normally brilliant. We get a 63%.

Then comes the dreaded Special which I've made no headway on convincing him to like. We get a 58%, which is generous.

We have two weeks before our next CDI, the WEF Dressage Classic, and Hans has no miraculous cures. Idy's work at home is splendid and we can't correct things when they aren't a problem. We repeat the same scores as at WEF.

I decide we aren't ready to do CDI's yet and for my final show, enter a national one, Dressage at Equestrian Estates. We do two Grand Prix, no Special. The first day he's in the mood to show and gets a 69%. The second day he's not and gets a 63%.

Roby's flying changes are confirmed so I also show him and he wins his two classes with 72%'s. So at least Rich's own horse is doing well.

Jason comes to every one of my shows and begins to tell me the results of my heroes, Isabell Werth from Germany and Steffen. He loves all sports and he's the only non-horse person I've met who acknowledges dressage as a sport and is interested in the players. He tells me my default face is a good thing as it intimidates the competition. Amused, I explain to him that it's not like tennis, me against them. We don't affect each other so intimidation isn't beneficial, but I appreciate the attempt to make it an attribute. Jen says it does work in the warm-up because everyone's too scared of me to get in my way.

· 34 ·

When I get home, I'm more excited to see Quiver than Jason because at least Jason got to visit often. He's the same heart-warming, intelligent, soulful, laid-back dog I fell in love with. Francine got a new horse, a mare named RendezVous, and of the eight horses I've ridden for her, I've never seen her love one as much as she loves this mare. She's funny-looking—big head, huge ears, scrawny neck and body—but her trot is phenomenal. We call her the Queen because she expects to be treated as such and the devil because the bones over her eyes stick out like horns. I soon shorten her name to RV, to which Francine protests saying, She's not a recreational vehicle.

Rich also bought a new horse, a schoolmaster for himself to replace his current one who needs to retire. Mythilus arrives from Holland soon after my return. He got two 64%'s at Grand Prix in Europe, but the first day I ride him I can barely stop. I can't trot straight down the long side with any semblance of control. He doesn't do anything naughty, just goes like hell.

I want to turn him out but Rich says the seller told him not to. I ask if we can try and he says he'd love him to be turned out, absolutely.

So we put him in the field closest to the barn and stand outside watching him. But he doesn't move. When we walk away, he leans into the gate. We go in the barn so we're out of sight, but when I peek back out, the whites of his eyes are showing. He's petrified.

He's the first horse I've met who's scared of turnout. I learn that a Mythilus is a type of Mediterranean oyster, which is a suitable name given that he acts completely vulnerable without his shell—us.

* * *

The next day, he's equally as strong. I stay on a twenty meter circle and do a zillion trot-walk transitions. Rich says, But ask for piaffe.

And it's exquisite. Apparently he knows the movements but not the basics.

After a week, I feel I have enough control to canter straight down a long side, but I need to do a ten-meter circle three times along the way to retain it. After ten days, Rich is dying to ride him. So he tries and we decide Myth needs a bit more time with me teaching him the basics.

He's such a kind horse. I realize that to him, trying hard means going faster. I want to sit him down over a beer and say, *Look, when I pull, it means slow down.* I can picture him slapping himself in the forehead and saying, *Ohhhhh!*

Rich tries to ride him a few more times, but we ultimately decide that I should be his rider for a while. I have no idea how they showed him Grand Prix, I cry almost every day I feel so incompetent.

One day Lendon says, Courtney, is there a reason why you just do walk-trot-walk-trot ad nauseam?

I can't stop, I say. I'm just trying to explain *stop* to him.

Let me get on, she says to my great relief.

She climbs on in her street clothes and reduces the work to even more basic walk-halt-walk-halt transitions.

Wow, she says. He's about as tough as they come.

My feeling of incompetence is somewhat alleviated to know that she feels the same way, but a feeling of defeat replaces it when I realize one of the greatest riders in the world can't ride him well.

Then I ride him in a clinic with Steffen. The theme of the whole lesson is *finish it*: until you can give away the reins and they stay collected, it's not done even if you need to go all the way to halt. Whereas Wyoming learned to complete the half-halt himself in response to light, momentary rein pressure quite quickly, Myth never does.

◆　◆　◆

Although Myth isn't close to being ready to show, my other horses are. Wyoming's rearing abates and he does Training and First Levels, consistently gets high 70%'s and remains undefeated the entire season. Roby continues to do well at Third Level. He loves to show and although his laziness continues to be an issue at home, it never appears in the show ring. He only scores below 70% once and ends up the National Third Level Horse of the Year.

RV does Prix St. Georges and Intermediare I. Her physical sensitivity and responsiveness to my leg and hand make her easy to ride well, but she's also emotionally sensitive to her surroundings. The method I find most reliable to relax her is not to pet or comfort her but to put her to work, put her mind on tasks instead of worries. She's a thinker so I direct her thoughts. The lowest score she gets all summer is 68%.

Idocus begins his showing up north the same as he did in Florida: he completely deflates. At the first show, we get a 62%. Then I try warming him up, taking a ten minute hack, doing a five minute touch-up and then going in the ring. He enters happy and doesn't deflate. I utilize this technique at the next two shows and his scores improve drastically. He gets a 70 and 71%. Then 74%.

After these shows, I've had enough time with many of my summertime horses to begin showing them so I often don't have time for Idy's little hack. The inconsistency of his scores, which are anywhere from 61 to 70%, reflect this.

As he did in Florida, Jason comes to all my shows. He gives up his weekends to accompany me, and it's not to be nice, it's because he enjoys it.

◆　◆　◆

One weekend, we go to Francine's Camp Dancing Bear in the Adirondacks. She calls it a camp because there are many individual cabins and space to sleep twenty-five. The driveway, which is two miles of two-track through thick woods full of deep potholes, steep ups and downs and narrow curves, leads to a discreet mansion that appears to simply grow out of the surrounding forest. It's all natural—they gave the builders and decorators strict instructions to have nothing artificial like paint, wallpaper or plastic—so every floor is stone and every wall is wood of different types. My favorite is the Birch hall.

Each room contains a fireplace you could walk into and each bathroom has a whirlpool. Seventy-eight mulched steps lead to a boathouse on the lake whose deck has a full kitchen.. Although it epitomizes discreet luxury, one feels completely at home.

The days are warm and we water ski while Quivvy frolics in the water. The nights are cool and every evening we bundle up and take the boat on the Walkers' traditional booze cruise. Jason plays pool with Francine's husband till four in the morning and we hardly talk horses at all. I'm reminded of the importance of a non-horse life as my shoulders relax for the first time in weeks.

On the drive home, I sink into a reverie. I can't imagine a better person than Jason for me. With Mike, I didn't feel like I deserved him but I don't feel that way with Jason at all. Not because he's any less wonderful but simply because he's elevated my confidence. I want to spend my life with him. It took me nearly five years to realize, but he's my one true love. When we get in bed that night I say, So where's my ring?

◆　◆　◆

Devon is the last show of the season and it's a CDI for both RV in the Small Tour and Idy in the Big Tour. The amplified atmosphere makes RV nervous. Her brain is scattered and she spooks at the slightest movement.

But opposite of Jambo, entering the show ring calms her. She breathes a bit easier after departing the noise and festivities around the warm up ring and entering the quiet of the show ring. She gets a 67 and a 68% which are both fourth places.

I have time to hack Idocus as I'm not showing a million horses and as it did last time, the energy of the show excites him and invites his show-off spirit. He gets a 69.5% in the Grand Prix and 70% in the freestyle, repeating the first and second places he got in 2000.

Francine has a celebratory dinner and in a toast to the table, she looks at me and says, 2007 is going to be your year, kid, I can feel it!

Idocus, Credit: Susan J. Stickle

· 35 ·

November 20th is my twenty-ninth birthday and Jason rents a hotel room at The Castle in Tarrytown, New York, on the 19th to celebrate. Its appearance is true to its name: it looks like it was built in medieval times, has big stone walls with turrets, towers and many little windows. We've enjoyed the delicious upscale restaurant before so staying overnight is a luxurious treat.

I take a shower because I came directly from the barn and after making a rare attempt to look elegant, I emerge to find forty-eight red roses and a bottle of champagne. I've often chastised Jason for his lack of enthusiasm over any holiday—I've received many presents in their shopping bags if I'm lucky enough to get one, and my family calls him the Grinch because he doesn't believe in giving Christmas gifts and loathes all Christmas music—but, combined with last year's trip to Jamaica, I'm very impressed.

He wraps his arms around me and tells me I look beautiful. Now I'm impressed with not only the gift but his tenderness; his eyes bathe me in love. He pulls me over to the loveseat and pours me a glass of champagne, hands it to me but tells me not to drink.

Happy birthday, Honey, he says. I love you so much…

I love you, too, I say.

Shut up, I'm trying to propose.

My hand goes over my mouth. He goes down on one knee and resumes. I love you so much. I want to spend the rest of my life with you. Will you marry me?

I can't get out any words. I just nod and go to hug him.

He backs off, smiles, raises his eyebrows and says, Say it, I need to hear the words.

I roll my eyes. Say it, he purrs.

After I get out a suitable acceptance, I call Greta, then my parents. My dad says he knew before I did because Jason called and asked his permission.

Then I call Francine. She congratulates me and I tell her that Jason and I have already discussed where we'd like the wedding to be. Would she consider letting us have it at Camp Dancing Bear?

Of course! she says. It will be great practice for when my girls get married.

Because Jason and I both have big families and his will come from New Zealand, we want to have a wedding week, our close friends and families to be able to stay with us the entire week before the ceremony.

• 36 •

Planning my wedding will have to wait because going to Florida is around the corner, and before we go down, I submit a Declaration of Intent to qualify Idocus for the 2007 World Cup which is in April. Although I know my chances of making it are very slim, there's no downside to declaring in case we come into our own.

The World Cup is based only on the Freestyle. The Grand Prix simply determines the order of go and doesn't count toward the placing, and luckily there's no Special at all, so a professional choreographer helps me upgrade Idy's freestyle from the one Lendon made in her basement. We use almost the same music, but it's much better quality, in the tempo of his footfalls and the pattern is determined by exact points instead of *round about A*.

The riders who declare and receive the highest averages at specific qualifying shows are invited to the League Finals to compete head to head and the top four riders in that will be selected to compete in the World Cup. There's no team; each person represents only themselves and their country.

◆　◆　◆

Rich realizes he has better luck riding Roby than Myth, so Myth accompanies me to Florida for the season of 2006-7. I share an apartment with Jen, Dave and their dog Lilly, and Jen's client rents stalls to me in White Fences.

Taking my place as nightly visitor is Betsy Tyler who boards with Jen. We had a moment of soulful connection years ago when I was teaching a clinic in Millbrook, New York. I was walking across the parking lot and saw someone in a car crying so hard the car shook. I tapped on the window to ask if she was OK and she told me she'd decided to leave her husband of twelve years. Things had been brewing and she finally decided she just couldn't live that way anymore. Something in the way she said it, the way the pain was so visible in her eyes, sent a fist into my chest that grabbed and squeezed my heart. I stroked her shoulder, told her I couldn't imagine the pain, to realize the life she'd built for herself was built on a faulty structure, but that the pain was temporary. We shared a hug through the car window that spanned minutes, hours, weeks, years. Feeling her pain brought me to tears. They say that eyes are a window to the soul but that was the first time I'd witnessed it.

Now she becomes part of our happy family. Her eyes tell me before her mouth does that she's happy now. She says the lesson I gave her at that clinic was perfect: it challenged her enough to take her mind off things but not so much to push her over the edge.

◆ ◆ ◆

My first show is in February, Wellington Dressage. I enter RV in the St. Georges and Intermediare I and Idy in the Grand Prix and Freestyle. I hesitantly enter Myth in the St. Georges and I1 as well because it's an Open show not a CDI. Although he's beginning to understand the basics, my control is still unreliable.

When I warm up, he does all the movements but his neck is so short his ears almost touch my chest, and if I attempt to let it out, he steps on the gas. A horse is penalized for a short neck because it appears the rider is constricting them, that their whole topline is tight indicating a lack of the desired suppleness. After forty minutes with no improvement, I walk, let my reins out and go to leave the arena. Klaus Balkenhol, who's our Team coach, is helping another rider and says, Where are you going? He indicates his prize list and says, You go in ten minutes.

I'm going to scratch, I say.

Scratch? Why? he asks.

I can't control him. I have to hold him in or he takes over, I say.

No, he looks good. You show, he tells me. Case closed.

I spend my last few minutes doing walk-halt, give. Canter-halt, give. Anything-halt, give. Giving the reins away is both to encourage him to not pull on me and to let his neck be as long as possible. His neck is literally wider than it is long so even at maximum length, his neck is short even if his topline is supple. I go in already embarrassed.

Although his ears almost touch my chest the entire time, we make no mistakes and get a 64.9% which is sixth place. It's certainly not great, but it's not as bad as I thought. The following day, I warm-up with more confidence, *know* I'll show, and although the places I can show some length of neck remain seldom, he gets a 71.8% and wins.

RV gets a 71.0% and is second in the St. Georges and a 70.2% in the I1 and is second to Myth. I also do an Intermediare I Freestyle on her which has an impressive entry: we halt at the beginning of the centerline, proceed to canter and do three separate pirouettes, left, right, left. This gains us points for difficulty, but we also have mistakes. She gets a 73.5% and another second place.

I have time to do Idy's little hack and he shows he appreciates it by earning a 70.7% in the Grand Prix. In the Freestyle, the use of the arena, inventiveness and musical interpretation get their own marks, so revamping it greatly improves our score. We're also able to highlight his strengths—the passage, piaffe, pirouettes, extended canter and changes—because the choreography was specifically designed for him, and although we need to show every movement, we can minimize showing his faults—walk, half-passes and trot extensions. He earns a 76.3% and wins both classes.

With the success of both RV and Myth, the owners and I decide to try to qualify them for the Pan American Games. The final selection trials will be our National Championships in Gladstone, New Jersey, in June. The twelve riders with the highest CDI averages are invited to our National Championships every year, but this year the top four will be invited to represent the United States at the Pan Am Games in Rio.

♦ ♦ ♦

Jen, Betsy and I grow closer. We celebrate and commiserate, we lament our failures and rejoice in our achievements daily. We go out and have fun, stay in and have fun. When American Idol starts, we watch it together every week at the house where Betsy lives, and Deen Benedict, the owner, becomes our "Florida mom" and treats us to her delicious home cooking during each show. I finally have the group of girlfriends to hang out with I always longed for. We're all riders, hard workers. They're down to earth and buy thirty-nine dollar shoes. Finally, people I fit in with.

One night, we're in a particularly raucous mood and go to a bar named Boonies, which is an appropriate name given its locale. We order our drinks by color: *make me something blue, something orange, something green. Can you make periwinkle?* We drink a few too many colors and the next day, we suffer together. But even suffering and regretting is enjoyable in this company. My own little clique. These are the people I want as friends. I not only want to be *with* them, I want to be *like* them.

♦ ♦ ♦

The Palm Beach Derby is a CDI held in March and will be my last show in Florida. On Friday, RV wins the St. Georges with a 72.4% and Myth is second with a 72.1%. On Saturday, Myth wins the I1 with a 74.2% and RV is fourth with a 70.5%. Very good marks to make the top twelve.

Myth's awards ceremony is at noon and I show Eubie in a Fourth Level class at 11:48 in a ring across the field. Not only is the timing tight to get from one ring to the other, I need to change from my short coat and helmet to my tail coat and top hat to be properly attired for the awards ceremony.

So as soon as I exit the show ring, Jason grabs Eubie and trots us across the field, I throw my short coat at him and he hands me my tail coat. We do the same switcharoo with the hats, all while trotting. Elias is holding Myth by the main arena and I leap off Eubie, onto Myth and head straight in to the awards ceremony where I'm greeted with laughter and jovial welcomes from my competitors. Most of them have come to understand that despite my default face, I'm not a bitch.

Wyoming continues his winning streak. He does the Young Horse Tests for Six-Year-Olds which originated in Europe as a way to assess the horse's talent for the future. It's easier to get high scores if you're on a nice moving horse because mistakes don't matter, they're only judging the horse's talent. He wins both days with 79 and 82%.

The Derby is in a huge open field so it's great for Idy's hacking. He enters the Grand Prix completely happy and doesn't deflate at all. His trot maintains maximum cadence and thrust. He gets a 70.0% for second place. Our freestyle is mistake free, earns a 75.5% and wins.

· 37 ·

Idy's high score at the Derby earns us an invitation to the League Finals which will determine who will be sent to the World Cup. The League Finals are in Burbank, California, three weeks before the World Cup and three weeks after the Derby. Steffen Peters is in San Diego which is two hours from Burbank and five from Las Vegas where the World Cup will be held., so although I know the chance is slim, I call him and ask if there's any way Idocus can stay at his barn.

Of course, he says, to my glee.

Then I start to think about it. If I make the World Cup or if I don't, either way I could train with Steffen for a month. Myth and RV are not only going for the Pan Am Games, I'm also beginning to school the Grand Prix work with both of them and could really use Steffen's help. I call Rich and Francine and ask them if they'd consider sending their horses. Both say absolutely. I'd also get a great amount from his help with Wy and I don't want to leave him unridden while I'm gone. The Malones would pay for half and I'd be responsible for the rest, but if I can figure out a way, the training would be well worth it.

I call Steffen back, aware that it's a great deal to ask and an improbable or impossible request. But I won't know unless I ask.

He thinks. Four is a lot, he says.

I know, I say, bracing myself.

I'm sure we can work it out, he says.

· · ·

That night, Jason takes me to one of our favorite restaurants in Wellington to celebrate.

Cheers, honey, he says with a grin.

I clink his glass but don't return the smile.

What is it? You got everything you wanted, he says.

But I have to figure out a way to pay for it. Rich and Francine will pay for Myth and RV, but I'm responsible for Idy once the help is used up and half of Wy, I say.

Call Lendon, he says. She always has ideas.

Of course, why didn't I think of that? I call her the next day and she says to let her think about it. Within an hour, one of her clients calls me with a fundraising idea: supporters from all over the country can sign up for different levels of involvement. For $100-$499, they get emailed journals of my travels and experiences. For $500 to $999 they also receive DVDs of my training and competitions throughout the year. For $1000 or more, they receive the journals, DVDs and a lesson with me on their own horse. I love the idea because it's not asking for something for nothing.

After tossing around names for the fundraiser for several days, we decide on Courtney's Quest. It's a huge success and I book the horses to fly to L.A.

◆ ◆ ◆

When Jason, Elias and I arrive at the airport to find that fourteen two-year-old mares will be our traveling companions, I panic. Like most breeding stallions are, Idocus is a pedophile. When I voice my concerns to the worker, a particularly fiery Irishman, he informs me in a not particularly friendly way that I'm not allowed to ask about or think in any way about the welfare, happiness, or general survival of any of my horses because that's his business and not mine. I'm reduced to enraged silence.

I cake Idy's nose with Vicks Vaporub to cover up the scent of those delicious fillies and watch, ready for disaster. To my amazement, the Irishman does an excellent job, keeps Idy's attention on him and puts him between Myth and Wy who are the only two geldings.

I'm always impressed with how trusting and adaptable horses are. Their ears are literally touching the roof of the plane and they're nose to tail with horses they don't know. Myth and RendezVous who are nervous and sensitive by nature, both chomp happily on their hay and seem completely unfazed. The only sign I see that Myth is the slightest bit insecure is that he leans toward Idy. He loves Idy and gets security from Idy's constant confidence. And Myth is the only horse who Idy doesn't get studdy with—squealing and puffing up. He treats him like a kid brother. They're ideal traveling companions.

The only one who's a little bit distraught is Wyoming, who came out of the womb with the certainty that he owns the world and all other beings should bow down to him. This is the first time I've seen him be the slightest bit uncertain and I think it's a good experience for him.

◆ ◆ ◆

When we arrive, we go directly to the L.A. Equestrian Center where the show will be held. The show grounds are enormous and house several permanent trainers and their barns, so although we're several days early,

Steffen arranged for me to have stalls in one.

When we put the horses in, Idy runs from one side to the other flailing his head with a huge erection. The stalls are double sized with slits between all the boards and he can see the surrounding horses which drives him berserk. So Elias takes him for a walk while Jason and I go to Home Depot and buy plywood to cover the slits. When they're up and Idy's back in the stall, he peers through small cracks and goes wild again. Elias takes him for another walk while Jason and I duct tape the cracks, and once he's in solitary, he finally settles and munches on his hay.

◆ ◆ ◆

After five days of just going hotel, barn, shady Mexican restaurant, repeat, I look in Jason's eyes before we go to sleep and say, I'm sorry it's all horses, honey. I wish I could do other things with you but I just can't.

Don't apologize. This is important. I want you to be there as much as you do.

I breathe deeply and exhale. Thank you. I love you, I say.

I know, he says and strokes my cheek.

I roll over and he spoons me. Good luck tomorrow, honey, he says.

I just squeeze his arms in reply as I'm already riding the St. Georges in my mind. I always start to mentally ride my first test of the next day when I close my eyes the night before a show, but I rarely finish. Nothing puts me to sleep faster than imagining a dressage test.

◆ ◆ ◆

Idy doesn't show till the weekend so I'm able to put all my focus into the other horses during the week. Myth wins every class of the CDI Small Tour: 71% in the St. Georges, 73% in the I1 and 75% in the Freestyle. In the I1 and the Freestyle, I have the confidence to ride with loops in my reins on every short side to allow maximum neck length so at least the judges can see that I'm not constricting him.

RV wins the non-CDI, or Open, St. Georges with a 69% and as I finish my ride Jason points to look behind me. The whole mountainous ridge is engulfed in flames and the sky is speckled with helicopters darting in and out of the smoke. I'm thinking *is it time to set all the horses free and start running?* but the Californians are basically yawning and saying, So *what? It's another forest fire.* Apparently it's a normal occasion for them to have a mountain less than a mile away spontaneously burst into flames. Everyone's more worried about the Hollywood sign which rests on the other side of the ridge.

In the I1, RV's light in the bridle and the expression comes easily. With most horses when they feel this way, I find the best way to maximize that expression is to relax and stay out of the way, just ask and allow. But RV doesn't work that way. She feels abandoned when I completely relax and although our score of 71.5% earns second place, I know she could have done better.

Wyoming only has one class and it isn't until five p.m. He prefers to keep his afternoons for lounging around and to get his work done in the morning so he's extra pissy. The judges tell you their thoughts right after the test in the Young Horse division and give each gait, the general impression and submission separate scores. They love his canter and give it an 8.7. They think his potential as a dressage horse is extremely high and that his training is correct so 8.9 on general impression. 8.5 on submission. Only 7.8 on trot. His pissiness prevents him from trotting his best because that would entail trying. He ends up with an 81.7% and second place.

I'm disappointed in Wy—not the results but him—but Jason doesn't see any reason for my disappointment.

How do you know he's not trying? he asks.

I know he can have an exceptional trot because I've gotten it on a few rare occasions. He could do it if he wanted to, but it's harder so he doesn't. I can't figure out what to do to make him want to try. I'm normally good at pinpointing a horse's specific needs, but his I can't. The only times I've seen him happy is when he was jumping.

You'll figure it out, Court. Maybe he resents being castrated.

• 38 •

Idy always gets extremely pissed when I put my show clothes on and take another horse. He bangs at the door and flails his head with his beautiful little ears pressed back into his neck. So after watching me take other horses to show countless times over the days, when I finally take him he's very satisfied. He's patient with his grooming (where he can often be a bully) and seems completely content. First I take him for a hack around the turned-out horses because it always excites him. Then I warm up for twenty minutes and hack him one more time around the barn before our five minute final tune-up. When we trot into the show arena, he feels good, fresh.

He maintains the cadence in the piaffe and passage, but we miss the one tempis. The first nine are good and then he trips behind and loses the sequence. He gets a 68.375% and ends up third. Steffen wins with 73%.

The mistake in the one-tempis was expensive. They're a coefficient so between the five judges, they count for ten scores. Added to a few imperfect transitions—this is top competition so of course the scoring is strict—this mistake earned our relatively low score. But in the awards ceremony all the judges come around me and say, There was only one problem with your test today. Do you know what it was? I say, The ones of course. They say, No, your test was lovely but his mouth was wide open.

If in every movement that his mouth was open, five judges took a point off, that's a lot of points. He never feels resistant in the contact so I haven't regarded it as a problem. Regardless, I'm extremely happy, more with him than the test—opposite of Wy. He was enthusiastic, honest and having fun. He was proud of himself afterward—neck up and arched, scanning his admirers with a soft look in his eye. This is particularly gratifying with Idy because he has to decide to work. Many horses can be bullied into submission but Idy would give me the big middle hoof if I dared to try. He tries hard and is honest in his responses because he chooses to be so.

• • •

The show's finale is Idy's League Finals freestyle—the reason we flew across the country. The weather is cool and the clouds threaten to spit on us which is ideal weather to energize Idy. We go for our hack by the turned-out horses and Idy shows off even more than he did before the Grand Prix; maintaining control is a struggle. The music suits my state of mind, cheerfully following a path without knowing the destination: *Follow the Yellow Brick Road.*

When we enter the showring, his enthusiasm doesn't abate at all. The ones don't just feel like skipping merrily along, they feel like exuberantly celebrating and the passage bounces so much I feel like I may hit my head on the rafters. Other than one very slow pirouette, it's mistake free.

This freestyle is difficult for me because it combines many difficult movements—one-tempis to two-tempis on a circle as well as twos to ones, ones to pirouette. Has many wonderful transitions—canter to passage, piaffe to extended trot. But for the first time, I feel I can just go with the music, like dancing, instead of calculating every single stride so we're able stay right on the music.

Steffen and Floriano win with 78.7% and I'm second with a 75.5%. I make the World Cup. Idy and I make the World Cup. I always hoped to represent the U.S. but to be able to do so on Idocus with whom I share so much history, so much heartbreak, is painful it means so much.

In the victory lap, we wear a big red cooler and passage next to Steffen and Flori in their big blue cooler. I say to Steffen brimming with excitement, I've never gotten to do an awards ceremony in a cooler before. In his very polite way, he looks at me like I'm a moron, but I'm delighted anyway.

• • •

After the awards ceremony, there's a press conference with the top four riders. One of the reporters asks me and Steffen how it feels having both of our horses at seventeen years old and if we think of the end of their careers.

My smile falls and seriousness grips me.

I'm aware of his age every single day. Even last year when we were getting 58%, I appreciated each day on his back, every time I got to be carried on that swingy walk, that I got to feel like a horse was made for me.

I often worry about when he'll decide to stop working. It may be a month from now or it may be five years, but whenever he doesn't feel the desire anymore, we'll stop. I know he'll tell me when he's done. Some horses, like Mythy, are non-stop pleasers, for anyone, every day, but Idy's not that way. He won't do it unless he wants to.

With the weight of equine mortality on my mind, I walk back to the barn to the bright cheery faces of RendezVous with her big doe eyes and new-found confidence, Myth and Wyoming with so much expectation, and am invigorated. I realize that this is only the beginning. I rave about Idy because I love him dearly, but each of these horses has something special in both talent and personality. Even Wyoming whose temperament I struggle with is an extremely lovable character. He's Jason's favorite. He's calm and cool, like he should have a leather jacket and slicked-back hair. Always lets you know exactly how he's feeling, and he does so with amazing clarity considering he lacks the power of speech. I call him my perfect specimen because he's anatomically perfect. I can't get over how lucky I am to be riding them.

Jason walks in as I'm resting my cheek on Mythy's muzzle. He strokes my back.

I love the smell of all horses' breath but Mythy's is the best, I say.

Why?

It's like a breeze over an alfalfa field: pure, fresh, soothing, I say.

◆　◆　◆

Jason insists that our celebration dinner won't be at our usual shady restaurant so we put on something other than jeans and drive out of town. You did it, honey, he says after we're seated and tells me not to expect to see him much in Vegas because he'll be at the tables. I tell him he better bring down the house because we're going to need the funds.

We sip our wine and enjoy the momentary feeling of completion before the next task demands our focus. He says he's surprised at the improvement in the score from yesterday. How did I get Idy to keep his mouth closed?

I shrug and tell him I cranked the noseband. I've gotten open mouth comments on my test sheets before but have never been so heavily penalized.

But you're in top competition now so of course they're going to be tough on the details, he says.

I know, but he actually feels softer in the contact and more supple in the neck when he has the freedom to keep his mouth a little open. He does it in the crossties with no bit in his mouth—stands there in his halter and gapes his jaw like he's trying to pop his ears. It has nothing to do with resistance; he's probably the softest horse in the contact I've ever ridden. But the judges can't know that, so tightening the noseband so he can't open it too wide is the lesser of two evils I suppose.

I tell him I'm finally getting comfortable and confident enough in freestyles to be able to adjust for imperfections. The choreography is planned, but sometimes you get ahead of or behind your music and need to adjust what you do, or you have a mistake and the freestyle gives you a chance to repeat the movement if you're clever enough to find a way. A good freestyle rider, like Lendon, is able to do something different to get back with the music or repeat a mistake. Everything didn't go according to plan this week—like Mythy's trot and Idy's slow pirouette—but I was able to adjust.

He knows I've always hated freestyles, struggled with the added challenge of staying with the music, and says, Of course you're getting comfortable with them. You do a lot of them and Myth's, RV's, and Idy's were specially made for them. You chose the music, like it, so it's natural with your love to dance to stay with it.

I look in his eyes, so logical, insightful, understanding. He looks back in mine. I don't wonder what he's thinking, simply let the feelings of the day wash over me. Then I realize both our cheeks are wet with tears. I didn't feel the impact of this event until now, sitting here, just the two of us. I was happy with the horse and that was the only thought in my mind, but now the impact hits me full on and both our tears are unstoppable. He tells me that before I finished my ride, he had to stop filming because his hand was shaking so much.

• 39 •

The United States Equestrian Federation, or USEF, is making posters of each of its World Cup competitors with their horse, so at 7:30 the following morning (at which time I'm sure I look striking) I meet the makeup artist. I know it's ludicrous for them to think anyone would want a poster of me, but nonetheless, I'm little-girl excited about getting the star treatment. He stares at me in appraisal and clucks unhappily. You don't pluck, do you, he says.

No, I apologize.

He shakes his head and asks, What do you normally use for makeup?

The stuff to cover dark circles, blush, mascara and eyeliner.

He waits for more. No foundation?

I shake my head.

No eye shadow?

I shake my head again.

He sighs and says, Well, what do you want done?

Just make me beautiful! I say.

He looks me over again and delves into the task.

When he's finished, he hands me a mirror and I barely know the person staring back at me.

Wow, I say, forcing a smile. Then I go to "wardrobe" and nothing fits. The photographer finally loans me the sweater she's wearing which is long enough to cover the waist of pants that are too big. Then Elias hands Idy to this person who's not me.

After fifteen minutes, the photographer's happy and I return to the barn as myself to check on the other horses. Klaus is waiting for me. You go home? he says as hello. I'm scheduled to take the red eye to New York tonight.

Just for three days, I say. Idy will have some well-deserved days off.

This is important, he says. You stay.

Of course he's right, this *is* important, but I want to check on my horses at home. I feel good about the situation they're in but it's hard to be away so long. I decide that if Lendon assures me everything's under control, I'll stay. She says, Courtney, they're *fine*. They can live without you for three days.

◆ ◆ ◆

So I accompany Elias and the four horses on the move to Steffen's barn on April 3rd. We turn into a driveway labeled Arroyo del Mar which slowly declines into a valley and the dust and brown of the road gives way to lush greenery. It feels like we've entered an oasis in the desert. A large pond with fountains is encased in a lovely grassy knoll and an earthen bridge connects the two sides. Trees dot the perimeter providing splotches of shade in an otherwise shadeless environment.

The grass is well protected—no walking or grazing on it—which Idy will be sad about, but there are acres and acres to wander and trails to hack to appease him. Steffen and his wife, Shannon, have a house on the farm and let me stay with them. They also provide a camper for Elias.

I give Idy a couple easy days and then work him in front of Klaus. Klaus is the opposite of Schumacher when it comes to contact—always tells me, *Give hand*, which makes sense with Idy because he resents pressure on his mouth. Overall Klaus is happy with our work. The piaffe, passage and pirouettes are very good but, to me, the canter isn't his exquisite Idy canter. Both Klaus and Steffen say if you don't know the horse, it's still a good canter, but it regularly causes mistakes in his one-tempi changes which are normally a strong point.

His trot extensions and half-passes are impossible to improve, but Klaus says that his good things far outweigh them and basically shrugs his shoulders. Then Steffen tells me something that surprises me: he says to focus on improving his good qualities. The extension is a seven no matter how much I work on it, but the piaffe or pirouettes, I can improve from being an eight to a nine or ten. It makes perfect sense. I've spent years trying to improve the trot half-passes and extensions, but why waste my time and his energy on something that's as good as it's going to be?

◆ ◆ ◆

After a few days, Steffen invites me to join him for a session with his personal trainer. I detest exercise. The only time I run is when I'm in a hurry to get somewhere. I can't get past the feeling that swimming laps, doing reps, or running and biking nowhere is a horrible waste of time. But he's damn good for a reason so I tell him I'd love to.

The gym is small; the owner runs it and is Steffen's trainer. He tells us to stand back to back and hands Steffen a weighted ball. Says to hand it to me over our heads, I'll grab it and hand it back between our legs. After several repetitions, we switch: I hand it over our heads and Steffen passes it between our legs. Then we hand it around our sides. He attaches our legs together with a gigantic rubber band and tells us to both walk away until the band won't stretch anymore. Then sideways each way. Then backwards.

I'm surprised when he says, OK, see you next week.

I tell Steffen of my previous abhorrence of exercise and he says him too, but having little tasks keeps our minds too occupied to think of what else we could be doing. I continue to go with him two times a week. He's not only helping me train my horses, he's helping me train me.

◆ ◆ ◆

Instead of trying to perfect the movements of the Small Tour to prepare for the Pan Am Games, Steffen zones in on Myth's and RV's particular impediments for the Grand Prix. The main obstacle I face with RV is the piaffe. She understands the movement but gets very backward in it; instead of having her energy forward off my leg and being ready to push out into passage, she bottles up, bloats and feels ready to back up. Steffen has me only piaffe from collected trot instead of from walk or passage. He also has me ask for it from just one strong half-halt instead of collecting the trot more and more until she's piaffing—or piffling, as Lendon calls almost-piaffe.

With Myth, other than simply continuing to get him more rideable and soft in the contact, we mainly focus on making the passage rhythm more correct. He gets unlevel—one hind leg stays up longer than the other which disrupts the consistent two-beat rhythm—so Steffen helps me with a bamboo pole which is a technique I've heard of but never experienced. He doesn't hit Myth's leg but holds the pole close enough that when Myth picks his leg up, it hits and makes a noise. For some reason, horses enjoy making a noise so they *try* to hit the pole. In this way, Steffen can encourage Myth's rhythm and by making him reach more, he gets more swing through the back and loft. The resulting passage is astounding. In Steffen's words, it's "PFI" which stands for Pretty Fucking Incredible.

I school the ones on the quarterline because he doesn't try to take over as much as on the diagonal where they are in the test. We can do several of them but I have to keep his strides very, very short. Steffen says they look bigger than they feel. He says that when he saw Myth in the clinic over the summer, he was skeptical about how well he could do at Grand Prix, not because of doubting his talent but because of the lack of rideability. He says, Now I think you're really going to wow some people when you come out with this horse at Grand Prix.

Remembering the first six months I had him, crying nearly every day and feeling totally incompetent, makes me appreciate my persistence. Maybe I'm not a good enough rider to be able to fake my way through it, but because of my need for the basics, I may be able to get 70% instead of 64.

• • •

Eventually I can get the PFI passage without Steffen and the bamboo pole. I can consistently get fifteen ones and his piaffe has been the one good thing since the day he arrived. Steffen puts a sticker on the door of my bedroom that says, *2008 Olympics: We'll Be Ready!*

I tell Rich and he points out that I've had Myth away for several months now and we've had great success in the show ring. Hopefully we'll be able to make the Pan Am Games. All the time he's speaking my heart is sinking like a lead balloon. Rich bought Myth as a horse for himself, he was never intended as a horse for me. The plan was that we'd both ride him; I'd show him but he was primarily a horse for Rich. So I fully expect this to be leading up to, *So, Courtney, when he comes home, it's really time for me to ride him more and for you to ride him less.* Instead he says, So, Courtney, let's face it, he's your horse now. You've made him into more than I thought he could be and you've earned the right to take him all the way if he can do it.

I almost cry out, out of surprise as well as glee. I would have been sad to have to back off on Myth, but I've always been aware that he's for his owner and have kept myself prepared for that. It's an immense sacrifice for Rich. He loves to ride.

• • •

The next day Steffen, Jason and I wander downtown, take a tour of the *USS Midway*—which is a retired aircraft carrier—and Jason and I discover

Steffen's passion for Ruth's Chris Steakhouse. When he calls to make a reservation, he begins with, This is Steffen Peters… and I tease, Do you think they're going to roll out the red carpet? You're only famous in the dressage world, Steffen.

To my surprise, when we walk in the hostess says, Hi, Mr. Peters, how are you this evening? And the waiter says, Are we having the usual this evening, Mr. Peters?

Steffen's a stark contrast to Lendon who would never go out to dinner. Once when the power was out, we went to Friendly's. In the six years I worked for her, that's it. One time. She only ever does horse things, never took a vacation, never even took a day off—was in the barn from eight to four every single day. She didn't even do clinics because they'd take her away from the barn. Steffen on the other hand, is on his first horse by seven so he can have his afternoons free to go on his boat or play on his 4-wheelers. He works extremely hard, gives up two weekends a month to teach clinics, but, like me, feels a non-horse life is important to maintain.

◆ ◆ ◆

Wyoming's snotty mood from the show hasn't subsided. I normally think he has a reason: he's growing, doesn't feel well, or I don't know, has a head ache, but he needs to get over excuses to be a top show horse. I've been successful training him thus far because I've been able to find my way around things without confronting them head on. He's given up on rearing since I learned to disarm that by getting him to put his head to the ground, but I can't disarm the attitude.

Steffen's seen me struggling with him day after day and one morning he asks if he can ride him. I'm relieved but I know it's going to be a challenge because Wyoming won't get to eat his lunch as his ride is at 12:15 and I'll have to wake him up from his mid-day nap.

As expected, when Steffen gets on, Wy has his tutu in a bunch. He snatches at the reins, bucks his butt up at anything Steffen asks, threatens to stand on his hind legs and is generally as disagreeable as possible. At first I giggle because Wyoming's like my naughty little boy and cracks me up, but then I think Steffen might come off and it's not funny anymore. That might get dressage some publicity: *Number Two U.S. rider for World Cup Causes Broken Leg for Number One Rider.*

Every time Steffen gets a glimmer of submission, he halts, lets the reins out and strokes Wy's neck. Watching Wyoming's reaction, it's strikingly clear that he couldn't care less. All my other horses have come to really want to please, want the praise, but to Wyoming it makes no difference if he's good, bad or otherwise. He's completely comfortable with himself and doesn't feel the need to impress anyone. When Steffen lets out the reins, Wyoming simply looks around cheerfully at all the other horses and checks out what's going on.

When Steffen gets off an hour and twenty-five minutes later without even cantering and Wyoming showing no sign of giving in, Wy drags me to the barn proud as a prince like he'd just won the Olympic gold.

The next day Steffen rides him in the double bridle and the ride is no less controversial. But once again, Wy couldn't be more pleased with his performance. Steffen doesn't try to beat him into submission or force him into uncomfortable work, he's just quietly persistent. There's only one right answer for Wyoming: straight through, round, swinging, forward. Period.

Wyoming's admitted to baby boot camp and Steffen rides him every day. And every day is the same thing: trotting (or something resembling trotting) around and around the jumping ring in a continuous temper tantrum with slightly increasing numbers of moments of decent behavior.

On day five, Steffen says there's a change in his attitude. Now it seems to be more of lack of understanding and the work being harder, so frustration rather than just not caring. And it's visible. He finally seems like he's acknowledging Steffen and they even do a little canter.

On day six, Wyoming's ears are at half-mast showing that he's thinking about Steffen, and when Steffen stops to praise him, his ears go up. There are still some exciting moments but more because Steffen is getting after him than because Wy's saying screw you, and he does some of the trot I knew he was capable of but couldn't get. The time to go comes too soon.

Courtney's Quest Journal
I have so far to go to be as good as Steffen is. That's really why this sport is a life-long process. The more one rides and the more feelings one acquires of the advanced movements, the better one can become. It all has to be instinct. And in order to train younger horses to Grand Prix, you have to know so many different feelings of so many different reactions to those upper level movements to move the horse along in a smooth progression. I feel so lucky to have these amazing horses, at all different levels and with different issues, and then to have this opportunity to have them all out here with me. I'm just breathing it in and storing it up for some day when it's a little stuffy.

◆ 40 ◆

The countryside on the way to Vegas distracts me from thinking about my destination. It's so different from anywhere I've been: all desert, strange rocks and attempted cactus forests. I ponder the reason why this huge city is out in the desert in the middle of nowhere.

Suddenly sirens go off. We're getting pulled over. When they get to the truck, they ask me to step out and it's not the police. I'm confused. They ask me where I'm taking the horses and I tell them the World Cup. They look around and ask me again. I tell them again. I ask who they are and they say the Nevada Department of Agriculture; they're concerned that I stole the horses and am intending to sell them to the slaughterhouse. I repeat that I'm going to the World Cup. They look at me dubiously, peer in the truck and ask my name. I tell them and they walk to their car.

While waiting, I go through spurts of giggling at the ridiculousness of the accusation and horror at the thought of spending the World Cup in a cell while Idy and RV breed in a shared pen. After ten minutes they come back, wish me luck and send me on my way.

◆ ◆ ◆

We drop my other three horses at a barn that Steffen arranged fifteen miles outside the city. Elias stays with them since he knows their care inside and out and one of Steffen's grooms, Nicole, will help me take care of Idy.

Then we go to the Thomas and Mack Center where the World Cup will be held which is right downtown, walking distance to the Strip. The stabling is set up in tents outside the building and the white lines stretching across my tackroom floor indicate we're in the parking lot. I scope the lot in search of places to let Idy wander and am disappointed in my findings.

After Idy's settled in his stall, I go to the vending area which, as in most sports arenas, is on an upper level behind the stands. The first thing I see as I come through the doors is the poster of me. I'm looking down and Idy has his nose on my cheek. The girl in the picture looks elegant which, added to her hair being longer, makes her look nothing like me. The store clerk doesn't recognize me, asks if she can help me.

The atmosphere is entirely different from any horse show I've been to. The thrill of being in Vegas is added to the excited anticipation of being at a major sports event like hockey or basketball, and the fact that I'm one of the players boggles my mind. This thought alters the purity of the happy giddiness I was feeling. The happy giddy feeling remains but is encased by a resolute, serious shell. I think, *I owe it to the audience to perform well,* and it's a responsibility I'm proud to shoulder. For once showing well isn't only about pleasing myself, there's an audience to please. This weighted lightness is a pleasant feeling, like a helium balloon contained in silver.

After wandering the entire loop, I return to the stable area to tack-walk Idy. The warm-up ring, which is in a big tent with temporary footing, is open to school in. A dimly-lit chute attaches it to the main arena and most riders are concerned that their horses will panic with this bizarre tunnel-like entrance, but I know Idy won't think twice about it. I'm only concerned about the inability to hack.

As I'm walking around, pleased that Idy's interested in the strangeness of these surroundings, the mother of Marlies—Idy's rider in Holland— comes up. She says that Idocus looks great and congratulates me, seems pleased to see him and isn't resentful or judgmental in the least. She asks if she can take some photos of him and I feel very connected to her. Perhaps Marlies loved him as I do, perhaps her heart broke like mine did when she lost him. We agree that Idocus is a great horse.

•   •   •

Jason and I dive right into Vegas life and that night, we join Steffen to see a hypnotist show in the Paris Hotel. The hypnotist calls several people to the stage, including Jason, and tells them if they don't feel they're becoming hypnotized, please open their eyes and leave. He instructs them to picture themselves floating on a cloud, getting further and further away. After about a minute, Jason opens his eyes and walks off the stage. Another man follows suit. Then another. Eventually there are only three left and he begins with simple requests: cluck like a chicken, make out with your hand, pretend you're eating an apple. Then he tells them to dance erotically with their chair. Give it a lap dance. Pretend you're having sex with it. Even though we know the *hypnotized* people are actors for the show, it's highly entertaining and we laugh with the rest of the audience because what they do is hysterical. When one woman begins to take off her shirt, he wakes them up.

On the way out, Steffen buys one of their CD's that supposedly helps with memory, and the next morning as I prepare to get on Idy, I ask him how it was. He says with a smile, Well, it made me fall asleep right away.

•   •   •

Schooling is open in the main ring from 6-8 a.m. and when Idy and I enter, we're in the midst of Kyra Kyrkland, Edward Gal, Jan Brink, Isabell Werth, and other famous riders. My stomach clenches and I'm seized by a feeling I've never experienced on horseback: nervousness. I keep trying to get out of peoples' ways and by not following the standard ring rules, they don't know where I'm going so I keep cutting them off. Finally Steffen, who's helping me, says what Lendon always tells people: everyone in the ring is equal.

I look around wishing I could watch all these magnificent horses and riders. Then I realize I'd rather be riding with them and my stomach unclenches.

Idy doesn't feel quite as energetic as he has recently, but he still feels loose and swingy. Most importantly, he tries, he *wants*. Steffen tells me that for now the trot must always be passage-y, exactly what we wanted to avoid with RV. RV naturally has a lofty, cadenced trot, so bringing it closer to passage makes it slow and loses the activity. Although Idy has great cadence in the passage, his natural trot is flat and unimpressive, so we try to put some of the cadence from passage into the trot. Our piaffe is as good as or better than it was at the League Finals.

Klaus was watching and when we get back to the barn, he tells Steffen that Idocus looked so good we should take him to Aachen this year. Aachen is in Germany and is the most prestigious show in the world. Steffen says, That probably won't be possible because she'll be in Rio for the Pan Am Games.

Klaus shrugs and delivers a Klaus-ism: She *must* take him to Europe to show this summer. I'm floored, both that Steffen is confident that I'll make the Pan Am team and that Klaus thinks we look good enough for *Aachen*.

◆ ◆ ◆

In the afternoon, the riders do a *Meet and Greet* where we sign autographs for the fans. I think including me is nearly as ridiculous as the poster and tell Idocus he better grow an opposable thumb and learn to write because he's the real star. But they want me to, so I'm happy to sit in the booth and pretend I'm a big shot.

Each rider has their own booth so people can choose who to go to, and I figure people stand in my line because they assume I'm someone famous even though they don't know who I am. The first person in my line is a teenage girl. Her grin shows a mouthful of braces and her cheeks turn red.

You're Jenny's idol, her mom says and pulls the poster of me out that I was sure no one would buy.

Jenny says, Your ride in the League finals was amazing!

Do you mind if we get a picture? her mom asks.

Many people in the line relate specific instances: my ride at Devon, the Derby, they're happy I have him back. Several also bring up Myth and my awkwardness renders me speechless. I want to express how touched I am and I know my silence makes it seem like I don't care. After Jason witnesses several instances that, like my default face, misrepresent the person I am, he comes to my rescue.

Do you have a horse? he asks a little girl. How long have you been doing dressage? he asks a middle aged woman. He's so good at small talk, he can talk to anyone. I look at him in appreciation. I sign, smile, and pose for pictures, and he talks.

◆ ◆ ◆

The following day, each rider has a specified twenty minute time period to school in the main arena. Tickets are on sale to the public to watch us school and the stands are surprisingly full. I just do a tiny bit with Idy, let him see the sights and do a couple diagonals of sequences because they've been a problem. He's as good as he's going to be at this point; working will only tire him out and he needs to be fresh.

That evening, my friend tells me all the talk in the internet chat rooms was about my pigtails. Since I chopped my hair off, it won't go in a ponytail and pigtails are the only way I can keep it out of my face. One person said, What's a thirty-year-old doing wearing pigtails? I'm twenty-nine anyway and I don't know if I'm enraged or relieved that they don't talk about my riding.

◆　◆　◆

I give myself twenty-five minutes to warm up for the Grand Prix because I can't hack and want to keep Idy as fresh as possible. As we go through the chute I'm totally focused, but as soon as we enter, the applause erupts on top of me. Any horse but Idy would have spooked. Immediately my default face is replaced by an ear-to-ear grin and I look up in the stands, see huge banners reading *Courtney and Idocus*, Lendon, Francine with her hands in a funnel over her mouth shouting something. I know my dad is here and several other people I don't allow myself to look for.

For the first time, I enjoy showing *while* I'm showing. I've always loved showing, loved the work it takes to show well, but I love it retrospectively and preemptively. During a class, I'm focused only on the second-to-second details and never think of the overall act itself.

Idocus, Credit: Susan J. Stickle

My face keeps the grin the entire ride, my default face never makes an appearance. The crowd's energy fires Idy up too making his piaffe and passage spectacular. His only mistake is a blooper in the ones and the crowd erupts as I salute. I lean forward and alternate between stroking his neck and patting it so hard it hurts my hand, and as the crowd continues applauding and screaming, my eyes remain focused on his neck and I do a half wave. When the score comes out at 67.833% as we leave the arena, I know we were punished for the open mouth again. The tighter noseband didn't work. Regardless, I couldn't be happier with my horse and the joy with which he performed.

◆ ◆ ◆

The first thing Jason says when I dismount is, Why did you do a half-assed wave to the crowd?

A big wave would indicate I think I deserve their praise, I retort.

Court, waving is how you show you appreciate the crowd. A big wave is acknowledging them, thanking them. I know you're humble but this looks like you don't care about the fans. It looks stuck up.

Like so many things, my actions don't express my intentions. I wish everyone could know my actual thoughts and feelings but they only have these brief glimpses to judge me on and I often appear awful. I vow to Jason that I'll wave after the freestyle no matter what.

Regardless of this reality check, I'm thrilled with the horse and with the test. It wasn't perfect but it was a test I can be proud of and earns eighth place. Isabell wins with a 74.791% and Steffen is second with 72.875.

In the evening I have an early dinner with my dad and Pam, Lendon, Francine and a small group of people who came just to see me. I know that many riders don't go out or even have a glass of wine before major competitions, but I need to. Trying to stay focused on studying my freestyle would be like trying to herd cats. Like needing to get dating *out of my system* before being able to commit to Jason, I need to get celebrating today out of my system before I can focus on tomorrow.

My dad looks like he's ready to cry all night, he looks like he's ready to laugh all night, and I reciprocate so much hugging that sometimes I don't even know who my arms are around. Francine says, What did I tell you about 2007, kid? Lendon says, Don't you think you should go back to the room now?

When I get back, I study the DVD of my freestyle ten zillion times and then study it some more. My dreams are set to *Goodbye Yellow Brick Road*.

◆ ◆ ◆

The freestyle is in the evening so I ride my other horses in the morning, as much to keep my mind occupied as to work them. When I get back to the Thomas and Mack Center, I go in Idy's stall, just stand and look at him. He lifts his head from his hay, just stands and looks at me. His eyes tell me that he shares the feeling of a helium balloon lined in silver. I give him a Sore-No-More rub down and then put my show clothes on while Nicole grooms him. Study my DVD while she tacks him up. When I get on, I know every beat of my music.

Although I think I'm prepared for the crowd's enthusiasm, it strikes me just as hard. Once again, a perma-grin settles on my face, but Idy isn't affected the same. He's tired and the cadence in the passage I do before I begin the test lags. The deflating I thought we'd gotten rid of is reappearing. The beginning of the test is piaffe and passage and it begins lackluster but to my surprise, instead of deflating, Idy's adding air, it gets more cadenced as we go. Many horses try harder in the show ring but Idy hasn't done that since I've had him back. But that's what he does; he rises to the occasion *because we're showing.*

In my two-tempis to ones on a circle, he has a tiny glitch in the ones, doesn't miss a change but has a minute bobble. I have two more sets of ones that are good but we designed my freestyle so that I can repeat anything that needs repeating as I go down the final centerline. The music has a beat that could suit any gait. So since the ones were my only mistake, I decide to repeat them. But I have a worse bobble and my halt from one-tempis is awkward and off timing.

I admonish myself for making a poor decision for a split-second before the crowd erupts. They're so close it should feel like they're on top of me, but it feels like they're carrying me along on a mosh pit. The lining of silver releases my helium balloon, and true to my vow I give the crowd several huge thankful waves. As I do, I have the courage to scan the faces in the crowd and look at the enormous banners of our names while Idy saunters out as if to say, *I know, I was beautiful.* His score is 73.2%.

I give Idy three apples and he accepts them but doesn't grab them, is perfectly regal. He's pleased but not bubbly like I am. It appears his helium balloon is still lined in silver and he brings me back to reality, makes me realize this isn't the end, it's the beginning. Next year is an Olympic year and we have a lot of work to do. The silver relines my balloon.

Our score earns sixth place. In the world. Sixth in the world. Isabell wins with an 84% and Steffen is third with a 77.8. Klaus looks as proud of me as my father did at my graduation party. Steffen's placing was fully expected but mine is a surprise, to me most of all.

By the time I take care of Idy and get cleaned up, our celebration doesn't begin until midnight and carries on till the wee hours. Francine brings bottles of champagne to our hotel and we spend the morning in raucous celebration. She explains the anxiety of anticipation during my ride, says you could hear a fly whiz by. She cried the whole time and at the end joined the crowd in their crazed screaming. When she called Rich at end, she had no voice. She says it was *my* crowd.

Idocus, waving to Lendon in the stands
Credit: Susan J. Stickle

◆ 41 ◆

After over four months of being away from home, I luxuriate in stepping into my old worn slippers—literally and figuratively. Back to the rocky, hilly, lush terrain I'm accustomed to after the flatness of Florida and the dryness of Vegas. Kissing Quivvy. Being with Jason for more than a week straight. Finally getting to plan my wedding.

A week after I get home, Francine invites me over for dinner. As usual her cooking is divine, and as usual, she stays perfectly white and chatters away the whole time she cooks. After dinner, she rests her chin on her fists and looks at me. I'm cradling her miniature dachshund, Lulu, with her head on my shoulder and it feels like Francine's looking right into me. She says, If you could have one thing for your wedding, something you'd never ask for, what would it be?

I rock Lulu like a baby and say, A Lulu!

She drops her hands to the table. Come on, she says.

I want a travel-sized Quiver, I tell her.

Her face softens and she smiles. Fair enough, she says.

◆ ◆ ◆

At the barn, I delve into the task of sifting through all the tools Steffen gave me. Figure out what I can integrate into my style and for what I can't make work, find my own technique to get the desired result. With Wyoming, I find the balance of the super trot Steffen convinced him he would do with how much he can consistently maintain during the half-passes and small circles required in his tests. Every once in a while, I ask for more cadence as I want to make sure he stays fresh to understanding that request, but more I try to find the trot he can be relaxed, confident and consistent in.

In typical Myth fashion, once he understands, he goes out of his way to do. In San Diego, we focused only on the ones and passage because they needed the most help, but now he does them when I don't ask. If I ask for a single change, he does three or four ones. If I half-halt too big in the trot, he passages. The half-halts are certainly still a daily discussion but they're basically reliable and effective. I'm able to go for really big canter and big trot and trust in my control instead of feeling like I'm racing toward the edge of the cliff.

RV's piaffe continues to improve. I'm able to do passage-piaffe-passage transitions as they are in the Grand Prix, and although they aren't perfect, they're showable. Her passage has always been good but incredibly inconsistent and now I'm able to find a smaller passage that she can maintain. For a few days, she madly shakes her head as if she has something in her ears and leaps into the rafters every time I ask her for a bit more expression, and then she decides to give me the army salute and say, Can I do more, please? She's always been a moody queen.

Idocus works with an immense amount of energy and enthusiasm. It warms my heart. This is the Idy I lost. His work is nearly flawless so I mainly work on the basics, find a balance between the feeling of his hind legs to my hand that Schumacher taught me and Klaus's *give hand*. This is lucky because the unfortunate result of being such a nice horse is the necessity to reproduce and spring is breeding season.

Chris and I aren't in agreement about what his breeding schedule should be because for her, showing is just a tool to generate breedings to create income and there's a specific season that breeders want semen. But breeding is hard on him and, of course, showing is all that's important to me.

He breeds to a phantom—a breeding dummy—and it's far from a high tech one set up specifically for him. It takes him several jumps to properly mount which screws up his sacrum as it repetitively slams the phantom, and it fatigues the muscles in his hind end which are required in both mounting and the Grand Prix work. I've been putting blood, sweat, more tears than I care to recall and every penny I earn into this horse for two and a half years, he finally comes into his own again and I don't want to lose that.

That's part of the deal though, so I'm keeping my fingers, toes and eyes crossed that it doesn't affect him as badly this year as it has in the past.

◆　◆　◆

Idy needs to do one Special to qualify for the National Grand Prix championships, and I want to find my boundaries with Myth and RV to prepare for the Small Tour ones—take some risks and see how far I can safely push things—so we do the ESDCTA show in New Jersey at the end of May. I also want to practice Myth's and RV's freestyles as Myth's gaits have gotten much bigger, much loftier, so we renovated the music to keep the timing right, and RendezVous has all new music because Francine wanted a *My Fair Lady* theme.

For the first time in months, RV doesn't lean on the cross ties in happy anticipation of work. When I get on, she once again shakes her head as if she has something in her ears and leaps through the air for no reason, so I realize that the reason she didn't try to bust out of the crossties is because she was frustrated. She knew she was at a show and couldn't do her best because something was bothering her. I'm sure I could just ride her through a careful test and she'd be ok but that would defeat the purpose of this show. I want to push the limits, see where they are. Why put her in the ring and have her feel frustrated just to go around another safe Prix St. Georges?

I scratch.

This is becoming an inconsistent issue so Francine calls RV's previous trainer to ask about it. He tells her it's exactly what she did with him when she had Lyme disease so we send her home to start treatment.

The judges reward the improvement in Myth's forward expression and he wins the St. Georges with a 73%. In the I1, I find out what my boundaries are by breaking them. Much of the test is done with a one-inch neck, which happens when I've passed the line and need to regain control, and we have a fantastic extended canter that ends with a couple of unrequired one-tempis. He still wins but only with a 71%. Now I know my boundaries. At the Championships I'll go to them but not through.

Although we tried to adjust the music of his freestyle to match his increased forwardness, it isn't enough. In all the trot work, I border on passage to keep it slow enough to stay with the music and although he has no mistakes, I'm unable to show him off. The judges' opinions differ a great deal. Lilo Fore loves it and gives it 77.5%, but Lorraine McDonald detests it, says the trot tour is boring, lacks creativity and she hates the music. Gives it a 72. Axel Steiner calls me out on the passage-y trot. He also says it's too test-like, which is true because when we originally created it, I wanted to keep it as much like the St. Georges as possible to keep it very simple. But now he can do more.

Although the judges' technical comments are exactly what I wanted and will help me a great deal, the differing opinions on my music reveal the unwinnable challenge of freestyles. It's hard to please everyone anyway, but I chose something very different that I love. It was a risk. Some judges will love it and others will hate it, but I have to listen to it eight zillion times so I figured I have to like it. He ends up a very close second with a 73%.

In the warm up, Idy feels better than at the World Cup, but as soon as we go around the outside of the show ring it feels like he's on tippy toes. The footing is different than in the warm-up and he makes it known that it's not suitable, it's too hard. His piaffe is barely a piffle. He doesn't make any mistakes and still wins with a 68%, but he was a pansy and gave about 25% effort so I go back in the warm up ring to discipline him, to get the piaffe he's capable of. But he piaffes exquisitely without any reprimanding which infuriates me more.

I take him to the barn and hand him off to the groom. I usually take his bridle off myself every day, give him an apple and lots of loving, but not today. I'm pissed at him. I never take horses' disobediences personally but this is personal. He let me down and he knew he was doing it.

Whereas normally I acknowledge him every time I pass his stall, I ignore him. He presses his shoulder against the bars, begging for my attention but I look away. At night check, I just throw his hay over the door and move on. I usually always go in and give him loving, tell him of his perfection. He grates his teeth on the bars, paws and tosses his head. I do nothing.

The next day is the dreaded Special, the test I need to qualify for the Championships and the one that the last time I rode got a 58%. Before I get on, I don't give Idy his customary neck scratch and ego stroke. He warms up great as he did yesterday, but I'm ready for the deflation as we enter the show ring. He doesn't complain at all, though, stays just the same. He might be the only horse in the world who understands the silent treatment. He gets a 71%, wins and gets us into the Championships.

◆ ◆ ◆

On the drive home, I tell Jason I'm having doubts about going to Rio for the Pan Am Games. Myth and RV are so close to Grand Prix, I'd really like to start it this fall and then maybe go to Europe and show over there.

He says, It would be a lot of travel to do Rio and then go to Europe. And I don't think Rio's that safe.

But it's the Pan Am Games, I say. How often does a rider get a chance like this—have the right horse at the right time? Part of me feels I'd be spitting in the face of fate if I don't go for it.

He shrugs. Up to you, Court.

I'd have to be away from my other horses for nearly five weeks. And from what I understand, we won't have much control once we get there as the country works on a bribery system.

Sounds like you don't want to go, honey.

But it's the *Pan Ams,* I repeat.

He chuckles.

When we get home, I find an email from the USEF asking the qualified riders to withdraw our applications for the Championships if we aren't prepared to go to Brazil. This adds even more weight to the decision. Myth is #1 and RV is #3 in the standings so there's a very good chance I'd be selected. But it seems unfair to take away our Championships after all our work.

I think I'll go for it, I tell Jason. It's such a hard choice but my personal rule of thumb when faced with a decision to do or not to do, is always go with the positive, always do. It just seems better to take action than to sit and wonder.

Glad I could help, he says with a smile.

I lie on the floor eye to eye with Quiver hoping he'll tell me what to do. He looks back in my eyes and it strikes me that Quivvy's the same as Idy. They're my soul mates. So human, so smart. I used to be sad that Quivvy didn't favor me, didn't treat me as Mommy, but I came to realize he's not that dog because he's not needy. He needed to learn to respect me, learn that I respect him. Once he did, he was the easiest dog to train because he's so smart. I can leave a half-eaten T-bone on the coffee table overnight and he won't touch it because he knows he's not supposed to. I taught him to wait till I say *OK* to go out the door when I let him out, and now if the door is left open and no one's in the room, he'll walk to it and just stand there, wait until someone comes in and tells him OK before going out. Just like Idy, once they want to be good, they just are.

Thinking of Idocus makes me realize another dilemma with going to Rio: Klaus wants Idy to go to Aachen which is July 5th-7th in Germany, and the Pan Am Games are July 14th-18th in Brazil. Although the dates don't overlap, there'd be a ten day stretch of time when I should be preparing Myth to compete but I'd be in Germany. I briefly consider having someone else ride him—that's what I'd do if it were Idy—but Myth is complicated. I don't trust anyone to ride him but Steffen and Steffen will be in Aachen.

I call Francine because she always gives me such great advice, expect her to cement my decision to go to Rio because it's her horse.

Mais, no, Courtney, of course you need go to Aachen. As far as skipping the Pan Ams, I'm happy to have my girl back to ride, but that's ridiculous to not let the top horses compete in the Championships. Then *national champion* is a joke, she says.

I'm sorry, I say.

It's certainly not your fault, the USEF made a bad decision. Dinner tomorrow? she asks.

She makes everything so simple.

My next call is Rich.

Well, that seems like the right decision, Courtney, he says.

I can't believe how cool both of them are being. After all the money and all they've sacrificed, they make it easy. Then I tell him that Klaus is going to Gladstone ten days before the show and I can go train with him if I want.

That's great. There's no sense in leaving Myth home to not be ridden.

• 42 •

So I scratch Myth and RV from Gladstone, but four days before competition begins, Myth, Idy and I go to the showgrounds to train. A long driveway bordering a golf course twists through a path of trees and leads to a magnificent barn that was built in 1913. It feels fresh and pure, quaint and solid. Jason looks over and sees my content expression. Happy, honey? he asks. I sigh, smile and nod.

Idocus bred three times in the past week so I do very little with him in an effort to not demand more of his butt. And pray. Klaus hones in on the passage with Myth. He has an amazing gift with knowing exactly what needs to be done exactly when it's needed. He tells me, *a little more forward, a little more bend, no leg now, just take back from the hand, bounce your seat* or whatever it needs at that precise moment. What excites me the most is that I *can* do what he asks because Myth has gotten amazingly rideable. I'm not yet clever enough or educated enough, or simply genius enough, to do what he tells me the millisecond he says it, but I *am* able to do it the millisecond after.

On the third day, he tells me he wants Myth to do an exhibition ride of the Grand Prix test on the final day of the show. Idy shows Thursday, Friday and Saturday, but the I1 Freestyle is Sunday and he wants me ride the test at lunch, have the judges score it and comment on it.

My stomach clenches. Are you sure? I ask. Absolute, he simply says, turns and walks away. So the following days, we work on the movements of the test.

When the competition begins, one of the judges who knows Klaus's intentions, Anne Gribbons, says, We only want you to move to Grand Prix if you're ready. This is a good horse. So just know, we're going to be brutally honest.

Honest, I like, but is the brutal part really necessary? I just smile and meekly say thank you.

◆ ◆ ◆

In Idy's Grand Prix, he feels completely crooked, like I'm riding two horses. His light week didn't help the joints breeding disrupted and the test is riddled with mistakes, gets a 65.4% for fifth place. I'm broken hearted, not because of the result but because I put him through something that was impossible for him to do and he tried, *for me.*

The Team vet, Tim Ober, spends two hours in his stall after our test trying to get the necessary chiropractic adjustments. He does acupuncture as well and gives him fifteen liters of fluids.

As Idy gets his fluids, the other competitors and Jason share commiseratory beers with me. I think horse people can always feel for each others' downs because we all have them. I tell them I'll get on the next day with the intention to show but will be 100% prepared to scratch the Special if he feels the same way.

Starting out, he doesn't feel awesome, but he can use his haunches and gets better as we go. I'm riding one horse. The movements aren't as easy for him as they normally are but he can do them, so I decide he's comfortable enough to go in and I won't be torturing him. He puts his heart and mind into it and we manage to pull off a very nice clean test worth 71.64%. Steffen goes right after me and gets the exact same score but wins the tie breaker. I'm immensely proud of my Idy, worship Tim's godly healing and am thrilled to get the same score as my hero, made even more impressive by the fact that it was in our nemesis test.

◆   ◆   ◆

Saturday is our Freestyle. Never before have I shown Idy three days in a row. His schedule is normally work a day or two then hack a day or three, so I worry he won't have the energy. But he warms up identically to yesterday—doesn't feel great at the start but gets better as we go. Mike Poulin stops me when I'm taking a walk break and tells me I'm a mustard seed so I can move mountains. I don't know what it means but his enthusiastic delivery motivates me.

Steffen goes right before me and gets a 76%. Idy's still not 100% himself physically but puts out 200% in effort. We have one bobble in the twos to ones on the circle like at the World Cup, but I learned my lesson to not repeat them and finish the final centerline with extended trot. My halt is square and right with the music. As I come out of the ring, Steffen says, I think you got it this time.

Just then the announcer says we all have to take cover because "swirls" are approaching. I rode obliviously to the music from The Wizard of Oz while the skies were turning dark and threatening and little twisters were bouncing around. Maybe that gave us extra points for inventive choreography because while taking shelter in the barn, the announcer comes up behind me and shows me my score—78%. Idy won.

Now more than at the World Cup, I'm struck with the realization of my achievement. All the hard work and struggles through my childhood paid off. I look out at the storm and realize that I don't need the barn to feel secure anymore, to feel connected to others. I have the mutual security I always craved without a shelter. Without a storm.

We wait for the weather to clear before having the awards ceremony and as Hilda Gurney, one of the judges, shakes my hand in congratulations she says, You're going to hate me for this, but I bred two mares to Idocus last week.

You're right, I think I hate you for that, I say with a smile.

But I'm so happy to see you riding him again and I'm going to make it up to you. I'm going to have you ride one of those babies some day. They're very nice mares.

Now that would really make up for it, I say.

I would be honored, she replies.

I'd be honored, I tell her.

Back at my stall, the commiseratory beers my fellow competitors shared with me on Thursday are now celebratory ones. Although they didn't win, they share in the glory of my unexpected victory.

My satisfaction, however, lasts as long as my beer. Tomorrow is Myth's exhibition and I'll be laying myself and this wonderful horse out on the dissecting table in front of the top people in our sport. My show is over but Saturday night is spent tossing and turning in anxiety. I saw a PBS episode that said nervousness comes from feeling unprepared; if you're confident in your knowledge for a chemistry exam, you won't be nervous, but if you feel you haven't studied enough or don't fully understand, you will. I don't feel prepared.

◆ ◆ ◆

I wake in the morning still concerned. Part of what has me worried is that Myth has never gotten to see the show ring before which he would have if he were showing. But as we enter the ring, he doesn't let the new environment affect him at all. His mind stays 100% on me the whole ride. I have to ride the extensions conservatively to avoid ending up in Kansas and the passage, as planned, I ride very small. We do thirteen ones instead of the required fifteen—not because he stopped doing them, but I stupidly stopped asking.

Then Anne Gribbons gives a commentary. She says the judges were happily surprised with the quality and flow of the test, the only thing overall she'd need to see is more power. She says, The passage is wonderfully level but it needs more lift. Hearing *wonderfully level* is music to my ears. The pure two-beat rhythm we've worked so hard to get has been achieved. She says she hasn't seen the other judges' marks yet, but she's sure the score would be hovering around 70%. That would have been second place in the Grand Prix on Thursday. The final score is 69%.

◆ ◆ ◆

Once again, my celebration is short-lived. I clearly made a good decision to forego the Pan Ams, but I won't be able to go to Aachen if I can't come up with the funds. Susie Dutta heard about my quandary and calls out from her tack room, Courtney, I've got an idea. You need help getting Idocus to Aachen, right?

Well, it would be nice, I reply.

Come on, I'm going to introduce you to someone, she says and takes me to meet the sponsors of Gladstone, Shereen and Jeff Fuqua.

This is Courtney, she says to them. She has to pay for her horse to go to Aachen. Would you be interested in helping her?

Shereen apparently has watched my progression since I just started and says they'd certainly be happy to help.

Now nothing can minimize my happiness. I have two International quality Grand Prix horses, RV is a very good Small Tour horse almost at Grand Prix, and Roby and Wy below her. Rich and Francine are making my unrealistic goal sheet possible. When I get home, Francine has Rich, his wife, Jason and me over for dinner. I keep waiting for her to say something about 2008, but she doesn't.

· 43 ·

My family planned an engagement party in Harbor Springs for the evening of June 30th so I can't travel to Germany with Idy who leaves for Aachen on July 1st. Not only does this alone petrify me, but he also won't have his travel buddy Mythy, who his love for remains mysteriously strictly platonic. Instead he has to travel with an Icelandic horse who looks like a pony. Idy does love ponies but in a strictly non-platonic way.

He breeds four times in the two weeks before we go so I arrange for the chiropractor to see him after each breeding. And Tim will be at Aachen so I'm as comfortable about the situation as is possible.

Being with all my siblings and my three parents gives me momentary reprieves from my anxiety. The theme of the party is Wine, Wit, and Wisdom, the idea being that everyone brings a bottle of wine and showers us with a bit of matrimonial wit or wisdom. We arrange ourselves on the deck with me and Jason in the middle surrounded by the guests and are given everything from hundred dollar bottles to boxes of wine while everyone tries to outwit each other with a bit of wisdom or two interspersed.

As we're wiping our eyes from tears of laughter one guest asks, Why did you and Jason decide to marry each other?

I look at her and wait for the joke. She's dead serious. I look at Jason and he smiles and motions for me to answer. The obvious answer is love. The obvious joke is a green card.

I clear my throat, shrug and say, He has great health insurance.

Immediately the jovial mood is rekindled as everyone knows a marriage will add me to his insurance.

◆ ◆ ◆

I'm sad that I have to leave our annual Fourth of July week-long sibling get-together early, but I'm excited to go to Aachen. Gib feigns offense and says, I see how it is, but leave the wine. Gray says, Kick some butt, sista!

Greta's the slowest to say goodbye and I go to the kitchen to find her. Is this going to be every year? she asks because Aachen is generally around the Fourth. I don't answer because I'm not sure how to. I hope so, but the Fourth of July in Harbor is a sibling tradition.

Only because if it is, maybe we should find another week, she continues. I should have known; she wasn't trying to guilt me, she was being pragmatic. Looking at her, I realize that each of my siblings has a perfect combination of Mom's idealism and Dad's pragmatism. She takes off her rubber cleaning gloves and hugs me. Good luck, Court. We'll miss you but I guess all those five a.m. walks up the hill paid off.

◆ ◆ ◆

Elias has to stay at home to take care of the other horses, so Betsy travels to Aachen with Idy as his groom and we think it will be great fun to take care of him together. I soon realize we were mistaken and miss Elias dreadfully when we end up with more of the mud-like poultice on us than we get on the intended destination of Idy's legs.

For some reason, this place makes Idy very anxious and he never settles. He paces and spins in the stall non-stop. I take him for walks and give him fresh hay which normally calms him down, but not here. I get nightly calls from the security guard at three or four in the morning and have to go walk him. The only reason I can come up with for his anxiety is that these barns must harbor strange old scents. They're a hundred years old, made of cement blocks and have built in feed bins. They're like no other barn that I know of that he's ever been in.

Despite all the wasted energy spinning in the stall, Idy remains full of vitality. He feels excited to be here, there's a big field I can hack him in to satisfy his craving to wander and the chiropractic work kept his bones in their proper places.

◆ ◆ ◆

Before competition begins, Steffen takes me and Betsy to watch a jumper class. As we climb the bleacher stairs, Steffen stops in front of me to say hi to someone. When he steps aside to introduce us, my jaw drops. The person is George Morris, my childhood hero—icon of the jumper world. Not only is he himself an Olympic medalist, he's also coached numerous riders to Olympic medals and is the coach of the United States show jumping team.

Steffen introduces me and George says, Yes, I know.

You know who *I* am? I ask in disbelief.

Yes, I like the way you ride. You don't do any gorilla riding, he says see-sawing artificial reins.

I giggle and tell him Idy simply wouldn't allow that. The people around us express their irritation at having us standing in the aisle, so we say goodbye to George and find our seats to watch.

As I'm accustomed to in jumper classes, you don't even have to watch the rider to know how they're doing. The crowd's moment to moment reactions tell you exactly what's going on. If a horse slows down, everyone leans forward and clucks. If he refuses a fence, they cringe, and if he meets a fence precariously but gets over, there are many cheers. I tell Betsy this must be what it's like to be a football fan; the crowd's enthusiasm feeds itself.

To my surprise, watching dressage here is the same way. If a horse has a mild spook or flinch, there's a collective gasp. If they don't halt square, an *aww* is audible. If an extended trot is extraordinary, you hear an *oooh*. The rider can feel the crowd's disappointment or appreciation.

The whole show experience is starkly different than it is at home. In the U.S., I stay at cheap motels and eat fast food, but here the show supplies each rider with a hotel room and has cars to drive us between there and the show whenever we want. Breakfast is supplied by the hotel and lunch is available any time on the showgrounds. Beer gardens, restaurants, and vendors—who don't just sell horsey products but stylish clothes, kitchen appliances, and house wares—open days before the show and are packed. The atmosphere puts Devon to shame in the party-like feel.

The sole disappointment about Aachen versus the U.S. shows is the lack of camaraderie. At the big U.S. shows, all the riders know one another and chit chat, say *good luck* or *how was your ride*, or *oh I'm so sorry but your braids look wonderful*. Steffen warned me that it would be different here but I wasn't quite prepared. There are no smiles and good mornings, no *how did it go* or *have a great ride*. I know when it's game time, I don't seem friendly and my default face is unfortunately less than welcoming, but back in the barn we're all friends. We're all working for the same thing, have the same ups and downs and as happened at Gladstone, we celebrate and commiserate with each other.

◆ ◆ ◆

Steffen introduces me, Betsy and Jason to a tiny restaurant for dinner, Italia Uno, which quickly becomes our favorite and we go there nearly every evening. On our third night there, the owner joins us at our table. He's Italian, lives in Germany, and speaks Spanish and French as well. The one language he doesn't speak is English and we attempt to converse in a mish-mosh of languages. I use the smatterings of French I learned in school, German from when I lived here and Spanish I picked up from the grooms, much to Jason and Betsy's amusement. Adrenaline allows me to fully enjoy it, but by the fourth night the midnight outings have taken their toll and I'm spent.

Perhaps Idy's energy was the effect of adrenaline too as on the day of the Grand Prix it begins to deteriorate. In all the piaffes, I have to creep forward to keep him active. His trot doesn't have the extra cadence we've found, but other than the ones in which he has a tiny bobble, there are no mistakes. Despite the anxiety and lack of rest, we put in quite a good test.

When the score comes out, though, it's only one percentage point higher than at Gladstone where I was mortified at our mistake-laden performance. Perhaps what people have been telling me for years about international competition but I resisted believing is true: scores are often based on the politics of past performances.

I don't see it as a bad thing at all, though. It makes sense that a rider needs to gain the judges' confidence by repetitively performing well in order to get really high marks. I've only ever shown in front of one of the five judges here whereas Steffen and Isabell have shown countless horses internationally over the years and all well. That consistency earns them the right to higher scores. Perhaps when they ride, everything starts as an eight and if a movement is particularly good, it gets a nine or a ten. When it's not very good, it gets a seven. I'm unproven so I'm automatically a six and if a movement is particularly good, it gets a seven or eight but if it's substandard, it gets a five. It's inspiring. I hope that one day I'll be an eight, that the judges will think, *Ah, here's Courtney, who gets good marks.*

All five of the judges give me eights on the rider score and Klaus tells me that in his conversations with them after the class, every one of them was impressed with how Idocus looked. So at least I'm starting in the right direction.

◆ ◆ ◆

After five nights of three a.m. calls from the security guard, lack of sleep is making me giddy and the night before the Special, Betsy tells him to call *her* when Idy gets beside himself. I also utilize a strategy I've developed to arrive rested when I fly internationally: I'll take a Tylenol PM when dinner is served just after take-off, sleep soundly until they serve breakfast just before arrival and wake up totally fresh. That's about four hours which isn't enough for tonight, so I take two.

My ride is at 10:32 and when my alarm goes off at 8, I wake up in a daze. I figure it'll wear off but by the time I get to the barn, I feel the same. I'm standing in the middle of the aisle not by my stall, doing nothing and Betsy comes over smiling. Good morning, sunshine, she says. Did you sleep well? Then she sees my look of consternation and says, Are you all right?

I nod and tell her about the two Tylenol PM's. I'm sure I'll be fine, it must just take a while to wear off.

But when I get on at 9:52, I'm no less hazy and my normal focus has vanished in a cloud. On top of my poor state of mind, Idy feels like a different horse. He's cocked and crooked and his hind end is gone. Several times throughout the test I have to think where I'm going which hasn't happened in years. Luckily I've done the test enough times that even if my mind is slow, my body knows where to go. And maybe I've jumped from a six to a seven because despite both of our issues, we jump to a 68% and eleventh place.

The top fifteen riders do their Freestyle and although I'm grateful for a chance to redeem myself, I have nothing to listen to my music with because I didn't think I'd make it. Luckily I threw the CD in at the last minute *just in case.*

Tim works his chiropractic magic to sort out Idy's crookedness, but we have another night of unrest. This time I insist the security guard call *me*, and at 6 a.m. when I'm returning to the hotel, the sun peeks over the horizon for the first time of my stay. Rain and wind have persisted every day thus far, but at 11:17 when I ride, the sun is glistening off of Idy's coat.

When my music starts, the crowd's laughter startles me. It begins with a flapper era voice saying, *Here she is boys! Here she is world! Here comes Mama!* and the crowd finds it hilarious. Their amusement amuses me and I can feel my body dance a tiny bit with the music. Unfortunately, Idy's lack of rest makes every movement subdued and unimpressive, especially the piaffe and passage. Our test is mistake-free again but the entire thing is lackluster. We're eleventh again with a 71%.

I'm satisfied with the result. It was the best we could do and got the score it deserved. I receive many nice comments from the judges as well as spectators but I know that from now on, even if it busts my piggy bank, I need to take a groom. I had a friend to help me and Steffen's groom fed Idy when she fed his horse in the morning but in the end it was only my responsibility. There was all the hand-walking and being there for the other two meals and stall cleaning and soaking hay and bandaging his legs in the evening. There was a great deal to see and do at Aachen that I wasn't able to do. Never again.

♦ ♦ ♦

As the show has progressed, the atmosphere has lightened up a great deal and by Sunday, it's downright friendly. Perhaps as the show got underway, the anxiety lessened so people were more open and got to know each other.

The final thing we do is the Closing Ceremony, which is required for all competitors including the jumpers and drivers who have a show simultaneously. If a rider doesn't feel safe taking their own horse, they can rent one, but they must ride. Isabelle rides a little donkey-like horse with an inverted neck which is amusing to see since she's normally on big impressive mounts. I ride Idy, who's highly entertained but too exhausted to do anything more than whinny and check everything out.

The ceremony takes place at 7:30 p.m. the final night of the show so one would think the people in the audience would go home, but every single one stays. Outfits of cavalry and Lusitano groups are added to the competitors so hundreds of horses and riders parade through a long trail surrounded by thousands of fans. We file into the stadium which is packed with yet more fans and walk around the whole perimeter right next to the wall. All the people look directly at each rider and wave, and when a rider makes eye contact with a person and gives them a special wave, their face lights up. Every single rider, no matter which country or discipline, is cheered.

Once we make our round, we all stand—or pirouette or levade—in the middle of the stadium while the fans sing us a song to say good bye, and everyone—I mean everyone—waves a white handkerchief. Tingles emerge in my throat and nose as I sit on my horse and have half a million people waving their white hankies and singing their hearts out. I take off my white glove and wave it as the other riders are doing but after a few minutes, I put it back on because I figure the song is nearly finished. Ten minutes later, however, as we're finally proceeding out of the stadium, they're still singing and waving. It feels as if the audience is commending each rider's hard work. They know this glory is never without sacrifice.

• 44 •

I come home with the same feeling the World Cup gave me: a euphoric sense of grounded weightlessness. Everything I've struggled for, yearned for, is coming to fruition. I'm getting married. I have three nearly Grand Prix horses and good ones following them. My dad loves *me*. I have a great group of girlfriends and fantastic clients. I feel like I used to be trapped in a house and all the doors were locked preventing me from following my path, and after trying each door I crawled through a window to find my way out. As my journey has progressed, people have begun to call to me, to lead me in the right direction. There's so much more to do but now I'm being helped, not hindered.

• • •

In July, Myth and I compete in our first official Grand Prix and get almost the same score as our exhibition ride at Gladstone: 68.3%. By August, RV's ready to make her debut and I enter them both in HITS on the Hudson—RV in the Open division and Myth in the CDI.

RV's the first to go on Saturday, and going around the outside of the show ring, the veins on her neck protrude in excitement and her enormous ears rest at half mast listening to me every moment despite the screaming baby, the water truck and the loose dog. I think she knows this is a special test. As we enter, I feel totally, as Francine would say, zen: calm, peaceful, focused.

Although she makes several mistakes that aren't common for her like missing the ones and breaking to canter in a trot extension, her piaffe and passage are quite good. Everything that's normally a problem isn't. When I come out, I ask Jason with a big grin what he thought. He looks at me apologetically and says, There's room for improvement?

That's exactly how it should be, honey. We're just starting. I hug RV's neck and let her saunter back to the barn. She's ridiculously proud of herself and checks out the people watching her like Idy does. She ends up with a 65% and wins.

Warming Myth up, he's right with me, soft in my hand and taking the half-halt from my seat. The judge rings the bell and as I pick up the canter to enter, a horsefly half the size of my palm dive-bombs poor Mythy. He, more than any horse I've known, can't stand bugs. They're the only things that make him angry. Twenty feet short of the entrance, it lands on Myth's neck so I halt, take one good whack at it, miss, and then have to enter to be within the forty-five seconds allowed.

I pick up the canter and go in on a crazed Myth. He bucks in the first trot extension and then runs like hell. Bugzilla rides on my top hat while I try to get Myth's eyes and brain back in his head—I'm surprised the judge doesn't eliminate us for having more than one rider. It sees another opportunity when we stop going fifty miles an hour for the piaffe and once again dive-bombs Myth's crest.

Surprisingly with all the mistakes and general hysteria of the test, he's still an extremely close third with a 64.3%—first is 64.6%. The judges' comments are all very positive. They say he just needs to get more relaxed and secure but are impressed by his quality.

We do the Special at 7:30 Sunday morning when it's too cold for monster-bugs. We have no mistakes, but it's not as fluid and expressive as it could be and I'm unable to do most of the movements letting his neck out. He wins with a 68%. I expect the Grand Prix to be just as the Small Tour was: it'll take time to get him secure enough that he doesn't feel he needs to try hard—which to him still means going faster.

RV's test is completely devoid of mistakes and as I leave the show ring, Cara Whitham, who's an Olympic level judge says, Very nice potential! I'm looking forward to seeing more of her!

Although I'm in the open division, the class was judged by the CDI judges, so even though the test was better than yesterday, the score is lower. She wins with a 62%.

When RV and Myth were far away from Grand Prix, it felt like Grand Prix was the destination, but I now realize there are two totally different journeys: there's the journey to get to Grand Prix and the journey of the Grand Prix itself. Getting it better and better, fine tuning, changing, all the ups and downs each movement takes before becoming solid. It's extremely inspiring to get those first Grand Prix done and then to go home and work on all of it.

• 45 •

For how excited I am about the journey with my horses, I'm ten times more excited about my non-horse journey: my wedding. All my years of emotional confusion, waiting for my one true love, he was across the Earth and the internet brought us together. Perhaps ten years ago, we wouldn't have found each other. Perhaps if we hadn't found each other, my mind wouldn't have been convinced to stop searching for the complexity in everything and my turmoil about riding would have continued.

Jason's parents, Cath and Kezza, make the five-hour drive to Camp Dancing Bear with us and question our choice of locale as we navigate the driveway. But when we reach the house, they understand that the journey is worth it.

The ceremony is on September fifteenth, but both our large families spend our "wedding-week" with us and our closest friends trickle in toward the end. Greta and her best friend become my wedding coordinators and continually chastise me for my lack of planning, but the week is just what I'd envisioned. The first few days we canoe, water ski and play golf, and as the weather gets progressively colder we play pool, sing on the Karaoke machine, have booze cruises, and bask in the warmth of the fires.

◆　◆　◆

The master bedroom has two choices for sleeping accommodations: one bed is inside next to the fire and another one is on a screened-in porch so you can fall asleep to the sound of loons and huddle for warmth under massive down comforters. Jason and I choose the latter and wake on the morning of our wedding to the sound of rumbling skies. Although it adds to the cozy feeling, it's a definite concern as the ceremony is to take place outside.

He and his groomsmen get ready in the boathouse while my bridesmaids and I pamper in the master bathroom and, obeying the groom not to see bride on wedding day ritual, we continually discuss the situation over CB's. Should we have the ceremony on the dock as planned or move it under cover? If we move it inside, where should it be? Maybe by this afternoon the weather will clear.

While keeping one eye on the weather, the other is absorbed in the pampering process. The mood as we get ready isn't that of a wedding day but of a group of fourteen-year-olds playing dress-up. One of my bridesmaids does everyone else's makeup while we circle around and discuss options: more blush? Blue or brown eyeliner? Red lipstick? When she's doing mine, Dave brings in a plethora of champagne, and to the complaints of the girls who are feeling the after-effects of last night says, Hair of the dog.

My hairdresser arrives, twists my hair up and decorates it with pearls. Then she goes to work on my bridesmaids while I bathe Quiver in the bathtub, to Greta's horror. When Jen's hair is finished, she stands in front of me with tears streaming down her face. I look like my father, she says to the agreement of everyone else. I tell her that her father must be beautiful and eventually our laughter incites hers. She and two other girls get their hair redone and are equally as disappointed in the results. They point out that perhaps my poor choice in stylist is due to the fact that any hairdressing impresses me after my own handiwork as I normally cut my own hair.

When I come out of the bathroom, my wedding dress is hanging by the window and the sun is peeking through the clouds bathing it in a light that can only be described as romantic. We stand in a circle admiring it, talking about how normally people only wear their wedding dress once but I'll wear mine again for our wedding in New Zealand. We'll get married on the beach, I'll cut it off just below the knee and wear flip flops.

Pam pulls out my cover-up when my back is turned and Greta, who went dress shopping with me, says, Uh, oh. She holds up a tulle jacket that just covers the shoulders and upper arms with puffy sleeves. After looking at it for a moment, I burst out laughing and explain to the bewildered bridesmaids that that's the cover-up I hated. I chose a straight-sleeved half jacket. My friend who arranged for me to get the Vera Wang dress because she does business with them, is far more upset than I am, calls and tells them she has a hysterical bride on her hands while Betsy and I stifle our giggles. I tell the girls I guess I'm going to be cold because that thing is hideous.

After I'm dressed, we all stand gazing at my refection. She's elegant, but unlike the World Cup poster, she's me. The dress is lovely. Off-white. Strapless. Floor length. No decorations or embellishments on the tulle fabric. It couldn't be more perfect in its simplicity. Francine comes behind me and drapes a beige mink shawl over my shoulders.

Although the rain continues to hold off, it feels as if the sky has storm-constipation and at some point it's going to come pouring down. Jason and I decide that it's too risky to take a chance of eighty-six guests having to scramble up the precarious steps if the storm explodes, so when the decision can no longer be delayed, the original plan is aborted. The ceremony will be inside.

My bridesmaids expect me to be upset by this turn of events but it doesn't matter to me in the least. We could all be in pajamas and dinner could be ordered pizza followed by store-bought ice cream and it wouldn't matter. The unparalleled feeling of all of the people I love most in the world gathered together to celebrate the depth of my and Jason's mutual love wouldn't be diminished.

Steffen, Jen, Betsy and Buttcheeks remove the furniture from the living room and the ceremony takes place in front of floor-to-ceiling windows overlooking the water. I take my dad's arm. Tears fill his eyes and his smile attempts to split his cheeks. At my graduation he was proud of my past and that our father-daughter relationship was salvaged. Now he's happy for my future and we're joined as two people, his concerns for my choices as his daughter are laid to rest and he couldn't be happier in the man he's handing my welfare over to.

It's a Wonderful World by Louis Armstrong begins and we start down the aisle. Francine, Rich, my friend from Andrews, Lendon. Every face I look at near and dear to my heart. I used to think the ceremony meant nothing to me, it was the marriage I looked forward to, but although it's the little piece of paper from the courthouse that makes us married, having all these people witness our vows to spend the rest of our lives with each other means more to me, consecrates him not as my husband, but as my life partner.

Then I look at Jason and our eyes envelope each other. I was such a freak to take so long to realize he was perfect for me and am extremely lucky he was so patient. He's like a tree, grounded in his convictions— honesty, loyalty, ethics. And me. He was right in his response when I said the rain was a good thing: we don't need luck.

You may kiss the bride.

It's a Wonderful World

In our reception, my dad, Greta, Buttcheeks, DP and Gib give speeches telling stories from our pasts, impressions of our love and making jokes about adjusting for the weather. Then Jason's dad speaks. He tells of Jason's upbringing, how they lived in a house built of discarded cardboard sealed with a slurry of cow manure. Jason got his first clothes, a stolen rucksack, at three years old and at six they had to wash it. Those who know his dry sense of humor laugh so hard they cry, but the faces in the crowd of those who don't know him vary from hilarity to confusion.

Jason then begins his speech by telling the audience they've had their laughs and now it's time to settle down, which gets more laughs. He says he never thought he'd be writing poems because he's flippant by nature, but I've had that effect on his emotions. He reads a poem he wrote when we got engaged entitled *5 Years*, a follow up to *11 Weeks*:

It seems like just yesterday we had our first date,
I remember our encounter; I recall you were late.
It was well worth the waiting, a beautiful sight to see
The more I grew to know you, the more you captivated me.
We have traveled a path and been down a road
That led to our engagement, what a seed we have sowed.
You gave me that chance and my words can't express
The pleasure you give me, it's pure happiness.
A marriage awaits us, a future together
The excitement engulfs me, I feel light as a feather.
My love for you got stronger and stronger each hour
Our love was a seedling, but it's now in full-flower.

How can I be so lucky to have this man love me so? How can I be so lucky to get to spend the rest of my life with him? I stand up and give him a trembling embrace. The clapping of the audience reminds me they're there and reluctantly, we release each other. Our first dance is to the Finn Brother's *Luckiest Man Alive* but I tell Jason it should be *Luckiest* Woman *Alive*. We agree on *Luckiest* People *Alive*.

Me and Quivvy

167

◆ 46 ◆

Our honeymoon is the Devon CDI and for four days, Jason and I are grimy and smelly with a thousand other people from seven a.m. to one a.m. He never suggests we should go away and I never consider that it's a sacrifice. It was a heavenly week and I never thought of my horses, but I'm happy to return to my equine journey.

Devon is the first Olympic Qualifier for both Idy and Myth. Idy will do the Grand Prix for the Freestyle and Myth will do the Grand Prix for the Special. The atmosphere, which has had a negative or positive impact on every horse I've shown here thus far, doesn't affect Myth at all. His focus remains only on trying to do what I want. Sometimes he guesses wrong and tries too hard, but his attention never strays to his surroundings. He wins his Grand Prix with a 68+%.

When I begin to warm Idy up, he feels weird—like he has a kink in his back. But whereas it used to be that if he didn't feel good, he'd get cranky, stop trying and I couldn't challenge him without instigating the middle hoof, now he willingly pushes through issues. He has a little bobble in the ones (as usual) and one large pirouette but goes to the top of the leader board with 71.04%. The very last rider, Ashley Holzer who's a Canadian Olympian, edges him out with a 71.2%. Although of course I would have loved to have won, I don't mind coming second to such an extraordinary pair.

Although Idy has a mistake-free freestyle, his nose goes to his chest and I struggle the whole ride to get his face on the vertical, but he takes the lead anyway with a 73%. Lars Petersen rides after me to *Big Bad Wolf* and the music, along with its suitability to the horse's piaffe and passage, is perfect. I little-girl enjoy his performance which earns a 73.4% and wins. So once again, I'm edged out of first and take second place, but when you walk away with your competitor's music in your head, you know the best performance won.

Myth's Special is Sunday afternoon so I school him lightly in the morning to take the edge off. One thing Idy's made me appreciate about Myth is that I never have to wonder if he's going to piaffe no matter how much work he does. The hardest thing about the Special with him is the order of the canter movements: extension on the diagonal to pirouette on the centerline, straight to ones on the centerline to another pirouette. Forward to on-the-spot to forward to on-the-spot encourages the short neck, but he stays with me and wins with a 73%.

As I give him his apple after the class, I look in his eye and realize the different loves I feel for him and Idy. I love Idy as one loves a husband: I respect him and revere who he is. I love Myth as one loves a child: I'm proud of who he is, want to harbor and protect him, love him with adoration versus the admiration I feel for Idy. I love them equally, only differently.

Mythilus, Credit: Susan J. Stickle

Idocus, Credit: Susan J. Stickle

◆ ◆ ◆

The first day I'm at the barn after Devon, Francine calls and asks if I have the Suburban I tow the trailer with and some guys to help lift.

Yes, I say. Why?

I have your wedding present and I think it's too big to fit in your 4Runner, she says.

In the afternoon, she parks her Suburban next to mine and the guys gather to help unload the present.

Ready? Francine asks. I smile and nod curiously.

She opens the door and pulls out a miniature dachshund small enough to fit in a hotdog bun.

A Lulu! I shriek and take her in my arms.

Come, she says and leads me to the lawn. We sit on the grass and I set her down to wander. She doesn't though. She stays right in my lap.

After fifteen minutes of sitting and admiring her, I put her on the ground and walk away to call her. But when I turn around, she's followed me. She already knows I'm mommy.

Viva following my boot, Credit: Stacie Lynch

When I get home, I present our family addition to Jason.

Oh, Francine, he says in mock disappointment. Well, what are you going to name him?

Her, I correct. I want something like Lulu: two consonants surrounding two vowels. Then it comes to me. I want Vegas to live on. Viva! I say.

OK, Viva it is, he says, already in love. She squirms and wants to come back to me. He hands her back, chuckles and says, Guess she's your dog.

• 47 •

Because of their successes at Devon, Klaus wants Idy and Myth to become known to the international judges in Europe in preparation for the Olympics, so I repeat Courtney's Quest and in the fall, Viva, RV and Wy join us for two months at his barn in Rosendahl-Osterwick, Germany.

Driving in feels like driving into a fairytale—not a pristine, perfectly planned out Cinderella palace type of feel but a cozy, welcoming, birds-on-your-shoulder type. The sensation it elicits is just peaceful. A long driveway is flanked by huge fields that are encompassed by a trail—which Idy will love—and quiet paved roads that will be perfect for hand-walking traverse between the neighboring farms. The driveway leads to a courtyard of brick buildings that contain housing for students. The apartments at Schumacher's were dorm-like and had an industrial feel, but these are spacious family-sized ones evoking the same feeling as the rest of the farm: warm.

After a day off and a day of tack-walking, Klaus watches my horses work. He doesn't teach me, just watches. He's happy with Myth and Idy, but RV does the ear thing after a bit of good work. He says when the blood gets pumping, it doesn't circulate as well in the head because of sinuses and the build-up in pressure is making her uncomfortable. Hence we need to give her lots of breaks, especially from very collected neck carriage. He massages her ears to help with the circulation and we vary the frame a great deal: head by her ankles, then up in show frame, then long and at the height of her shoulders. And it does get better. I'm thankful he thinks creatively and puts his whole heart into the effort. It shows he believes in her.

Wyoming loves Germany and has the best attitude he's ever shown. I tell Klaus my main objective with him is to introduce him to piaffe and the next day he asks to get on. After about three minutes of basic work, he stops and says, This horse is very smart. Piaffe will not be a problem, he will know it.

• • •

Ashley Holzer, a Canadian Olympian, invites me to the Elite Auction in Holland the first Saturday evening and I never would have guessed the building we enter would house horses. It's like Aachen in vendors but more sophisticated. You can be measured for tailored clothing, buy not just kitchen appliances but entire kitchens or bedrooms. You can buy a car. The tables are set with bottles of red and white wine and the dinner, brought by wait-staff, is delicious. All the Dutch people enthusiastically welcome me and don't let me pay for a thing because they recognize me as the rider of Idocus.

The whole evening is a party with occasional distractions of watching horses. One of Ashley's friends is gorgeous and used to be an erotic dancer—now she has four kids and is happily married but she still has the moves. Which she shows us and I try to mimic. When she lays back erotically on the wall with an inviting expression, I flail against the wall with a face combining scary and mentally disturbed. When she leans on a table and coquettishly displays her cleavage, I lean on it looking like I'm not feeling well as I try to squeeze my tiny breasts together. I'm pathetic, but I have a glorious evening in my ridiculous attempts and the silliness they bring out in our whole crowd.

Toward the end of the evening, I tell Ashley I'm sad that she's leaving and ask if she has plans to come back.

No, but let me introduce you to someone I think you'll hit it off with who lives in Amsterdam, she replies and leads me to a vendor who makes tailored clothes for fashion as well as riding.

This is Jose, she says.

I learn that Jose used to be an accomplished Grand Prix rider but was heartbroken when her horse died and decided not to ride anymore. She'd always designed and sewed her own clothes so when left without a passion, she made a profession out of doing so for others.

Her eyes are playful with a twinkle like Francine's and we chat for fifteen minutes before a customer interrupts us. Ashley was right. We hit it off and she invites me to go out in Amsterdam.

◆　◆　◆

At the beginning of the following week, the horses' jet-lag kicks in and I come to understand why the general rule of when to arrive at an international show is two days or two weeks ahead. The first few days they're still on the previous time zone and feel good, then the battle of adjusting begins and two weeks are necessary to ensure a horse will be fully on the correct time zone for competition. RV's mind is in another galaxy, Wyoming's is like a brick and his body's crooked like a corkscrew. Myth is uncharacteristically mellow but no more supple and I just take Idy for a nice long hack to be safe.

After a few days, they're recovered and we begin training.

Klaus explains the technique we're going to use to teach Wy piaffe: we're going to first teach him passage and then get the piaffe from that. I've never heard of this method. Most trainers first teach piaffe from the walk or trot and only after the horse becomes comfortable with it do they teach passage. And they continue to keep the two movements completely separate, only combine the two when the horse knows each. Klaus feels that with many horses this confuses the rhythm: piaffe is quick and passage is slow so it's unsettling to the horse to go between them if they know each separately. They lose confidence and become frantic as they struggle between the rhythms, so he teaches piaffe from the passage so the change of rhythm happens naturally.

So the first thing we need to do is teach Wy passage. After several days of trying to get passage-y steps and getting the old screw-you, I ask Klaus to get on. Many times, I see a horse trotting around looking like a plow-horse and then they burst into a phenomenal passage, so I know he can get anything to passage. Like with Mr. Schumacher, I don't see Klaus doing anything. Wyoming leaps hither and thither, pins his ears and once in a while Klaus shouts, Weltmeyer, which is the name of Wy's sire who Klaus blames for giving him the attitude. Suddenly Wyoming explodes into an enormous passage, keeps it a few strides and then returns to a normal trot, then enormous passage. Klaus pats him, says, Sehr gut, and gets off.

When I get back on, I ask for passage expecting a half-assed effort, but bam: enormous passage. Not too much, Klaus tells me, He's not strong now.

He uses the same rationale to help RV. Although her technique for piaffe itself has improved, the transitions between piaffe and passage continue to be a struggle. He has me do passage to just one or two steps of passage on the spot and then passage forward again. Although passage on the spot isn't piaffe, this method will allow her to find the rhythm naturally at the same time as the necessary strength is developed in a gradual way.

She still does the ear thing sometimes so it appears it's not her sinuses—or at least what we do doesn't help—but Klaus works well with it, appreciates her many amazing attributes and accepts that it's simply something we have to deal with. The question to me is whether we can work with it because if we can't, she can't be international, but apparently Klaus has no doubt as he tells me we have to think about the World Cup for her.

With Idy and Myth, Klaus just tries to perfect the details. With Idy, he has me *give gas*, or amp up, the passage before going into piaffe instead of getting into the piaffe and then asking for more activity. Myth requires just the opposite. He has a fantastic piaffe but when he goes to the passage afterwards, it stays flat for a few strides like forward piaffe while I activate it. Instead, I need to add power to the piaffe at the end so that I already have the loft as I begin the passage.

Courtney's Quest Journal
It's so special to have these four wonderful horses and be able to practice piaffe and passage on all of them to very different extents and styles. I can just feel myself getting more clever in those movements which is where my education needs to continue. I mean, I've gotten to ride five trillion half-passes in my life, but how many piaffes and passages have I gotten to ride? Such a tiny amount relative to the other movements because out of the hundreds and hundreds of horses I've ridden, only a handful of them can do it. I don't know how I got to be so lucky, but I'm living it up every minute while I have the chance!!

In the stables, we have a horsey soap opera. RV has become smitten with Wy who she lives next to with only bars separating them. She's always had a thing for him, but now she's shameless—makes doe eyes at him as she plants her behind right up against the bars toward his face, and when she sees him from a distance, she makes a sexy Janis Joplin-y nicker. Her hussy theatrics are endless. Wyoming isn't quite certain how to react to her but he's not going to ignore the attentions of a lady either so the interactions between them are quite amusing. Poor Idy only gets to be the voyeur across the hall and Mythy's so innocent, he has no idea why everyone else is acting so crazy.

· 48 ·

The Global Dressage Forum, which examines the world's top riders' and trainers' techniques, is held two hours away from Klaus's barn and although I can't go for the whole day, I make a point to go to the section on creating freestyles because how many I need to make this year is daunting and I hope to get some ideas.

Imke Bartels is the speaker. She had the music specifically *composed* for her and the pianist who composed it plays the music while they explain how each section came about. I'm dumbfounded by the genius of the musician, but this sort of thing is way out of my budget. Although it's interesting, it certainly doesn't give me ideas but only serves to daunt me further by learning what other people are doing.

When the forum ends, I need to unwind. Amsterdam is only an hour away, so I call Jose and she says, Let's go out, girl! As I enter the city, I find myself in a maze of canals—I can't believe it doesn't sink or at least flood. Never before have I experienced a city that has the fragrance of nature: the water and the abundance of flower markets—for which the city is famous—bring fresh air into the traffic and congestion of a big city.

We wander the Red Light District and peruse the girls in the windows. Go in a sex shop and pretend to select dildos, attempt to see a peep show but don't have the guts. Instead, Jose tells me I must experience a coffeeshop which I learn is a dope-selling bar. We sample several varieties as I hack up a lung, then we get hungry. She has a box of Stroopwafels—

waffle-like cookies sandwiching caramel—in her car. We eat a whole box and I fall in love.

I return to the barn refreshed. As it always does, my non-horse life improves my horse-life, eliminates the self-imposed pressure I allow to creep up on me. I'll do the best I can on my freestyles with the inferior brain and funds I have.

• • •

The Stuttgart CDI, November 14-17, is Myth's introduction to the international judges. He does the Grand Prix for the Special and Idy does the one for the Freestyle. Only Idy goes on the first day and although there's no place to hack in an indoor show and leaving the soap opera at home eliminates his spring chicken attitude, he gives his all and his passage has more amplitude than it did in warm-up. I'm determined to not have a mistake in the ones because although I've had no mistakes in them at home in who knows how long, it's become a usual event in the show ring. So I override the first change, there's a weird bobble and then fifteen beautiful ones. The only mistake is the bloody ones. Again.

We're also nailed for the open mouth and end up eighth with a 66+%.

That evening, I write to my Courtney's Quest contributors to tell them about the test then go on to write about the highlight of my day:

Isabell and her sponsors sat at lunch with me and Jason. They were, of course, smitten with Viva. I showed Isabell her trick: "Sit", and the first time I asked her to sit, Viva almost sat, so I told her she was good and gave her a treat. Isabell wasn't impressed but I explained to her that when training an animal, sometimes you have to reward even if it isn't perfect and then the animal may try harder the next time. Then I asked Viva to sit again, and this time she actually got her butt on the floor. I think that then Isabell was very impressed, although Jason insists that her expression wasn't one of awe at my training abilities, but one of incredulity at my stupidity. Still, I'm expecting her people to get in touch with my people regarding some lessons for her.

While writing it I occasionally chuckle, so Jason reads over my shoulder. He says, Honey, I find that hilarious because I know you but some of those people have never met you and sarcasm doesn't always transmit over the written word.

They do know me, though. I write them all the time, I reply.

He reads again and says, Well, I guess they know you don't have people. I wouldn't send it, but whatever you think.

I press send.

Later, as Jason spoons me and I spoon Viva, I'm woken up by party noises that have suddenly emerged on the street. When I look out our third floor window, I see it's a bunch of riders, some still in their breeches. Jason, who's still lying in bed, says, Who *is* that?

175

I guess Europeans haven't heard that dressage riders are boring; it's the riders! I respond through giggles.

Although I don't go down, I get to enjoy the party—much to Jason's chagrin—until the wee hours. They sing German drinking songs and break glasses, have all sorts of fraternity party type fun. Although sleep would be nice, their appreciation of non-horse fun invigorates me.

◆ ◆ ◆

Myth is the first to go the following day. Although at most shows the Grand Prix for the Freestyle attracts the more competitive field, here the Special does.

About five minutes into my warm-up, he becomes extremely light in the bridle which causes problems because it's so uncharacteristic. When I ask him to passage forward, he breaks to canter. When I half-pass, he goes extremely sideways and barely forward. Klaus watches as I struggle to figure out how to ride this new horse underneath me and finally shouts, Give hand more! More!

I do, and immediately he passages more forward instead of cantering. I feel like slapping myself in the forehead the way I imagine Myth would if I could verbally explain to him what pulling on the reins means. It's so simple.

He stays just as sensitive in the test and although I do give hand and avoid mistakes, I keep expecting him to grab the bit and take over. But he doesn't. In the end, I realize I could have trusted him more and gone for more expression, but he still gets a 69+% and ninth place. I'm thrilled to be at a competition where you need over 70% to be in the ribbons. The five above me are all right around 70% and Isabell wins with a 75%. What pleases me the most is the confidence and trust Myth displayed.

Then Idy does the Freestyle. In the warm-up and around the outside of the show ring, he feels great—soft and energetic. I feel the perma-grin from the World Cup settle on my face when I see the stands are packed to watch this glorious stallion I adore so much. But as soon as the music starts, his nose goes to his chest. It's even worse than at Devon; it's as if we're preparing to somersault.

I don't feel embarrassed. I don't feel upset. I feel hurt. He's one of the very few horses I think is intelligent enough to know what he's doing and the fact that he chose to do this feels like a slap in the face. He only does this in the freestyle and it occurs to me that maybe he's grown tired of the music or has decided he doesn't like it. If I had to do some stupid dance to P Diddy or New Kids on the Block—which I can't stand—I wouldn't be overly eager either. But I have no money to change it so we just have to deal.

◆ ◆ ◆

Jason and I join Klaus, his wife Judith, one of his students from England—Laura Bechtolsheimer—and her parents for dinner that night. Laura's upbringing was the opposite of mine: her parents are wealthy and have always been immensely supportive of her riding, have given her not only a string of fantastic horses but her own farm. My initial feelings of jealousy are immediately vanquished by her attitude. She fully acknowledges how incredibly fortunate her situation is and seems to genuinely appreciate it, doesn't take it for granted in the least.

And despite the difference in our backgrounds, our personalities are strikingly similar. We share a sense of humor and spend the evening honing a fake plan to trash-talk the top riders so they perform badly: *Steffen, your fly's open—Isabell, his tongue's out.*

Honey, Jason interrupts with a chuckle, the Balkenhols have a good plan for your child bearing. Judith?

Well, you must plan around the competitions, of course. You want four, right? So every two years: after these Olympics, two years later after the WEGs, two years Olympics, WEGs.

She says it as if it's a no-brainer. I jokingly thank her for making our plan and say, But we want to just be married a while, maybe begin after the WEGs. Then I go back to creating devious plans with Laura.

As we leave the restaurant, I'm quite certain I've made a life-long friend. We may not see each other for ten years but it won't matter. Just like tonight, it'll be easy.

◆　◆　◆

The next day, Myth does his Special. Although he isn't as mysteriously light in the bridle as he was for the Grand Prix, he's still light for my normal Mythy. As I trot around the outside of the arena, one of the judges gives me a big grin which I take as an encouraging sign and grin back. The entrance, halt, trot off are beautiful and I think, *Ah, this is what it's all about.* Then we turn left to come to our first extension and low and behold, there's a new sponsorship banner hanging on the inside of the arena fence. This is shocking for poor Mythy as he's seen the arena for the past four days with no signs inside the ring. Now banners hang in several places so little spooks and losses of balance pervade the test and we come in last place with a 65%. Coming in last is humbling but I'm very happy with Mythy. He was often scared but the movements that weren't by the signs were excellent. He gets a few 8's, one 9 and several 2's.

When I tell Rich about it, he points out that it's not a situation I'm likely to have to deal with often as normally shows go to a great deal of effort to keep the ring identical every day. Don't worry about it, the important thing is you were happy with Myth, he tells me.

◆　◆　◆

Rich calls again two days later and says he has to talk to me about something. Look, he begins with a voice full of gravity. Sweat formulates in my arm pits and I begin to pace as far as the cord will allow. Here it comes. He says Myth is doing very well and although he bought him as a horse for himself, he realizes that he's a great horse for my future and, more importantly, the horse has a great future. He proposes that I find someone to buy him for me for the price he bought him.

For a good Grand Prix horse in a pre-Olympic year he could easily ask over a million dollars and his willingness to part with Myth for such a reduced rate is incredibly generous and supportive of me, but finding someone to buy him for me is frightening. And if I don't find someone, he feels it's only fair to the horse to sell him anyway.

I was always prepared for Rich to take him over, but then I'd still ride him. I didn't prepare myself to sell him, to say goodbye.

Jason somehow understands my garbled, gasping lamentation over the phone and suggests Francine.

She likes riding her horses and Myth isn't her type, I sob.

What about a syndicate?

Now I stop. Wipe my eyes. That might be possible. Several people buy equal portions and then we have a "Myth account" into which they each put an annual amount.

We come up with a list of four people and I immediately begin to compose emails to them. I saw Alex Rukeyser, Paiute and Jamboree's owner, at Devon last year and although she's been out of horses for years, that made me think her interest was rekindled. I send her an email saying that I may be completely wrong but telling her my suspicion and asking if she'd like to be a part of Myth. She responds immediately saying that I'd guessed right and she'd love to be part of my dream. I don't hear from any others but go to bed hopeful.

◆　◆　◆

Two nights later though, I still haven't heard from any of them. As I sit in front of the computer trying to will an email into appearing by staring at the screen, the phone rings. I leap up thinking maybe they've decided to call instead. Maybe Rich changed his mind. Maybe Ed McMahon is calling to say I won a million dollars. It's Francine. She says she wants me to have the chance to be competitive with RendezVous at the same time as another Grand Prix horse but she misses riding her when I'm away so often. It's only worth the sacrifice she makes if RendezVous can be internationally competitive.

I've always believed in RV, but two things make me apprehensive: the ear thing and I think it will take a year for her to grow strong enough to do well because she's not a compact bundle of muscle like Myth. She says, Let's see how she shows and take it from there.

Between the sad thought of having RV go home and the terrifying thought of losing Myth, plus anticipating that this will be Idy's last year, I feel extremely vulnerable. I've been incredibly lucky to have such great horses these past few years and perhaps this is the rainy day I stored up all those wonderful moments for.

I'm more thankful than ever to Harmony Sporthorses for making Wy my own.

◆ ◆ ◆

Klaus says that Appelhausen will be a good national show for RV and it's close enough that we can trailer in and not get stalls. The weather is even worse than all the other days in Germany—freezing rain and wind that will blow an open door off your car. Klaus's daughter Belli shows another horse three hours before RV's time, so RV sways around in the frigid trailer while she waits which exacerbates her natural tightness. But she loves showing and in the test goes the same as she has at home with no ear thing. To my surprise, she gets a 66.4% and Klaus says, See, I told you it looks better than you think.

As soon as I get off, Jason calls and tells me that Harmony Sporthorses is interested in buying Myth and to call Leslie when I get home. Between these two things (and the cold), my hands are shaking so much I drop my phone. If RendezVous can get upper 60's even now when she's not feeling her best and her piaffe and passage aren't confirmed, I feel confident that she can be internationally competitive.

As soon as I get home, I race to my apartment and call Leslie. I sit down, stand up, walk around, sit back down. She asks his results, how long I've had him, his vet history.

I say, I have to tell you in case you want a horse to go to the 2008 Olympics, he's green at Grand Prix so I don't think he'll be ready for the Olympics. He'll peak for the 2010 World Equestrian Games.

She just says, We want no part of a syndicate but we'll buy him outright.

I repeat thank you like a broken record. Now he's a horse who's truly for me. I'm about to run to the barn to tell Mythy the news but then I realize I need to disappoint Alex and my ecstasy becomes slightly pained. I write her an email and she responds immediately again. Says she's so disappointed, is there another way she can be part of my dreams? I respond that a good young horse would help. She replies that she'd love to buy one.

◆ **49** ◆

My last competition in Germany is the Frankfurt CDI, December 15-16. They only have room for one competitor though, so I have to choose a horse. Klaus says Myth must go because the international judges know Idy from Marlies as well as me but they've only seen Myth once. It's a risky choice because Frankfurt offers no Special so Myth has to do a Freestyle, which he doesn't have. Idy's choreography is much too difficult for him but I figure I know the music so well I can wing it, so my first competition aboard Harmony's Mythilus is Frankfurt.

Although I feel fairly confident in adjusting the freestyle for him, the ring itself is intimidating: little horse-eating Santa statues and bushes pruned into rearing horses surround it, and the banners which so terrified him at Stuttgart hang on the inside of the arena. Many top riders on extremely experienced horses have a great deal of trouble in the ring including the infallible Warum Nicht of Isabell Werth who only scored 69% because of so much spooking. When we go in, Mythy's eyes bulge and he says, *Are you sure?* I say, *Yes, Mythy, I'm sure*, and he says, *Let's go for it!*

As we go around the outside of the arena for our Grand Prix, I think, *I'm gonna show you judges some neck—no comments on short neck.* So I ride differently. In my attempt to let the neck long I allow the balance to go on his forehand, and not only do my extensions, passages and half-passes go from 8's to 7's, I have several mistakes. It gets a 66.958% for seventh place. Myth was perfect. I could have shown him off but I messed up.

I can't forgive myself for riding badly but I take comfort in the fact that nothing terrible happened that would clue Myth in to the fact that it wasn't a fabulous test. For him, it was a good confidence-building experience and for me, a good learning experience.

The top six are required for the awards ceremony and since I'm seventh, I sit with Gil, the USEF High Performance Director, to watch the final rides with my thoughts on my impending banana and Nutella crepe (heavy on the Nutella). Gil speaks German and after an announcement, he turns to me and says in an eerily calm demeanor, Run. Get ready quickly.

Turns out the top eight are required for awards.

We race back to the stable, wake Myth from a luxurious nap in his shavings and fresh manure and begin throwing equipment around in an effort to get it on him. Klaus puts on the dirty bridle, Gil attempts to find some hair beneath the shavings that should be his tail, and I show my naked buttcheeks to all the passers-by as I get from my jeans into breeches and filthy boots. All the while I'm saying we're never going to make it, but I'll be eliminated if I don't.

Klaus runs poor Mythy to the indoor and Jason shows his rugby skills by throwing our little dog at high velocity with impeccable trajectory into a stall while I strangle myself with my stock tie and try to get my buttons in the right holes. We get there right as they're awarding the winner. The doors are closed and a crowd blocks the way. My hair, which is once again a length which can only be contained by pig tails, is standing hairy carry and when I look down at Myth's braids, only one is properly encased in its rubber band.

I'm less than pleased at the prospect of parting the crowd to interrupt a nice awards ceremony, but Klaus says, Smile, and we clamor through the small children who are trying to get a glimpse of the beautiful winner. We barge in just in time to gallop off at the back of the pack in the dark—the done thing in Europe is to do the awards in the dark under a spotlight.

♦ ♦ ♦

Despite his less than confidence-building final experience in the show ring, Myth feels just as sure of himself for the Freestyle as he did for the Grand Prix. And I *ride* instead of being a passenger. We make several mistakes as my winging it is less than stellar and two of the judges penalize the music because it isn't suited to the horse, but Myth bravely accepts the bizarre maneuvers he's unaccustomed to and gets a 71.4% for another seventh.

When I come home, I'm sad to only have a few days left with Klaus but I'm excited to return to Florida. As often happens, I wish there were two Courtneys.

Courtney's Quest Journal
I've been truly thrilled with my time here... Klaus's training, temperament, and family feeling have been wonderful, and I think the shows were exactly what we had hoped for. All the horses improved, and for sure, so did I.

♦ 50 ♦

Eighty degrees and sunny is a welcomed change after two months of freezing rain in Germany. I arrive in Florida a few days before Christmas and Betsy, Jen, Dave, Jason and I have a luau, wear leis and celebrate the holiday basking by the pool and drinking pina coladas. I've always loved a white Christmas but nothing could be better.

I need to earn as much money as possible to make up for so many months of being away and incomeless this year, so whereas I normally have twelve horses in training, I take sixteen and teach extra lessons when I can. There's not much time for anything other than our weekly girls' night watching American Idol and the occasional evening at Boonies, but just being here is social. I live with one best friend and am walking distance to the other.

♦ ♦ ♦

Our first big Florida CDI is an Olympic and World Cup Qualifier. We're scheduled to leave for the show on Thursday and on Tuesday night, I wake from a dream that a huge conch shell is being shoved down my throat. I weep in pain as I realize I really do feel like a conch shell is being forced down my throat. In the morning, I get up and ride a few horses and then collapse back in bed certain that I'll be fine by American Idol at eight. But when my alarm goes off at seven thirty, the conch shell has been joined by a heavy metal band playing inside my head.

I delay moving the horses to the show grounds until as late as possible on Thursday, but when it's time to sit up, putting on my breeches seems an impossible task. Luckily Jason can guide me to my proper horse and when I'm on, I feel almost human. As always, riding reduces any ailments—or at least eliminates acknowledging them. Between each horse, I regret not making a will but when I get on, I think I may make it through the day. I buy a new stock tie because mine won't fit around my swollen throat, but I'm determined to show because it's a qualifier.

Other than some to-be-expected miscommunications and bobbly moments in the passage and piaffe, RV makes no mistakes in either her first CDI Grand Prix or Special. She comes in ninth and sixth with two 65+%s. The judges' comments praise her potential and say she just needs to get stronger and more confirmed which bolsters my confidence in her future.

Myth gets a 71+% in the Grand Prix and Idy's right on his heels with a 70+% for second and third places. For Myth's Special, the wind makes the surrounding tents into flapping monsters which instigate a couple of panicked spooks. These spooks are accompanied by outstanding quality, however, and he wins with a 69+%.

Idy decides to carry himself for the Freestyle this time and keeps his face on the vertical. He gets a 76% and wins. In the awards ceremony, my body realizes the show's over and the fog which usually steps aside when I'm on a horse, takes over. As is the custom, before our victory gallop the national anthem is played and I place one hand over my heart and stand patriotically with my fellow competitors. Suddenly the photographer loudly whispers, Pssst, Courtney! Courtney, you can take your hand off your heart now! Start the victory gallop! and I realize the anthem has ended.

◆ ◆ ◆

The sickness forces me to spend the next several days in bed but only a golf ball-sized goiter remains to accompany me and Betsy to Holland the following weekend to look at horses for Alex. I tried several while I was in Germany but none was exactly what I'm looking for.

The first horse we look at is a four-year-old stallion. The rider brings him into the arena, pulls down the stirrup and looks at me expectantly. Standard practice is to watch a horse being ridden before getting on, so I just look back at her. She asks if everything's ok and I tell her I'd like to see him go before getting on. She says the horse is young and can't do too much so she doesn't want to tire him out for me. She'll video so I can see when I get off. I jokingly say I want to make sure he's safe and insist that she get on.

As he trots around the arena, I think I've found my horse. He's dark bay and stunning. Elegant and powerful, like a fancier Idy. Then he picks up the canter and it's even better than the trot. It's as if his front legs are reaching for a spot ten feet in front of him.

Just when I'm about to ask to get on, he slams on the brakes and stands on his hind legs. The rider hugs his neck to stay on, he touches his front feet to the ground for a millisecond, rears again and starts walking on his hind legs. He's tipping, looks like he's going to flip over and she leaps off. A couple people immediately rush in to catch him and she looks at me, sheepishly shrugs and says, Young horses, you know, and asks if I want to get on.

We go to five more barns but the highlight of our trip is our night in Amsterdam with Jose.

◆ ◆ ◆

When we get home, the goiter is only the size of a large marble and after the show, a couple days in bed and then a weekend of traveling, I look forward to an evening on the couch with a glass of wine and the girls debating who our next American Idol's going to be like an upcoming vacation. Since I didn't ride my horses for three days, it's straight back to work and the anticipation of girls' night gets me through the day on Monday. I think it's going to get me through Tuesday as well but Betsy calls. She's not coming. I burst into tears. No Idol?

Court, you're stressed because you're doing too much. I tell her no, it's just that I love our girls' night and always look so forward to it.

She says, Don't you think you need a day? I tell her I'll have one next week and try to convince her to come to Idol.

Sorry, honey, I can't, she apologizes.

◆ ◆ ◆

The Palm Beach Derby is the first weekend in March and will determine if Idy and I make the 2008 World Cup which will be in 's-Hertogenbosch, Holland at the end of the month. Most of the other horses go too, but I scratch Myth because a couple weeks ago he seemed lethargic which is very out of character. I was worried about him so my vet gave him an immune booster which we later discovered has a chance of causing a positive drug test.

The first day Wyoming, who's seven, does the Developing Horse Prix St. Georges which has all the movements of the St. Georges but in a different pattern and is only for seven to nine-year-old horses. He wins with a 70%. The time spent not showing and just building strength was as valuable as I'd hoped. The attitude remains, but his movement is finally consistently good.

RV begins her warm-up feeling confident and powerful, but after twenty minutes she suddenly has an ear attack. By show-time, it's dissipated but not gone. We canter in, have five good strides and then she goes leaping through the air. Her test gets 8's and 1's throughout and we end up with a 61.7% and don't place. Once again, I'm forced to question her international future.

Lendon comes into the barn and finds me stroking RV's cheek, trying to telepathically figure out the issue. She begins to ask me something but when she sees the black cloud over my head, stops and puts her elbows on the stall door. Gazes at the two of us. Eventually she asks, Any idea what causes her to do that?

No. We thought it was Lyme. Then we thought it was sinuses. We tried injecting her neck to alleviate any arthritic pain. Had her ears checked. I'm out of ideas. What if this happened at the World Cup?

I don't know, Courtney. Maybe she's a horse for Francine. Or a mediocre Grand Prix horse. Maybe she just can't do what you ask without discomfort.

But she's so talented.

Talent doesn't mean she can do it. She walks in the stall and takes my shoulders, makes me look at her. It's fine if she can't be an international Grand Prix horse. Not everyone can be a Mythilus.

She waits for me to digest this thought. Finally I nod. OK? she asks.

OK.

She gives me one more shake of the shoulders to make me look her in the eye. Pauses, then asks what she came here to ask before treating my angst with a dose of realism and acceptance. What time can you look at a horse?

I don't bother to ask why, just tell her after Idy.

◆ ◆ ◆

As Idy struts majestically around the field that surrounds the show rings, I think, he *can* do the work comfortably, Myth *can*. If either of them were unable, it would be extremely difficult to find a job for them in which I'd be confident in their happiness, but RV would be perfectly happy with Francine as her rider. It makes no difference to her if she's international or not, and Francine would be happy to have her girl back. The realization that I'm the only one who cares greatly reduces my angst.

My peaceful frame of mind remains in the show ring as does the enthusiasm generated by Idy's hack. He makes no mistakes and is second with a 72%. As we leave the arena, however, curiosity takes over.

I sit down next to Lendon and she points out a little bay horse who looks like a PRE, Pura Raza Espanol, being ridden by Pati Pierucci. I ask her what I'm looking for: is he for sale? for a certain person? one of her young riders? She says, Just watch.

After a few minutes she asks what I think. I tell her he has an impressive trot, great shoulder action and good ability to collect. When he sits more, which I think he has a talent for, it will make his canter very good as well.

She doesn't say anything for a moment and we just watch. Then she asks if I want to take him in training. I look at her in surprise and say absolutely. I expect a big conversation, an explanation, some sort of plan, but she just smiles, gives me the owner's address, tells me to go there after the show and leaves.

◆ ◆ ◆

I pull into a driveway with a sign that says Hampton Green Farm. There are large pastures on either side populated by PREs which are recognizable by their conformations and long manes. The drive leads straight to the entrance of the barn and I park my car alongside others. As I get out, Lendon yells, Yoo, hoo, from a deck above the barn and waves me up.

She leads me into an apartment and a sophisticated looking blonde woman introduces herself as Kim Boyer. She's a breeder of PREs and the horse I watched, Grandioso, is her top breeding stallion. She says she's decided to change riders. Pati's been great for developing Hampton Green and they've had a great time doing it, but Grandioso needs a rider who can take him all the way. When she told Pati, Pati said if she couldn't ride Grandioso, she wouldn't ride the others.

I say, That's understandable. If you know the best will be taken away from you, why bother? I'd do the same thing.

She smiles, nods and says, I'd like to keep her involved, but I'm sure Grandioso needs a more advanced rider. And I think it's especially important that the judges already recognize you as a serious competitor because we're still facing some prejudice against the breed.

What I appreciate more than anything is that she hasn't said anything bad or complained even a tiny bit about Pati. If people focus on criticizing their previous trainer, I shy away under the assumption that they're judgmental and inherently negative.

She says, Riding a PRE takes a special finesse. When I saw you ride Mythilus I wasn't convinced. Then I saw you ride Idocus and because he's sensitive, I thought you might be able to ride a PRE. Then today I saw you ride that mare in the Grand Prix who looks like an overgrown polo pony. She's so sensitive and requires such finesse, then I knew.

We both laugh at the description and I ask about his breeding schedule as that's been such a problem with Idy. She says she has plenty of frozen semen and will only breed her own mares so she won't need to breed him for a long while. Competition is his priority.

I tell her I'd love to be his rider.

◆ ◆ ◆

The next day, Wy does the open Prix St. Georges and wins with another 70%. In RV's Special, I compromise on the collection of her frame to avoid the ear thing and of course the quality is severely diminished. We end up with a 64.440% and don't place again.

Francine and I agree that sending her with me and sacrificing being able to ride her herself isn't worth it. If she continues to be uncomfortable in high collection and it causes the ear thing however infrequently, she can't be international because we can never count on her. I'll continue to show her when I'm home and hope it becomes a non-issue, but she won't go all over the world with me unless it does.

When I get on Idy for the Freestyle, he's a different horse than he was before the Grand Prix. The enthusiasm is replaced by mild contentedness and instead of strutting through the field, he saunters. The test is clean but lackadaisical and gets a 72+% which is third place. Despite the less than stellar test, the score gets us into the World Cup.

◆ ◆ ◆

My celebration evening is slightly different than 2007: a glass of bad champagne with Betsy as we fly to Holland for another horse-hunting trip. I recently received a video of a three-year-old Dutch Warmblood gelding who shows an abundance of the hind leg activity along with freedom of the shoulders needed in top dressage. So much so that it's worth a trip to see him. His name is Arthuro. He's medium sized, bay, has perky ears and intelligent eyes. Has been ridden twelve to sixteen times. It's raining when we see him and the excitement caused by the storm attacking the indoor roof enhances his spectacular movement. He's exactly what I want.

Klaus's farm is close by so I go to show him the video. He raises his eyebrows and approves but says not to ask for that movement when he's young; it'll be there when he's more advanced. Then he asks about my other horses. Of course he knows that Idy made the World Cup, but I tell him the other horses will do the CDI in Florida the week before I leave. He says, No, Courtney. This is an Olympic year. You must stop and focus. You are working too hard and never stop. You are looking too skinny. We need you to only think about Olympics.

Betsy told me I was doing too much but I never thought of it in terms of affecting the Olympics. I took on a great deal this year to make up for the lost income, but what's the point of my being away and chasing the

Olympic dream if I'm not able to do my best? The time spent riding the horses doesn't suffer—as soon as I'm on, my focus is solely on that horse—but at the end of the day I don't have the energy to reflect on the training, health, freestyles, the horses' diets and my own fitness Also, after sixteen horses my body must become fatigued so without realizing it, I must ride a little sloppier—not think if my shoulders are back or if my right leg is too far forward. I decide it would be better to rely on a credit card at a pivotal time like this. As Betsy and I drive silently away, she takes my hand and is too kind to say I told you so.

When I get home, I heed Klaus's advice and focus only on the eight horses I brought. I enjoyed every extra horse and student I'd taken on so I didn't realize I was overdoing it, but I feel the difference like taking off a heavy backpack. Before I can think only of the Olympics, though, I need to think World Cup.

Because I'll be traveling so much, I decide to leave Arthuro—whose name we change to Atomic, aka Tomtom because that's the navigation system that guided me to him—with Klaus. Between him and Grandioso, excitement for my future adds frosting to the cake of my present. Francine and Rich actualized my goals initially and by doing so, gave me the experience that allowed sustaining them to become independent.

Idocus, Credit: Susan J. Stickle

Harmony's Mythilus, Credit: Susan J. Stickle

RendezVous, Credit: Terri Miller

Harmony's Wyoming, Credit: Susan J. Stickle

• 51 •

Idy and I go to Klaus's barn two weeks before the World Cup begins. Viva acts like she's come home and I settle back into my apartment. Of course the reason I came early was to let Idy settle, but the added bonus is getting to know Tomtom. I knew he was beautiful but he also oozes personality—is sweet, intelligent and curious. One day while I'm grazing him, I gaze in his eyes and wonder if someday, we'll be doing a World Cup together.

◆ ◆ ◆

On March 26th, Idy moves to the World Cup stabling in 's-Hertogenbosch. It lacks the charged atmosphere of Vegas but boasts the sophistication of European shows I'm growing accustomed to. Idy embraces the curiosity of his surroundings with enthusiasm. The stabling and rings are in an enormous building and to get to the warm-up, we walk by ringside restaurants, beer gardens, shops, even an escalator.

For the Grand Prix, he feels as energetic and expressive as he ever has and comes in seventh with a 70.125%. For the Freestyle, he doesn't feel quite as energetic but as he's come to do regularly, increases his expression as we go. As we come into our first double pirouette, he takes a funny step and turns quickly. I think only to fix the pirouette and when it's recovered, I think, *Shoot, did I do one or two?* I listen to my music, find it's still in pirouette, continue around and finish on time.

I leave the show ring feeling proud of our performance, of the improvement from last year, and am still smiling when I get down the mile long corridor to exit and see Jason. He's making a very unhappy face and I think, *Oh, it must be good! He's trying to look unhappy to surprise me!* He says, Honey, you did a triple pirouette. My hand goes over my mouth.

A double pirouette is the maximum allowed for the welfare of the horse. The cost of my mistake is that all five judges were required to give a zero on the pirouette and a maximum of five on both choreography and technical difficulty. I find humor in most things, but I find none in this.

Klaus comes up and lays a hand on Idy's crest. I look down and slump, ready for him to lay into me. I've never felt so horrible. I let down my horse, my nation, my many supporters. Klaus says, Don't worry, it's nothing. Everybody makes these mistakes. I made so many mistakes, I cannot tell you. Tomorrow you just think it was a dream and you go on. It's nothing.

I look at him tear-faced, both grateful and disbelieving. I'm so sorry, I say.

It's nothing, he repeats.

When I get my score sheet back, I see my score was brought down from a potential 74% to a whopping 63% and dead last.

At the end of the night, I see the judges and they say, Why? Why? Why? It was so good! When they see my grief they tell me they've seen a great many top riders do things like that. I want to say, *In the World Cup?* but I decide to spare myself that pain and just take their kindness.

When I get back to the hotel, I dig into my jar of Nutella with a spoon and have a glass of jack and coke as I write to my Quest contributors.

Stupid, Stupid, Stupid. I don't know how I've gone thirty years under the illusion that I'm a reasonably intelligent human being. Today, that illusion was shattered with twenty thousand witnesses.

• 52 •

Courtney's Quest Journal
Between being naturally blonde and having two left feet, I'm accustomed to the fact that I make more mistakes than my share (although usually not with horses and usually not of this magnitude). It's these times when I'm especially grateful that I've been able to keep some balance in my life... that I have an amazing husband, friends, family... people

who think the World Cup rates equally in importance with the local bass fishing tournament.

Although I'm extremely embarrassed, Idy thinks he won the World Cup and returns to Sunnyfield full of himself and proud. My focus turns to the Olympics. Unfortunately Idocus has to delve straight into breeding, but Chris is nice enough to limit his availability so that at least we have a month before the Selection Trials in June to sort him out.

He and Myth need to be fit enough for the Hong Kong heat—racehorse fit according to the vet—so they each go out twice a day: work once and do hills once. Idy goes on a diet and loses a hundred-sixty pounds, and I adopt a conditioning regiment for myself as well. I don't have Steffen's personal trainer and still find real exercise abominable, so I walk Quivvy for an hour each evening, find that reading while riding makes thirty minutes on a stationary bike bearable and before I drink sangria and play poker on the boat, I go for a swim.

Helping with my fitness are also the hand-walks I take Grandioso, who I call GR, on. Although he's been working well enough, I feel he doesn't give me that extra effort. He does just enough and not more. All my horses hand-walk for twenty minutes a day in addition to turn-out and riding, and normally my grooms do it, but I decide I need to do GR's myself. I feel he knows me only as *that girl who rides me* and I need to develop a personal relationship with him.

The time isn't spent all lovey-dovey trying to get him to like me but developing respect—the basis of a strong relationship. I want him to pay attention to my body language. If I stop, I don't want to have to pull on the leadshank at all; he should see that I've stopped and stop. If he doesn't, I give the lead a quick jerk to say *hello, pay attention to me*. Same when I go forward: I carry a whip in my right hand and if he doesn't walk when I do, I reach behind my body and give him a little fwack.

In this way, I teach him to constantly be tuned into me and not be distracted as stallions can be. After a few days, he looks at me differently. He's assessing me—trying to figure me out. In a week, he's tuned in. And after ten days, I get the extra effort under saddle that I was missing.

• • •

Although I add a bit of fitness work into my days on the boat, they remain mainly a source of fun and relaxation, and one afternoon, Jen joins us with the intention to water-ski. As I finish my swim and near the boat, Viva races excitedly around the sundeck begging to come in. We finally got her a life-preserver with a handle on it because she always wants to get in the water and we aren't confident in her swimming abilities.

I tread water while Jason puts it on and gently sets her in. She automatically doggy-paddles, so he lets go of the handle and I swim a little away. She swims toward me, but then her head stays above the water and her body does a full three-sixty pulling her head with it. She swims a bit more and the same thing happens—she's like a broken rudder. I grab the handle, hand her to Jason and say maybe we should try without the preserver. I stay close and when he sets her back in the water naked, she panics and desperately tries to climb onto my head.

When we recover from our laughter and Viva's happily in my lap, I say I guess she's no Quivvy; she'd rather be a sun-bathing beauty.

Then we begin our water-skiing. I go first and, figuring it will help my fitness, I go for an extra long time. After Jen and Jason's turns, I go again. The next day, I'm so sore it hurts to shampoo my hair and muscles I didn't know I had in the front of my neck hurt.

◆ ◆ ◆

In addition to getting all of us fit, my immediate need is to create a freestyle for Myth. After sampling several possibilities, Marlene Whitaker from Custom Freestyles designs a whole piece based on Cat Steven's *Sad Lisa* because I told her a specific piano/violin part in it captivates me. I love it but I want to get judges' feedback, so I take him to the ESDCTA show which is in May a month before the Trials. I also take Idy and Wyoming.

Unfortunately the footing is so hard it bothers all of them. I think Idy remembers the silent treatment, which happened at this same show, because he doesn't complain at all and wins the one class we enter with a 71.8%. Wyoming on the other hand, acts like it's impossible to move. In the St. Georges, as I would with any other horse, I try to band aid his stubbornness and he says *ha, gotcha*! When I realize my mistake and try to blatantly fix it, he has a major temper tantrum. We get third with a 64%. I don't make the same mistake in the Developing Horse test and although I know I don't have the 70% horse he can be, he behaves better under protest and wins with a 67.8%.

Myth is also particularly sensitive to the footing, which makes him extra strong in the contact, but unlike Wy, he doesn't complain. In the warm-up for our freestyle, he's oblivious to the one-tempis—simply doesn't do them—so I get after him. Then in the test he's so sorry, so very very sorry, that often if I ask for a single change, he does ones. He's the sweetest horse on the planet and wins with a 70%.

The judges, Axel Steiner and Cara Whitham who are both Olympic level, give me the feedback I wanted. They say it needs more drama, more ups and downs. This makes sense because the goal was to make it beautiful and not dynamic in order to downplay Myth's strongness. Also, when I sit in my car with a good sound system and give myself totally to the music, it's an extremely emotional piece, but for the judges with the poor speaker systems and not knowing what to expect, the emotional experience is subdued. They say they were on the edge of their seats waiting for the build-up to come to a climax but it never did.

Marlene immediately goes to work making it more dramatic for the Trials.

◆ ◆ ◆

I come home to find a DVD of a horse named Zygosch sent by a Dutch dealer. He's four years old, 17.3 and jet black. He was only broke five months ago so he's very green, but I like him a great deal. He has one of the best canters I've ever seen.

Harmony Sporthorses owns his sire, Rousseau, so I call Leslie and ask if she'd consider buying him for me. She sends me to try him and I fall in love. He's a rare combination of super sensitive and level-headed. She buys him and we send him to join Tomtom at the Balkenhols.

I'm almost as excited about my youngsters as I am about my Grand Prix horses, but it's time now to think of the 2008 Olympics not the 2016 ones.

◆ 53 ◆

The Olympic Selection Trials are in San Juan Capistrano, California, over two consecutive weekends—the Grand Prix and Special are ridden the first weekend and the Grand Prix and Freestyle the second. I want to go two weeks early to let Idy adjust to the time difference, and I don't want to not ride GR and Wy for a month so Steffen, whose barn is only an hour and a half from the show, makes four stalls available for me again.

Despite his own need to prepare, Steffen takes time to work with my extra horses. He says that Wyoming's trot has progressed to international quality and his changes are exceptional. But then, as he always does, Wyoming throws a temper tantrum. As usual Steffen's unperturbed, but it upsets me a great deal. *Focus only on the Olympics.* How can I when Wy causes me so much angst, stresses me out? Remembering his love to jump, I ask the manager who's a jumping rider to jump him the next several days. He's not only pleased as peaches to do it, he's good at it.

With GR, we work on establishing one trot: maintaining a consistent rhythm and cadence. He wants to go from enormous loft to tiny pony trot and back. Steffen says to keep the small one and I have to work hard to do so.

When I was here before Vegas, doing what Steffen wanted was a struggle. Now I feel much more competent which offers a great sense of achievement because there's seldom a gauge on how much one's own riding has improved, especially at this level when any changes in the way you ride are so minute. In the past year and a half, I've become a little bit more coordinated, have a little bit better timing, am a little more instantly effective.

◆ ◆ ◆

Although riding four horses instead of twelve reduces some exertion from my fitness regime, many other activities make up for it. I hand-walk all my horses instead of just GR, Steffen has a pool in which I do laps and a tennis court which my groom, Allana, helps me utilize as she needs to get fit, too. She's just as fervent yet spazzy as I am and just as amused at the ridiculousness of our efforts. Although I'm like a T.rex with a racquet, it's good exercise if for no reason other than the giggling.

One evening we're having a particularly intense game and in her effort to return one of my special curve balls, she sprains her ankle. She's a trooper and continues to be an excellent groom but we agree that it's a good thing I want to hand-walk myself. Then I recruit Jason who actually plays tennis, and after several days I write to my Quest contributors:

I'm feeling really good, really fit. I've kicked Jason's behind in tennis twice now so I guess I'm pretty good, even though his behind is very little. I mean, he does give me three serves. And I start each game with thirty points already. Well, and my boundary lines are the outside ones, the ones for doubles. And if my ball's going long, it's part of the rules that he has to try to hit it on the full if he can. But other than that we're totally equal.

◆ ◆ ◆

Despite feeling that I'm riding better, I have awful rides on Myth for several days. He's completely crooked to the right, stronger in the contact than usual and can't do any of the canter work properly—sequences are rarely clean and I'm forced to do the pirouettes with a one-inch neck again.

I find Steffen working on his computer by the pool and tell him of my dilemma. He says, Let's try together tomorrow. Don't worry yet. We still have eight days. He sees my look of consternation and adds, This is the most frustrating sport, there's no doubt about it.

Even though I thoroughly know this, hearing it from him somehow eases my burden. It seems as if everything's easy for him and to know that he struggles sometimes like the rest of us mere mortals is soothing.

The next day his help does improve things but Myth's still not nearly as supple and powerful as he was before coming to California. Steffen tells me again not to worry. He says every person competing at the Trials will be praying for a particular movement to work or some mistake to not happen. I ask if my prayer can just be for canter work or if that's too broad. Then I ask him what his prayer is. He hesitates and says, With Lombardi it's that he stays honest in the piaffe. I say, And for Ravel? The only answer is a smile, which I return and tell him he better just get those shavings out of the tail.

195

• • •

Although Tim's godly hands aren't available to work on Myth, the local chiropractor does similar magic. For three days in a row, Myth's joints are eased back into alignment and each day, he becomes more supple and rideable. His improvement remains rapid afterwards and by the time Klaus comes, he's back to how he was before we came.

Klaus watches both horses go and says they both look very good. Idy looks more elegant with his reduced girth size—fitter and younger—and I'm now able to add some power to Myth's movement and retain control. Which horse would I want to take? I say that if Myth continues to improve at the rate he has been, he should go. But Idy's so solid, if he's going better at the time, we should take him.

Absolute, you take the best horse, Courtney, he says with a smile.

He also works with GR and when I walk into the ring, he makes his low expectations because of the breed clear. He doesn't say much at the beginning but as we go, he repeats with increasing enthusiasm, This is good. He is very good. Ja, super. And at the end of the ride, he says, This is a very interesting horse for the future.

• • •

The day we leave for the show, Idy goes for a wander in the woods and Myth does ten million half-halts in the ring. I've done everything I could to get each horse as prepared in their particular way as I know how. I have no regrets, no wishes that I'd done this or that, and we're all as fit we can be. Now I just have to see what I can do at the show.

• 54 •

Courtney's Quest Journal

Through all of these hectic, exciting, stressful times I often become suddenly and poignantly aware of how incredibly lucky I am. I must have the most amazing support group around me. My husband is truly astonishing… he gives up his weekends to schlep around with me, working in the barn, making DVD's, returning phone calls, organizing hotels… whatever helps. And my assistant Jennifer and supergroom Elias make it so I never have to worry about my horses' care at home; they're so dedicated and after so long with me basically know what I want before I say it. They NEVER cut corners, and I'm extremely particular about the details of care. My owners… the ones who stay behind hardly say a word of complaint that I have had to leave them so often, and the ones who send their horses with me pay those incredible bills without giving me the slightest angst (although I cringe to send them sometimes). Lendon who's always there to offer great advice and is so creative and willing to be helpful in logistics. Steffen who basically arranges my entire trips to California and even opens up Hotel Peters for me. And then all of you! I remember writing about how great of a team Debbie McDonald has behind her. But she ain't got nothin' on me! I feel like the cell phone commercial with "the network" of a million people following them around making sure they have connection everywhere! I've been extremely touched by the support sent to me from all over the country... both financial and emotional. Thank you all so much for accompanying me on this amazing journey. Let's hope it takes us far from home!

The afternoon of June 18th, Steffen and I move our horses to San Juan Capistrano. My assumption that this show will have a different vibe from any I've been to isn't contradicted. A grandstand surrounds the single show ring and only riders I've idolized since Lendon was just a picture in a magazine populate the barn. They don't act as if we're competing against one another but as if we'll compete to find the best Team to represent the U.S.

There's a hunter/jumper show held simultaneously, so the million small ponies competing in it will add enthusiasm to counter the reduction in Idy's energy due to the heat that's supposed to blanket the weekend. The walk to the warm-up is a dirt path next to a road with plenty of interesting scenery, so his curiosity and need for adventure will also be sated.

♦ ♦ ♦

This is the first time in a decade and a half that Olympic teams will consist of three members instead of four. Previously the fourth ride allowed the lowest score to be dropped from the Team total, but to reduce the time necessary, the IOC, or International Olympic Committee, has done away with drop scores.

The top twelve horses in the country will compete to earn one of these three spots and a reserve rider will also be taken. Each Grand Prix counts for 35%, the Special counts for 20% and the Freestyle for 10% of the total score.

My goal with each horse for the first Grand Prix is a solid, clean, perhaps unexceptional test. Idy's fairly steady. He may be slightly better or worse than usual but I basically know what to expect. With Myth, I don't. He's capable of getting a 73 or 74% when he's on my aids and I can go for it, but if I try to go for it when he's trying to take over, we'll make many mistakes and do poorly. It's not worth the risk. At the rate he's continuing to improve, I'll have a better chance at success if I take chances next weekend.

♦ ♦ ♦

The high on show day is ninety degrees. The heat has no effect on Myth but Idy finds it quite uncivilized to have to sweat like that, so I work him lightly in the morning and before we show, do twenty minutes of light warm-up, one piaffe and a lot of walk.

Entering the arena, it feels that conserving his energy helped. The first piaffe gets 8's and 9's and he even has a major spook at the beginning of the first half-pass. But then he begins to feel the heat. I don't push him, ride more to avoid mistakes than to impress the judges because the heat is like a heavy cloth weighing down all his limbs, inhibiting his movement, and if I push I might instigate blatant rebellion. We do manage to avoid mistakes, but as we leave the arena he jigs and struts, spooks again. My hand ceases its patting and regret courses through my veins as I realize that he had energy, he's *racehorse fit*. I rode like a pansy. His score is 69%. It could have been 72% but I was a wimp.

I used to have to compromise with him—if I said *you will* or *you must* or got after him in any way offensively, he'd say *you know what, I'm just not interested*. But now he does allow me to get after him when he deserves it. His willingness to take corrections has grown but my carefulness has remained.

After I take his bridle off, Steffen pokes his head in the stall and says, He's feeling the heat, isn't he?

He is, but, Steffen, I could have pushed him through it. I would never have accepted deflation from any other horse. It's a serious problem; I'm often too easy on him simply because I love him so much.

Sometimes you just have to love them the other twenty-three hours of the day, he replies.

Debbie McDonald, an Olympian I've always admired, stands beside Steffen and says, Don't be so hard on yourself. It was still good and it's only 35% of the final score.

As Allana takes Idy, he gets excited by a horse passing by, screams and dances around, tries to drag her out of the stall. I feel like a fool, like a man who finds his wallet is gone after being seduced.

Debbie follows me under the portable canopy Steffen brought, sits beside me and doesn't say anything. I tell her I'm so mad at myself, more for not doing my best after all the immense support that's been given to get me here than for how it affects my Olympic chances. I know it was by no means horrendous, but the least I can do for the people who've made it possible for me to come here is my very best. I didn't ride well.

Courtney, we've all had enormous help to get where we are. No one can do it by themselves. And none of us does everything perfectly, there's always something we wish we'd done. But everyone knows that. They support a human being.

She waits for me to look at her, takes my hands and says, Now you can show your best on Myth.

◆ ◆ ◆

Although the disappointment in myself remains, she's right; I can show my best on Mythy, and I don't let it alter my plan to go for a conservative and mistake-free test. We achieve just that and although there are many comments on the short neck, I'm sure if I'd tried to let it out more, we would have had many mistakes. He gets a 70%, which isn't much better than Idy but I feel I rode him the best I could so I'm happy.

The end results of the first day are: first Steffen on Ravel with 75.7%, second Debbie on Brentina with 72.6%, third Steffen on Lombardi with 70.6%, fourth Myth with 70.2%, fifth Idy with 69.0%, sixth Michael Barisone on Neruda with 67.3%, seventh Leslie Morse on Kingston with 65.4%.

◆ ◆ ◆

Idy's the very first horse to go in the Special the next day. I forego my love for him for the hour and when he complains about the heat in the warm-up, we have words. Then he puts in a solid clean test for 70.2%. It's a great credit to him that now I can get after him and he rises to the occasion. He's been doing Grand Prix for nearly eight years and still (or perhaps I should say again) gets inspired and does a great job.

Myth feels more on my seat than he did in the Grand Prix and I'm able to put my hands very forward on the short sides so at least the judges can see that he's in self-carriage. One section of the test is very similar to the pattern of the Grand Prix: down the centerline, pirouette right, pirouette left, trot at H and extend. Only in the Grand Prix, the extension is on the diagonal and in the Special it's down the long side. I gear up and prepare to go for it, to take a chance. And I do—straight across the diagonal. Off course, two point deduction from each of the five judges.

Somehow this blatant mistake is less disappointing than yesterday's with Idy. I had a brain-fart, made a human mistake, but I didn't choose to ride badly. It's embarrassing but Jason points out that I've done worse: the triple pirouette.

When the final results are in for the class, I'm grateful that my mistake didn't affect the placings. Steffen and Ravel win again with a 75.7%, Debbie is second with 74.1%, Myth is third with 73.1%, Idy's fourth with 70.2%, Steffen and Lombardi are fifth with 67.2%, Leslie is sixth with 66.9% and Sue Blinks and Michael both get 66.4% for seventh and eighth.

Courtney's Quest Journal
I really think I need to go and dye my hair brown for some artificial intelligence; this blonde thing just isn't working out. What in the #@!* (heck).

◆ ◆ ◆

The next day, both horses have a well-deserved day off and Jason and I lounge by the pool. For the four days before we show again, Idy mainly hacks. I do a bit of work and demand quality, but rest will improve his performance.

I have a tough choice with Myth. His muscles are tired so they need rest but he's a horse who must stay working or he gets extremely strong. The compromise I make is a dangerous one with a horse you're not sure is a hundred percent confirmed but it's the only option I have: I only work on throughness and basics—won't do any movements until the final day.

On Thursday at two in the morning, we're woken by a horrendous screeching. An announcement tells everyone there's a fire, to take the stairs and proceed to the parking lot, which we do more to escape the noise than because we believe there's truly a fire.

Jason, Debbie and I sit on the sidewalk and discuss how cruel it is for them to have a drill during the Olympic Trials. Then Jason points out that who cares about dressage anyway. Debbie replies that at least it wasn't Saturday morning.

We sit outside in our PJs for an hour, and as we make our way back to our rooms, we find out there was a real fire.

◆　◆　◆

Idy's the second horse to go in the Grand Prix and as soon as I get on, he's cranky—tight and snippety. I can't figure out why, but he mans up and does his job to put in a solid, clean test. He only gets a 69.9% and I'm surprised by the low score. All the judges had him at 70-72% except Uwe Mechlem, the German judge, gave him 66%. Mechlem is a good judge and Idy was a bit cranky in the contact, so perhaps he saw there was a little tilt in his head, which should be vertical, or some inconsistency so everything got marked down a point or two. The score is barely better than for the first Grand Prix but I'm happy with Idy as well as myself.

As I rehearse Mythy's test in my mind a final time before getting on, a deep calm settles over me. When we enter the warm-up ring, everything but the horse beneath me fades away. It feels as if the last week's work, the last month's work, the last decade's work, culminate. The good that I so wanted to be, worked over twenty years to become, is at my fingertips. My body and his are connected. It's not like a centaur after all. I don't think and he does, the synapses in our bodies connect. Right before I go into the competition arena, Lendon says, Are you going to go for it? I affirm with a monotone, Uh huh, and trot in.

He takes over a little bit outside the arena and I do major haunches-in right, both because I want to get the right half-pass sharp as it's been difficult, and to reiterate the half-halt. Then we enter. He's perfectly steady and waiting for me every step. I'm able to let his neck out completely; I barely need the reins at all.

As I do the final salute, tears sting my eyes. I cannot thank my horse enough for his amazing heart and spirit, and as we leave the arena, I have the courage to give a photographer two thumbs up. I've never before been so proud. When tests are good, I'm normally happy with the horse but I don't think of how I did unless it's bad. Now pride in myself—the hard work, self-discipline, patience, constant striving—to accomplish what we just did joins the gratitude to my horse. Then my score is announced: 75.208. Steffen went right before me and got a 75.25. He comes up while my tears are still threatening and says, You had the winning ride. That was amazing. Every step, amazing.

Harmony's Mythilus, Credit: Mary Phelps

The results of the class are: first Steffen and Ravel with 75.25%, second Myth with 75.208%, third Debbie with 73.0%, fourth Steffen and Lombardi with 70.0%, fifth Leslie with 70.3%, sixth Sue Blinks and Mark with 70.4%, seventh Idy with 69.9%.

As we're waiting for the awards ceremony, Guenter Seidel comes up and places a hand on my knee. Says, That was the most beautiful Grand Prix I've ever seen.

He's been in three Olympics, has seen the best in the world, and I don't know him well so there's no reason for him to come up to me at all. I don't know what to say. This should feel like a dream but nothing could feel more real. The sweaty horse beneath me who has no idea what he just gave me. The bustle of excited people. Reaching the pinnacle that countless people have allowed me to achieve like an oxygen tank on a climb up Everest.

Klaus says, That was the ride of your life.

I reply, So far.

He loves this because he takes it as attitude, but I'm utterly serious. I know there's even more in this incredible animal. When I can convince him to simply not try too hard, his suppleness and power will shine. Right now there's a cloak of control subduing that power. I strive to remove that cloak.

Harmony's Mythilus, Credit: Sara Lieser

• • •

That evening, there's a benefit fundraiser for sending the Team to Hong Kong. It's the Beijing Olympics, but the equestrian events will be held in Hong Kong because of the space required. The fundraiser is a sophisticated party with a Chinese theme.

The silent auction boasts many valuable items including several luxurious trips and a custom made bronze statue. Robert Dover and Guenter Seidel auction off seeing their tattoos of the Olympic rings which requires removing their shirts and three women pay $40,000 each to see them do so.

As Jason and I mingle with the crowd, Uwe Mechlem comes up and tells me what a great ride I had on Mythilus. I thank him and say, But you didn't like Idocus? He replies, Well, that was the beginning of the class. At the beginning, I was a little low, but then later on I got higher.

I nearly choke on my wine to prevent my laughter forcing me to spit it out. His surprising honesty combined with his accent make the situation hilarious. Although I'm not certain I'd see the humor if it weren't for Myth.

Before we leave, Robert comes up to give his congratulations. Robert is flamboyantly gay and Jason says, I like your back, to which Robert gives him a sultry stare, smiles and replies, How much?

◆ ◆ ◆

That night, anxiety about Myth's Freestyle the next day disrupts my sleep. I've never ridden to the changed music because the Grand Prix test absorbed all my focus as it counts for 70% of the final result. Although Myth has essentially made the team unless he doesn't do the freestyle at all, I dream of William Hung and other American Idol contestants who believe they're great but are awful. I worry that I'll be a joke like them.

I wake in the morning, though, a little groggy but feeling calm. It's almost as if I've stepped outside myself, as if a machine studies my DVD and implants the information into me.

Idy's the first of my two horses to go, and riding to his music is like walking in well-worn slippers. He gets a 75.4% and takes the early lead. When Jason finds me in the tackroom to hand me a bottle of water because I'm horrible about staying hydrated, he sees I already have a bottle in my hand. He looks at me waiting for a smartass comment but I just close my eyes and start my DVD again.

Debbie goes just before me and rides to Aretha Franklin's *Respect*. The crowd goes wild and she gets a 78.75%. I enter the arena of pumped-up fans with my understated, beautiful, emotional freestyle that I've never ridden, and although the stark contrast in mood and the success of her energizing the crowd should shake me, the machine persists and I'm unaffected. As we near the end, I realize yet again what a genius Marlene is. We stay on the music every stride and successfully express some of the emotions sought.

The machine disappears when my music stops and I give the crowd many heart-felt waves. The numerous responses from my Questers have made me realize how much people care and want to be part of things. I wave to them not as distant fans but as close friends. They make living this dream possible, therefore they *are* a great part of it and are celebrating our joined success. His score is 78.05%. King Peters goes next and cements his role as Team leader with a 79.5.

Then we're whisked away to a press conference in which Viva and Debbie's small dog star. All the horses are checked once more for soundness and the horses and humans are drug-tested. Ravel, Brentina, and Mythilus are the Team. Idy's fourth and Lombardi's fifth so they'll go to quarantine as well, but the USEF needs to take a reserve *rider* in case something happens to me, Steffen, Debbie or Brentina, so Michael and Neruda will go, too.

Steffen Peters, me, Debbie McDonald, Viva and Halle Berry

• 55 •

Courtney's Quest Journal
For the question of how it feels... right now I feel utterly exhausted, a very contented and happy exhausted. But this morning, when I walked into the barn and Steffen and Debbie (who I've recently come into the habit of fondly calling Deben and Steffie) said, "Good morning, Teammate!" to me with a big hug, it was a pretty elated feeling.

As soon as the official Team is chosen, the hectic process of preparing us for the Games begins. The Team vet, Rick Mitchell, goes through each of our horses' supplements to make sure nothing illegal will be unknowingly given. He even checks to make sure the ointment Allana's using on her sprained ankle is safe. The USEF spends three hours teaching us how to deal with the press and one of the things they instruct us to do is to take control of an interview by requesting to call the reporter back at a certain time. I utilize this strategy a great deal because I get wake-up calls from reporters every morning at six the following week. Apparently the East coast reporters haven't figured out the time difference.

Several non-horsey reporters call as well as horsey ones. One lady says, So I watched you on YouTube and it doesn't really look that difficult, but it must be difficult. I mean, how difficult is it really... what you do? Another one says, So you rode two horses in the Selection Trials. How do you decipher between the two? I can't resist replying, Well, how do you decipher between your two brothers?

After my morning wake-up call, utter chaos begins and our days are spent figuring out logistics, packing, doing paperwork, giving necessary vaccines and doing interviews. Quarantine will be in Aachen, so essentially we're planning for two trips. It's imperative that our horses remain on their same diets and the feeds in Germany and Hong Kong are different both from the U.S. and from each other. Luckily my feed sponsor, Purina, had faith in me and sent feed to both places weeks ago.

After four days, when I reach for my conditioner in the shower I notice it's hand lotion. For three days I conditioned my hair with lotion and never noticed. Although I'm used to working far harder than I did over the trials, the intensity of emotions and constant focus drained me, left my brain unable to process information.

◆ ◆ ◆

Wyoming flies home with Elias and will go to Scott Hassler while I'm gone. Kim decides to send GR to quarantine with me in order to limit the amount of training time lost, so on July 10th, he joins Mythy, Idy, Viva and me on a flight to Aachen. We fly on a KLM 747 Combi which carries the passengers in front and the horses in back with the cargo.

Courtney's Quest Journal
Right now, we're crossing over the whole United States, then over the Atlantic Ocean, then we land in the middle of Europe and we get to train as a team, amongst other teams. And then in a couple weeks we go on to Hong Kong... I've never been so far east! And then we get to compete for the real gold, silver and bronze medals... us against them, but even more, us AND them. How amazing. And then we get to come home! I love my home and so look forward to being there and getting back to all my wonderful horses,

friends, clients, and dogs there... and the greatest feeling right now is that after I get to live this amazing dream, I get to go back to all of them.

Idy and Viva

◆ ◆ ◆

The U.S. Team arrives in Aachen days before any other countries' and it's strange to be on the enormous showgrounds, normally so vibrant, all alone. When quarantine begins, a hundred horses have to get their paper work checked, get a nose swab for flu, blood drawn, wormed, sprayed and have their equipment weighed before they're allowed into the barn. If one horse is found to be sick, any horse who's been exposed to it can't enter quarantine either so all the horses need to be separated.

The organization for accomplishing these requirements is genius. The horse enters a barn which is comprised of three rooms. In the first room, blood is drawn. Then they go into the second and their nose is swabbed. In the third room, they're wormed and sprayed. It's like a full detail car wash.

As I approach with Idy, he gets very excited and I can tell what he's thinking: the shed into which horses are walking doesn't look like a barn with stalls in it and it certainly isn't a riding arena since the horses are being led instead of ridden. Therefore it must be a breeding shed. Anticipating his unexpected good fortune, he tosses his head, lunges forward and dances around. Each room we enter, he looks around madly for the phantom/girlfriend. But all he gets is a needle in the neck, a cotton bud up the nose, and force fed some paste. Idy exits disappointed, but after spending two days spinning in his stall completely wild—he still hates Aachen and refuses to settle—he goes into the quarantine barn, lies down and has a good long nap.

Courtney's Quest Journal

It's very exciting seeing everyone come in today... all the teams in their appropriate apparel. Isabell, Nadine, Andreas and everyone kept asking where is Viva, but unfortunately lockdown sanitation actually applies to tiny little adorable dogs too, not just big slobbery stinky ones, so Viva has to man the fort in the hotel room. I don't think the wrist band around the neck we did at the Trials will quite do the trick here...

♦ ♦ ♦

I go to a Gala put on by the KWPN for the Dutch Team where each team member answers a couple of questions. When Anky van Grunsven is asked if she has concerns about the heat of Hong Kong, the travel or the politics, she answers no but she *is* worried about the nose swabs, that the vets would be sticking swabs into her horses' nostrils and she's worried there'd be something on them that would cause her horse to have a positive drug test.

Our horses from the U.S. have now been nose swabbed four times and I'd never think of that. The swabs are completely sealed, sterilized cotton, but perhaps being number-one in the world and the one to beat is paranoia-inducing. I can't quite imagine someone saying, *We've got to find a way to take down that Courtney Dye. What can we do to take her out?*

♦ ♦ ♦

Some of the riders with only one horse are bored out of their minds because, like all riders, they're used to being busy, so I'm glad I have three to keep me occupied. With three horses to ride, hand walk and check on as well as going to the gym, keeping up on the articles I have to write for magazines and planning everything for the horses going home, the horses *at* home, and the one going to Hong Kong, I never get everything I want to done in a day. It's just like being at home so it's good for my focus and relaxation.

Although GR is the only horse at Aachen who's not qualified for the Olympics, he gets a great deal of attention. Everyone is curious about his role because he looks so different—he's a hand and a half smaller than most of the horses and his mane falls below his shoulders. Many of the competitors ask, What *is* that? But Klaus is unfazed and works with him nearly as much as our Olympic horses. He's my little rockstar, with rockstar hair and a rock-star attitude.

Idy also develops an attitude that benefits his work. He's inspired because our barn is mostly mares, has an extra spring in his step and our entire sessions are spent showing off for the girls.

One night beginning at eleven, we're allowed to school under flood lights to practice for Hong Kong where the classes will be held after dark. Idy's completely unperturbed as I expected, but I'm concerned about Myth. Unlike Idy who thrives on adventure and the unpredictable outside world, if Mythy could just curl up with me in a little nest safe from all the vulgarities of the outside world, he'd be completely content.

But much to my relief, he's exactly the same as he is during the day. As long as he has a security blanket—in this case, me—he's confident. As we walk out of the arena, he stops and turns his head to investigate an approaching shadow. I look at his face—so open, so honest, so loving— and think, *You're taking me to the Olympics*. Often, people talk about their Olympic horse as if the riders take the horse. No, he's taking me.

Courtney's Quest Journal

I did go through a little bit of a frustrating time when we got here, not because of anything with any of the horses, but because my right leg went on strike for a while. It just wouldn't do its job no matter how I tried to convince it. I think we've come to terms now, but I really wasn't in a position to compromise so it was very irritating that it chose this exact time to become lazy. But things like that happen from time to time with every rider and we have to be constantly aware of them in order to ride as clearly and justly as we can. It's the frustration of the sport, so similar to golf in that the smallest technical change can have a huge impact, and I'm sorry to find out that going to the Olympics doesn't magically change that! Darn!

◆   ◆   ◆

Aachen is close to Klaus's barn so I take advantage of the proximity and visit my babies one morning. Seeing them makes me fall in love all over again. Tomtom has improved a great deal from when I last saw him. His rider says he's very smart and learns quickly. Zygosch was uphill at 17.3 when we bought him and I think only his front end has grown an inch and a half. He's so uphill, he looks like a giraffe.

I have lunch with the Balkenhols and then return to ride my boys. When I walk in the barn, I find Allana holding Mythy and a woman I don't recognize looking at his shoulder. Allana tells me that when he got up from a nap, he hit his shoulder on the permanent cement manger that protrudes from one corner of the stall and there's a cut and it's swollen so, since Rick went back to the U.S. for a couple days, the Canadian vet is checking it.

She says to rub Surpass on it, don't put a saddle on him for a couple days and it'll be fine. We call Rick as we don't have Surpass and he says good, he doesn't feel comfortable with us using it anyway. He explains that the withdrawal time isn't precise so there's variability as to when it's not detectable in drug tests. The USEF says seven days (and we have five weeks) but whereas the USEF allows a threshold, CDI's don't. No matter how little is found in the horse's system, the horse will be disqualified. Therefore he doesn't want to risk a trace amount being present and having a positive test. Instead, we just ice it several times a day.

◆ ◆ ◆

That evening as I hold a Dixie cup of frozen water to Myth's shoulder, Debbie pulls up a stool and plops down to chat with me. Then Michael leans against a stall and Steffen sits on a trunk. Allana and Michael's groom can be heard laughing outside. I breathe in deeply, look at them chattering away and think, *What a great feeling it is to be part of a team—to be all working together toward a common goal.* We love riding horses because it's always a team, always the two of you, but riders rarely get the chance to be on a team with someone we can have a beer or go to dinner with, which we do nearly every evening.

I tune into the conversation and it's about where to go tonight. Michael says someone told him of a restaurant we should try, so after showering, we pile into a van designated to haul the teams around. It takes us most of the way, but Michael doesn't know exactly where the restaurant is so we decide to find it on foot.

I walk next to Steffen and we hear a ruckus behind us. When we turn around, Debbie and Michael are crawling out of a tipped-over porta potty laughing uproariously, so we walk back to ask what happened, how did it tip? Eventually Debbie manages to say it *was* tipped over and they crawled into it. Why? I ask. She just shrugs, continues laughing and points to Michael, who grins and shrugs, too and we carry on.

The jovial mood continues at dinner and lasts throughout the evening. I crawl into bed that night thankful for making the Olympic Team not just for the riding, but for getting to be part of this group. Opposite of Young Riders, I've found kindred spirits.

• • •

Before we depart for Hong Kong, we take a team field trip to Klaus's old police station. He was originally a mounted police officer and in Germany, the police officers train their horses in dressage, sometimes even have small competitions amongst themselves. Klaus's gold medal Olympic horse, Goldstern, was his police horse originally and continued to work as such all the way to Grand Prix.

We're amazed at how they train their horses. A huge ball, which people normally use for exercising, is thrown at the horse's head, shoulders and rear end while the horse just stands there. Fifty rusty cans are attached together and thrown at the horse's feet and jingled over their bodies. Then the horse canters around as the rider drags the cans behind them. One exercise Viva loves is when the horse trots and canters around the ring while we throw tennis balls at them. Although her mouth is too small to grab the balls, she chases them with vengeance. The horses seem to enjoy the crazy exercises. It's a game like recess at school, and we decide we're all going to send our two and three-year-olds here to be broke.

• 56 •

On July 30th, we get on a plane headed toward the dream that began when I was nine years old. Jason gets us an upgrade to business class with all the miles he's accumulated following me from place to place, so we're served champagne and silently toast.

As I look out the window watching Amsterdam become smaller and smaller, I think I should feel like this plane is taking me not only to another country, but to another phase in my life. Although I'm well aware that luck was the final factor in my making the Team—I had the right horse at the right time who stayed sound and woke up on the right side of the stall, the right owners, the right trainers—my goal was to be as good as an Olympic rider and I've achieved that. I should feel a sense of accomplishment, have a change in goals. But I don't. What I love about dressage is the constant ability to improve and my goal to do so remains the same. It's certainly not that I don't feel as good as an Olympic rider, I just know I can still improve a great deal—same as I always have.

When we arrive in Hong Kong, whereas normally the vegetables and other perishables are unloaded first, the Olympic horses are given priority and we watch from our windows as they're deplaned. Rick's allowed to be with them for the entire trip and we're still in baggage claim when he calls to tell us they're safely in their stalls; the roads were closed to traffic so the horses could travel directly to the equestrian center.

An Olympic welcoming committee greets us and supplies a van to take us to the venue. As we pull in, I'm captivated by the view: Hong Kong skyscrapers with a backdrop of mountains—a big city nestled in the wilderness. There are a great many places in the world I want to visit, I have to pick and choose, and the Far East would have been at the bottom of my priorities. At first I thought it was unfortunate that the Olympics weren't in Greece or Italy, Finland or Brazil—places I want to visit—but now I realize it's very fortunate. I wouldn't have seen this part of the world if the Olympics hadn't brought me.

A multitude of guards watch us closely as our things go through an x-ray machine, and as we walk to the barn, staff outnumbers everyone else—competitors, grooms, vets, chef d'equipes and coaches—ten to one. Security guards for each nation, including ours, wander discreetly around and before entering the stabling area, which is separated by a fence, we're required to use hand sanitizers and walk over a foot-sanitizing rug. The intensity of attention to each person's security, each nation's security, magnifies the importance I already attributed to this event.

The stabling is composed of two barns connected by an aisle of several open-air wash stalls. The barns sit on either side of a lunging ring and as we walk in, a cool breeze welcomes us. Air conditioning makes it a good ten degrees cooler. Mats cover all the floors, the horses hang their heads out of enormous stalls and a large machine constantly makes ice to fill the boots all our horses wear after work. Steffen, Debbie and Michael, all of whom have been to previous Olympics, say that Hong Kong is by far the best venue.

◆ ◆ ◆

Although there's an equestrian Olympic village, our significant others wouldn't be allowed to stay with us there so, rationalizing that happy athletes are more likely to get medals, the USEF took the extra expense of getting us rooms at the Sheraton. Before we go to them, we're each given a large suitcase labeled U.S.A. filled with Olympic clothing and a gift bag from the Hong Kong Jockey Club. One of the gifts is a silk embroidered box containing two matching bracelets—one for you and one for your biggest supporter—accompanied by a poem:

You worked harder.
You went further.
You never gave up.

Along the way, many people
Helped you find your strength.

Your moment to shine
as an athlete is now,
but your opportunity to
inspire and change the lives
of others as an Olympian
is only just beginning.

In this spirit,
We honor you with this gift,
To treasure and to share.

It's as if they're talking directly to me. Then it strikes me that every competitor must feel this way. Every single person worked harder, went further, never gave up. Every one of them was helped along the way. I feel as if I was trudging up a hill alone and when I got to the peak, an entire village is welcoming me on the other side.

As I try on each item of clothing—tee shirts, sweatshirts, jerseys, shorts, sneakers, a swimsuit cover-up—Jason flicks on the TV and of course the Olympics are on. They're interviewing Michael Phelps and he's wearing the same jersey I have on. My breath catches. We're on the same Team. The riders aren't the whole of my village; every athlete from every sport—archery, long-jump, running, gymnastics—they all constitute my village.

◆　◆　◆

At dinner that night my rookiness is highlighted by my amazement at our circumstances. The rest of the team seems to take them in stride, are more focused on what we're here to do than the specialness of our current state of being. Slowly their business-like attitude rubs off on me and I think, *Yes, I'm here, I found my village, but I'm a part of their village, too. I need to do my part to contribute to its success.*

I vow to lay it all out there on the first day. Normally I begin with a conservative test-—make sure it's clean, that my horse has a good experience and the judges have a good impression—then I take a little more risk each day. But the Team test is the *first* day, so to help the U.S. medal, I need to take the risks that make a brilliant test possible our first time in the show ring. Besides, it may be my only time *to* show if I'm not in the top twenty-five who make the Special.

I ask what everyone else's game plans are. Steffen and Debbie say they'll just do their best as always and Michael says, To not ride. We apologetically toast to that and I ask how they think we'll do. Holland and Germany will of course get gold and silver as they always do, but the Danes, the US and the Brits all have strong teams so there will be a good fight for the bronze.

Steffen smiles and says, That's why we just have to go for silver.

◆ ◆ ◆

The horses have the day after we arrive off and I take Mythy for a long handwalk to scope out the venue. As we walk out of the barn, I hear a horse grunt and shake. A Brazilian rider leads a horse out of what appears to be a stall and the horse is covered in footing. I ask him why and in broken English and with a lot of smiles, he says we can let our horses roll in there. After he walks out, I peer in. It's a fifteen by fifteen foot space, rounded so the horse can't get his legs caught. Although Mythy won't use it, it would have been perfect for Idy and I'm impressed that our hosts thought of such details to suit each horse's individual needs.

In preparation for monsoon season, countless drains surround raised arenas which are made of exquisite footing. We follow a path made of the same exquisite footing and find we're in the midst of the cross-country jumping course. Although I'm very happy to be taking Mythy to the Olympics, I can't help thinking how Idy would have loved this place. It has components to suit all his needs.

After meandering through the extensive fields full of natural jumps, we check out the indoor. It used to be a ping pong hall, has a high arched roof, a grandstand and is air conditioned to provide some relief from the heat. Also in anticipation of the heat, misting tents in which twenty giant fans are fed by hoses to create a fine mist, speckle the venue. Two horses are being bathed in one and stand contentedly with their noses to the fans, but Myth isn't so eager. He enters resolutely, doesn't balk, but I get the feeling he enters only to please me.

When we get back to the barn, grooms and riders in U.S.A. apparel are hanging paper American flags on each stall. All the equestrian disciplines are stabled together and although we don't know each other, the unified team feeling radiates. George Morris is the coach of the show jumping team and I expect him to be pleased and impressed that I made the Team. Instead he just acts like it was expected.

◆ ◆ ◆

The next day, the horses are supposed to have an easy day and I get on Myth intending to work him lightly, but when we walk away from the mounting block, he feels out of balance. I halt to let him regain his composure, but when we walk again, he still feels wobbly. I keep waiting for him to outgrow his sea-legs but I need to hold the reins short our entire walk to the arena because it feels like he may fall down if I let them loose.

Rick planned to meet me at the ring, and when I arrive and tell him about it, he says that when the plane took off in Amsterdam, Myth almost sat down so perhaps he strained a muscle. Let's see him trot.

He feels weird but sound. Rick says he looks fine, do a bit and we'll see how he is tomorrow.

Perhaps he didn't *strain* a muscle but he always stays very rigid while traveling and this is the longest flight he's been on, so maybe they're tight. I work just enough to get the blood pumping and work out any kinks.

The next day he's the same.

Rick can't see anything and encourages me to work him so, as I always do when concerned that something may be bothering a horse but am unsure if what I'm feeling isn't just in my mind, I ride him as if nothing's wrong. Make my normal corrections and insist on the same quality.

He does everything fine. If this were a horse I hadn't ridden before, perhaps I wouldn't be concerned, but this isn't my Myth. Something's wrong.

Rick asks me to explain what I feel. The best way I can describe it is it's like feeling someone else's vertigo: they look fine from the outside but they feel like the world is wonky.

He waits for me to continue. I can't. It's an indescribable sensation. I feel as if the ground we're walking on is a tightrope and we may fall off any time.

I wait for him to give me some possible explanations. He can't.

We both leave perplexed.

♦ ♦ ♦

I barely do anything with Myth the next two days, am consumed by anxiety and barely notice anyone's presence but Jason's and Rick's. Of course my teammates see Rick scrutinizing him several times a day, know I'm not working him and that we're searching for something wrong, but we don't talk about it. They don't ask, recognize my anguish and allow me to rely solely on the one closest to my heart: Jason. He can't empathize with my soul-deep concern but he believes me. I feel like Rick thinks I'm crazy. Myth is pooping, eating, drinking, is sound, nothing obvious is wrong. But something is.

I stand by the arena and watch the other competitors school and prepare. The soft, harmonious power that both my American counterparts display. The laughter and joking amongst and between teams. Sadness about being unable to be part of the excited seriousness that pervades the venue joins the agony of concern for my horse.

As Steffen and I walk to the van to go back to the hotel, he says, Court, don't you think you should do more with him? He looks fine.

My pace slows. But, Steffen, he's *not* fine.

Think about the Team, he says.

I stop dead, feel like having a four-year-old's temper tantrum. Does he think I don't *want* to ride? That the thought of letting the Team down

214

doesn't add weight to the horror of knowing something's wrong with Mythy?

First I'll think about my horse, *then* I'll think about the Team, I snap and storm ahead.

Jason and I take the subway instead of the van and as I sit quietly in the hum of Chinese chatter, I begin to regret snapping at Steffen. If he and Debbie don't know what's going on, how can I expect them to understand my misery? I expect them to blindly support me when they see the risk our country might suffer. Am offended that Steffen would put the country before my horse when he hasn't a clue how I feel my horse may be in jeopardy.

Although I know it's unwarranted, I can't shake the anger.

◆ ◆ ◆

Rick decides to go back to basics in his search for what could possibly cause my insistence that something's wrong. Temperature: normal. Respiration: normal. Heart rate: lub, dubdub, lub, dub, lubdublubdub. Not normal.

I don't know whether to be glad we found the cause of the problem or horrified that it's his heart, and Rick gives me no indication which is the proper reaction. The three of us simply go to the clinic to do an EKG.

Gel is gooped onto probes which are attached to Myth's chest, and I watch as a computer regurgitates a squiggly line onto paper. Rick says, Hm. I stare at him, waiting.

Myth has atrial fibrillation, he tells me and when he sees my lack of comprehension adds, An irregular heartbeat. I swallow and wait for him to continue but he ponders the paper and marches away.

My horse with the heart of gold has a broken heart.

I suffer for fifteen minutes before he comes back with the Olympic Veterinary Commission. They assure me that Myth is fine and say many horses compete at Grand Prix for years with this condition. I ask, Did it happen during take-off? Doubtful. Is it because of the stress of so much travel? There's no way to know. Sometimes horses just standing in a field get A-fib. There's no known reason.

They want to do a cardiac ultrasound to check his heart structure, so ultrasound gel is slathered onto his chest and another probe is moved over his heart as the vets look at a computer screen. I stare at it too and although they make an occasional grunt or *hmm*, to me it looks like fuzz on a TV screen interrupted by occasional solid masses or lines.

Finally, Rick puts down the probe and tells me that his heart structure is fine.

Is that good?

Definitely good. Courtney, his heart is healthy. You can compete him like this.

He sees refusal beginning to formulate in my expression and continues, Or we can try to convert it back to regular rhythm.

How?

The only possibility is a drug called quinidine which has a sixty percent success rate. It's administered by inserting a tube in his nostril and pumping the medication into his stomach. It may work the first time but can be tried a total of nine times every four hours.

As the tube is stuck down Myth's nostril, tears soak my cheeks. He has no idea why we're doing this to him but accepts the torture without complaint. His eyes focus on me, then at the person inserting the tube then back on me. What a dear, sweet, kind animal.

When all the medication is in his stomach, another EKG is done and once again we watch the computer draw a squiggly line. It gives the vets no better news.

At eleven p.m., we've done the third dose and the EKG reports that the heart is maintaining its erratic rhythm. They tell me to go back to the hotel and when I begin to protest, explain their rationale: if I'm gone eight hours, I'll miss one dose and hopefully arrive to a healthy heart.

I lie in my bed thinking I never should have left. Maybe, as Jason pointed out, I couldn't do anything but perhaps I could help him not be scared. Like how Lendon's presence comforted me when I broke my arm.

There's no change when I return.

Again and again, they stick the tube down Mythy's nose and each time fills me with agony. Of any horse in the world, he deserves the pain we're inflicting on him least. Each EKG, my eyes flicker back and forth between that damned piece of paper and Rick's face. On the eighth dose, the squiggles develop somewhat of a pattern and Rick begins to smile. Then the beat reverts to dub, lubdub, lub, dub, lub, dubdublubdublubdub.

We're getting somewhere, he says offering me a ray of hope.

After the ninth time, the beat doesn't become completely regular but regular in its irregularity; instead of lubdublublubdub, lub, dub, lubdub, lubdub, it's lubdublubdub, lub, dub, lubdublubdub, lub, dub. The vets begin to bustle about, wipe the gel off Myth, roll the machine away and fill out paperwork as I watch them completely baffled. Finally Rick tells me it's much better, I should ride him.

I'm not convinced and just look down, tears dripping off my nose. The head of the veterinary commission—a grandfatherly type with light blue, direct eyes—confirms this advice and all the vets repeat their initial assurances that this won't affect his performance.

◆ ◆ ◆

The Team always has breakfast together and as I watch Michael tell a story and Debbie and Steffen laugh, I feel my aloneness for the first time. So far, I've been in a purgatory over which I had no control but now it's my decision: to ride or not to ride. I want to lean on them, to get their understanding support if I need to scratch.

Steffen was my closest friend amongst them and I realize that the anger I felt toward him is gone. It's been replaced by sadness. Sadness that we haven't talked about our spat, that I've lost one of the people who's affected me the most, is the most responsible (besides Lendon) for getting my riding worthy of being here. Thank goodness for Jason who's absorbed an ocean of tears, but I want my Team.

◆　◆　◆

For three days I battle with the decision of whether to ride or not and work Myth conservatively. His lack of coordination decreases every day and each ride feels better, but he still doesn't feel like himself. If it were Idy or Wy I could depend on them to tell me, but Mythy never complains. He'd try his hardest if one of his legs disappeared. I need to decide. *I* need to decide. It's up to me to ensure his safety.

Rick finds me in his stall and I tell him I think I should scratch. He says not to be silly, reiterates that it can't do harm. I listen but don't hear him.

When he leaves, I lay my forehead on Mythy's shoulder and Michael's voice comes through the bars, If the vets say you shouldn't scratch, you shouldn't. As much as I want to ride in the Olympics, you should be the one riding down that centerline. The Team needs you.

I look at him. This is the team attitude I so cherish—sacrificing what would be the most beneficial to you for what would be best for the nation. But the horse doesn't have that choice. I tell him I hope I can but it's a huge relief to have him here if I can't.

◆　◆　◆

The next day, the head of the veterinary commission watches me school. Myth once again feels better than yesterday—not completely normal but the daily improvement gives me hope, a glimmer of confidence that he'll be OK. As I dismount, the vet walks over and tells me he looked very good, how did he feel? Like my first phone call with Lendon, my gut says to trust him.

So I ask. If we were to compete in this heat, with this stress, could it hurt him? Not like could he have a heart attack and drop dead, but could there be long-term damage?

He puts a hand on my shoulder. Says, Let me put it this way: my daughter loves her horses to such an extent she'd die before putting them in danger. If this were her horse, I'd tell her to ride. There's no chance it could cause harm.

I look at him and his eyes don't waver. I give one nod and with six days left, I begin to prepare wholeheartedly for the Olympic Games. Finally, I can feel part of the Team.

Courtney's Quest Journal
Although it's far less preparation than I'd hoped for and under far less desirable circumstances, there are two things that ease my concerns very effectively... first, Myth proved at the Selection Trials just how confirmed he is now. I don't need to practice the movements. I need to have a fit, comfortable horse and the test will be fine... less impressive, but it'll be fine. Second, Myth has a heart of gold. He has the biggest heart I've ever experienced, and that's the biggest responsibility I hold. He'll give his heart and soul ten times over and I never have to fear that he'll be wimpy or say no. And if he complains the littlest bit, I'll listen because he'd never want to complain.

• 57 •

Because the competition is at night, we need to get the horses accustomed to being ridden then, so our schedule is leave for the barn after breakfast at seven, ride the horses, come back to the hotel around eleven or twelve and then go ride them again at eight or nine in the evening. Myth continues to feel slightly more solid each day, and although Klaus is our coach, Steffen helps me as much as possible. Like Lendon, he's not one to discuss his feelings and I know if I attempted to discuss our spat, he'd clam up and it would make the situation worse. So I simply accept his good-will and our return to both a good student-teacher relationship and friendship.

The schedule leaves the middle of the day free, so we immerse ourselves in Hong Kong culture. The city's famous for tailored clothing, so Jason gets measured for a suit and I have my favorite shirt copied in a different color. We buy Rolex knockoffs and wander through local markets where we're barraged by vendors. My dad and Pam came as did Jason's parents and we spend an afternoon lounging by the pool.

One night the U.S. Teams from each discipline take a boat across Victoria Harbor to Hong Kong Island to celebrate the birthday of Jim Wolf, the USEF'S chef de mission. As we float across the harbor, I watch the moonlight dancing across the water, listen to my teammates laughing as they pass around a cowboy hat that looks like an American flag, and can finally feel what I did in quarantine: appreciation for being among kindred spirits. Everyone seems to have left their Olympic seriousness in the hotel room and the evening is spent in jovial enjoyment of each other's company and being in Hong Kong.

We choose a waterside restaurant where the choices of dinner—squid, shrimp and several types of fish—are swimming in aquariums, which horrifies Debbie but Jason and Steffen are highly amused.

After we've selected our victims and Debbie has ordered off the menu, Jim gives a speech. He says the best present he could get would be personal best performances by everyone, not just the athletes but the support staff as well. If we do that, he's certain we'll be successful both on and off the field of play. He tells us that how we conduct ourselves is more important than how we actually place in the competition, but winning medals is certainly our goal. More than anything, let's be thankful that we get to be part of the Olympic movement and enjoy it.

Enjoy it. That's the last way I'd categorize my experience thus far, but tonight makes up for my two weeks of misery. I look around at the rest of my team—vets, grooms, body worker, USEF staff, jumpers, coaches, teammates. Everyone seems to embrace this concept. They're already living it, but it affects me differently, reminds me how fortunate I am to be here.

After several hear, hears and toasts amidst and between tables, enthusiastic banter resumes. Steffen comes up, gives me a special cheer, To Mythy, and puts the cowboy hat on me. His toast, the easy congeniality of it, amplifies my feeling of content.

Steffen Peters and me

Although my heart and mind want to continue to revel in the scene surrounding me, my bladder demands my attention. Now. I scamper the ten feet to the single bathroom but Debbie's in it. As I wait, distracting myself by watching our dinners swim around, Jason comes up and nudges me. His expression is mischievous and he grabs a rather large shrimp. The door to the bathroom stops about two feet above the floor to allow air to circulate and he throws the shrimp under then bolts back to the table where he sits with everyone else as if he never left.

Debbie shrieks as if Freddie Krueger's after her and charges out before her pants are buttoned. I charge in and by the time I return to the table, she's scrutinizing everyone's hands because no one would tell her who the thrower was. She sees the humor of her terror and makes her investigation extra thorough to the amusement of everyone else. When she gets to Jason, her jaw drops and she looks in his eyes, says, It was you!

When we get back to the hotel, no one wants the evening to end so we go upstairs and continue our celebration at the bar until it closes. As I walk back to my room hand-in-hand with my wonderful husband, I think now I'm following Jim's orders to the fullest: enjoying it, and my hard times have made me appreciate the sensation even more.

Debbie McDonald, me and Steffen Peters

* * *

The three hour plane ride to Beijing prevents us from going to the official Opening Ceremony, but there's a far smaller one in Hong Kong. One rider from each discipline will march, and to choose among the three of us, Steffen, Debbie and I each write our name on a sugar packet and Klaus draws one.

He draws my name and says, Keep this because it's all your luck, then he throws it to me. I'm a terrible catcher but it's a horrendous throw. It hits Steffen in the shoulder and ricochets to the floor. We stare at the sugar packet aghast and Klaus looks at me like a guilty schoolboy caught by his teacher and trying not to laugh. Luckily given my current circumstances, I'm not superstitious and can only hold it in for so long before I burst out laughing followed by everyone else.

As I march surrounded by the other countries' riders, every single one of whom has worked just as hard as I have, striven for the same passion, I'm filled with a great sense of pride. Not pride only in myself but pride in all of us: we represent the best in the world. We compete for our countries individually, but we have a unified heart.

Then I look up in the stands, see Debbie clapping with her hands over head, Steffen with his fingers in his mouth mid-whistle, Klaus grinning from ear to ear, and humility is added to my pride. They're all so much better than I am. I have so much more to learn.

In an Olympic Ambassador program I attended in the midst of my worries, they told us the Olympics are about the glory of pursuit, not the pursuit of glory. So true. My joy came, not from chasing my Olympic dream, but from working every day to become as good as an Olympic rider. Isabell who's won several golds, doesn't stop working, striving to be better. Our glory will continue long after the Games.

* * *

Several days before competition begins, the show ring is set up for us to school in. The judges' booths are Chinese style houses, ponds with bridges lie behind them and bushes shaped like dragons are scattered around the enormous stadium. Everything has a Chinese feel.

The only thing that doesn't is the mammoth Jumbotron TV screen that hangs over one end of the stadium which panics many horses because it appears a two-hundred-fifty hand horse is coming straight at them. The Germans want it turned off but the Dutch say it should stay on and win the battle.

When I get on Myth, I intend to keep the work light and just let him see the surroundings as he worked hard for a few days after having several days off, but as soon as I'm on, I know he's in the zone and wants to work. The surroundings have zero effect on him and he feels the most in control of his body he's been since our arrival, is expressive and energetic. The lack of practice may make putting the test together difficult, but his energy and enthusiasm eliminate any lingering concerns about his welfare.

◆ ◆ ◆

The normal strategy is to have the weakest member of a team go first so in this case, it's me. I'm the fourteenth rider of twenty-four to go on the first day.

As I repetitively do my mental rehearsal, I memorize all the details I need to think about: in the corner before the left extension make sure he's light on the right rein, take your time to go straight and balance him before beginning the canter zig-zag, bend him a little before asking for the canter from passage.

And it pays off in the test. I have the time, the calm and the focus to think of everything so I'm able to ride to the best of my ability. Myth is just as business-like as I am and is unfazed by the environment, the Jumbotron or the applause. We put in a solid clean test and as I salute, the thought of how strong his erratic heart is chokes me up. I can't imagine anything bringing two beings closer than what we've gone through together, achieved together, and an immense amount of respect and admiration for him are added to the adoration I've always felt. He's a champion, through and through. Every horse has their difficulties, but there's not a horse on the planet I would trade for my Mythy.

Although the ride certainly wasn't as brilliant as the one in San Juan Capistrano, given the lead-up circumstances, it couldn't have been better. The score is 70.485%.

When we get to the gate, I dismount and give Myth's expanding and contracting nostril a long kiss, breathe in the delicious scent of his breath. We did it.

Allana takes him and I'm ushered to a fenced-in maze lined by each nation's media. As the rider walks through, each nation asks a question or two. The first reporter says, Over 70 percent; what will you aim for individually?

I reply, A medal, of course! which gets a chorus of laughter. I wait for the laughter to subside and continue, I don't think I'll go for this or that. I'll ride aiming to win and do the best I can.

Well, what do you think you have a chance for? she asks.

Now it's my turn to laugh. Gold!

When I reach the end of the lineup, the rest of the Team is waiting, beaming at my success. I'm simply satisfied—not excited and not disappointed. This competition isn't just for me like a World Cup which is only individual, and I'm satisfied that I did my job for my Team, for my country. And now I'll most likely get a chance to move on to the Individual.

When I get back to the hotel, I get an email from Lendon congratulating me. She says, It was good but wimpy. Go for it the Special!

I momentarily regret that I didn't succeed in carrying out my original plan, but then I realize that I did lay all I felt we could out there.

Harmony's Mythilus, Credit: Susan J. Stickle

Courtney's Quest Journal

I was sitting here, contemplating how to begin this journal. Then it occurred to me; at least I don't have to begin it with "Stupid, Stupid, Stupid!" Yes, that's a relief.

◆ ◆ ◆

My dreams that night are of being in a hot-air balloon and waving at Rich, Francine, Lendon, the Malones and countless nameless people. I feel the weight of a hug a thousand strong. Share a beer with Mythy who tells me no atrial fibrillation could damage *his* heart.

When I wake, the satisfaction with my ride has turned to soul-deep joy. Not only did I do my job for the Team and the country, all the efforts of the countless people who've helped me to get to the Olympics weren't in vain.

The Team's in a good position to medal and I know Debbie and Steffen are very solid, so I can just sit back and enjoy supporting them. I spend the day sweating off ten pounds by the rooftop pool, trying to find the vendor who sold me the fake Rolex which already broke and find a small authentic Chinese restaurant to have lunch with Jason's parents.

When I get to the venue that evening, Debbie's groom is doing a final spit polish on Brentina but there's no sign of Debbie. She's supposed to get on in fifteen minutes. When I ask where she is, her groom tells me she likes to be alone for an hour before major competitions and Jason mocks my concern, asks if I thought she forgot.

Warming up, Brentina looks better than she did at the Selection Trials and Steffen's theory of going for silver looks possible. Nerves begin to flutter in my belly—to watch and have no control is excruciating. Debbie's husband says, Welcome to my world. I'm buying stock in Depends.

Her groom gives her boots a final polish and she trots into the ring. As she does, Brentina's ears flicker and she spooks. Debbie walks and pats her to give reassurance, but when they trot forward again, Brentina remains tense.

I keep waiting for her to settle but it gets progressively worse as her test goes on. Her passage looks like she's jumping hop-scotch and her extensions are a mish-mosh of tempos. She's been in much more intimidating atmospheres so I can only assume she's scared of the Jumbotron. Although she didn't care about it in schooling, horses are often much more confident when they have company.

When Debbie comes out, there are no words to comfort her. She's not crying, she's bawling. She keeps saying she's so sorry she let us down and we can't convince her that she didn't. I tell her they're horses, not machines and she couldn't have done anything.

Although we're heartbroken for Debbie, Steffen still has to ride. Debbie puts on sunglasses (although it's almost eleven p.m.) and comes out to support him. He puts in a solid, clean test for 70% which, with my score of 70.485% and Debbie's of 63%, puts our team fourth.

Myth and I are seventh place individually and when I go to pick up my test, the secretary says, Seventh place, how does it feel?

I half smile and say, Well, I'd rather be ninth behind Debbie and Steffen where I belong.

Sadness for Debbie, her horror made worse by the fact that this is Brentina's last show before retirement—the last show of America's darling horse— dilutes the joy I feel.

• • •

The next day, the trauma of Debbie's ride goes from bad to worse. The press announces that Brentina was *unfit to compete*. Her tension caused her to look uneven but nothing could be further from the truth. Debbie's love affair with that horse is like mine with Idy. She'd no sooner put that mare in jeopardy than she'd put her own baby in front of a moving car. I write a letter defending her for publication by the news website, Dressage Daily.

They not only blame Debbie, they question Klaus's ethics and concern for the welfare of the horse, the very traits I admire most in both of them. They epitomize love and respect for the horse.

To prove them wrong, Debbie schools Brentina out in the open so everyone can see that she's sound. Although Debbie still wears sunglasses to hide her eyes, Brentina looks as brilliant as she did before entering the show ring and I notice with satisfaction that vets and fellow competitors are watching and quietly talking.

• • •

That evening when I take Mythy from Allana to show the Special, he drags me down the aisle in his excitement to work. His enthusiasm makes him extremely strong but he has more expression than I've ever gotten. I vow to let it be so in the test. Keeping control and letting the neck long will be a challenge, but it's time to go big or go home.

And I do. As I trot away from X down the centerline, his trot feels divine. In order to maintain the impressive momentum, I compromise on the half-halt and he gets stronger and stronger. This is also what he does when he's tired: he tries too hard, which to him of course, means going faster. We manage to have no mistakes but the control is questionable and the harmony is negligible.

Although the risk didn't pay off, I don't regret trying. Myth is barely over a year into his Grand Prix career and he isn't ready to show maximum expression at the same time as being in self carriage. Plus, the past two weeks have caught up with him.

This in no way disappoints me but excites me for the future. We end up

Harmony's Mythilus, Credit: Susan J. Stickle

with 70.8% and eighth place. The judges range a great deal on my test. One
has me in third and one thirteenth.

Debbie, still in her sunglasses, congratulates me but Steffen says, Why
didn't you do more steps of piaffe?

I did thirteen. The test calls for twelve to fifteen and by doing the full
fifteen, I could have shown off Myth's fantastic piaffe. But I didn't. Now

that, I regret.

◆ ◆ ◆

Two rest days separate the Special and the Freestyle and although most horses do a little work on the first day, Myth gets a well-needed day off. He works harder than most horses because he needs to in order to stay supple, and I think the down time will serve us better than one more schooling session. The rest days between each class sounded like a help but in reality, they just mean a longer period of concentrated work because we're always preparing for the next thing.

I only do a tiny bit the second day and find that the day off didn't help. Rick's in our aisle when I come back and I tell him that Myth's tank is empty; if this weren't the Olympics, I'd scratch. He says, Well this *is* the Olympics.

Case closed.

I walk over to Myth's stall to take him for a graze, but he's napping. I look at Rick. He looks back at me, then turns and walks away. I sneak away too leaving Myth to his nap and spend the entire evening listening to my music. Jason goes to dinner with his parents and brings me leftovers. I convince myself that the better I know the music, the easier Myth's job will be.

In the morning, my studies are resumed with increased vigor and only paused for the van ride to the venue where I sit on a tack trunk and begin again. When I finish, I realize Jason was videotaping me. I say, That will be interesting: six minutes of doing nothing.

For your Quest contributors, he says. Some people will find how you prepare interesting. Allana and Justin were laughing and fooling around right next to you and you didn't even notice.

When I get on, Myth's tank is no more full and my incessant listening didn't make his job easier. The quality of his movement is at about sixty percent and we have several mistakes. Our score of 69.55% is the lowest freestyle score I've gotten in many years (barring my infamous triple pirouette) but I'm happier than I was after the Grand Prix or the Special because now he can rest. I feel that I prepared him the best I could and he did the best he could. What more could I ask?

When I get to the exit gate, a drug tester is waiting for me. Which horses will be drug tested are chosen randomly and I've been selected many times before so I know that Myth sometimes takes hours to pee. I apologize for this fact, leave him with Allana and watch the remaining rides.

Steffen's freestyle brings tears to my eyes it's so lovely. He gets a 76.5% and third place. Mythy and I get fourteenth. Even when he's physically compromised he's seventh, eighth, and fourteenth in the world. What an incredible, incredible horse.

The individual medal is determined by the average of the Special and

Freestyle scores, and Anky wins gold with 78.68%, Isabell gets silver with 76.65%, and Heike Kemmer from Germany just edges Steffen out of bronze by .305 of a percent with a 74.455%. Mythy's thirteenth with 70.175%.

As the Dutch national anthem begins, I look around, and even though Anky's not American, a great elation fills me. Tears stream down many faces as they hear their anthem and watch their flag rise and I imagine the emotions that must be gushing through them. Every rider knows how incredibly much work, dedication and sacrifice goes into this achievement and to see someone stand on the podium, having everything culminate into being the best in the world, American or not, is extremely touching.

Courtney's Quest Journal

It's been fantastic to be here and to experience and see everything. Of course I wish that we could have maintained and increased the quality going into the freestyle, but I know there's nothing more we could do and I wasn't about to push the horse for more than I knew he had. He did way more than could be expected of him, and now he's saved for a great future.

• 58 •

The next morning, Gil calls and wakes me up. He says Myth's drug test was positive for Selbinac, come down at eleven for a meeting. I hang up unconcerned and laugh to Jason at the ridiculousness of it. I don't even know what Selbinac is.

When I get down to the meeting, I find all our vets and USEF staff doing internet research trying to figure out what the drug is because none of them have heard of it either.

Then the official document comes. It's *Fel*binac, not *Sel*binac. No one's heard of Felbinac either so everyone begins their research again, but this time they can find it: it's a topical anti-inflammatory mostly used on humans and wouldn't even *help* my horse. Rick says that Surpass would be a more effective anti-inflammatory and much more attainable as Felbinac isn't even approved or available anywhere in the U.S.

We're told the FEI won't publicize anything until a B sample confirms the results, and Jim tells me not to worry; the B sample will surely be negative, the A sample must have been contaminated. Don't tell Debbie and Steffen because there's no need to worry them needlessly.

Worry Debbie and Steffen? I knew that *I* could be disqualified from the Individual, but I had no idea that the *Team* could be punished.

The Team placing could be taken away? I ask.

Jim sees my panic, apologizes and assures me it couldn't because a precedent had been set: a show jumper got eliminated from the individual competition but the team placing wasn't revoked. Myth was tested after the freestyle and they can't know if the drug was in his system for the team test even if the B sample comes back positive. Which it won't.

So why shouldn't I tell Debbie and Steffen if it wouldn't affect them anyway? I ask.

They're the first people I want to tell. I didn't talk to them about Mythy not because I wanted to hide anything, but because I was lost in my own pain, struggling with what was the right decision. I have no control over this. They should know.

They're both dealing with enough, Courtney, Gil says. Debbie's dealing with her heart-breaking ride and Steffen just narrowly missed a well-deserved medal.

Jason squeezes my knee and I don't say anything more till we're walking back to the room. I tell him I feel like a traitor not telling my teammates. He says, But the USEF is right; they have enough to deal with in their own traumas, especially Debbie, to have to deal with yours, too. The USEF has been doing this a long time and they're confident it won't be a problem.

When we get to the room, I collapse on the bed and though I can't believe there's anything left, the hoses in my eyes turn on once again. Jason sits down beside me, wipes my tears and says, Why do bad things happen to good people? I smile because that thought had flickered and died in my head. I tell him that *way* too many good things have happened to me to even start down that line of thinking. Maybe this is the bad after fifteen years of good and will earn me fifteen more.

This rationale turns the hoses off and after sitting up and staring at my knees for five minutes while Jason strokes my back, I call Leslie. After several calls regarding the a-fib, I feel like she only ever hears from me with bad news. She's a relatively new owner and I seldom talk to her—I've only ever seen her twice—so I worry that she'll be dubious of my ethics. But she doesn't even consider the possibility of guilt, says that's ridiculous. She's not only supportive, she's sympathetic.

◆　◆　◆

In the afternoon, we have another meeting and the FEI tells us that the Team would, in fact, be disqualified if I am. The precedent case was during the time when there were four members to a team and only three scores counted, so if I'd been disqualified in those years, the other team member's score would simply count instead of mine and the team would be placed accordingly. But there's no drop score so without mine, the team would only have two scores and be ineligible.

I scan each face in the room hoping there's good news to go with the bad. Finally Jim reiterates that the B sample will be negative and because of this, I'm reminded to not tell Debbie or Steffen.

Seeing Debbie in sunglasses that night at dinner and her groom's unhidden puffy eyes negates my impulse to ignore the USEF's instructions and tell them. I spend the dinner painfully pretending everything's all right. Luckily neither Debbie or Steffen are chatty either and Mike and Klaus obliviously banter.

◆ ◆ ◆

The plane ride home the following day is quite the opposite of my plane ride to Hong Kong. The excited anticipation for what lies through the next door is replaced by feeling like I've walked through that door to find a huge, fanged and taloned monster and am cowering from it. When we leave, the B sample result isn't in yet so the FEI says they'll inform the USEF of it and the USEF will inform me.

After the horrible and suffocating drama of the previous three weeks, walking into my house is like crawling into a cocoon. The drama still exists but it's out there. I put on my favorite jammies, and Jason and I make spaghetti as we list0en to our cooking music: the soundtrack from Garden State. After we eat, I snuggle with my big white dog and little black dog on the couch, revel in their warm, puppy dog smell and their wonderful love. I sleep a dreamless sleep in my own bed.

◆ ◆ ◆

The next morning, I make an appointment at Cornell University for Myth to have his heart electronically converted back to a regular rhythm on September 5th. Feeling good about this and refreshed from being home, I answer the phone momentarily forgetting about my horrible situation. It's Jason from his office. He got a Google alert of a news article about me that says the B sample was positive. Vibrations start in my belly and travel through my innards.

With shaky hands, I call Jim. He's surprised that no one called me and says they've been busy researching the drug. They found that it's often used as a coupling agent in ultrasound gel so perhaps Myth was exposed to it during treatment in the vet clinic. They investigated getting it tested, but Rick pointed out that the batch we used is gone so we can't. He says I can defend myself in front of an FEI Tribunal at the beginning of September by phone. Or if I want I can go to Lausanne, Switzerland, and do it in person.

I call Jason back and we agree that there's no choice. I'll appear in person. My reputation and the value of my lifelong dream are on the line and I need to come face to face with them and let them see my genuine desire for what's right.

Then I call Debbie and Steffen. Debbie simply says it was a horrible Olympics. I say, But you saw everything that was done with him apart from what was done in the clinic. Surely you know I'm innocent? She says that honestly she hardly noticed anything after her ride but she doesn't believe

I'd do anything purposeful. Steffen says he's behind me all the way.

Courtney's Quest Journal

It breaks my heart that people out there might believe that I doped my horse. All these mothers and little girls who write to me and say what a great role model I am. And now they'll think this? Did I let them down? It's awful, it's horrible. Never have I felt such impotent rage.

◆ ◆ ◆

Courtney's Quest Journal

You know, my mom used to always say in difficult situations, This builds character. I'm so F*#! ing sick of building character... if I get any more character I'm going to spontaneously burst into a cartoon. I'm sure some day I'll see the value in this. No, actually, I sort of already do. That was one of those philosophical things I was going to bring up before... it certainly makes you not take things for granted. The feeling that you never have to think about your reputation, if you just do what you feel is right, then why would you have to worry? Well, now I realize, you cannot take for granted that your reputation relies only on your actions. Sometimes shit happens.

Within an hour of Jason's phone call, I begin getting emails from strangers saying they know I didn't do it. Just like the USEF and USOC, they see it only as a mystery to be solved. This is a great relief, but I'm painfully aware that the people who believe I did drug my horse wouldn't write so the only people I hear from are those who believe in me. The journalists who call and email throughout the day know me well enough from past years to assume my innocence and interview me apologetically and compassionately.

When Jason gets home, I'm calm, comforted by the well-wishes, and he's all business and wouldn't think to comfort me if I needed it anyway. He's already been in contact with John Long, the CEO of the USEF, who recommended contacting another rider who fought a drugging accusation successfully for suggestions on how to proceed. She gave him the contact info of a chemist she used and the lawyer who represented her.

Although I maintain the heart-felt belief that the Tribunal must find me innocent because I am, I'm comforted by Jason's immediate full-bore effort to accrue every bit of information in my defense. The lawyer, Andrew Temkin, joins the effort with equal vigor. He works for Skadden Arps, which is one of the top-rated law firms in the U.S., and says he'll do the case pro bono because he believes in my innocence and thinks it's a worthy cause. We know the zero tolerance rule makes proving innocence nearly impossible because even if I prove that I didn't give the drug and wasn't negligent, I need to prove beyond a reasonable doubt where it came from.

The chemist says that an Olympic venue employee could have rubbed a medication containing Felbinac on his arthritic knee in the morning, used a broom at the show, my groom used that same broom and then patted Myth. The testing procedures have become so sensitive that this tiny amount would show up in Myth's system. The amount of Felbinac found wouldn't be enough to affect a rat. The biologically effective dose for a human (who's one tenth the size of a horse) is approximately 7,500-100,000 ng/mL and the quantity found in Myth was 14 ng/mL. All the evidence suggests that the trace amount found was most likely a matter of contamination so that's what we're basing our defense around.

Courtney's Quest Journal
I'd contentedly accept this unearned tarnish on my name in order to catch some real offenders. Doping is so stupid. It's like cheating in cards or tennis, or anything else... it's not putting your best skill against the others' best skill so it makes the competition invalid anyway. I want my horses to BE healthy, I don't want to cover up their unhealth.

◆ ◆ ◆

Spending my days on horseback allows me to forget my anxiety for a while, and I experience the benefits of the Olympics. I feel like I should send Isabell a thank you letter because watching her helped my own riding so much. She rides with such feel and suppleness. I don't think there's ever a tight muscle in her body even when her horse is bucking or scooting, which happened from time to time. In the past two years, I've ridden with several top trainers who are all good but very different from each other. I've worked hard to master each of their techniques but watching her somehow allowed me to find my own way of riding—combine the techniques to find my own method. I no longer am riding the horse for the movements but riding the movements for the horse. Playing around with the horse's body in order to put them in the position to truly carry themselves, have their back totally soft and swinging and have the contact with the bit be communication rather than control.

Meanwhile Jason and Andrew continue doggedly amassing evidence. Andrew makes a binder to give to each Tribunal member clearly mapping out our defense, the professionalism of which reminds me that he is, in fact, a top lawyer. In addition to the chemist's report and a letter from the FEI vet describing Myth's treatment in Hong Kong, we include numerous character references from prominent equestrians including Debbie and Steffen.. Although it doesn't change the fact that the drug was in his system, we hope bringing attention to my reputation for solid ethics will convince the Tribunal that I wouldn't allow this to happen.

Jason's furious that the media is saying I'm accused of *doping* when I'm actually charged with *illegal use of medications* which constitutes a lesser offence, but it makes no difference to me. If I'd knowingly given my horse an illegal drug, it's cheating no matter what vocabulary you use.

Courtney's Quest Journal

So I'd just like to say thank you to everyone out there for their support. Although sending me to the Olympics turned out to somewhat resemble slow roasting me on the spit of my lifelong dream, the amazing emails and support I've gotten even through this rigmarole, have been like a cold cloth on the burns. Makes it bearable... makes it so much less hard (not easier, but less hard) when you don't feel you're alone. So thank you.

• 59 •

We leave for Switzerland on September 5th, the day Myth was supposed to be converted at Cornell. I'm actually glad we need to postpone because I want to be sure of the necessity to convert before I take him. The specialists all tell me that most horses adapt to this condition and after time, function completely normally. Most of the horses who spontaneously lapse into atrial fibrillation, however, are young and Myth is fourteen. But I want to give him time to adjust if he's going to. Any time you put a horse under general anesthesia, which is necessary for electronic conversion, there's risk, and I don't want to take that risk unless absolutely necessary. With all the added factors in Hong Kong, i.e. the travel, the heat and the pressure of upcoming competition—which means schooling for the test instead of just schooling—I don't feel it was a fair indication of how the a-fib is truly affecting him.

As we fly over the ocean, I write to my Quest contributors:

I feel that we've done everything we could to prove my innocence and if they choose to not clear my name, then I can live with it with no regrets. It simply is out of my further control and it's fine.

When we get to the FEI headquarters, we're guided to a conference room. I'd imagined the hearing would take place in a courtroom and I'd sit on the stand, but seven of us sit around a large table: the FEI attorney, three Tribunal members, Andrew, Jason and me. Everyone is congenial and I realize that for them, it's just another day at the office.

Andrew begins by explaining the person I am. He says, Mrs. King Dye has a reputation in and outside the international dressage community for her honesty, her adherence to fair play, her outstanding work ethic and commitment that the welfare of her horses always comes before personal ambition or gain.

He presents my character references and continues, The preface of the EADMC and, subsequently, the values the FEI officially endeavors to uphold include: ethics, fair play and honesty; health; excellence in performance; character and education; fun and joy; teamwork; dedication and commitment; respect for rules and law; respect for self and other participants; courage; community and solidarity; and the principle that doping is fundamentally contrary to the spirit of the sport. Ironically, all of the values and principles can be used to describe Mrs. King Dye and are present in her character.

He goes on to report the facts of the Olympics, Myth's a-fib and the subsequent proceedings. He says, Neither Mrs. King Dye, nor her veterinarians, Drs. Mitchell and Ober, knew what Felbinac was prior to the positive A test. Moreover, Felbinac is not approved by the U.S. Federal Drug Administration and therefore cannot be sold or obtained in the United States where Mrs. King Dye and Myth reside. In addition, there is ample proof that Myth was not suffering from any lameness in the months before or during the Olympic Games. Accordingly, Myth was not being treated with anti-inflammatories of any kind.

Rick calls in at an appointed time and describes the possibility of exposure to Felbinac in the vet clinic through the contact gel during his ultrasound or several EKGs. He says that my horse's welfare was unwaveringly my top priority and that I was prepared to forego competing in the Olympics for the welfare of my horse. He relates instances of our carefulness to avoid illegal substances in order to prove that we weren't negligent: he checked the ointment the groom was using on her sprained ankle and wouldn't allow us to use Surpass five weeks ahead of competition because he wasn't absolutely certain it would be completely out of his system in time. The chemist also calls in and recounts his findings which prove that the drug in no way helped Myth in the competition and appears to be contamination.

When I give my testimony, my prepared speech sits ignored on the table and I speak from the heart. I say I can't tell them where the drug came from because I don't know, I want to figure it out as much as they do. I would never purposely dope my horse, and Rick was incredibly careful so we weren't negligent. I'm innocent and I hope they can find a way to not punish me.

The Tribunal members wait to make sure I'm finished and I just look at each of them. I can think of nothing else to say. Andrew clears his throat and begins his closing statement: Within the time allowed by the accelerated proceedings in this case, Mrs. King Dye has made every possible effort to identify how the prohibited substance entered Myth's system. Although she cannot, we have provided indisputable evidence that the drug entered the horse's system through contamination. There is uncontested and corroborated proof that neither Mrs. King Dye, Myth's support team, nor the U.S. Team veterinarians intentionally or accidentally administered

Felbinac.

He goes on to say, Section 2.1 in the FEI Rulebook states that: It is not necessary that intent, fault, negligence or knowing use on the Person Responsible's part be demonstrated in order to establish an anti-doping or medication control violation. But section 2.1.3 states: As an exception to the general rule of Article 2.1, the Equine Prohibited List may establish special criteria, including but not limited to specific thresholds or extenuating circumstances, for the evaluation of Prohibited Substances that can be produced endogenously and/or be ingested from the environment or as a result of contamination. If such special criteria or circumstances apply, the detected presence of a Prohibited Substance in a Horse's Sample shall not automatically constitute a rule violation.

In this case, we have a horse who innocently tested positive for a banned medication in a trace concentration that resulted from environmental contamination and which was detected using sensitive analytical equipment. This should be found as an exception to Article 2.1.by 2.1.3 and should be applied to release Mrs. King Dye from liability.

Then the FEI lawyer gives his closing statement. He says, This case is simple. The FEI has a zero tolerance rule and the horse tested positive for a banned substance. The Person Responsible cannot prove that an outside source, without her knowledge, constituted exposure, therefore she should be found guilty.

In less than ten seconds, their case is summed up.

◆　◆　◆

On the flight home, I write to my Questers:

Although I cannot go into the details of the trial, I feel comfortable assuring you all that it seemed pretty clear that they all completely believed that I've done nothing wrong... didn't knowingly or negligently allow my horse to be given Felbinac. Even the FEI prosecutor gave me an apologetic look and shrug as we left the room as if to express he didn't believe it but he had to do his job. I think they have a real difficulty now... I truly don't think they want to punish an innocent person, but they have a challenge in finding a way not to do that around the zero tolerance rule. They said they would have a decision by September 19th at the latest. I must say, they were all nice. You know how you sometimes feel that people are doing things for some ulterior purpose, not for the true betterment of the sport or genuine ideals? And often you feel that with the higher authorities? I didn't feel that at all. I felt that everyone was genuinely listening to all of the arguments and wanted to do the right thing for the horses and the sport. So now it's time to wait. But as I said before, we did everything we could to give them the chance to see the situation for what it really was. There can be no regrets, and if my name is cleared, then we'll celebrate and be thrilled because right can be accomplished despite all the red tape to be cut through. And if my name is not cleared, well, then we've been on another great adventure, made a friend, and learned a lot along the way. Maybe we'll take it further, maybe we won't. But for those of you concerned that I'll lose my joy about the sport or become tainted by this experience, never fear. There's still good even at the top of this sport and that was great to see. It would take more than this for me to become jaded about this sport!

◆ 60 ◆

The week after I get home, I barely think about the drugging at all, although Jason pragmatically reminds me to do so from time to time. Instead, my focus turns to assessing the necessity of converting Myth. In order to do so, I try not to collect him too much to see if he can balance himself without my help. Take him for walks to the field over uneven terrain to see if I feel comfortable on a loose rein. When he's been home nearly three weeks, he feels no more stable. He's had ample time to at least begin to adjust if he's going to, and since he's no different than in Hong Kong, I'm confident that the added stresses didn't exacerbate the problem. Conversion is necessary.

On September 19th, the very day the Tribunal is supposed to deliver their decision, I take Myth to Cornell University Veterinary Hospital. When we arrive and are waiting to be shown to his stall, he noses the ground and drags me from place to place. He's curious to see what's in the trash cans and around the corner. When he's free in his stall, he hangs his whole body over the door to see what's going on and reaches his neck around to make friends with his alpaca neighbors. The way he acts reminds me of Idy: simply loving the adventure.

When he first came to me two and a half years ago, he was extremely introverted and to see the confidence he now exhibits makes my heart grow and my chest contract. He's still heartbreakingly sweet, but otherwise his personality's completely different.

When the initial ultrasound is done to make sure his heart structure is good, ten staffers and students stand behind him to view the screen. He cranes his neck around and looks at them with his big eyes and perky ears as if to say, *Why are you all back there when I am so obviously up here?* He wins all their hearts and afterwards, one often stops by his stall simply to pet his neck or kiss his nose.

◆ ◆ ◆

Courtney's Quest Journal
Being here with Mythy really puts it all into perspective...the ruling of that prohibited substance case seems so inconsequential while sitting here in the hospital with my horse. (Well, the Malones' horse of course, but you know what I mean...mine by love).

Before they begin prepping him, the cardiologist stands next to me as I gaze at Mythy nosing the shavings in search of something to eat. She says the wobbliness I describe has never been heard of as a symptom in a-fib in horses. It's normally a strictly human symptom in severe cases. I don't know what to say so I don't take my eyes off Myth and say nothing.

She waits and then tells me that owners aren't normally allowed to watch because it's a difficult sight to stomach. My head spins toward her, panicked. She looks at me, pauses and says, We'll make an exception for you, but if you become too upset we expect you to leave. She squeezes my arm and walks away.

The techs come and lead Myth into a large padded stall with a windowed wall which Jason and I stand behind with a dozen other viewers. They look at the cardiologist and when she gives a nod, Myth is given a shot. He wobbles and falls on his knees. Stays there swaying for a second, then collapses on his side. I expect his eyes to momentarily fly open in a panic, but they don't. His body simply slams into the ground.

I feel how people describe an out-of-body experience: my soul exits my body, escapes the impending implosion of this container of too much pain. Jason comes close behind me and puts his arms around my neck. Tears slide from my unblinking eyes but I don't react.

Pads are placed between his legs to prevent them from striking each other and several EKG leads that connect to a machine in front of us are attached to his chest. The cardiologist presses a button and Myth's body lurches. My body lurches. I knew what would happen. I *knew*. But seeing his body lie lifeless then be wracked with a million volts of electricity causing every muscle to suddenly tighten was unimaginable. I wasn't prepared. I couldn't be prepared.

I can feel the cardiologist's eyes on me. I don't look away from Mythy, attempt to smooth my features. My peripheral vision sees her look at the paper and shake her head. I wilt into Jason. My soul has returned to the misery of my body. Three more times, the excruciating process gets a shake of the head. It's become hard to breathe in the strength of Jason's grasp but I want him to squeeze harder.

They can shock him a maximum of seven times. On the fifth one, she pauses long enough for me to look at her before she shakes her head. After the sixth, the shake comes before I can pull my eyes away from Mythy. The seventh, she just looks at the paper. And keeps looking. Then she nods and turns around beaming, darts over, Jason releases his grip and she throws her arms around me. My trembling has turned to shaking and all the viewers cheer as if we won a war. Many faces are wet with tears.

Before Mythy gets up, I call Leslie and leave her a message. Tell her as I soak the phone, that I finally have good news. The process was like having a baby: painful ecstasy.

When Myth stands up, the first thing he does is try to eat a towel on the ground, then a paper.

• • •

As I lean my face between the bars of Myth's stall watching him enjoy a mound of hay, the cardiologist comes and listens to his heart. Perfect, she tells me. The relief I was feeling mingled with sadness over what this wonderful creature had to endure turns to joy, pure happiness. All anxiety leaves my body and pure contentment settles in. The difficulty is all behind us. He's a hundred percent healthy and we have a great future.

Jason comes down the aisle and puts his arms around me, joins me in gazing at my finally healthy horse. All good? he asks unsure of what to make of my wistful silence. I just turn and hug him, nestle into his chest and nod. After holding me a moment, he kisses my hair and says, Come with me. There's something you need to see.

We look out the window of the reception area and he points to a trailer in the parking lot. It's small and has an open top, out of which huge antlers are visible. They move a little bit as if munching hay so I tell Jason something must be lying down and snacking. Then another set of antlers of equal size appear. I squeak in surprise, look at Jason in excited consternation and he sweeps his arm as an invitation for me to go investigate. I dart out and peer into the trailer. They look like two dwarf moose—enormous antlers adorn short, squat creatures.

An elderly gentleman with denim overalls and a brownish-gray beard sidles up with a big grin, pops a peanut in his mouth and says, So what do you think?

What *are* they? I ask.

He stares at me in mock disbelief. Well, on December 25th you'd miss 'em, he says and laughs a soundless laugh. He sees my confusion and says, Reindeer, of course!

I stare at them in a whole new light. Mythical creatures versus mysterious livestock—although their manure remains unchanged.

I smile and point to the bigger one. Rudolph? I ask.

Course not, Rudolph has a red nose. That there's Blitzen. And he doesn't go anywhere without Dasher.

I ask him what his purpose for having them is but before he can answer, Jason calls me back in and says the cardiologist wants to speak to me. As I walk away though, he gives me a wink and I have a feeling his answer would have been, *To deliver the presents, of course!*

The cardiologist tells me Myth's care instructions, says to tack-walk him for a month and be careful not to get his blood pumping for a couple weeks after that. He was a staff favorite and everyone was thrilled it worked out. They hope to see him in the next Olympics. I smile in reply. The Olympics are the last thing on my mind.

As I sit by his stall waiting for him to recover, I check my emails. One is from the USEF. Apparently the Tribunal has delayed making their decision. Jason says that's a good sign, but I shrug, gaze at Mythy with puppy-dog-eyes and say, Who cares?

The next three days are spent in bliss on horseback for eight hours a day. I take Mythy on long walks to the field and rejoice in being able to do so on a loose rein. I also hack Idy because he's been uncharacteristically lazy. I have the vet check him and he's amazed at the perfection of his condition and soundness. When I voice my concerns about him getting old, the vet says, Well, he's going to get old, but not yet.

Although this eases my mind somewhat, the fact that he doesn't feel as inspired as he used to bothers me. Maybe his body doesn't feel old but he's just tired of the ring. He's entered in Devon but whether he goes is up to him. If he wants to show, he will, but if he wants to hack then he'll do that. He's far more than earned the right to decide.

♦ ♦ ♦

On September 22nd, the USEF emails me the Tribunal's verdict: I'm disqualified from the Olympic Games. I don't cry; I'm crushed but resigned. A fourteen page attachment accompanies it summarizing each part of the hearing and explaining the Tribunal's thoughts, though, and as I read, I get angrier and angrier. Toward the end, my anger turns to rage. The statement says:

The Tribunal finds the evidence of the Person Responsible and the U.S. Dressage Team Vet to be credible and believes that neither the Person Responsible nor anyone on her behalf or related to the USEF has knowingly administered the medication to the Horse. The Tribunal further accepts the Person Responsible's and USEF arguments that they have done almost everything in their power to ensure that no rule violation shall occur.

I gasp for air and don't bother with tissues. Then, a deep calm settles over me.

Courtney's Quest Journal

I was infuriated for about the first fifteen minutes after I heard the news. It was the first time I felt that way. I mean, they know I'm innocent... how can they punish me? But then I realized everyone handled everything correctly. I actually really appreciate the Tribunal's expression of their belief in my innocence; they didn't have to be forthcoming with that. They could have just said, "Drug in the blood, no explanation, here's the sentence." The thing is, their job is to uphold the rule, to the letter. What a hard position to be in. They know I'm innocent but they're bound to follow the rules prescribed to them. I feel that the wording of that rule needs to change. That's the good that I hope will come out of this circumstance. Perhaps this example, so clear, will be the catalyst to change that wording so that no one in the future finds themselves in this same situation.

✦ 61 ✦

I wake the next morning at peace. Unlike the triple pirouette, I can't be mad at myself, infuriated at my own stupidity. This wasn't my fault or anyone else's. There will be other Olympics. So I put it behind me and turn my focus to what I can control: Idy's future.

He's normally a very forward-thinking horse but his laziness and lack of interest have persisted, so I let him choose his own program. If he wants to do a bit of piaffe, we do that. If he wants to get out of the ring and go for a wander, that's what we do. If when we get to the field, he wants to show the world how fast he can go, we do. Although he's never naughty and the work he chooses to do is very good, I don't have the heart to force him to practice the movements of the test so I scratch him from Devon and decide that his show career is over. Idy has always been very clear about what he wants so I have no doubt.

To ease up on his workload and initiate the proper next phase of his life without losing him, I have my assistant Jennifer ride him as he would be perfect to educate her. But when she asks him to go forward, he stops and backs up, kicks out at her leg or simply pretzels his body around with his ears pinned.

Then Francine says she'll sell the talented six-year-old she recently purchased and put the money toward buying Idocus. But when she tries him, he does the same thing to her. When I get on intending to school him, he's perfect so I can't. They're both very good riders so he's clearly informing us of his offense at being made a school horse.

Chris decides to send him to DG Bar Ranch in California where a Young Rider will lease him and he'll breed. I beg her not to, tell her he's very naughty when other people ride him. My father even says he'll give me fifty thousand dollars towards buying him. Only the drugging has instigated such impotent rage; I *know* he'll be miserable without me. I'm responsible for his happiness and I can do nothing except tell the new trainer of his likes and dislikes.

I lead him onto the trailer and beg his forgiveness, tell him I'm so sorry, he relied on me and I failed. As the trailer pulls away, sadness at losing my soul mate is amplified by guilt of him losing me. The powerlessness to control his retirement makes me infinitely thankful to have complete control of Mythy's. He'll remain my baby and be preened and pampered until he's twenty-seven or forty-two.

Two weeks later, the Young Rider sends me a video of her riding him. He looks happy as a pig in shit. She's perfect for him: quiet, precise and clear. And he's perfect for her: he won't allow her to be otherwise. I had fully convinced myself that I alone could make him happy—after seeing the video I even briefly thought that perhaps his naughtiness was showing *me* that he's no school horse. Typical person overestimating her own value. I watch the video four times and each time my smile grows. Jason and I open our special bottle of hundred dollar Silver Oak wine to celebrate.

The celebration continues over the weekend as since I missed our Fourth of July get-together, all my siblings fly to Burlington, Vermont, and stay with Gray. We find a dog-friendly beach and repetitively throw a stick for Quivvy to swim after. Viva takes turns chasing and being chased by Gray's two Siamese cats. We go for sushi, spend an evening at the bowling alley and go dancing. Always followed by card games till four a.m. I leave exhausted but refreshed. Finally, life can get back to normal.

◆   ◆   ◆

Two months before I leave for Florida, I begin to ease Myth back into work. When I begin trotting, he doesn't feel a hundred percent sound and I assume his body is just wonky after all it's been through. But after a few days, I realize it's not improving and he simply isn't sound.

Since I've known him, he's had a thickening of scar tissue in his suspensory origin but it's never bothered him. He's never had more than three days in a row off, though, so the scar tissue always remained warm and flexible, but so many weeks of only walking due to his heart eliminated the gentle stretching that allowed it to be so.

Rick explains that the scar tissue became tight so when he started trotting again, the ligament was strained. It needs a month of rest but will be fine. When I ask why we should rest it when that's what made him lame, he explains that it's an acute injury and needs time to heal. We'll bring him back extra slowly.

◆   ◆   ◆

In the meantime, my future international horses occupy my focus. GR does his first show and gets 68% and 72% winning his two Prix St. Georges. Francine and I treat RV's Lyme disease with tetracycline instead of doxycycline and are hopeful that will remedy the ear thing, and her new horse, Willy, consistently gets low to mid 70's at Fourth Level. I make arrangements for Tomtom and Zygosch to join me in Florida, and although I'm disappointed that the lack of Idy and Myth will prevent me from redeeming myself at the 2009 World Cup, I head south with great anticipation for the future.

I share an apartment with Jen and Dave again and Betsy lives down the street with our Florida mom. Although a great deal has happened in the past year of my life—making the Olympics, being wrongfully convicted of illegal use of medications, Myth's heart and losing Idy—nothing changes with our happy Florida family. We fall back into our weekly routine of watching American Idol, sipping cosmos and munching on goat cheese and fig preserve crackers before the big Southern meal made by Deen, our Florida mom. Apart from being with my own siblings, being with them makes me feel the most like a part of the whole, a perfectly fitting piece of the puzzle.

One night, Betsy and I go to Nicole's for dinner. We fall into a fit of laughter over nothing as we often do, but when we recover she looks at me silently. Her seriousness takes me by surprise and I look from one of her eyes to the other. She takes my hand and says she knows I keep a positive attitude for the public but it must have been so hard for me. I squeeze her hand and assure her that I wrote my heart, that I've never bothered being upset by things I can't control. You can't choose the hand life deals you but you can choose how to play the cards. She says, Court, you make me want to be a better person.

Bets, *you* make *me* want to be a better person, I tell her and she rolls her eyes in response. Betsy, you do. You're so accepting of people's faults, patient and endearing. Sometimes I say what I think without considering that it may hurt people's feelings. I need to develop a filter and you're my role model.

I love you a gazillion, she says.

I love you ten gazillion, I reply.

We listen to the live musician in comfortable silence until he plays a Barry White song and we're overwhelmed with the urge to dance. Some friends join us on the tiny floor and in this moment, I feel fulfilled. The non-horse part of my life was greatly diminished in 2008 but I vow to prioritize it in 2009.

◆ ◆ ◆

Zygosch and Tomtom begin traveling over on January 5th and are required to spend three days in quarantine. After one day, I get a call from a quarantine worker and am told that Zygosch simply won't settle; he leaps around the stall, ignores his food and won't sleep. I ask if he can see other horses and she says yes. I ask if he can see Tomtom and she says no. I tell her I don't know the horse so don't know if it will make a difference, but my only suggestion is to let him see Tomtom.

The next day, I call to check on him and am told that he immediately ate and slept and is completely normal. Jennifer and I discuss the hopeful necessity of getting a miniature horse to live in his stall with him and take to shows. Or a potbellied pig.

When they arrive, getting to know their personalities makes them even more dear to me. Tomtom twists his neck as if he's trying to look at the sky with the down-turned eye when he's walking around on a loose rein, and Zygosch gives a whinny that sounds like it got cut short, as if he's surprised, every time a horse comes or goes. He has scars all over his head because apparently he didn't understand his height. While Tomtom has remained his 16.2, I hope Zy's finished growing at 18.2.

Their enthusiasm to work and learn makes me lament Wyoming's complaining even more. Even though he's talented at the movements, I feel I have to *make* him do everything which takes the joy out of the work for both of us.

Since he was three years old, he's shown that he loves to jump so I begin taking him to a jumper to ride each week. Seeing him galloping over the field with his ears perked and doing playful mini-bucks after the fences makes me know that jumping is his calling. Just as some people hate biology and some have a passion for it, and some people are baffled by how I can find joy out of going around in circles in a sand ring all day when to me it's the most life has to offer, Wyoming's heart is simply with jumping.

The trainer loves him and purposely lets Wy's lack of knowledge put him in precarious positions, but he never once considers refusing. As a green older jumper, he's worth substantially less than as a talented, well-trained dressage horse, but I sell him as a jumper as his happiness is worth the hundred thousand dollar difference.

With my unexpected income, I take everyone to dinner at the Players Club. Betsy, Jen and I decide to make an evening of it and wear fancy, slinky dresses and five-inch heels, which with my two left feet are a challenge to walk in and only look good when I'm sitting.

After dinner, we go upstairs to the dance club which we normally avoid and make fun of. As we do the white-man's-overbite and mock the melody-less rhythm, Betsy slips and grabs my arm, I grab Jen's and the three of us bite the dust. We lie on the beer-soaked floor unable to get up because of our laughter, and when we eventually recover, I need to remove my shoes to be able to stand. At two a.m., the bar closes and the three of us leave carrying our shoes, go home, open a bottle of Prosecco and pick shards of glass out of Betsy's feet.

◆ ◆ ◆

The next morning I walk into the barn a bit bleary-eyed but excited. It's the day Myth begins to trot. As we walk around for twenty minutes soaking up the early morning sun and listening to the cacophony of birds, I once again appreciate my winter circumstances. Every day, Betsy and I say, Another day in Paradise. I get to be in the Florida sun when it's too cold in Connecticut and in Connecticut when the Florida sun becomes too hot. My circumstances in general are pretty darn fortunate: I get to make a living doing what I love all day which Jason reminds me not everyone does.

As we walk by the arena mirror, I look at Myth's large belly and depleted topline and imagine him becoming Olympic-horse fit again. I pick up the trot hoping he's perfect but trying to be prepared for if he's not 100%. After five strides I haul him to a dead stop and stare down at his shoulders in disbelief. He's not only still lame, he's lam*er*. I take a couple shallow breaths and try again. Same thing. Still sitting on his back, I call the vet.

He ultrasounds the suspensory ligament and says it's completely healed. The lameness, he says, is in his stifle. So much time off is what caused it and the only way to make it better is to work him. It will either get better or worse but it's my only option. Take it slowly, but he needs to move.

◆ ◆ ◆

While I painfully ride a lame Mythy, the others horses' show season gets underway. GR consistently scores 68-70% in the Small Tour CDI's, Willy continues to win the majority of his Fourth Level classes and the rest of my horses bring home more blues and reds than any other color.

By February, I feel RV's ready to show. Unlike Wy, she loves dressage, loves to show, and she begins the test feeling solid, supple and powerful. But half way through, she has an ear attack. Francine and I agreed that I shouldn't compromise on the frame to see if I can ride her through it, so I don't. She does all the movements but they're riddled with leaping and head-shaking. She gets a 63%.

After that, we try a new technique: I school all the movements with a long, low neck and only pick her up for ten minutes at the end as we would need to at a show. After three and a half months of schooling like this every day, we not only avoid the ear thing but improve the connection and our hope returns.

I'm also confident that Myth will be back in the show ring as 98% of the time he's 100% so work is definitely making him better. Although I greatly look forward to this occurrence, I decide to spend the summer enjoying my non-horse life. Many of my horses are young and there's no point in taking them to shows just to show, and the older horses are all between levels: two are beyond Small Tour but not yet Grand Prix and Willy is beyond Fourth Level but not yet Prix St. Georges. The only show I do is the Small Tour Championships in the middle of June on GR where he repeats his consistent Florida scores and gets an overall fifth place with a 69 and 70%. Then he just needs to work on the Grand Prix.

◆ ◆ ◆

Over the Fourth of July, I join my siblings for our week-long get-together in Harbor Springs.

Because of all of our separate requirements—Gray wants to be on the water, Greta wants to be close to town, Gib wants it cheap and I want it pet-friendly—we end up with an atrocious house close to town with a lovely lawn that borders the water, I bring Quivvy and Viva and we pay very little.

We have to walk through a bedroom to get to the only bathroom which could pose a problem, but we figure we'll be outside all the time anyway so who cares.

Back row left to right: Gray, Gib, Jason,
Front row left to right: Gray's wife Karen, me, Greta, Gib's wife Barb, and Viva

But it rains and is freezing the whole week. We play games, go to a movie, play more games and finally resort to going shopping. I buy an electric fly swatter both because the flies are horrible in the house and it'll be entertaining. It looks like a tennis racquet and fries the fly on contact. I dare Gib to let me touch his tongue with it and know he will because when he was seven years old, he'd eat a live minnow if we dared him. When I visited him at college, he swiped a cockroach skittering across the seedy bar we were hanging out in and ate it unprovoked.

I inch the racquet ever so slowly toward his protruding tongue and he never wavers. When it makes contact, there's a spark and a loud snap, he lurches and says, That didn't hurt, but I can barely understand him because his words are so garbled. Hilarity consumes us and from there it becomes chaos. Somehow I end up with Gib's whitey-tighties over my pajama pants and Jason tries to pick me up with them. We have a double chin contest as much of my family sports one. Take pictures of each other smiling and compare the lack of lips we inherited from our father. When there's a break in the rain, we bundle up and barbeque, after which Gray and Gib take off

245

their shirts, push their bellies out as much as possible and have a contest for whose is bigger complete with measuring tape.

When the week is up, the sun comes out and Greta cries. I tell her next year will be divine, plus we'll find a better house. We put on our sunglasses and bikinis even though it's 64 degrees and spend our final hours shivering in the sun.

· 62 ·

The rest of the summer is spent taking full advantage of my newfound horseshow-less weekends. Jason and I spend the night at a casino hotel twice and go to Vegas for a long weekend. We spend whole days on the boat and join Betsy and her boyfriend to sample wines in Napa Valley. Go to Camp Dancing Bear, visit Greta in Chicago and Gray in Burlington.

As fall rolls around, Grandioso can reliably do eleven ones and his piaffe and passage are fantastic. Francine decides to send Willy to her trainer in Europe because it's much less expensive than Florida, but our technique with RV continues to find success and I'm confident she can finally be international. Myth isn't 100% yet, but he's consistently progressing with work.

One day, Jennifer comes in the indoor while I'm riding Tomtom and tells me Myth isn't feeling well. He's restless and isn't wolfing down his alfalfa which is strange. They'll take him for a walk and keep an eye on him. An hour later she comes back and tells me he's a little worse—keeps looking at his sides and hasn't pooped, which are clear signs of colic. I tell her to give him five ccs of Banamine to ease his discomfort, but an hour and a half later, his discomfort returns.

He's not bad enough to cause panic, but it's the end of the day and instead of having my staff check him every hour, I feel he needs to be constantly watched, so we take him to the vet clinic.

By the time I leave at 8:30 in the evening, he seems to be resting a bit more comfortably and I'm glad I took him to the clinic so I can rest easy and not worry; he's in good hands. When I get into bed, I go straight to sleep.

In the middle of the night, the phone rings. It's the vet. He tells me he's so sorry, they lost Myth. My heart stops. I don't believe it. Really don't believe it. He had an inoperable mass in his colon and they couldn't save him. What do I want to with the body? I'm silent. Cremate or bury? Silence. Courtney?

I don't know, I don't know, I don't know. I've never done this before, I don't know. Can I tell you in the morning?

Of course. I'm sorry, Courtney, we did everything we could.

I know.

I try to crawl inside Jason, suffocate the pain. Then I push him away; I deserve to be smothered by the pain. I thought I failed Idy, but this is my consummate failure. My dear friend and partner who relied on me, trusted me.

At 6:30, I call the owner of the farm in Millbrook, New York, where I moved my horses at the beginning of the summer and ask if I can bury Myth there. Absolutely.

I stand staring blankly out the window at the rain. How suitable. The earth lost a great soul and is weeping her loss. Jason stands behind me and wraps his arms around my neck. I turn and nestle into him, fold my arms between us and let him squeeze me.

I call Leslie, I call Rich. I want to wallow in my hole and grieve but the press needs to know. The world needs to know. I can't find enough words, can't find enough tissue. When my fingers finally compose something somewhat send-worthy, emails begin to flood in almost instantaneously and I'm comforted by the fact that I'm not alone. He touched many people's lives, was loved by many. He was closest to me but multitudes share his loss. The endless string of emails is a deserved tribute to Myth.

Many of the emails talk about Rainbow Bridge which Google tells me is a mystical place under the rainbow where animals who die wait for their people to join them. Although it's a nice story, it does nothing to ease my pain. I can't find comfort in the unreal.

When I get to the barn, my staff is as bleary-eyed as I am. We hug and cry and commiserate our astounding loss. Then his body arrives. It's shockingly lifeless. As they drag him into a hole in the earth, I keep expecting him to react, to wake up in a panic. I want to hold his head, feel its weight, tell him I love him. While they cover him up, we each settle into our own reverie, our own pain. Then he's gone, under a thousand pounds of earth. Gone.

We pull all the bouquets we each brought for his funeral apart and place the hundreds of flowers over his mound, say our goodbyes to our dear, beloved, kind, sweet, magical Mythilus. Stand hugging, offering what consolation we can to one another in our shared grief. Then I realize the rain had stopped for us for the first time all day.

His resting place couldn't be more beautiful, overlooking the gorgeous farm with horses playing in the field in front of it. He'll look on the field where I anticipated retiring him.

Then we go back to the barn and open a bottle of wine to toast to darling Mythy, end our day of grieving his death with celebrating his life. The rain has started again.

Courtney's Quest Journal

I find it extremely comforting to think of Myth free in a big field with long grass and a shining sun, looking down on us and wondering with his ever curious and innocent expression, why we're crying. I'm not religious but I cannot imagine a soul like Myth's not being rewarded in a simple and perfectly joyous way. It has to be.

As I drive home, a rainbow appears in front of me reaching from ground to ground. I've never seen a rainbow in Millbrook. Tears blur my vision as I swerve to a stop on the side of the road and convulsions wrack my body as I shout to the Mythy under the rainbow that I love him endlessly, am so sorry for all the pain he had to endure during his short life and if there's one thing I look forward to in death, it's seeing him again. The arc of the rainbow remains in front of me for nearly the whole drive.

When I get home, I order a tombstone:

Harmony's Mythilus The biggest heart, the kindest horse, loved by all.

Harmony's Mythilus, Credit: Sharon Packer

The fact that the world chose to show me the story of Rainbow Bridge isn't unreal provides some consolation. Perhaps Myth does get to frolic in the field I envisioned him living out his final decades in and is free from all the world's pain. This possibility doesn't ease the pain, but it ignites a dim candle in the tunnel that was pitch black.

Ten days after Mythy's last breath, Elias calls me on the horses' day off and says RV hurt herself. He was grazing a horse and could see her munching on grass in her postage-stamp sized paddock, she did a feel-good squeal and buck and he heard the fence crack. She's lame so the impact must have hurt her. I tell him to call the local vet and have him call me after he's seen her.

An hour later, the vet calls as I'm unloading the dishwasher. He says hello, how are you, bla, bla, bla, and then he tells me RV broke her leg. The snap Elias heard was her pastern, not the fence and she needs immediate surgery. I crouch to the floor and gently set down the plate I'm holding. The responsible trainer I'm supposed to be battles for control with the heart of a devastated little girl. I ask how long the recovery after surgery is. She'll be in the stall wearing a sling and can't move for six to twelve months. Can we ride her again? Probably not, we're aiming to get her sound enough to turn out. He's going to email the x-rays to Rick as the surgery is complicated and he wouldn't trust it to someone else. I listen silently but my chest feels like it's being squeezed like a wet washcloth.

I call Francine. It rings four times before she answers. She says, Oh no, oh no, oh no, oh no. Her normally strong voice is meek, vulnerable, makes me think of a drowning kitten. I tell her they'll do surgery.

The vigor in her voice returns and she almost shouts, No! I will not have her suffer! She moans in physical agony. Put her down, Courtney, put her down, she whimpers.

Are you sure?

Of course. I'll come right away and be there in an hour but do *not* wait for me.

The line goes dead but the phone stays to my ear, my eyes locked on the receiver. My instinct to keep her alive was selfish. It would save me the agony of losing her but it would prolong her torture. Mythy could have found simple joy while being slung in a stall for a year, but RV certainly could not. Francine's decision to put her down was a kind one I never would have been strong enough to make.

The vet arrives at the barn moments after I do. Munching on her hay in the stall, RV looks totally normal. Except she's holding up her leg. She looks over at me, ears perked, and then resumes eating. I'm struck by the thought, *today's the day she's going to die.*

The vet says we need to figure out where to put her down. When he sees my confusion bordering on irritation, he explains that we'll need to move the body. Logistics.

We don't want to make her walk so we can't take her outside. Her stall is at the end of an aisle close to the indoor so we consider asking her to hobble into the ring and have a tractor get her body there. Then Elias points out the possibility of doing it right in her stall. It's one of two stalls that has a door to the outside as well as to the aisle. The door leads to a small deck that's five feet above the ground, and the barn owner says we can arrange the cradle of the tractor below the deck so she can be pulled right in.

We put on her show halter and the vet tells me it's my job to aim her head so she falls down to the right. As I grasp her head, I realize that arranging all the logistics kept the responsible trainer in control and with their completion, the devastated little girl takes over. The vet enters with an enormous blue syringe and RV looks at it in relief. Syringes have always eased her pain. A memory flickers in my mind: when I was four years old, my hamster started seizing and Gib told me he'd take away all the pain, so I handed him Hammy in relief. He took him outside and lopped his head off with a shovel. I was horrified but Gib said, No more pain, and walked away.

No more pain, I tell RV.

The vet warns me that she may twitch when she goes down. He keeps talking but his words sound as if he's speaking through water, slow motion in an incomprehensible language. He stops as if waiting for a response and when I do nothing, he shifts her hind end so she has space to fall.

Then he gives her the shot. Her eyes go blank. She jerks, relaxes, falls. I collapse to my knees holding her head. It's heavy. Warm. Her eyes flash open. She struggles to lift her head. Kicks her legs. Is still. I curl over her head and she tremors, fighting for life. Then she's gone. I put my hand over her nostril. She's gone. I crumple over and stroke her cheek. No more pain, no more pain, no more pain. I feel a hand on my shoulder and a voice says, It's time to put her in the tractor.

I gently set her head on the shavings and stand looking at her. A man steps in front of me, puts his hands on my arms and says, You shouldn't watch. I look up at him, am about to protest, then nod and leave the stall. As I hear the chains being hooked around her legs and jerking her into the tractor, I hug myself and hum as if quieting a baby.

When all is quiet, my legs stumble down the aisle and sunlight blinds me as Francine and I grasp each other. She resumes her mantra of oh no, oh no, oh no. I know I'm supposed to comfort her but I have nothing. Two horses in ten days after thirty years of never losing one.

The tractor carries her up to a grave next to Myth's and we place her favorite treats in the hole with her—bananas, sugar, and horse cookies.

Francine also wants her best cooler buried with her and as I place it in, her legs are at awful angles, her head is twisted on her neck. My face crumples in agony and I can't breathe. Jennifer pulls me away from the hole and we try to squeeze each other's misery out. As the tractor begins to fill the hole, I look angrily at the driver and try to shout to him over the tractor's rumble that the dirt should be gently placed on her, not heartlessly dumped. The last thing I see is a hoof. Unlike Myth's quiet burial, gasps for air and unabashed groaning accompany RV's. We order a gravestone like Myth's:

RendezVous,
A true queen, loved so deeply.

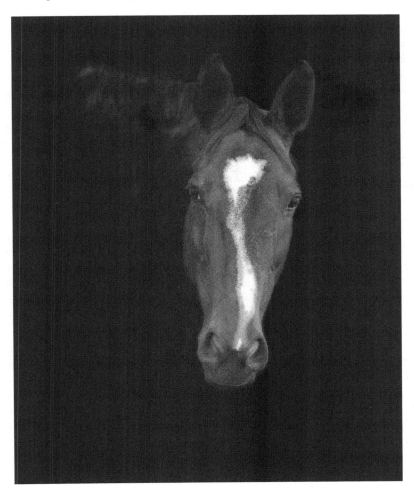

RendezVous, Credit: Sharon Packer

251

· 64 ·

I don't think I can go on. I can't. But Tomtom, Zygosch, Grandioso, my other horses need me. I have to. But I can't. But I have to.

I'm wilted. I need water. I need inspiration.

I ask Isabell, Klaus and Hubertus Schmidt—another German rider I've always tried to emulate—if I can come to their farms to watch for a day. Betsy says she'll go with me and eight days after RV dies, we begin a tour of inspiration.

We get off the plane in Amsterdam at 8 am and drive to Klaus's. As I sit in the corner and watch him train, I immediately regret taking this trip. Something I've always loved about Klaus are his relationships with his horses, and watching his closeness to them, his understanding, is like digging at my wound with a spoon. It's precisely what I lost.

I continue sitting there, not because I want to but because my limbs won't move. My eyes move blankly in their sockets following the motion, torturing me with the repetitive picture of my loss. After four horses, a tingle of life begins to course through my veins. After six, I begin to be inspired. I was sad for the relationships I lost, but I have other relationships to covet.

If my body were a thermometer and my inspiration level began at my toes, my visit to the Balkenhols brings it up to my waist. When we get to Hubertus's farm the next day, instead of the level going down before it goes up, the first horse initiates its rise. What I admire about Hubertus is that he doesn't ride the fanciest horses but he consistently does well because he rides whatever's under him superbly. After we watch this happen time and again for a whole day, my inspiration level is to my shoulders. Making any horse be the best they can be is the joy of dressage.

That evening, we drive two hours to Italia Uno, eat too much truffle Carpaccio, drink too much Limoncello and continue where we left off in our efforts to communicate with the owner.

The next morning, my excitement plus the Limoncello makes me feel sick. We're going to see my hero: Isabell.

As we approach the farm, a foal runs in front of our car and an old man pursues it carrying a lead rope. They disappear around a barn and we scramble out of the car to join the chase, but by the time we catch up, the old man has the lead rope around the foal's neck. He blows air, shrugs and grins at us. I explain why we're there and ask him where to go. He looks at me blankly and says, No English. Papa de Isabell. When I pointedly shrug and ask, Isabell? he points toward one of the barns.

We find her talking to someone as they look in a stall. When she sees us, she says, No Viva?

I tell her sorry, not this trip, thank her profusely for letting us come and comment on the amazing facility. She says it was originally her parents' farm and they still live in the house and work the land, but her sponsor did the upgrades. Then she takes us outside to see her Olympic retiree, Gigolo, fat and happy in a paddock. How Myth should have been.

She's not riding because she's pregnant, so instead of the benefit of watching her body move like in Hong Kong, we get to hear how she thinks.

The first horse, she explains, was bred to be a carriage horse but she liked him so she bought him. She keeps saying, Rounder, rounder! but despite the rider being very capable, the horse continues to have his head in the air like the carriage horse he was bred to be. After forty-five minutes of suppling exercises and trying to get his face on the vertical, she tells the rider to put him away. She looks at me, shrugs and says, Some days you win, some days you lose, and proceeds to the next horse. This strikes me. Not only is it heartening to know that a god like her faces the same struggles I do, she accepts that it's just a part of training and not her own failure.

The next horse is Warum Nicht, barn name Hannes, one of her two top competition horses. I recognize the girl on him as the groom at all the shows and assume that the rider will return and get on, but the groom keeps going. On a walk break I ask about it. Isabell confirms that the girl is normally her groom but she wanted to ride Hannes while Isabell was unable. I ask if she has riding experience and Isabell says not really, but she has a good feel. I'm floored that she'd let an inexperienced groom ride her top horse, but it appears the girl has learned a great deal from watching because she's quite good.

Then Hannes poops. To save the footing, the manure must be removed and Isabell, still teaching, gets up. I tell her I'll get it but she waves me off and walks toward the picker. I hurry to cut her off and take the picker from her hand. She looks at me, lets go and walks away still teaching. I look at the picker and frown. It's like a dustpan at the end of a pole into which you push the manure with a three-prong hoe-like contraption. Klaus had an identical one. It takes me four trips to the manure bin to get the whole pile.

We watch several more horses and are equally as awestruck. Her teaching and the way her horses are trained are impressive, but what inspires me is her attitude. She's of course excellent in competition, but I believe wholeheartedly that she'd ride the same out in the field with no competition in mind as she would preparing for the Olympic Games. She just does her thing. She rides talented horses because of course it's the most fun to make a great horse exceptional, but I get the feeling that if she couldn't have great horses, she'd get joy out of making mediocre horses good. My inspiration level becomes immeasurable.

In the airport on the way home, Betsy and I have champagne and caviar and toast to the success of our trip. I taste the caviar and tell her it's a good thing I find it disgusting because I could never afford it. She says it's unfortunate that she adores it. We almost miss the plane because we lose track of time sipping our champagne and recounting each moment of our journey, but as we fly over the ocean, dreams of my future dance through my head and I awake rested instead of being more exhausted from enduring the torture of nightmares.

When I get home, I send Isabell an American pitchfork with a wide base into which the pile can be scooped all at once so only one trip to the manure bin is required. The note says, Germany may have us beat on good cars and horses, but the U.S. has you beat on pitchforks!

• 65 •

The inspiration that the tour instigated is amplified by the Malones saying they'll buy me a new Grand Prix or coming Grand Prix horse. With this being added to my current international prospects, I go to Florida feeling that the hole of my terrible loss is sprouting flowers.

The more I get to know GR, the more we appreciate each other. He's smart and opinionated like Idy, but also like Idy, I feel he's working for *me*, because he wants to, not because that's what he's trained to do. And his attitude toward me has grown from seeing me as *that girl who rides me* into treating me like a best friend. He always nickers when he sees me, shows he's happy to see me, as Kim says, in a very stalliony kind of way. He's exceptionally talented at piaffe and passage, and as I suspected it may, understanding collection more and making *butt down* a normal way of going, increases the quality of his canter a great deal.

Zygosch's sensitivity, good mind and raw talent make him incredibly easy to train. As I always do with young horses long before they need to learn flying changes as a movement, I simply go across the diagonal and ask him to change leads. It doesn't matter if they change late, buck or take one stride of trot, simply that they learn that changing leads isn't bad. As we spend years teaching them to stay on the counter lead, they're often stressed out when we ask them to change leads and I find that this reduces their eventual anxiety. When I do this with Zy expecting him to flub his way through it, he does a perfect change as if he's been doing them all his life.

Although I'm giving him time to grow into his body, Tomtom begins his show career in January getting 72% at First Level. GR does Intermediare II which has piaffe, passage, and ones but less than in Grand Prix, and gets 65 and 66%.

At the next show two weeks later, Tomtom gets 73% and GR gets 67 and 68%. I apply with GR for the $25,000 Carol Lavell Advanced Dressage Prize, which is awarded to a combination they believe has international potential, and win.

Grandioso,, Credit: Susan J. Stickle

◆ ◆ ◆

I live with Jen and Dave again and although we fall back into our routine of having fun going out and staying in, Jen and I spend many evenings lamenting her dog's ill health. Lilly's seventeen years old and time is finally taking its toll. Jen says that when she has no more quality of life she's not going to force her to live, she'll help her to die. So when Lilly becomes incontinent and dementia prevents her from recognizing us all the time, Jen can put it off no longer. She calls me gasping for breath and says it's time. She spends the next hour feeding Lilly whatever human food she wants, endlessly scratching her belly and trying to make it the best hour of her life in whatever way she can. The vet, Betsy and I meet her at the house and sit in a circle around Lilly. Jen holding her head and Betsy and I holding Jen's arm and knee. The vet draws out a big blue syringe identical to the one that ended RV's life, lets Jen say her goodbyes, and injects it. I expect the tremors that RV had, but Lilly just exhales and is gone. Like she's saying thank you. RV's life was taken early; she was injured at twelve years old, we took her life and she fought for it. It was Lilly's time and she knew it.

Of course Jen is devastated. We're all sad to lose Lilly, but I'm relieved. It was so much less painful to watch than RV's. We'll be saddened by our loss, but we can know that she knew we were helping her. I try to console Jen with this information but, as expected, she's inconsolable and needs to be alone with her pain.

After giving her a long hug while Lilly's body is still in her lap, I sneak upstairs and make the only meal I can cook: penne with artichoke hearts, kalamata olives, pinenuts and lots of goat cheese. We sit around the table exchanging stories that begin as fond remembrances of Lilly but lead into funny anecdotes about our other dogs. The time Betsy's dog stole Quivvy's enormous bone from my room and proudly carried it upstairs clunking on every wooden step to show it off to the other dogs. Viva's swim technique and the joyous puppy-zooms Quivvy occasionally embarks on.

The next night, we experience lingerie night at our shady haunt, Boonies. The wait staff, many of whom are overweight and have an inconsistent array of teeth, wear lingerie over their clothes. Some patrons do as well and we agree that next time we'll join in.

On our way home, Jen breaks down again. I'm reminded of a question Francine asked me when one of her dogs died: *Why do we do it? We* know *they're going to die before we do and it's so painful.* I answered that the amount of joy they give us in life is much greater than the sorrow caused by losing them. Just as it did with Francine, thinking of her loss in this way eases Jen's pain, reminds her to think of what she gained from Lilly's life instead of what she lost by her death.

◆　◆　◆

Two weeks after Lilly dies, Betsy joins me on another horse-hunting trip to Germany. After several times to Europe to look for a horse for the Malones, I haven't found a suitable one but in the middle of February, I finally do. She's an eight-year-old Dutch Warmblood, not the fanciest mover but like Steffen says about Ravel, she has no holes. What sets my heart on her is that, although not so strong in the contact as Myth, when you pull she slows down but her legs remain quick. I can tell the trainer's been zoning in on the passage because she does it all the time: if I want to half-pass, she passages. If I ask her to walk, she passages. Also like Myth, she's quick to do what she thinks you want.

Greta visits the weekend after I get home from finding her and as we sit in the sun on the deck imagining a pool, I tell her that Leslie will come on Tuesday and watch the video of the horse I hope to get her approval to buy. And GR is doing his first Grand Prix and being awarded the Carol Lavell Prize at the Derby next weekend. She says it's good to see me excited again. It was a tough year, Court, but you're a tough girl. Here's to a better 2010, and we toast to that.

We go shopping and spend ridiculous amounts of money. Rent a cabana on the beach in Delray. Have dinner with our dad at Charlie's Crab. On Sunday, her grade-school friend joins us for a glass of Sav Blanc by the pool and tells us about an animal-rescue program she's involved in.

· **66** ·

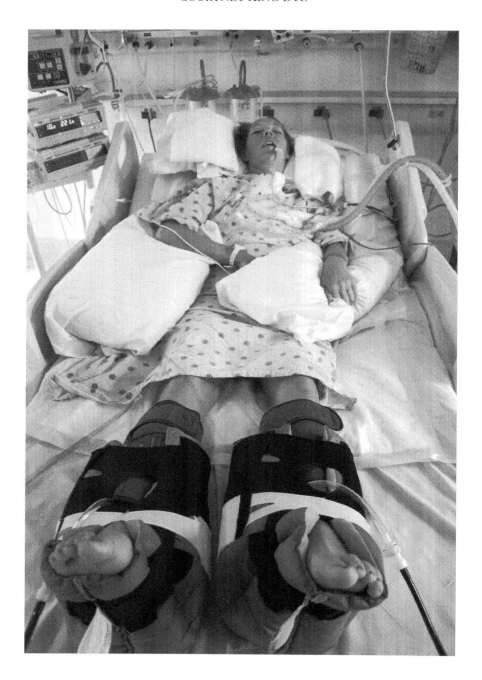

◆ 67 ◆

Myth is lying on the ground dead and I'm embracing him, soaking his neck with tears. My Grammy's voice says, Did you vaccinate him?

I say into his neck, Yes!

For what? she asks.

For blue amoebas! I say with an of course intonation.

Well, you should vaccinate for pink *amoebas.*

My head jerks up. I take a foot long, metal syringe and plunge it into his neck. He leaps up and gallops off, bucking happily.

I'm in the cabin of a fishing boat. The worn benches are pale blue and so are the walls. An old man who I know is Jason's Grandpa (though he's dead and I've never met him) stands looking out at the dark and stormy sea. My Grammy says, You must not go to him. He's going to die. Don't try to stop it.

He's my son! I shout in agony.

You can't change fate, she says.

Tell me how it happens, I beg.

He's fishing on the other side of the world. The weather is fine. Their boat is captured and boarded. He jumps and drowns.

I'm in Japan, wearing a kimono. I'm adopted. They tell me I have an arranged marriage. I tell them I can't. I don't know why, but I can't. Grammy's voice says in my ear to play along and go to my room. She and Jason's Grandpa are waiting there and have my western clothes. I scrub off the white makeup, pull off the black wig and climb through the window.

I'm in Spain and am asked to lead the Spanish cavalry because I had success with an Andalusian which is a Spanish horse. I don't want to, but they want to force me. I've learned the benefit of playing along from my experience in Japan so I do and then sneak into a room with a tinged glass door. A large table occupies the room full of models of buildings, mountains, horses cloaked in armor. Like a blueprint of their plans. Grammy and Jason's Grandpa are there and usher me to another smaller room. Then another. And another. The rooms get smaller and smaller until they disappear.

• 68 •

A voice says, You're at the Kessler Institute for Rehabilitation in West Orange, New Jersey. It's April 5th, 2010.

◆ ◆ ◆

A dark haired, freckled, woman's face leans close to me and says, Say Laura when they ask who you want your therapist to be. L-A-U-R-A, *LAURA*. Her voice travels around the room, doing things. She tells me how she was in the Olympic trials for bobsledding. I want to stay awake because I'm interested but I can't.

◆ ◆ ◆

A reddish-haired man with a goatee leans over my bed and says, Say *ahhhhhh*. Say *ahhhhh*. He's funny looking. I open my mouth to say ah, but nothing comes out. He says, Stick out your tongue. I do and he's happy.

◆ ◆ ◆

It's the middle of the night. I stare at Jason, asleep on the pullout chair. Eventually he looks at me. I try to motion for him to come over with my left index finger but my hand doesn't listen to me and just lurches spastically. Jason gingerly crawls in bed with me and falls asleep.

◆ ◆ ◆

A woman says, You're at the Kessler Institute for Rehabilitation in West Orange, New Jersey. It's April 9th, 2010.

◆ ◆ ◆

My siblings surround my bed and Greta holds a board with letters on it. They say they know I have thoughts and maybe since I can't say them, I can spell them. Gray says, What's my name? I spell it and they're overjoyed.

◆ ◆ ◆

The stuffed dachshund Pam brought me as a Viva replacement lies on my chest. Jason holds up the spelling board and asks what I want to name it. I contemplate the dog. Something like Viva but a boy. I smile and point to V, rest. I, rest. J, rest. O, rest. K. Vijok. Jason looks at me dubiously and asks me to spell it again. I do and my body shakes in soundless laughter. He gazes at me and his forehead gathers. He asks me to spell it once again and I do accompanied by the laugh. He asks if I want to name the dog Vijok several times. I find it hilarious that he doesn't believe me so each time my body shakes more. His face looks concerned and he asks me to point out the year of my birth. I do. Our wedding year. The current. I'm pleasantly surprised by how pleased he is.

◆ ◆ ◆

I stare at the huge poster of me giving the two thumbs up on Myth. I miss him. When Jason comes in, I point to the board indicating that I want to say something and he holds it over me. How is Myth? He's silent. I wait. Ask again. He looks down, Myth is dead, honey, he says and gives me an awkward hug. How? He gets tears in his eyes as he replays the occurrence for me.

I only remember Myth happy in a field.

◆ ◆ ◆

I ask Jason what happened to me. A horse tripped and fell while you were riding him in Florida, honey. You got a traumatic brain injury and were in a coma for a month.

I've seen the leaves beginning to sprout out the window so I know we're up north. And they tell me every day we're in New Jersey. Jason explains that I was in intensive care in Florida, but after three and a half weeks they flew me to Kessler because not only is it a top rated hospital, it's close to Jason's work.

I think he's mistaken. I clearly remember driving to Millbrook that day.

◆ ◆ ◆

A woman walks in and says, You're at the Kessler Institute for Rehabilitation in West Orange, New Jersey. It's April 19th, 2010. She takes my blood pressure, temperature, heart rate, feeds me several pills. Hangs a bag of brown liquid over my head and attaches it to a tube protruding from my stomach. When she makes to leave, Jason says, Say thank you, honey. The skin on my forehead gathers and I say something resembling thank you. She bustles back to my bedside, strokes my cheek and says, You're welcome, baby. You get better now, you hear?

By the end of the day, I'm trying to say thank you for all your hard work, and within a week, after the nurse takes my vitals and feeds me my pills she asks where we are, what town we're in and what the date is instead of telling me. I become aware that the right side of my body doesn't work properly and begin to know my schedule: occupational therapy in which they focus on my arms and upper body, physical therapy in which they focus on my legs, rest, speech, then occupational and physical therapies again. And then my family orders dinner and eats in my room. They asked if I want them to go out to eat because they're concerned that I miss eating, but I don't. I want their company.

Large portions of my days are also absorbed in gazing at my walls. Every inch of every one is covered with photos, posters of my best rides and banners that say things like, We love you, Court. A collection of eight by tens of me, my siblings and our pets doing funny things attracts most of my attention. One day, Gray comes in as I'm focusing on a photo of me holding a cosmo to my cheek and winking. I tell him that I want to be that girl. You *are* that girl, Court. You just can't do that yet. I smile and repeat, Yet. Adopting this frame of mind amplifies my natural instinct to work hard. Instead of just waiting for my body to heal, I'm in control, I *am* that girl.

That week when Betsy comes to watch American Idol with me, I proudly tell her I can't drink cosmos *yet*. As she scrunches on a chair and we stare up at the tiny monitor that hangs above my bed, I realize she lives in Florida and we're in New Jersey. She tells me she flies up every week because we always watch AI together of course. Jason crawls in bed with me and we discuss who we like: Crystal? Lee? Casey?

Everything else in my life is new and strange, but this feels normal.

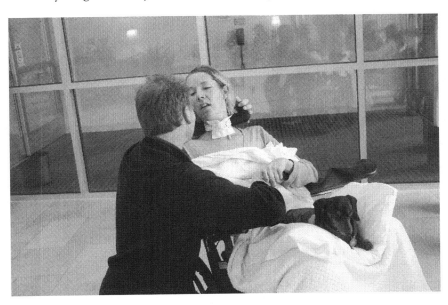

Jason, me and Viva

265

· 69 ·

One afternoon as I gaze at the banners and photos on the wall, my mom asks if I saw Grammy in my coma dreams. I nod and say she was with me the whole time. Her eyes widen. I clarify, Not her body, but she was guiding me through all my dreams. It was preternatural.

Greta says, You mean supernatural?

No, preternatural.

She gets the spelling board because she thinks she can't understand my speech and I spell it: P-R-E-T-E-R-N-A-T-U-R-A-L.

That's not a word.

I nod emphatically and begin to laugh.

She gets out her iPhone, Googles it and when she finds that it is, she asks why I choose to use such big words all the time. I tell her I want to show people I'm not stupid. I'm aware of how impressed people have been when I do tasks I think are simple, like picking the requested sibling out of a photo, sticking my tongue out or saying where we are. I think that if I use big words, they'll know I'm not stupid. I tell her, I want people to know that my brain may be fucked-up, but my mind is fine.

She says, Court, you've always had a fucked-up mind.

Yeah, but it's unchanged. Just this stupid Righty needs to get with the program, I say and give my right arm a swat. She says I need to be nice to Righty, strokes him and says to treat him like one of my horses: Good Righty, You can do it, Righty. I join in the stroking and say that perhaps we can cajole him into behaving if not submitting.

· · ·

The next morning when my neurologist, Dr. Fellus, does my exam, he asks me to squeeze and release his finger with my right hand. I obediently squeeze but can't let go. I say, That's good, Righty, just a little more, Righty. His eyes go from me to Jason and back wondering if I'm suffering from delusions.

I further confuse him when my fingers eventually unclench by asking him why he always wears a bow tie. I often hear my therapists laughing about it and, more than being curious, I think they'll find the fact that I ask him when he's unconvinced that I even know who he is, very amusing. I need to repeat the question three times before he understands and then he gives a very scientific answer: a tie could drag in things when he leans over which, on top of being an unnecessary risk, is unsanitary.

When he finishes his explanation I make a very serious face as if to say *ah, that makes sense*, and then burst out laughing.

He gazes at me and asks Jason if my giggling gets in the way of my therapy. Jason says yes, it often prevents me from continuing an exercise.

Dr. Fellus tells him he wants to put me on a medication to prevent this because my giggling may be an effect of the brain injury.

I want to explain that I just find it funny when I tell my body to do something and it does something completely different and then the laughter makes my body act even worse which I find more hilarious. It's a terrible and debilitating cycle. But I can't explain so instead I giggle.

Although disturbed by my giggle fit, Jason is skeptical of the need for medication so they agree to keep an eye on it.

As Dr. Fellus proceeds with his exam, my mood turns serious and I'm silent, lost in my thoughts. When he finishes, I make a noise to prevent him from leaving. He pauses and when I do nothing, makes to leave again. I say um and he waits. After a moment, my eyes raise to his. Will I be able to ride again? He sits down next to my bed. Well, that's up to you, he says. All four lobes of your brain were injured. You can ride again, but if you hit your head, it won't be two times as hard to come back, but five times.

My eyes drop down again. That gives me my answer. Recovery isn't easy now and five times harder? I won't ride again. I got an education *in case something happened* and something has.

Without knowing how his words impacted my life—eliminated the force which has driven me since I left the womb—he goes out the door. Jason sits on my bed and takes my hand. My eyes connect with his and then peruse the photos of my family. Pets. Jen. Betsy. There are so many non-horse parts of my life. I have a degree in literature and like to write. I also like to travel so maybe I could be a hotel critic.

I ponder the many possibilities for an hour before Jason wheels me to therapy but come to no conclusions. My session begins with the treadmill and I practice walking at a tenth of a mile per hour. A harness supports my weight, Laura lifts my right foot forward, Kara helps my left and Rich holds my hips. They continually give me guidance, but as hard as I will my body to follow their commands, it won't.

Always before, if I worked hard enough, if I *thought* hard enough, I could improve, but I've been on the treadmill several times and have gotten no better. My face contorts, my mouth gapes open, forehead crumples and I collapse in the harness in tearless misery. I feel frustrated, I feel defeated. My therapists are accustomed to my amusement at my body's refusal to obey so they're shocked, but no amount of talking, encouragement or offering support can pull me out of the shroud I've crawled into.

That evening, Jason's mom sits by me as I scrutinize the photos on the wall. Gib sticking his belly out. Us posing in our ridiculous Snuggies (which are wearable blankets). Viva and Quivvy posing for the camera sitting side by side to show their drastic size difference. The final passage in front of American flags in Myth's 75% ride. Me staring up at Idy's head. Posing with my arm around GR. She asks how I am. I say, I'm sorry. I'm sad. She takes my hand and says, Don't apologize. It's normal to be sad. Then we fall back into comfortable silence and I return to searching for comfort in my photos.

Over the night, I become tired of being sad. I've tried and failed to think of something else I'd want to do. I want to ride. I'm left no choice; I'll strap on a helmet and take my chances. I return to therapy with renewed vigor. I just need to work *harder*. My therapists are relieved at my return to normalcy and happily welcome back my game face—what they call the ultra focused expression that I refer to as my default face and which got me the reputation of bitch when I rode.

◆ ◆ ◆

Soon after my day of depression, Greta asks if I want to read the emails that were sent to me after my accident. An influx of well-wishings flooded my inbox right away and DP, who'd flown from New Zealand to be with Jason the moment they knew I was in a coma, printed them all out and filled three enormous three-ring binders. There are also two three-foot by two-foot Tupperwares full of cards.

Some are from people I knew long ago and many are from people I've never met, from countries as far away as South Africa, Japan and Brazil. Many people who were in Wellington at the time talk about the incredible feeling that permeated the entire Derby. How Lendon accepted my Carol Lavell Prize and the crowd was full of tears. How everyone wore a green ribbon—the symbol for brain injury—and many people wore helmets when they weren't required to. Bracelets reading Come Back Court were widely dispersed.

As I begin making my way through the emails, I realize it's not only the horses I don't want to give up, it's the equestrian community. Then I look at my current emails and I'm still receiving at least five a day. Knowing that so many people out there care is like a warm blanket on a cold night.

When Jason sees my incredulity and how touched I am, he says he's been keeping the public aware of my progress on my website but has always limited the amount of detail he goes into to respect my privacy. Do I want to say anything? I tell him to tell everyone I said hello and be open in explaining how I'm doing.

Thinking about everyone's reaction to my being in a coma makes me curious about that time. Jason tells me that my family members each dropped everything and were with me the next day. They rented a house near the hospital and took turns staying. He set up shifts amongst everyone, including Lendon, to make sure someone was with me twenty-four hours a day. Although many people wanted to see me, he had to be very strict in limiting visitors to close friends and family because my rest was his priority, so in addition to my Florida family and staff, he only allowed Francine, Kim and Steffen to visit.

I'm extremely touched and amazed to learn that the closest people to me continue to watch over my responsibilities as well as my happiness. Lendon oversees my riders and horses, Betsy still comes every week and Greta continues to fly in every weekend. So many people coming together, ensuring that every facet of my life is covered. In my horrible circumstances, I couldn't possibly be luckier.

I also become poignantly aware of my good fortune in siblings. Everyone tells me how incredible Jason was in overseeing my welfare with a fine tooth comb and my friends have been amazing, but I chose them, I *know* they're amazing. I had no say in selecting my siblings and they're each perfect in their own way.

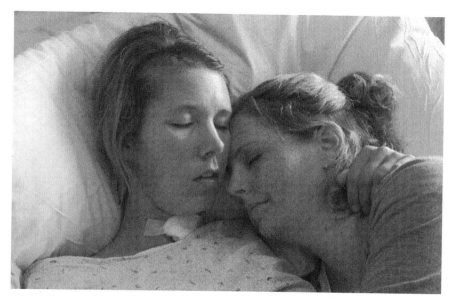

Me and Greta

• 70 •

My siblings take turns coming to Kessler so that someone is always at the hospital, both to be with me and to lend a hand to Jason who still needs to work.

We keep a small apartment at the Marriott Residence Inn for them, our parents—who also make frequent trips—and our dogs. When the weather is nice, someone pushes my wheelchair to a grassy spot bordering the parking lot where Quivvy can have his puppy zooms and Viva can have her sun baths. I often lament to Jason that they don't recognize me but he insists they do.

To prove it, he shows me a video of Viva visiting me in ICU. He says the girls would wash her at the barn, Betsy would bring her to the hospital and one of the nurses would let him sneak her in in a backpack. I watch her nestle close to my body, very calmly with the noises of all the machines attached to me, wag her tail and scratch at me trying to get my attention. Jason puts her next to my left hand which gently explores her body. He says that when I pet her, my hand was the most delicate it ever was. Then he walks around and touches her to my right hand, which doesn't move. My left hand simply reaches over my body and searches for her. Although I know it's sad, it's kind of funny to watch.

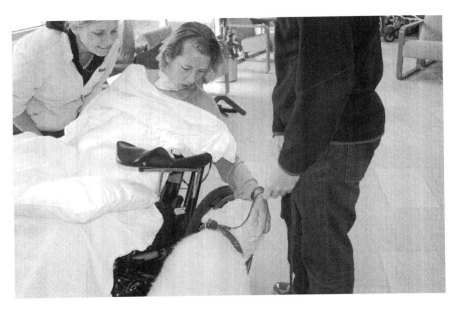

Greta, me, Quiver and Jason

I want to watch the video again but my dad says we need to go to my swallow test to see if the stomach tube can be removed. Although I don't wish I could eat, it hurts and I want it out. I failed the previous time so nerves settle in my gut as if I'm taking a final exam in school.

As we stand in line, I ask to see the folder he's carrying of my medical records which he was instructed to give to the swallow test monitor. On the cover is a photo of me from the first day I arrived: my mouth hangs open, my hair is dirty and tubes hang out of my nose. I chuckle and say I'm surprised Jason still loves me because I was so ugly. He belly laughs and says, Well you *were* a whole lot uglier than that.

When we go in, they put a metal apron on me and x-ray my throat as I swallow things of decreasing thickness as the thinner the substance, the greater the risk of choking. They begin with crackers. Then applesauce. Pudding. Ensure. And finally water. Everything goes down smoothly until the water. I'm fearful this means another failure, but the stomach tube is removed and a thickener, which is rather gross, is simply added to my drinks.

My speech therapist begins to watch me eat dry turkey sandwiches for lunch every day and after a few times successfully doing that, I'm allowed to eat normal well-chopped food. Jason asks what the first meal I want is and without hesitating, I tell him steak. So he buys a food grinder and chops a filet mignon. When I graduate to unchopped food and can finally eat with my family, I'm surprised at how emotionally satisfying it is. Combined with the recent removal of the trach from my windpipe because I can breathe on my own, I feel much less like a patient.

A week after my stomach tube is removed, Lefty's able to muddle his way through my first entry on my website:

May 13
Hello everyone!
Thank you for your cards, goodies, flowers, and emails! I'm sorry I can't respond to them all, but please know I'm getting and appreciating all of them.
I'm awake and tube free now! For those of you worried that I'm becoming depressed, do not concern yourselves; I had to take a test on if the reason I giggled so much was a disorder! It's hard for me not to giggle when I'm struggling to do something that was once easy for me like walking, talking, or eating!
It's difficult not to be sad when I think of how much it sucks what happened to me, how much I'm missing out on etc., but I've become aware that I'm not only lucky to be alive, but to have all my memories (except the final few days) and senses intact.
I'm very lucky to have the constant support of family (including husband- thank you, thank you, thank you!) friends, and dressage enthusiasts.
Much love and appreciation to all.
Ckd

• • •

A few days later, my feeling of being a patient is further diminished by my therapists approving my first day trip away from Kessler. Gray accompanies me to therapy to learn how to safely transfer me in and out of an artificial car, but we run into an issue once we get into the real car: my wheelchair is designed to prevent my head from flopping around and the car is not. We learned how to transfer but not how to be transferred. To remedy this, they finagle a pillow to support my neck and Jason holds his hand to my forehead to eliminate the forward/back.

My mom, siblings, Jason and I go to a bowling alley and I'm given a contraption to allow me to play: I set the ball on the top of an arch and when I push it, it travels down the lane and hits the pins. Gib wheels me out, Jason aims the contraption, puts the ball on it, and I push. This technique allows me to begin with a strike followed by a spare.

Gib's thumb, which we call an 'um because it's half a thumb—a third the normal length and twice the normal width—won't fit in the hole, so he puts his two fingers in their holes and balances the ball against his forearm. Greta, who took a bowling class in college, gives humorous coaching to Gray: Swing your hips, stick out your butt, close one eye.

As I watch their interactions a thought strikes me: my mom named her art shop Quarters because that's what we are. If one of us were missing, we wouldn't make a whole. I can't imagine not having a Gray, a Greta, not having a Gib. It must have been incredibly hard to face the possibility of having no Courtney.

We're extremely different but we share the important things: values, ethics. A sense of humor. Although perhaps we wouldn't agree with my parents' individual parenting techniques, the combination of them was perfect. Together they made four (or at least three) wonderful children.

We go to a park for a picnic lunch afterward and spend a glorious afternoon in the mild spring weather. As they situate the food on a picnic table, I say, Is everyone OK? but no one hears me. Although I'm able to form words now, my lungs remain too weak to project them, to give them volume. I try again and the force with which I try to yell pushes my head off its support and it falls toward my chest.

Greta rushes over to re-place it and as she wipes off the drool that escaped she says, Yes, Court, why? clearly touched. Everyone else has gathered around and I say, 'Cause I just kicked all your butts! and laughter makes my head roll off its support again.

Gib says he guesses they know the real Court is back, and that's how it feels. Two and a half months ago I was motionless in bed. Six weeks ago I couldn't breathe and a month ago I wasn't able to speak. Ten days ago, I couldn't eat.

Dr. Fellus explained a brain injury this way: the path of communication hits a road block and instead of waiting for the traffic to clear, the brain finds another route. My brain is clever and is finding another route very rapidly, so it won't be long before I'll be able to walk and speak normally again. Debbie visits me at the hospital and I tell her that although I may not be able to do the 2010 World Equestrian Games, I'll try for the 2011 Pan American Games and I'll definitely be ready for the 2012 Olympics.

◆ ◆ ◆

I begin to take regular trips to the hotel to hang out with everyone. Gray gets me a children's card-holder since I can't hold a hand and we play card games, board games and watch movies. Like we always have.

Another great thing about being able to go to the hotel is getting to watch American Idol on a normal size TV, and when the finale's on, we plan to meet Betsy there. Jason pushes my wheelchair to room 229 but after going to our room nearly every day, I'm quite certain we're in 221. When I point this out, he reminds me I'm brain damaged and unlocks the door.

As it begins to open, I see a blonde dart by and Betsy's brunette so I tell him we're definitely at the wrong room, but he doesn't pause. When we get inside, my whole American Idol crew jumps out and says surprise. I'm flabbergasted. They flew in from three different states to be with me. Deen pulls out her famous mac 'n cheese, Betsy presents our traditional snack of fig preserves and goat cheese and Jen hands me a mock cosmo since I can't drink alcohol.

As we sit down to watch, pure contentment overcomes my excitement. Like my real family, the extent they go to to add some normalcy to my life is astounding. If I close my eyes and just listen to them banter, I can almost forget where we are because a fortunate thing about my injury is that there's no pain. If I don't move and don't speak, I feel absolutely normal. When I open my eyes, Betsy's looking at me. It doesn't matter where we are; *this* feels normal.

◆ ◆ ◆

Everyone flies out the next day and my focus returns to my own scheming. While Jason's been busy planning my surprise American Idol night, I've been planning a surprise party for his fortieth birthday. He's left his family and all his close friends. *For me.* And I'm determined to make it as special as he deserves.

His parents have come to the U.S. to celebrate and I plan to cloak the party in a lunch date with them at our house which is two hours away. Cath will do all the cooking and decorating but I'm dependent on my siblings and the hospital staff for help with the rest.

I want a poker theme and have Greta order shirts for all the guests that say *Roll the Dyes* on the back over two dice. On the front is a photo of Jason from his modeling days doing his make love to the camera look, and Gray has playing cards made of pictures of him in several poses, shirtless and in surfer shorts.

There's normally an eight o'clock curfew at the hospital for live-in patients, but Dr. Fellus says that although I can't stay away overnight, I can ignore it. I can't send the invitations because Jason regularly looks at my BlackBerry to keep track of my business and sees all my emails, so my occupational therapist tells him I need to bring my phone to therapy as pushing keys is an exercise in finger dexterity, I give her the contact info of people to invite and she emails them from her account.

The day before his birthday, I point at the ceiling and say in my slurred speech, I wish I could do something special for your fortieth, honey, but I'm in here.

The plan is to meet his parents for lunch at our house at noon so the guests are due to arrive at eleven thirty. That means we shouldn't leave until ten o'clock but Jason wakes up at six thirty and wants to get on the road. By the time we have breakfast at eight, we're dressed and he's antsy. I need to figure out a way to postpone.

When the nurse comes in with my pills and to take my vitals, she says my blood pressure's high. It's normally very low, so she takes it two more times and then says there's something wrong with the machine so she has to do it manually. When she heads out the door after finally getting it on the fourth try, she winks at me and Jason says, I could have done that better myself and I'm not a nurse!

That postponed us a half hour, but it's still too early to leave. I have a problem with constipation and I happen to have to try to go four times that morning, but at nine fifteen Jason's impatient and I've run out of tactics to delay our departure. Once we get on the road, I beg him to stop at Panera for a lemonade. He says it's out of the way but I bat my eyelashes, say please honey, and he relents.

As we get close to the house, we're on time but Jason's dying to pee. The plan to get me in the house is that Jason will drive to the front door and help me inside while Jason's dad gets the wheelchair. Then Jason will push me down the hall and when we go around the corner, everyone will scream surprise. But the bathroom is at the end of the hall so if he leaps out and runs to the bathroom, he'll catch the guests off-guard.

To my relief he runs to the woods bordering our house and pees on a bush as I watch the guests peering at him through the window and laughing. Then we drive to the front door and unload me as planned.

When the guests scream surprise, Jason says, You bastards, to many slaps on the back from his poker buddies and jokes about his age. Everyone plays yard games and humors me by letting Lefty have a go who, though my good hand, only works at about seventy-five percent. DP, Buttcheeks and Jason's siblings call on Skype and partake in the Jason Jeopardy game his sister created.

Greta tells me that after seeing Jason completely absorbed in my welfare for the past three months, it's so good to see him enjoying himself. Finally I could do something for him when he does so incredibly much for me.

· 71 ·

I began pleading for release from inpatient status as soon as I was allowed out in the world but Jason's party, which was June 5th, makes me want it even more. I see no reason to return to the hospital to sleep. Occasionally a chatty nurse visits me as I lie awake in the wee hours—which aggravates Jason greatly—but I've never needed one.

But when Dr. Fellus sets a release date of June 25th I'm not so sure. Maybe I've never *needed* a nurse, but it's a comfort to know they're there if I do, and when I'm in the hospital Jason can leave me any time he has to. His office has been wonderful about allowing him freedom and much of his work is done remotely, but he does need to visit clients. Plus if I go, will my recovery suffer?

Dr. Fellus assures me it won't as I'll continue to do outpatient therapy five days a week. I'll simply do one longer session of each therapy instead of two shorter ones. Jason says he's already spoken to my working student at the barn, Koryn, and she'll help us when we need her. He wants to sleep in a real bed, have a real kitchen, not have a curfew and a wake-up time if we don't need them.

So he moves our belongings to our little apartment at the Marriott, but the first night I spend out of the hospital is at Camp Dancing Bear. Gray brings non-alcoholic champagne and we spend the first night absorbing the warmth of the fire and each other's companionship. Even though we've spent many evenings together, the whole atmosphere is different. Everyone's a little more comfortable, a little less focused on me, my state of being and state of mind. I watch them play pool and try to sing on the Karaoke machine—we all have atrocious voices so it's quite amusing. I try too which makes it even more amusing.

The next day is sunny and warm so we traverse down the seventy-eight stairs to the water. Jason holds my left arm, Gib holds my right hand and Kezza holds the wheelchair behind me for when I need to rest.

As I recline on a deck chair watching my brothers play like ten-year-olds on the floating trampoline, Jason kneels down beside me. He cuts the leather strap from around his neck where my wedding bands have hung since my accident, takes my hand and wordlessly puts them on me. He leans in, kisses my lips and says, I'm so happy you didn't die and I can replace these. We wrap our arms around each other, try to pull the other into ourselves, ourselves into the other. *My* honey, I tell him. *My* wife, he responds.

Kezza pulls the boat up to the dock and Jason helps me sit on the edge, lifts my legs over the side and hands them to Greta who takes them and helps me slide down to the seat. We watch the boys take turns waterskiing and trying to dump each other on the tube. Take booze cruises minus the booze and I have a go at pool and foosball rationalizing they're therapy.

◆ ◆ ◆

Just as non-horse things used to benefit my riding, my weekend away from therapy acts as a reset button and when I return, I attack stimulating my recovery with a vengeance. In addition to physical and occupational therapies at Kessler, I hire my inpatient physical therapist to come to the hotel and walk with me twice a week. The Malones donate $100,000 to the International Brain Research Foundation, or IBRF, to cover speech and other therapies including the hyperbaric chamber where I lie in a coffin sized metal container into which pure oxygen is delivered at a high atmospheric pressure for a half hour, laser therapy where I sit in something that looks like a salon hair drier and my head is lasered for twenty minutes, and neurofeedback where I try to control a computer with my mind—like get a bowling ball to hit pins.

I also begin to do hippotherapy which is therapy on horseback: the horse's movement is utilized to improve motor functioning. Over the previous months, I've received several emails offering hippotherapy services and although I'm content to utilize any or all of them, Jason insisted on doing the proper research: are they licensed, experienced, reputable? He speaks to several and finally settles on one because she used to work as a physical therapist.

Although initially I was gung-ho to ride, the day before the appointment, nerves kick in. I'm not afraid—luckily the coma made me forget everything about the accident—but I know it will be a highly emotional experience. Lendon has always been my rock. The waves of my life have been tumultuous but she's stood firm and unchanging, so the first phone call I make with my labored and often incomprehensible speech is to her.

I'll be there, she says. When is it? After I tell her, she's ready to get off the phone but I realize I need to say something else, need to *hear* something else. Lendon? I say.

Yes?

I love you.

I love you, too, Courtney.

I knew she did, but hearing it relieves me. I've told her I loved her many times in cards or poems, but she's never said it to me. This doesn't erase the nerves but it's like encasing them in a balloon: they can collide with any object and bounce off intact. It's not like protecting them in armor or a cage where they can't be touched. They'll be touched but remain unscathed. On the drive to the barn, I make a rule for myself: riding is just another therapy like neurofeedback or putting pegs in a hole. Loving the horse is completely separate. So I pet Dude's face but no more. The therapists tell me it's ok to cry, but once I get on, it's like coming home. We work on different things, like saying my bonnet is blue and reaching for Dude's ears, but it absorbs my focus the same way a transition from piaffe to passage used to. When I get off, I love Dude to pieces and, like the hyperbaric chamber, my skin simply soaks in the benefit. It's pure emotional therapy.

My next ride is on a brutally hot day and Dude tries to stop by the fan every time we pass it. After the third time he stops, I shock everyone, especially me, by kicking poor Dude. Unlike dressage horses who are trained to respond to the rider's aids instantaneously, therapy horses are trained to ignore everything the person on his back may do in order to make riding safe for people with little body control. Dude obediently ignores my pathetic one-legged kick, but I'm mortified. The therapists find it hilarious and assure me that it was nothing compared to what some autistic kids do to Dude. They say, I guess you can't take the trainer out of the girl!

Me on Dude with Meredith Bazaar (foreground) and Sara Gruenwald Goodstone .

Hippotherapy is added to my regular schedule and I ride once a week. The therapist also recommends yoga and when I tell her I detest yoga, that when I tried it before my accident they said to concentrate on my breathing for two minutes to initiate relaxation and I spent the whole time thinking of what else I could be doing with those two minutes, she says she'll come to the hotel and do it with me. I'll try anything to get better so despite my reservations, I take her up on it. To my surprise, it's both enjoyable and helpful. I've had a problem sleeping since my injury and I've always said that my body slept for a month, it's rested, but after starting yoga I'm able to sleep till three or four a.m. instead of one or two.

Loving Dude

⋅ 72 ⋅

Hippotherapy sustains me by supplying the beloved horse scent but my heart yearns to see my own horses. Jason agrees to take me to Millbrook to watch Lendon work with them but he warns me that I may not remember how to train. Although I tell him that's ridiculous, I can't help but worry. But as I sit next to Lendon teaching my girls, I occasionally tug at her sleeve and ask her to add something for me. Instead of being sad that I can't ride them as I thought I might, my feelings are not about what I lost, they're overcome by the pleasure of seeing the horses.

My goal becomes to be able to ride one of my horses by my birthday, November 20. That gives me two and a half months, but I'm realistic. Everyone told me it would be a long time, so I don't expect to be able to train them, just walk them on a loose rein before Jennifer rides them.

After my last horse leaves the ring, Jason drives me to the top of the hill to visit Myth's and RV's graves. As we make our way to their headstones, the summer breeze plays at my hair, the scent of fresh grass fills my nose, the sun warms my cheek and I appreciate the gloriousness of their resting spot once again. As I stand at their graves, I think not of their accomplishments but of their personalities, how their lives were stolen at such a young age and they missed out on many years. A sadness deeper than any I've experienced since my accident settles over me. I shed no tears, but all life drains from me.

On the drive home, I'm struck by a realization. Many people commend me and say how amazing it is that I'll try anything to get better, and I always thought that was silly. Of course I'll try anything to get better, who wouldn't? But after visiting the graves, I'm tired of working on myself. I spend all day every day working to get better. I blow in a contraption thirty times a day to help build my lungs, make sure my belly expands when I breathe instead of my chest, chew food on the right side of my mouth as well as the left, think of keeping my left shoulder down, try not to twist to the right. I even work on myself when I'm asleep as Jason says that when I sleep talk, I often pause and repeat a word several times in order to get the pronunciation right. And my days are filled with therapies: speech therapy, physical therapy, occupational therapy, hippotherapy, neurofeedback, etc. I'm tired of trying. It strikes me that I don't want to try because I'm sad and some people are sad all the time. How awful. Those poor people.

My sadness lasts for three days and for three days, I do nothing. Then without deciding to, I realize I'm thinking of how I breathe, how I chew, where my shoulder is. Working toward getting better is in my nature. It used to be in riding and now it's in recovering. Why live if not to improve? Recovery may take a while, but the harder I work, the sooner it will happen.

Blog

Patience with myself has never been my forte, but I finally accepted that, in this race, I'm the tortoise. It may be slow, but it's steady and it's progress and I know that's huge. I WILL win this race! Lendon made a good comparison for me. She asked me to remember how many months of just the most rudimentary basics I did with Myth, and he ended up a star. Right now I have to relearn the basics, too. And rushing it never helps. When asked if I'm aware of how special I am in the way I'm handling this, the answer is easily "no"! I don't feel special at all! I have a lot to be thankful for, but beyond that, this is simply what life is for me right now. I'm happy with what I have. I go with the attitude I've always had... You can't control what life throws at you, it's only how you deal with it that you can control.

· 73 ·

When Kim Boyer offers me tickets to the World Equestrian Games which are in Lexington, Kentucky, at the beginning of October, I initially say no because I need to keep working on myself if I'm going to ride in the Olympics in two years. But as the time draws near, I remember that sometimes giving your nose a break from the grindstone helps more than unrelenting work. Besides, there are plenty of exercises I can do on the road.

Jason has to work and he's not interested in watching dressage unless I'm riding, so Betsy goes with me. Traveling with her is much easier than with Jason because at rest areas, she can accompany me into the bathroom instead of Jason's and my technique of wheeling me into the men's room as quickly as possible while I cover my eyes with my one working hand.

The first night, we have dinner with Kim and Lendon at their hotel where most of the riders are staying. We leave the wheelchair behind as I want to walk as much as I can, and to make this possible, Betsy walks connected to my left side, puts her right arm around my waist and holds my left hand with hers so I can lean on it.

As we sit down at the table, Lendon asks how I'm holding up. I tell her I'm happy to be here but it's a good thing that what I told the Malones— that Myth wouldn't be ready for the Olympics, the goal would be the WEGs—wasn't true because he's dead and I'm brain injured. She says, Well, it's a good thing *you're* not dead.

Throughout the evening many top riders, who I'm surprised even know me much less acknowledge me, come up and say they're so sorry to which I smile and reply shit happens. Belli Balkenhol gives me a Pandora bracelet with a charm representing bumps in the road and although the Balkenhols have always remained close to my heart, I'm reminded of just how caring they are—thinking of me all the way from Germany and unsure if I'd even be at the WEGs. Isabell's apology is accompanied by a hug and despite Kim and I lamenting my inability to compete GR here, I go to bed feeling that for how much my brain was injured, my heart was rewarded.

◆ ◆ ◆

The next day, as Betsy supports me and we make our way through the crowd, people wave and blow me kisses, several I don't know call me by name and tell me what an inspiration I am, how my blog has helped them through their own troubles. I've kept writing simply because the public cared so much during my injury, the least I can do is bring them on the whole journey if they want to accompany me, so it's very gratifying to know that sharing the steps along the way is actually helping people.

When we pass by the schooling ring where only team members are allowed, Rick Mitchell bustles over and invites us in. I don't have the proper credentials but the security guard recognizes me and ushers us through.

After we watch Steffen school and begin our journey out, I notice many people peering over the fence and through the bushes trying to get a glimpse of the riders, and when we get to the general area, lunchtime makes it chaos and there's barely room to walk. Lendon walks in front of us with her elbows splayed to prevent anyone from knocking into me and says over her shoulder, Pays to have fat friends, but I'm awestruck by the masses of fans and their enthusiasm.

When I was first injured and people asked me about making helmets a rule, I said of course I'd recommend wearing one but if people want to put themselves and their loved-ones at risk, it should be their choice. But after seeing how many people watch, how many idolize the team and how many recognize me, I change my mind. It should be a rule. Especially at the top levels because that's what people watch, what influences people the most. We aren't only responsible for ourselves and our loved-ones, we're responsible for the multitude of passionate viewers who will mimic us. If my thirteen-year-old daughter sees Steffen Peters show in a helmet, she'll wear one, too. Just like teenage boys wear their pants on the ground because that's what they see the hip hop stars do, people—both adults and teens—will do as they see the riders they want to emulate do.

I hope my accident will show people that their reasons for not wearing a helmet—bad hair, a hot head, or forsaking tradition—are meaningless when compared to protecting the brain. Potentially a large audience could be reached because whereas countless people get brain injuries while riding every year and no one hears about them, an Olympian getting one was widely publicized. A person at the highest international level being badly injured while riding shows that being injured has nothing to do with level of skill. Not only is it possible for an Olympian to be hurt, my horse did nothing naughty—he didn't buck me off or bolt or spook—he simply tripped and fell over his own feet. Therefore it shows that the quietness of the horse is inconsequential as well.

For twenty years I only rode young or dangerous horses in a helmet and my hope is that others will learn from my mistake. If my injury saves one life, it makes it seem worthwhile. The Riders4Helmets campaign was started as a direct result of my accident to promote safety and I decide to join the effort wholeheartedly.

◆ ◆ ◆

When the competition begins, I'm allowed to stand by the entrance on a platform reserved for team members when the U.S. riders go, and I tell Betsy that being injured has its bonuses. When Steffen goes, I'm glad for

281

her support because excitement makes my knees shake so much they'd never hold me. For the piaffes I cluck, for the changes I lean my shoulders a bit, when Ravel's umph declines I can feel the urge to kick. I ride every step with him. I don't wish I were with him, I cheer him on as if he were me.

When he does his final salute, I'm relieved. It's finished and it was spectacular. Then he becomes him again and my elation is just for him instead of the hypothetical us. I grasp his wife and her tremors match my own. Then Ravel's owners. Together, our shaking would be an earthquake.

As Betsy and I make our way out and the crowd is quieting down, someone in the stands shouts, Courtney, you *are* part of the team! I look down, feeling embarrassed and undeserving but immediately regret not blowing her a kiss and showing my appreciation. When I express my regret to Betsy, she says that because of my blog, people know my heart, they know I'm a good person. I tell her I always wished they did when I was a rider and people thought I was a bitch. Be careful what you wish for.

I watch every ride and can feel my body asking for every movement, but rather than being a torturous sensation, it's a joyful one. When Belli rides, I wave the German flag and when Laura Bechtolsheimer goes, I wave the British one. No matter the country, great riding gives me great pleasure.

The U.S. gets fourth place and they invite me to their celebration dinner. I'm honored to be included and promise that next time, I'll be a part of the team. I happily listen to them critique their own rides and praise each other's, dissect competitors' rides and comment on the positive and negative qualities of certain horses. It's a relief that the conversation isn't about me or noticeably geared toward allowing my participation at such a low volume. In the circumstances that should make me the most aware of my loss, I forget about it.

◆　◆　◆

On the day of the Freestyle, I get a text that George Morris, who's remained the coach of the show jumping team, wants to see me. He's sent me many postcards since my accident that always end with advice we use for riders that also applies to my recovery like *always think forward* or *look where you want to go.* When we meet, he's the first person who doesn't apologize for my circumstances or commend me for my multitude of therapies, and when we say our goodbyes, he says he'll see me at the 2012 Olympics. I leave him feeling invigorated because he focuses on the future and doesn't lament the past.

As Betsy and I make our way ever so slowly toward the ring, I tell her that Freestyles have never been my favorite—to ride because they're hard and to watch because you can't compare movement by movement. But Steffen's nearly changes my mind. It doesn't satisfy the analytical part of me that yearns for comparison but for the first time, the fun factor supersedes it. It's pure magic and earns him the bronze medal.

He does his victory gallop in a helmet and dedicates it to me which, beyond being extremely emotionally touching, does the job of showcasing safety to all the thirteen-year-old daughters out there. The world watches the American hero with a medal around his neck and a helmet on his head.

* * *

The whole trip is more powerful than my tour of inspiration and although Jason says my thoughts of riding in the 2012 Olympics are completely unrealistic, I'm determined. I ask the Malones if they'd still be willing to buy me an international Grand Prix horse if I'm ready and they say yes. I ask Klaus if he'd have stalls for me the following winter and he says he'll make them available, *absolute*. Although I loved every moment of the entire trip, I'm glad to go home and get my nose back on the grindstone.

• 74 •

When I come home, I resume my vigorous bordering on obsessive efforts toward recovery with added drive, but by October 20, a month before my birthday, I'm nowhere close to being able to walk on one of my horses safely. I write on my website:

I thought it was great to have a goal but boy does it suck to realize you can't meet it. But then I realized I'm very lucky. I'm the only one who cares if I meet my goal. I'm so lucky, I know all my family and close friends don't care at all, but also I don't have to worry about my business. I have a great rider and my clients continue to be incredibly supportive of my situation. I'm so, so lucky. I face no pressure other than my own, which is huge. Don't get me wrong, I'm still gonna work as hard as possible to get better as quickly as possible, doesn't change that!

Because all my entries are like this—seeing the good in the bad and continually focusing on my good luck—I get several emails asking if my positivity is a show for the public and if privately I have dark days. I try to set the record straight by saying:

It's asked occasionally if I put on the positive show for the public. The love shown by the entire community means a great deal to me, but I'm far too busy getting better to worry about what the public thinks of me! How I feel is this is just how my life is right now. I'm so thankful that I have my clients and workers and a rider who I believe will stay with me no matter how long it takes. So I'm pretty lucky I don't have to worry about the future. It may take more time than I foresee, but I know that's ok.

◆ ◆ ◆

Lendon and an equine lawyer created a medical fund for me immediately after I woke from the coma, and the many generous donations to it allow me to outfit a gym in the house. We hang a large mirror and install a bar in front of it to hang onto for balance, buy an exercise mat, several weights and a treadmill. I call it my room of inspiration and decorate it with the horse photos I previously banned from being displayed in my house: huge photos of me riding Myth and Idy, my magazine covers, trophies and ribbons as well as my favorite photos of horses I've ridden over the years.

Room of Inspiration

We make the house more handicapped friendly as well by strategically placing handle bars throughout. Betsy's mom gives us thirteen thousand dollars to redo our bathroom to make it safe because, although Jason needs to help me shower now, I need to plan for when I can do it on my own, which will be soon. Non-slip flooring is installed and we put in a raised toilet and a shower head that can be slid low enough to reach from my shower-chair or high enough for when I stand. Handle bars that match the faucets are built into the shower and by the toilet.

We make a new home to accommodate my temporary new life and by doing so, we can spend more time there. After living at the Marriott full-time for nearly five months, we pack all my New Jersey therapies into four days instead of five so we can sleep at home three nights a week. On top of the many exercises I do in my room of inspiration every day, I buy a system that allows me to do neurofeedback at home and a muscle stimulator to put on my right shoulder each day. I also ride a mechanical horse near my house once a week in addition to continuing hippotherapy in New Jersey in the hopes that by asking for the movements, muscle memory will kick in.

Although riding on my birthday would have been the most ideal gift, receiving the home improvements are the next best thing. I feel like a sixteen-year-old who instead of receiving the keys to a brand new car in the driveway, gets an envelope with keys for a car that will be hers when she turns seventeen.

♦ ♦ ♦

On November 18th, two days before I turn thirty-three, Francine calls while we're driving home from the Marriott and asks if I want to have my birthday dinner at her house. Jason says we can't because he made reservations at The Castle. Drinks then? she asks to which Jason says sure.

We pull in their driveway at six thirty and our reservation is at seven thirty so Jason says not to dilly-dally. Francine greets us in the driveway and Jason apologetically tells her that we can only stay for a half hour. She furls her eyebrows, scolds, Come on, that's not fair, and tells us to go to the dining room for champagne.

Jason supports me as Betsy did at the WEGs, and for the two steps that lead down to the dining room, he stands at the bottom and holds my shoulders. As I look down and concentrate on where to place my feet, the brim of my hat blocks my peripheral vision and when I look up, thirty of the people I love most in the world scream surprise: Francine, Lendon, Rich, all my siblings, my dad, Jennifer, Betsy.

I just stand there, my cheeks fighting to close my jaw enough to smile, unsure of whether to laugh or cry. I was surprised at my American Idol party but this feels like my heart is exploding into a million pieces. One by one, Jason transfers my arms around each person to hug and support me.

Jason and Francine congratulate each other on the excellent result of their plan and Francine ushers us into the living room where several tables are set and wait staff bustles about. Jason leads me to a sofa and everyone surrounds me as I open presents. Many are fabulous but they all pale in comparison to the gift of everyone's physical presence. As we sit down to dinner, I make a toast as loudly as I can: Here's to another year. What better way to celebrate continuing to be alive?

When we get up after we've eaten, Francine comes over, wraps her arms around me and holds me. As we stand there trying to squeeze all our joys in and all our miseries out, her husband Pete comes over and joins our hug. Jason jokingly asks what's going on here and joins in as well. Then Rich and his wife come over and we make room for them, too.

As the six of us stand squeezing each other with our heads down like a huddle, Francine says, Do you feel that? I mutter a noncommittal, Mmmmmmm. It's amazing, she continues, You can *feel* the love in this room. I love you, kid.

I love you, Pete says.

I love you, Rich says.

We all announce our love for each other and I know they're not talking only to me. They mean it collectively. Francine's right, the love is palpable.

After our ten minute love-fest, we retreat to the game room and Francine, Viva, Lulu and I sit on a sofa to cheer the boys on in pool. When I was in the hospital, she told me as soon as Righty could beat her in arm wrestling, she'd buy me a horse. She took me to dinner every Thursday the first few months I lived at the Marriott and tested Righty each time, so she asks how he is now, eight months later.

Getting there, I reply. But you need to visit when I'm in Florida because by then he'll whoop you.

Of course, she says. I'd expect no less.

We stay until three in the morning and when we get home, Greta gives me a card. On the front is a photo of a mouse wearing a football helmet approaching a mousetrap and the inside says *older and wiser.*

• 75 •

There's no question about me spending the winter in Florida because not only is walking through snow and ice impossible, the spasticity that makes my right arm clench like a wing and my right leg refuse to bend is exacerbated when I'm cold. But when I say *on the drive down to Florida,* Jason says, You're not considering taking your car down, are you?

Of course I'm taking it, I tell him.

Court, all the doctors have told you recovery's going to take a long time. I roll my eyes—which he hates—and tell him that yes, originally I thought a long time was four or five months, but does he really think I won't be able to drive a year after my accident? He spreads his arms and emphatically shrugs. I hope you are, but I don't think there's a chance. I finally convince him to take it down so that at least we have something for him or my siblings to drive. But I know I'll prove him wrong.

I share a house with Jen and Dave again but Betsy also lives with us as, without a job, she has time to be my caretaker. I, who was raised to be independent from the day my memories began, can't walk unattached to another person so someone needs to be with me twenty-four hours a day. I feel incredibly lucky that my best friend is able and willing to schlep me around, help me shower, help me dress, make my food, separate my million pills into breakfast, lunch and dinner in an enormous pill container, etc. etc.

It's hard to not let my life revolve around horses in Wellington, but I'm fortunate that because I make my own schedule, I can revolve the horses around my life. Which is therapy. With proper scheduling I can fit in a great deal, and maybe being very busy will encourage my body to sleep.

Palms West Hospital does my occupational and physical therapies, and my speech therapist from New Jersey continues to teach me via Skype. Vinceremos, like Starlight where I rode up north did, refuses to charge me a cent for hippotherapy and, on top of my regular physical therapy, a therapist who's starting a business teaching uninjured riders to use their bodies better, offers to help me privately for free.

I also bring my mat, muscle stimulator, elastics and weights to do exercises at home six days a week as Jason tells me it's important to have a rest day. What I can do every day though, is art, which everyone tells me will help Righty. He, with Lefty's help, makes pottery sculptures for people who've helped me a great deal: Greta's cat for her, a fish for Jason, Betsy's dog for her, a giraffe for Lendon, a dachshund for Francine. He also paints GR for Kim, Zygosh for Leslie, Tomtom for Alex, Gray's two Siamese cats for him, a pheasant for Gib.

Clockwise: Greta's cat, Betsy's dog, GR, and Gray's cat

The close proximity of everything in Wellington—ten minutes instead of an hour and a half—allows aqua therapy to be added to my schedule and I'm still able to teach my girls on my horses nearly every day.

Although I love to work with Zygosch, his sensitivity will make him the last of my horses I'll get on, so the Malones say that they'll lease me a starter horse to be able to advance on as my recovery progresses. I tell them a Grand Prix horse would be ideal since I know my body will need to get used to the movements again, but Intermediare would be fine. We find one who's easy on the body, passes all the hippotherapy tests and has an excellent piaffe and passage. We vet him and formulate a contract but Leslie's traveling so she plans to sign it when she gets home.

◆ ◆ ◆

In addition to working on building the strength and coordination of my body, some parts need to be manually loosened because they tighten up compensating for my abnormal moving pattern. I normally hate massages but Dr. Fellus wanted me to get them regularly at Kessler, so we called it muscular therapy and when I lived in the Marriott, I got one once a week. Betsy recommends a masseuse she's used and I go.

The next day, because so many people have raved about its effects, I get cranio sacral work done. He tells me that it will release toxins from my body. That I'll feel deep emotions, maybe things I don't know bother me will appear and make me cry. It's ok to cry. I wonder if perhaps sadness about my accident will appear.

I lie down and he sits behind me, gently feels my skull. I wait for the deep emotions. And wait. Nothing. When he finishes, I tell him so and he says that with the release of toxins I may feel its effects in the next couple days, so I leave disappointed but hopeful.

That night, Betsy and I go to dinner at The Players Club and I have snapper with onions and lemon sauce. No ice cream? Betsy teases as when we came last year, I ordered ice cream for dinner. We have a ridiculously satisfying dinner and as we're walking toward the door, a Barry White song comes on. We stop and look at each other. Then I start moving my hips left and right with the rhythm. Betsy turns to face me, holds both my arms and we move our bodies with the rhythm. Kind of.

Although we must look ludicrous—kind of trying to dance not on a dance floor—no one gawks. Although several people hoot and cheer us on. When the song ends, we make our way to the door and she asks if I feel anything yet. Nope, not yet, I reply.

As she does every night after she tucks me into bed, she hugs me and tells me she loves me to which I reply, I love you, too, Mom. She sets the clothes I'm going to wear the next day on the bed, asks if I need anything else and says, Maybe the cranio sacral work will make you sleep. We blow each other kisses and she walks out the door.

At three thirty in the morning, my stomach starts rumbling. I try to ignore it in the hopes that it will settle but by four, it's urgent. If I don't get to the toilet, I'll poop in my bed, which is extremely bizarre because I still suffer from constipation. We installed a door bell and keep the button that rings it by my bed so that if I need assistance in the middle of the night, I can notify someone. So I ring it, Betsy runs in and helps me to the bathroom.

She pulls down my pants, helps me to sit and walks out the door.

Bets? I say.

Yeah, Court?

I feel funny.

It feels like a million pounds of water are converging on every part of my body, like a silent very loud noise is infiltrating it.

I see bare knees, very close. Then Viva walks beneath them. I remember I'm on the toilet and try to get some toilet paper to wipe.

Betsy's holding my chest screaming, Jennifer! Jennifer Baumert! I need help!

Dave comes in and takes Betsy's place holding my chest. I hear Betsy saying, Yes, she's awake. No, she's not responsive. She gives our address. Comes back in the bathroom and tells me an ambulance is on the way.

I acknowledge this information and keep trying to get the toilet paper.

When she sees that I'm aware of my surroundings, she kneels in front of me and her face reveals that she's in more agony than I am. I look in her eyes, try to telepathically comfort her. When her features don't soften, I attempt to vocally assure her that I'm OK. The words come out comprehensible but even more garbled than usual and the crease between her eyes remains.

Dave says, Give her a sheet. I shake my head and grumble, Hot.

For modesty's sake, Jen, give her a sheet!

He's concerned because I'm naked but I grunt, I'm not modest, I'm hot.

Soon, an EMT kneels in front of me and tells me to watch his finger. He asks me to tell him my full name, which I do. The date? I don't know the date so tell him it's Friday. The president? Obama. He turns to Betsy and asks if the seizure was grand mal. She says she doesn't know what that is and when he explains it's when a person's body is wracked by convulsions, she replies in the affirmative. He nods and makes a note on his clipboard.

When we get to the hospital, they wheel me into a room and leave me to scan my surroundings. I become absorbed in contemplating the many machines—machines that keep people alive. The ingenuity of human beings boggles my mind. If my accident had happened fifty years ago, I would have died. Who invented a tracheotomy to make you breathe? A brain pressure monitor to assess whether surgery is necessary? A stomach tube to feed an unconscious person? Bodies themselves are amazing; my body *knew* to put me in a coma—to shut off everything not imperative for survival so it could put all its energy into the functions that are. Although I often say *my stupid brain*, in reality I know it's doing a stellar job.

Eventually a nurse comes in and checks my vitals. When he writes the results in my file, he looks at me, back at the file, back at me. He taps his pen on the clipboard, gazes at the file and mutters my name. Then his pen stops and he looks at me, says my name again. He thinks he heard about me. Was I in the Olympics, got thrown by a horse and suffered a TBI?

I explain that I didn't fall off; the horse fell, my head slammed into the ground and my brain bounced around in my skull. He continues to look at me, trying to gauge how I feel about this and when he sees my matter-of-fact expression, he chuckles. Says his wife rides—not dressage, jumpers—but my accident deeply affected the whole community. I tell him I hope dressage will follow in the jumpers' footsteps: as soon as helmets were required to show, no one would think of getting on a horse without one at home.

Then a doctor bustles in. She looks at the clipboard and shines a light in my eyes, asks if there's any pain. I tell her just in my left hand. She gives a slight smile when she sees the nurse is in the process of inserting a catheter there (although I feel that only professionalism prevents her from rolling her eyes) and asks several more questions. Has this happened before? Am I on anti-seizure medication? When was my brain injury?

It takes two hours to work up my blood and give me fluids so it's before seven when we get in the car. The Riders4Helmets Safety Symposium, at which I'm supposed to speak, starts at nine so I tell Betsy we can still make it. The crease between her eyes increases and she says, Really, Court? I put my hand on hers, assure her that I feel fine and point out that there's time for me to rest a bit before we go anyway. She visibly disagrees but, typical

291

of sweet Betsy, doesn't argue.

She puts me to bed and within minutes, nausea sets in. There's no chance that this will settle so I ring the doorbell, Betsy runs in, I tell her I'm going to puke and she grabs the closest thing to her—the laundry bin. I dry heave a few times and then it comes out. And keeps coming. The onions from dinner come out my nose.

We don't know if I should go back to the hospital so I tell her to call Dr. Fellus. He says absolutely, so Betsy wheels me to the car and we go back to the emergency room where they keep me the whole weekend. Jason got on a flight as soon as he heard I'd had a seizure although I told him not to bother as there'd be nothing he could do. I'm glad he ignored me. He says sleeping in my hospital bed at Palms West is much better than at Kessler because there are so many fewer tubes.

When I go home, Betsy says, No more Barry White, and I say, No more cranio sacral. Guess those were the toxins.

◆ ◆ ◆

Blog

I guess my body was saying, "Slow the bleep down, you stupid bleep". I'm kind of slow, but now I get it. I didn't respond to the gentle suggestions, so it had to go to the extreme. Slow down. I've been doing so much, trying so hard to get better, I never gave my body a break. So now I'll do less. It's hard for me but my body showed me that it needs it. So I've spent the weekend in the hospital recuperating. So much I missed out on, but I guess it's what my body needed.

So unfortunately it may take longer, but if that's what it takes to eliminate seizures, it's worth it. I'm lucky all my clients are loyal and all my horses are young, so a little more time, it's hard, but it's not catastrophic.

I'm not willing to forego any of my therapies because they're what will make me better, so I decide to only teach my horses once a week. I miss seeing them every day but it makes the day I do a special treat. And if it will make me able to ride them sooner, it's a worthy sacrifice.

The other thing that may have contributed to my body demanding a rest is that it still refuses to acknowledge the value of sleep. None of the sleeping pills Dr. Fellus has prescribed work at all—I've tried two types of Ambien and several drugs I can't pronounce. My therapist tells me to put all electronics at least fifty feet away from me at night so for two weeks I do, but then I just lie there twiddling my thumbs when I wake at three and have no phone or iPad.

So I try Melatonin. I give that two weeks as well before giving up on it. My body's reaction nullifies—or perhaps solidifies—my theory of you can sleep when you're dead. So I try to take a nap every day. I never fall asleep but just the rest refreshes me.

• 76 •

Blog

Not that I'm thanking my lucky stars for my brain injury but I think I've come to a good place with it. I don't know if it's because the seizure took away some of the urgency to recover, but now I've come to feel ok with it. Don't get me wrong, I fully intend to get back to my previous level of riding! Work hard and continue the fight, nothing can beat nature away!

Thank you all for writing to me. I've realized I'm touching a lot of people, and I can think of this accident as helping others. I thank all of you for showing me this accident isn't simply something to get through, in a way it's a blessing because it's helping many. I'm soooo lucky to have the support I have from my husband, family, friends, strangers, clients, horses, and the great staff I have. I have so much to be thankful for, it far outweighs one measly thing to be unthankful for!

It takes two weeks to regain what strength I had pre-seizure, then I go back to work increasing it. I need someone to guard me for most of the exercises I do at home but some, like touching each finger to my thumb, I can do on my own.

One day, while Jason's in the shower and everyone else is gone, I'm sitting on the sofa practicing picking up and putting down my right leg and suddenly my bladder threatens to burst. The bathroom is on the other side of our large house, so the distance combined with my muted voice eliminates any possibility of screaming Jason's name reaching him.

I've started trying to crawl in therapy so I ease myself to the ground and inch toward the bathroom. The carpet ends after about twelve feet and the floor turns to tile which is agony to my knees, but I really need to pee. I make it to ten feet from the bathroom and can hold it no longer.

I sit in my pool of urine and when the shower turns off, call Jason's name. He runs out dripping and in a towel, kneels by me and asks if I'm ok. I rub at my red knees and nod, hanging my head. Court, you shouldn't do that, he says. I ask him if he'd rather I peed on the couch thinking it's a hypothetical question, but he simply says, Yes. Safety first, ok?

My head, still hanging, nods. Court, look at me, he says. It's not worth taking a chance, is it? If your right arm gave out, your head would crash into the floor. My eyes meet his. He's right. Pee on the sofa would be a preferable dilemma to cleaning brain matter off the floor. It's not worth the risk.

After he sees my remorse, he smiles and says at least I made it safely to the tiles where cleanup will be easier.

He helps me to the shower and as I sit down, I think of how incredibly fortunate I am in my life partner. He couldn't be more perfect in any way. I knew that before, but my injury magnifies it. He's rational, responsible, thorough and patient as well as easy-going. He could have continued to chastise me but he made light of the situation as soon as he was sure I wouldn't do it again. Although very caring, he's not overly sympathetic, never makes me feel like a patient. The fact that our relationship hasn't changed at all is amazing in itself.

People ask me if he's upset that I ride and I tell them, on the contrary, he wants me to be happy and knows that riding makes me happy. Instead of being aggravated by my multitude of therapies, to which he has to take me, he encourages them. He even continues my therapy at home by challenging Righty to do tasks such as try to punch him, make the thumbs up sign from my 75% ride, flip him off.

That afternoon as we hold hands on the drive to hippotherapy, Righty takes his wedding band off and puts it back on. He's impressed and says, Good on ya, Righty, but I'm assuring myself that we're married, that we have each other for life. I've never questioned that we would—to me it seemed like, *of course* he'd stay with me in the hospital, we're *married*, but now it strikes me that sleeping in those horrible circumstances is incredible.

And how can he love me so deeply now? I'm so much less than the woman he married. I say, I love you, honey. He glances at me, squeezes my hand and says, I love you more. I reply, That's not possible.

When he helps me out of the car at Vinceremos, I take him in an embrace. He's caught off guard at my rare show of emotion and asks what's up. I say, How can you put up with it all? You never get frustrated with me but aren't you sick of taking care of me? He tells me not to be silly, as we always have, we're just adapting. He lets me continue holding him but his emotions don't match my own. Eventually he teases, Are you done yet? I smile and tell him, One more minute.

As we walk into the barn, I feel complete: the man I love holding me close and the scent of sweaty horse I've always cherished filling my nostrils. The curious faces poking out of the stalls remind me of how I felt at eight years old when riding was just a dream—loving them not as athletes but as genuine, honest, loving, non-judgmental, glorious, magical creatures.

The Vinceremos therapists were very thorough in selecting the right horse to suit my individual needs. First they looked at me stand: how much strength and balance did I have? Did my hips tilt forward or back? Right or left? Did my shoulders? Then they selected several horses based on their barrel size as I need a wide back to give me maximum stability. We watched each one walk to judge the cadence as the more bounce the walk has, the more core strength is required, of which I have none. Tommy had the flattest stride so he became my Florida Dude and soon has come to expect the apple I give him during my post-ride love session.

Every time I've ridden so far, someone has led the horse and a person has stood on each side holding my knee. We'd practice things like arm swing: if I allow Tommy's movement to determine where my arms go, they

Left to right: Stacey Brown, Jane Burrows, me, Arlene White,
Maurette Hansen (between Stacey and Jane) leading the horse

swing as if I were walking on my own feet. I'd stretch my arms out to the sides and twist as far as I could each way to open my pelvis. Stand up in the stirrups and try to sit back down as gently as possible to exercise my quads. We'd stretch out various muscles and practice speech.

But today, they let me loose. They all maintain their respective positions but no one touches me or the horse. I weave through poles, which requires not only steering but challenges my weight transfer. Practice stopping and starting because I struggle to keep my body from falling back during the first strides as my core is weak and my hips are stiff. I even attempt to do a shoulder-in, which if I somehow managed to ask for correctly, Tommy wouldn't have a clue what I wanted anyway. Nevertheless, I have a blast and when we finish, I tell him he was such a star, it's a two-apple day but he better watch out because next year I'm going to ask him to piaffe.

◆ ◆ ◆

On the way home, the sappy mood I came to Vinceremos with is replaced with my more normal work-mode frame of mind and I tell Jason of the new concept I plan to try out. My speech therapist told me that doing speech while exercising would stimulate my cerebellum which controls motor skills, so while I ride my stationary bike that evening, I read words from one of my speech sheets aloud. The next day, my balance feels slightly better so I delve into this technique whole-heartedly. When I bike, I read lists and when I'm on my treadmill, I sing my favorite songs—my renditions of which are quite amusing.

Within a week, the improvement is substantial enough to get a cane. Thus far I've felt lucky that my progress, although slow, has been steady whereas many people with brain injuries often have setbacks, but this is the first time an improvement has occurred within days instead of over months. Although someone still needs to guard me, I anticipate being able to walk completely independently soon, and under the pretense of trying to make my handicap invisible, I get a camouflage cane and joke it's so that no one can see it.

Soon I'm taking daily excursions on the sidewalk with Betsy or Jason on guard, and as I begin to work on my own independent mechanics, I realize that training my body is strikingly similar to riding. I always told my students to pick one flaw and focus only on that until it becomes instinctual, *then* focus on the next thing. But my natural inclination has been to try to think of everything at once so nothing is becoming instinctual: heel first then toe, right hip forward, bend the right knee, left shoulder down, don't lean forward, long step with the left, look ahead, shoulders back, step more quickly with the right leg.

Another similarity that applies to both riding and my recovery is that simply hearing something a different way can make a huge difference. Therapists have always told me—even on the treadmill at Kessler—to shift my weight to the right, but try as I might, I couldn't do it. Then my therapist at Palms West told me to leave my left toe on the ground longer, which was a struggle to do, and I realized that my left leg is always in a hurry to take its step in order to avoid taking weight on the right.

So one day as we walk around the block, I think only leave the left toe on the ground and ignore the right leg altogether. What do you know, this makes my weight shift to the right. Also as in riding, fixing one thing often fixes others: my left leg takes a longer step and my shoulders are more even.

I write about this epiphany on my blog and when I wake at three in the morning, I get many responses that this mentality can be applied to many sports and thanking me for spelling it out so clearly. I open one with no subject expecting a similar commendation but am shocked to read: *Now you know what it feels like to not be such a good rider, BITCH!*

My initial inclination is to not answer but I can't stop thinking about it. Why would she write that? Why does she hate me? Maybe, like when a person insults someone else to make themselves feel bigger, she's just upset at her own circumstances and is taking it out on me. Misery enjoys company. After two hours, I realize that the only way to put it out of my mind, is to respond, so I write:

Dear Alys,
This doesn't even hurt me. It just makes me sad that you're filled with so much
negativity. I did start out a bad rider, so I can empathize. I worked really hard to become
the rider I was, it wasn't easy. But I know I'm blessed with the natural feel it takes, too,
and I'm thankful for that. I wouldn't wish a brain injury on anyone, no matter how
much of a bitch they were, and you don't even know me. I'm not a bitch, especially just
because I could ride well.
I hope your life is touched by some positivity.
Ckd

After I press send, she's gone from my mind.

• 77 •

As March approaches and with it the one year anniversary of my accident, I realize that Jason was right: a long time is more than a year. Things would be so different now if I hadn't been injured. I may have competed in my first WEGs, had another fantastic Grand Prix horse under my butt—I still don't know what Leslie said about the video of that mare. I would have been showing Tomtom and Zygosch, maybe be pregnant with my first baby. A deep anguish settles over me and when I cry, tears emerge for the first time since my accident. Greta calls in tears herself as the day has reminded her of what we all went through.

The Derby is always the first weekend in March and I dreamed of showing there, saying *I'm just late!* I thought I was being realistic intending only to do Training Level, but I've just started trotting with a leader and two guards. I didn't make it a goal because of how disappointing missing my birthday goal was, and I'm thankful I didn't. It's much easier to be woken from a dream than to accept a failure.

Instead, I give a speech to fundraise for the Equestrian Aid Foundation which gives money to people injured in equestrian accidents. I was extremely lucky that a medical fund was made just for me because my accident was so widely publicized, but not everyone is so lucky. No one ever hears about the farrier who got kicked, the groom who got trampled, the fourteen-year-old who broke her back.

I'm doing the speech because it's a phenomenal cause, but doing so warms my heart—makes me appreciate not only the public's amazing support of me personally, but the equestrian community's efforts to take care of one another. The EAF is like a million arms intertwined to catch a falling person. It's as if a doctor said, *Clear!* and shocked my heart, which was having trouble beating this morning, back to life.

In the evening, I have a Celebrate Life party. The guests think we're celebrating *my* life, but in fact we're celebrating everyone's. I give them each a tee-shirt that says *Wel*come Back, Court on the front and Make Lemonade on the sleeve because that's the only thing to do when life hands you lemons.

It's a genuine party. Jason concocts many interesting drinks and although many people try several, Jennifer tries them all and ends up trying to juggle limes, which Viva thinks is great. Jason takes my cane and enacts a rendition of New York, New York complete with the cane maneuvers. Although I'm still on non-alcoholic champagne, enjoying everyone else's boisterousness makes me feel I've rejoined real life.

It's a perfect day; like Mythy's funeral, it started out mourning my loss and ends in celebrating what I still have.

Blog

I know from Facebook that some people still wonder if my positivity is a show for the public. The reason I keep this blog is that the amount of caring people showed meant so much to me, I felt they deserved to accompany me on the whole trip if they wanted. That includes the ups AND downs. Sorry there aren't more downs (not really!) but I can't make them up. I'm so lucky to have a great husband, family, friends, distant supporters, clients, workers... It sucks that it took my accident to enflame the attention to safety, but it showed people that the unexpected has to be expected. I saw the horse's owner the other day, and there was nothing I could say to take away the guilt she was feeling. In retrospect, I say to her and everyone else, that horse did a favor for everyone. I may be slightly injured, but through that he's possibly saved many people from injury or death. So we ought to be grateful.

◆ 78 ◆

At the end of March, Jason and I spend two weeks in New Zealand. His mom willingly helps care for me—which I deeply appreciate as it allows Jason to feel comfortable doing things with his friends that I can't do—and walks with me every day. This is my substitute for physical therapy and I find a version of occupational therapy in fishing: after Jason and Buttcheeks lift me into the boat, Righty reels while Lefty fishes. Other than those two things, I do no therapy the entire time.

One day, DP says he has a surprise for me and tells Jason where to take me at a certain time. We find ourselves in a music studio, are served tea and biscuits and sit down to wait for my surprise. DP asks what I think it is and I jokingly say, Bono! Ten minutes later when I'm mid-bite, Dave Dobbin, the New Zealand equivalent of Bono, enters the room. My biscuit fights my esophagus's efforts to push it down and I splutter out his name as a question to DP thinking perhaps he just happens to be here and isn't my surprise at all.

Jason is as shocked as I am when Dave sits down and proceeds to chat with us like a stranger we hit it off with at a party. We talk about fishing, different parts of the world, his kids, writing. He turns from the untouchable superstar floating light years above me into someone I could imagine having over for dinner. He sings two songs of my choice and signs a CD to Cortny. I tell him it's lucky he's a good singer because his spelling sucks, which he finds highly amusing. As we leave, I tell Jason that being a brain injured Olympian definitely has its perks. It was interesting enough to entice arguably New Zealand's most famous person to meet me.

When we get home, I make a copy of Dave's own guitar out of clay, Righty scrawls a thank you letter and I send them to him from Cortny.

Blog
I was very happy because I thought maybe I would have regressed during my vacation, but my physical therapist was amazed how much better I was, even my speaking! Yesterday I had my occupational therapist measure me for strength, flexibility and coordination, (which she does from time to time), and I was vastly improved in all three! Yay! I should take a vacation more often as this same improvement happened after I went to WEG for a week! Work hard, play hard... and often!

◆ ◆ ◆

The first day I teach my horses after my trip, one of my clients sits next to me and tells me I should ride her horse, Roxy—she's perfect. Although I appreciate the offer, I'm unsure of how to react because although I've never been afraid to ride, I've only ever ridden therapy horses. Roxy is a dressage horse and it frankly makes me nervous. I utter a non-committal thank you and continue my lesson.

Over the next days I ponder the idea. It would be fantastic to have a horse in my own barn, to be able to ride three or four days a week instead of going to New Jersey to ride once a week, but I can't bear the thought of finding myself in the hospital again. When I go to Vinceremos and tell my therapist about the offer and my anxiety, she says it doesn't matter that Roxy's a dressage horse. It's the personality not the training that makes a good therapy horse and she'll come over to judge her suitability.

So the next day, my groom holds Roxy on a loose lead while tennis balls are thrown at her neck, sides and butt. An umbrella is opened in front of her face and a plastic bag released into the wind. The therapist says she's not testing to see *if* Roxy will spook but how she will if she does. Putting her head up and gawking, stepping to the side or flinching and freezing are fine as they won't cause me to lose my balance, but a shimmy to the side or remaining nervous aren't ok. Roxy's sensitive so she does react but she just flinches and doesn't do any sudden movements. The therapist says she wishes they had one like her at Vinceremos.

Jennifer plans to get on first, to mount like me and ride like me to make sure Roxy's safe, but Roxy's nervous about the strange mounting procedure: someone holding her head, two people on the mounting block (Jennifer and someone to hand her leg over the saddle) and another on her right side (to receive Jennifer's leg and place it in the stirrup). She won't move close to the mounting platform and continually flinches when a person moves.

I lose hope after four tries, but the therapist is unperturbed. She says Roxy handled all the hippotherapy tests so well, she'll be fine. After eight tries, Roxy stands close to the mounting block and sighs. They lead her in a ninth time to be sure and she scratches at a fly on her leg. Jennifer kicks her in the butt as she mounts, as I often do, and rides with a spazzy right leg and a stiff right arm. The owner's description of perfect was an understatement.

When I get on, initially her sensitivity makes me nervous but after fifteen minutes I know she'll try to take care of me. She's the first horse I've ridden who gives me the strong sense that she's considering *me*, not just the rider. She's trying to figure me out: when she walks forward, she feels me momentarily lose my balance so she slows, then when I cluck, her ears flicker and she very gradually increases her tempo. I fully believe that if she were scared of something, she'd take the chance of being eaten before leaping to the side and dumping me.

I begin to ride her four days a week and do a combination of hippotherapy—which is using the horse's movement to help motor skills—and therapeutic riding—which is riding within your disability. After stretching out various muscles, practicing arm swing and twisting my torso each way, my grooms let me loose and I do shoulder-in, haunches-in, leg-yield, half-pass. Half the time, I don't think Roxy even knows what I'm asking for, she just guesses.

I've only met one horse with a heart like Roxy's: Mythy. Always trying to be good and putting their whole heart into pleasing the person on their back. Roxy has the heart of a therapy horse and the training of a dressage horse.

The owner of my farm in New York has a special mounting block built for me, and when I get back, I take lessons with Lendon once a week. Together we experiment with different ways to use my body the way it is and ways to improve it. It's great to be a beginner again.

◆ ◆ ◆

In addition to being able to ride at home, I find a place near my house to do physical and occupational therapies. I also continue to do speech via Skype, so the only thing I need to go to New Jersey for is to get a check-up from Dr. Fellus which I do in mid-June.

When I walk in, he says, Ah, a cane. How long have you had that? I feign surprise that he can see it despite its camouflaging and say that being a trained professional must give him a keen eye. Then I proceed to show him my gangsta walk and my sexy walk, which are strikingly similar except for the facial expressions. He gazes at me deep in thought and as I sit down, directs a question more at Jason than me: do I still have a giggling problem?

Jason smiles and says yes, but I tell him I wouldn't call it a problem. It's not like I'd laugh at a funeral; I laugh when I think something's *funny*, which is often. I was always giggly, it's just more noticeable now because whereas before I'd be able to continue doing what I was doing, now it leaves me momentarily paralyzed. His eyes keep going from me to Jason to make sure we agree and when Jason just shrugs, Dr. Fellus is forced to accept this explanation.

He makes some minor adjustments to my medication and does a physical exam: tests my strength by having me push through resistance and tests my coordination by having me do things like touching each finger to my thumb. Although it's difficult for me to be impressed with my current state, he says I'm doing far better than the MRI pictures would indicate.

On the way home, Jason and I stop at the grocery store and whereas normally I'd stay in the car, I insist on going in. I push the cart and as we traverse the aisles, I'm able to work on my walking while the cart supports my balance. Righty puts everything in the cart, other than the eggs, and attempts to enter our debit card pin when we check out. It takes over an hour to get our twelve items, but when we leave, I feel like I've accomplished something at the same time as working on myself.

It strikes me that I'm bored of the gym. I do the same thing every single day: go on the treadmill, do my many exercises, go on the stationary bike, repeat. So I begin to use functional tasks as therapy such as folding laundry, doing the dishes, wiping the counters, even cleaning the floor. Most of these things need to be redone, but it feels good to set out to accomplish a task.

Part of what increases my gym time and makes me restless is that many activities I so enjoyed in Florida aren't possible in Connecticut. The flat sidewalks being replaced by hilly streets eliminates my daily strolls around the block, so instead I've been forced to go on the treadmill. Now Jason and I go for walks around the yard. I also buy a tricycle and we drive to a park with a flattish path on which to ride, and to make up for the lack of aqua therapy, I put on a life preserver and Jason guards me as I swim by the beach of our boating lake.

My therapists are quick to adjust my program to reduce my boredom and still satisfy my natural and unyielding will to improve. They utilize activities to aid recovery instead of exercises. My physical therapist has me jump on a trampoline, dance and attempt to swing a golf club. My occupational therapist has me throw and catch a palm-sized beanbag and try to knock down finger sized pins with a tiny bowling ball. My speech therapist has me make a goal on the table and try to blow a feathered ball into it instead of repetitively blowing into a contraption and chew gum instead of doing reps of biting on a stick.

At home, Jason hangs a pillow from the wall so Righty can try to punch it. He throws a ball for me to kick while I sit on the sofa. I get a jewelry making kit and put beads on a wire, make meatballs and mix sauces. In addition to starting every meal eating with Righty and keeping a journal in which he writes the date each day, I begin to write cards to my sister every week. Mostly I write her poems like:

Roses aren't always red
They're sometimes white or pink or yellow.

And violets aren't totally blue
They're really more like purple.

But one thing that will always be true
Is that I fuckin' love you!

Of course there are certain exercises that can only be done in therapy or my room of inspiration, but the work is far less incessant and I begin to look forward to going into the gym instead of it being a looming monster I force myself to tackle every day.

Blog

Ok, time for another little physical update. I want to express how I really am since reading my writings may make me appear much further along than I am. Although in general I still work on the same issues, I thought a little more detail would help make the picture clearer.

Walking is still a problem of course, but my focus has mastered certain details like having the steps with my left leg be as long as my right to ensure my weaker right leg carries weight, keeping my gait a little narrower so my feet brush each other instead of having three feet between them like King Kong in order to have a wide base of support. I've gotten to be fairly independent with the camo cane. Jason used to have to guard me if I walked ANYWHERE, but now, bless his heart, he feels comfortable staying sitting on the couch while I go to the bathroom.

My speech is getting better. A guy at a restaurant the other night asked if I was from Spain! That's quite a compliment! Yes, he was ninety-four and had trouble hearing, but it's a start! Sometimes when I'm saying difficult words, I just feel like my tongue is this big gobby blob in my mouth going wherever it wants. I think he's lazy, but I have to treat him like an athlete, exercise him and get him stronger. He doesn't have a brain, so I have to mold him.

I've always been realistic about the possibilities of making it for major competitions, that the stars had to be in the right alignment and the possibility of not making it was there. I want to be as realistic about my recovery and its possibilities as I was about competitions. At first I didn't want to acknowledge full recovery may not happen but I don't want to lead anyone on, not even myself. I know I may not make a full recovery, and I know from my joy teaching that I'd be content if I didn't. Of course I'll try as hard as I can to make it and I think I will, but I know if I don't I'll be happy doing what I can.

◆ ◆ ◆

When the Fourth of July approaches, I have full belief that my week in Michigan will benefit me as my previous weeks off have, so it's the first vacation since my accident I've wholeheartedly looked forward to. I may not be able to play tennis or golf with the boys as I normally would, but I can lie in the sun and shop with Greta.

The photographs on the advertisement for our rental house made it look far better than our 2009 house but they were only of each room. Each room *is* much nicer but the layout couldn't be more ill-suited to my state of being. The entrance leads to two sets of stairs: one goes up to the bedrooms and the other down to the living area, so my only source of independence is taken away as someone needs to guard me whenever I need to go up or down.

The first day we go to a dog-friendly beach. I lather up with seventy-proof sunblock because my anti-seizure medication makes my skin sensitive to the sun, and Greta and I lay back watching Quivvy frolic in the water while Viva lies flat on her back between us.

Jason goes into town to get us sandwiches and when he returns forty-five minutes later, he asks what the red splotches on my skin are. Greta takes her sunglasses off and we peer at them. When we press one, it momentarily turns white like tanned or burnt skin does. I used my sunblock and she used hers so, figuring that perhaps mine didn't work, I put hers on. But fifteen minutes later the blotches are worse.

At two thirty my beach day is done and since the house is a half hour away, so is Greta's. I apologize, say now we have good weather and she still can't take advantage of it because of me.

Although I'd be content working on my computer while everyone else does their desired activity, that would defeat the purpose of the intended together-time so when I suggest it, they say absolutely not. Instead, we go to a tennis court and Gray guards me while Jason and Greta take turns tossing a tennis ball for me to hit from ten feet away while the other person plays a game with Gib. I figure fishing is one thing I can join in on, but despite the boys' vigilant moving of a large umbrella to block my skin from the sun, in three hours we have to pull in our lines.

On an overcast day, we hit the town for the final activity I'm sure I can do: shopping. But I'm unbearably slow. By the time Greta's ready to move on to the next store, I've just begun looking around. I also need to be constantly guarded because people who are absorbed in their shopping may obliviously knock into me.

On the final night as we sit around the table playing cards, Gib tells about the time he was sitting in traffic and the car beside him was rear-ended. The driver jumped out of his car with a crowbar to threaten the other driver who was a sixty-year-old woman.

I begin to tell about my experience of being caught in stop and go traffic between two infuriated drivers brandishing guns at one another, but Jason begins a story over me. When he finishes I start again amidst everyone's laughter but he begins another anecdote in response to a comment. I yell as loudly as I can, Listen to me! You always talk over me! He looks at me and everyone is silent.

I get up and proceed angrily away, frustrated that I can't suitably stomp. I grab the banister with my left hand and proceed up the stairs with no guard. As soon as I sit on the bed, Jason comes in. I glare at him as if I'm going to sizzle him right there and my chin begins to quiver.

Court, he says and tries to hug me.

Don't touch me! I shout.

Ok, he says putting his hands up as one would to show a dog there's no threat.

The quivering in my chin reaches my lip and I stare at my knees. You always talk over me, I say.

I'm sorry, Court, you've never told me that before.

I've never told you because it's not a big deal, but you always do it.

I'm sorry, he says, I'll try to pay more attention.

My eyes close and tears drop on my knees. Eventually I look up at him. This has been a horrible vacation, honey. I'm sorry. You've hardly gotten to golf, play tennis, go for bike rides, anything. Greta can't shop or sit in the sun. Gib tried to include me by fishing, but he does that all the time when he's not on vacation, and I couldn't even do that.

I take a deep trembling breath and tell him now he can hug me. He comes over and I coil into his arms letting all the emotions I didn't know I'd bottled up seep out. I tell him I don't mind for me—I've gotten comfortable that for now I can't play tennis, bike, golf—but I'm ruining all your vacations. You can't do what your vacations are for. I know you'd all say that you want me here, that it wouldn't be the same without me, but I can't help feeling that if I just happened to not be here, you'd all have a better time.

Court, he says.

I tell him not to say anything, I know they'd never choose for me not to be here but I feel like I should have just made up an excuse to not come.

As he holds me absorbing my anguish, Greta calls, Everything ok? I give Jason a squeeze, send him on his way and walk over to the mirror. My eyes look at each other and scan the rest of my face. My mouth smiles and the left side turns up more than the right, the left eye scrunches more. The front part of my hair they shaved to put the brain monitor in is an odd length. A little Dennis the Menace-y. My gaze returns to my eyes. Searching. They used to be an abyss. I'd stare into them, try to find what they contained. Now they're just eyes.

Jason comes back in, drapes his arms around my neck and waits while I search my face. Eventually he asks, Ready?

We walk back in to raucous laughter at a ridiculous definition Gib made up for Balderdash and I lose myself for several hours enjoying the family mirth. At three a.m. when everyone's heading to bed, Greta sits down and takes my hand, looks at me with her puppy-dog eyes and asks if everything's ok. I shrug and explain why I was so upset. After confirming what I anticipated hearing, she says it was good to see me get upset. Sometimes she thinks I'm just obliviously going along, not facing the agony of the life change. She's sad I took it out on Jason, though, because he's been amazing.

My eyebrows knit and anger fights with pain as I demand, Why does the fact that Jason's handling it well make him *amazing* and the fact that I am make me *oblivious*?

She stops, her mouth drops and her eyes flicker between mine. I don't know, she says. I guess I just relate to him more because we went through everything together. I'm sorry, Court, you *are* amazing.

We wrap our arms around each other and that night as Jason spoons me and I lie listening to him snore, I think of what it must have been like to be them, watching me lie there in bed, not knowing if I'd wake up, thinking of our last time together. I definitely had it easier: sleeping and completely unaware of any problems, free from worry. I snuggle a little closer to Jason and realize how they'd feel if I didn't come this year. It's too close to what could have been permanent. I'm glad I came.

◆ 79 ◆

This time my week away doesn't substantially improve me—perhaps because it was so sad—but I come home feeling cleansed. I was tortured by the sensation of being a burden but now I understand that I'm not only still loved, I'm still a valued part of the whole.

Although the equestrian community will never be incomplete without me, I try to maintain a sense of value within it by contributing what I can. I write monthly training columns for the magazine *Dressage Today*, teach, mentor people who write about their riding in an online journaling program. But soon after I get home, Lendon amplifies my ability to feel like a relevant member of our society by asking if I'd be willing to join a program she's thinking of starting: Emerging Dressage Athletes. The goal of it is to develop America's youth, to give kids learning opportunities even if they don't have the funds this sport demands.

There will be several clinics throughout the country every year which many trainers will donate their time to teach small portions of, but the clinics won't be just for riding, they'll cover overall equestrian education. The kids will learn about footing, shoeing, breeding, therapies such as massage and chiropractic, human fitness and sports psychology. The ten best kids throughout the year will be selected to participate in a Horsemastership Week—one in the winter with Robert Dover and one in the summer with me.

Lendon has always been good at coming up with ideas, but I have to say this is one of her best brain children. I was incredibly lucky to have her, but so is the world.

◆ ◆ ◆

Lendon continues to come to the barn to teach me once a week and I think she enjoys trying to figure out how to get the desired response from my body nearly as much as I do. Since my right arm is so rigid, the following she taught me years ago is impossible and she wants to find a different technique to not disrupt the horse's mouth, so one day she has me take both reins in my left hand and try to ride Western style. When my right arm flops around at my side like an unhinged wing and Roxy has no idea what I'm doing, she says, Well that didn't work. I've always appreciated her lack of ego, but it's especially valuable in her efforts to figure out my mysterious body.

Instead, one of my clients buys me a machine to ride that moves like a horse. It's designed to work the core, but I have Jason or Koryn hold the other end of reins and act as if they were the horse's head so that every day I can practice convincing my arm to relax enough to follow.

If left to my own devices I'd fall into the rut of using only the same exercises every day both to help my body—shoulder-in right to demand that the right leg works, shoulder-in left to encourage the right arm to relax enough to allow the bend, etc.—and to evoke enjoyment. But Lendon has me do things that would never have occurred to me, like turn-on-the-forehand and turn-on-the-haunches, a swing which is walking a certain number of steps back, a certain number forward and a certain number back again. She keeps things fresh.

One day when I come in on Roxy, Lendon's scribbling on a piece of paper and after several minutes, she calls me over. She says she made up a dressage test and wants me to memorize it:

A	*Enter working walk*
X	*Halt, salute, proceed working walk*
C	*Track right*
M to R	*Shoulder-in right*
R to B	*Renvers right*
B to P	*Shoulder-in right*
P to F	*Haunches-in right*
A	*Halt, reinback five steps*
K X M	*free walk*
H to S	*Shoulder-in left*
S to E	*Renvers left*
E to V	*Shoulder-in left*
V to K	*Haunches-in left*
A	*Down centerline*
D to E	*Half-pass left*
E to G	*Half-pass right*
C	*Track right*
B	*Half circle right*
I	*Halt, salute*

I enjoy doing the test so much it's like a slap in the face. I don't know why I never realized how much I miss showing. I didn't consider doing Para dressage because I was investing myself fully to getting back to able-bodied, but it strikes me now that working toward tests *helps* therapy, it hinders nothing. Recovery is an incredibly slow process—over a year has passed and I can't even trot without someone leading the horse—and Para provides a way to let riders strive to be the best they can be in whatever state they're in. This is the best I can be *right now* and Para offers me a chance to compete while I work my way back to the Grand Prix ring. So I decide to take full advantage of this opportunity.

◆ ◆ ◆

To ensure fairness, Para is classified into several grades which are determined by what the rider is physically capable of. Grades go from 1a, which is walk only for the most impaired, to IV which includes walk, trot, canter, lateral work and medium paces for the least impaired. To classify competitors into their proper grade, their mobility, strength and coordination are assessed off the horse. The testing is done completely on the rider's functionality on the ground and not on the horse at all.

After some research, I find that classification will be available at the HITS on the Hudson show in September where my horses are going anyway. The tests are standard physical therapy tests I've done many times before in which each limb, the neck and the trunk are tested individually.

For my legs, a plastic sheet with six three-inch circles is laid on the floor and I'm told to touch each one in order with my toe increasing the speed as much as I can. Then do the same thing with my heel. For my arms, I'm instructed to touch my nose and then the classifier's finger which she continually moves to test my accuracy. Again, increasing the speed. For my trunk they tell me to turn my body each way as far as possible as if I'm looking for something behind me, and for my neck I need to look toward the ceiling, the floor and each direction without turning my upper body.

Each task is given a score between zero and five: five equals normal accuracy and speed and zero is attempting the task but being unable to accomplish it. They tell me my final result puts me between 1a, which is walk only, and 1b which begins a little trot. As they discuss which Grade to put me in, I tell them that although I can't trot on my own now, I don't anticipate showing till Florida and surely I'll have progressed by then. So we put me in 1b.

· 80 ·

Now instead of just trying to progress toward a vision of what I once was, Para provides me with immediate goals. When I sit on a chair or in the car, I try to put all my weight in my left sitting bone because my body refuses to do so in the saddle. I practice twisting my torso all the way to the left because I did so poorly with that in the classification, and when I ride my trike, I try to force my heels down as I want them to do in the stirrups instead of allowing them to do what they insist on which is imitating a ballerina.

When I get to Florida, I resume taking walks around the neighborhood but now I do so without a cane. In order to do this safely, I wear a large belt which Betsy holds onto while she keeps in step right behind me like the caboose of a choo choo train. I also wear an inflatable plastic sleeve that goes from wrist to armpit to force my arm to stay straight instead of curling up, so two times a day the neighbors get quite an amusing sight.

In addition to my walks, I go for a trike ride nearly every day. And continue doing occupational and physical therapies. I also begin to see a chiropractor once a week and he adds many exercises to straighten out my crooked body to the ones I'm already doing.

But despite my vigilant efforts, by March I'm no closer to being able to trot on my own. I've even developed another hindrance: clonus. The spasticity that causes the rigidity in my arm and leg now causes them, when at all fatigued from work or sleep, to bounce up and down of their own accord. I've named this reaction Thumper because when on a hard floor, that's the sound my leg makes. It stops me several times each walk but is especially active when I ride.

I thought I'd improve but I haven't. I've gotten worse.

♦ ♦ ♦

Although I hoped to be able to show in Florida, with my current classification doing so is impossible. Classifiers are only at certain large shows, CPDIs, and I missed the only one in Florida, so I'll need to travel. Then an idea begins to formulate: many CPDIs are Paralympic qualifiers and if I have to go to one to be reclassified anyway, how cool would it be to have been in the 2008 able-bodied Olympics and then in the 2012 Paralympics?

The closest qualifier to me is in Houston, but unlike in able-bodied dressage, the rider is allowed to borrow a horse on whom to qualify for the Selection Trials. So I write on my blog and Facebook that I'm interested in competing and get an enormous response from Houstoners with offers for mounts. I send Jennifer to try them—to ride like me and do all the hippotherapy tests we did with Roxy—and after two days she chooses one named Nicolai.

Although my income would have previously allowed me to afford such a trip, the accident not only caused enormous therapy bills, it drastically reduced my income. To help make the trip financially possible, Nicolai's trainer organizes for me to have an apartment with two bedrooms at The Solana senior living home that's less than the price of a single hotel room, and a generous stranger arranges for me to borrow a car instead of renting one.

Although this help greatly diminishes the major expenses, they aren't eliminated, and there are still things like paying for the help Koryn gives me, our plane tickets, food and entries. To allow me to pay for these things, the incredible public comes to my aid once again. They generously give to Courtney's Quest Continued in which I'll send journals of my journey like I did for the able-bodied Olympics.

♦ ♦ ♦

I want to go ten days before the show begins to get to know Nicolai, so on April 16th, Koryn and I get on a plane headed for Houston. Although I trust Koryn with my safety wholeheartedly, some practical matters that I know Jason would be able to remedy concern me. For instance, the shower. There's a built-in seat which is great, but it's tile so I'm afraid my butt will slide around. However that's the least of my worries. I write to my Questers:

The core of my anxiety comes from the fact that I would be letting so many people down if I don't succeed. The support—financial and emotional—has been astounding. I hope that Houston will be the beginning of a wonderful journey to bring you all on, but the fact is there's the possibility it will be my only stop. In Houston, I have to get a 60% or higher to qualify for the Selection Trials. It should be doable, but I haven't ridden much lately. I'm trusting my previous competitive knowledge and abilities.

When we get to the Solana, I was right: my butt slides on the shower seat. We consider laying a towel down, but then the water wouldn't drain and my private parts would be in a soapy pool. Having Koryn hold my shoulders, but although neither of us is abashed at *my* nudity, being naked together would be quite awkward. In the end, we cover the seat with cupboard lining that's normally used to prevent glasses from sliding, and it works perfectly.

My practical concern is remedied and when I meet Nicolai, my larger worry is somewhat alleviated as well. His barn name is St. Nick for good reason and I know it will only be my fault if I fail.

The first day, we discover there's not a mounting platform I can use. So after scrutinizing many options as Nicolai waits patiently, Koryn helps me carefully climb a tall mounting block onto a picnic table and then climb a smaller mounting block sitting on top of the picnic table to mount. Although two people are needed to hold me so three of us stand on the picnic table and several people position themselves on the ground, Nicolai doesn't bat an eyelash.

The first thing we need to do is videotape my freestyle. Nicolai's usual rider was videotaped riding the choreography, but Marlene wants me to do it as well because a horse goes differently for each person. Lendon stands in the middle bellowing, More forward! Go!

Nicolai goes slowly because he thinks he needs to take care of me, and I realize I'm doing what I always tell people not to: nagging. I keep him going, remind him not to stop rather than having a dead-quiet leg and only using it to tell him to go. I'd normally kick him if he didn't respond to a light squeeze but I don't because I'm afraid he'll trot and my body can't handle any jump. So I squeeze, squeeze, squeeze, inviting him to ignore my leg. To eliminate my fear, Lendon has Koryn put him on a lead line so I can correct him without being scared of not being in control. After I give him one kick, he's perfectly happy to go forward.

◆ ◆ ◆

The more I experience Para, the more I appreciate the opportunity it affords.

Courtney's Quest Continued

I just was walking down the hall sans cane working hard on my walking technique as usual, and I remembered an awful dream I had a couple weeks ago. I had an accident and was paralyzed from the waist down. I was all geared up to work at getting better and I realized that there was nothing I could do. That's one way I feel extremely lucky. I know that with time and hard work, I'll be fully functional. Para is great for me to be the best I can be right now, but I imagine its value is infinite to those who are permanently disabled. Even though our bodies won't cooperate, we still have that drive, the focus to excel. Many people have this and Para gives us a way to exercise that drive.

Beyond satisfying my competitive urge, the whole show environment Para includes me in fills me with a sense of belonging. I've been to many shows as a trainer, but somehow it's different to be in breeches. I feel like one of the kids on the playground instead of the teacher.

I even get a feeling of being on a team because in Para, two riders can share a horse. I'm sharing St. Nick with Sydney—a fourteen-year-old girl— and she, her mom, grandma, Nicolai's trainer, owner, Lendon, Koryn and I paint our fingernails sparkly gold and call ourselves Team Gold.

As days pass, several of my Questers join Team Gold as well and by the day before the show begins, nearly all of them are members. Scott Hassler sends a photo proudly displaying his golden fingertips and Gib even paints his 'um nails. The most resistant person to join the Team is Jason, but before we crawl into bed, he at least lets Koryn paint one pinky.

◆ ◆ ◆

When I come out of my bedroom on the morning of show-day, Lendon's sitting on the couch and the first thing she says is, Know your test? As if I'm a ten-year-old doing my first competition. I smile and give her an *of course* expression.

We go to the show early to watch Sydney's ride—which gets a qualifying score so Team Gold is off to a stellar start—and in the time before I get on, Jason and I go for a walk. Although the extensive hallways in the Solana provide a perfect path for my walks, I want to take advantage of the added challenge of the uneven dirt footing full of hoofprints and hoses over which to navigate, so every day I walk the perimeter of the stabling as well. Upon our return, Lendon asks again, Know your test?

The plan is for Koryn to warm Nicolai up until ten minutes before my ride time. That will give me three minutes to get on, five to practice the things I know are difficult and two to walk from the warm-up to the showring. Hopefully little enough time to avoid Thumper.

As soon as my seat hits the saddle, Lendon asks *again*, Know your test? I assure her that I'll have plenty of time to think about it because it's all walk.

But I go off course in the very first movement. I'm supposed to turn right off the centerline, start across the diagonal and at X, turn up the centerline. But in warm-up I was practicing the two things I've consistently had difficulty with: turning right off centerline and free walking the diagonal from right to left. I did them together—repeatedly went right off the centerline to free walk on the diagonal—because I was trying to make the most of my few minutes before Thumper set in. So that's what's in my mind and that's what I do. Much to Lendon's chagrin.

And I guess ten minutes of warm-up is too long because Thumper goes crazy. Nicolai patiently ignores the annoying thumping on his side and, although I do the left volte too small, he goes exactly where I tell him to. He's a star.

I'm not nearly as close to him as I was to my previous show partners, but as we halt and salute my gratitude to him is overwhelming. I wish my right arm worked well enough to give him the pats he deserves, or at least to hold the reins while Lefty does. Instead I just lean forward and Lefty strokes his neck as far down as my body permits while he holds the reins.

I get a 62.7%, which isn't great but it's above the required 60% to make the Selection Trials, so although I'm disappointed in the test, at least the immense support to get me here wasn't in vain.

As soon as I get off, a classifier comes up and asks what I thought. I tell her that besides the embarrassment of going off course, I just don't know what to do about Thumper. I tried to keep my warm-up short to not tire the leg out but at this rate, it seems I just have to get on and go straight in the showring.

But, Courtney, I saw you walking for a long time this morning and that causes fatigue as well. This is competition. Get a wheelchair.

My jaw drops. How stupid of me. I've been doing a ton of walking, utilizing my ample time to work on my technique, trying to initiate muscle-memory. How did I not connect that to fatigue?

◆ ◆ ◆

So that evening I resort to using the wheelchair, which since I've been able to walk, I've detested. Other than appreciating the fact that it gives us the ability to get good seats at concerts and sporting events, I resent the feeling that it promotes my ailments and delays recovery. But now I welcome the rest it affords my leg. Three days won't make a big difference in the overall scheme of things anyway. Save therapy for when I'm done.

Thumper still appears in the Individual test but not nearly as continuously. And I stay on course. Added to these improvements, a suggestion Lendon made helps a great deal: she told me I had my reins too short. With Righty's inability to follow, this made Nicolai quite uncomfortable and he got a little twist in the neck. Plus I was telling him to go forward but holding him back. A longer rein eliminates the neck twist and encourages him to have a bigger walk which allows us to earn a 65.6%.

I write to my Questers saying that Team Gold is definitely working and maybe if more of them join, I'll get a 68% in the Freestlyle.

◆ ◆ ◆

I love my music. Marlene sent me several options and most were extremely boring—I couldn't see how you could provide excitement, show changes of feeling, of dynamics, when it's all one gait. The biggest change we show is going from medium walk to free walk. But then she sent me Kung Fu Panda and it made me smile the whole time. It does what Marlene tells me great Freestyle music should: it enhances the horse's movement. It provides a bit of bounce to the steps which adds a feeling of the energy we lack.

Not every horse would aptly fit the music but it suits the appearance of Nicolai's attitude: playful. He's round and wide with a relatively short neck and a perky expression. It wouldn't suit an elegant, streamlined horse with a big sweeping walk or one who appears regal like Idy, but it's perfect for Nicolai. Marlene refuses to charge me a cent for it, says it's my welcome back present.

The choreography is designed to avoid doing the things that are difficult for us so we never turn right off the centerline or do a free walk from right to left. I'm tempted to ride with a shorter rein to appear and feel more put together, but I know it's better to have a more relaxed topline and a bigger walk and risk appearing sloppy.

And the sacrifice pays off. Nicolai's walk is the most expressive it's been—I think he feeds off the music as much as I do. The test is smooth and flowing and perfectly on time. I have the most fun I've ever had in a Freestyle and win with a 69.4%.

Me on Nicolai with Koryn, Credit: Susan J. Stickle

More than anything else, I'm thrilled with the improvement. I know that right now I'm a terrible Para rider, but I was a terrible able-bodied rider at the beginning, too. My love to progress has been slightly sated with working on my recovery, but the meals of visible improvement have been so infrequent, it's becoming famished. Today is like Thanksgiving. I was able to drastically improve the score each day so my belly is full of the satisfaction of blatant improvement, and it's hungry for more.

· 81 ·

On the way home, I contemplate my life thus far. Some people believe that everything happens for a reason. When I was young, I believed that too, but time convinced me that we control our own destiny. We choose how to react—whether to focus on the negatives or the positives, whether to make the best of a situation or let it swallow us up—and that decides our course of action which leads us to the next step. But maybe they're right. Maybe it's all meant to be.

It's as if my whole life has been designed to accommodate a brain injury. My best friend is able to be with me twenty-four hours a day. I couldn't *design* a better personal assistant than my working student. My sister is extremely good at and takes as her own responsibility things I'm unable to do such as cleaning the house, packing and unpacking for my yearly trips to Florida, clothes shopping. I'm married to a wonderful man who loves me just as deeply and couldn't be any more perfect at caring for me. Financially, the public has made my medical care possible and my business is able to continue without my presence because my husband oversees the books, my mentor continues the training and my staff is exceptional in both work ethic and character.

Beyond the perfection of the people in my life, my own history has helped enormously in my current circumstances. The fact that I'm an Olympian (regardless of my disqualification) allows me to remain popular as a teacher and even got me special treatment from the doctors. If I'd just met my goal of being as good as an Olympic rider but hadn't gone to the Games, no one would have cared, but everyone views *an Olympian* as special. That I have that title made people interested when I was first injured, and perhaps my degree in Literature didn't help my career, but knowing how to write allowed me to share my journey. Which helped many people. Promoted safety. Instigated life-saving measures.

Made the world a tiny bit better.

Perhaps it was meant to be.

• 82 •

Courtney's Quest Continued

6/10/12

I was just wondering how Jason can be so patient with me, so unbelievably helpful. I'm amazed that the way I talk—like a three-year-old—and the fact that I can't go out the door alone, can hardly do anything alone, doesn't aggravate him. I wonder if I could be so patient. But then I remembered something I'd written in my old journal:

9/25/96

I've been very conscious lately of people with disabilities or disfigurements. I notice people in a wheelchair or with one arm or one walking oddly. I notice the mentally retarded, the ugly, the obese and literally feel a strain on my heart and tears in my nose. They must be so much stronger than I am. I think if that were me, I'd just live in my own self pity and almost embarrassment. It's horrible I know. I just get this overwhelming feeling of wanting to heal them. I want to give the chair-ridden a chance to run, to ride a horse. I want to give the walking dysfunctionals a chance to strut down the street. I want to give the ugly a chance to get whistled at, to be helped first because they're pretty. The obese I want to give the chance to be swung up into a man's arms or to be able to impress a girl with athleticism. I cried to see a man with one arm itch his hand with his teeth. I want to give him a chance to clap his hands to the music. I want to be able to see them all without noticing their disabilities.

I guess you don't know till it happens.

Epilogue

Although a rider is allowed to borrow a horse to qualify *for* the Selection Trials, they're required to compete the horse they'd take to the Games *at* them. Before I went to Houston, a trainer had called me and said she had the perfect horse for me to take: extremely quiet and excellent walk. So I tried him. I could easily do shoulder-in, haunches-in, half-pass, make the walk bigger or smaller. The riding was all easy, so my hippotherapy trainer came to test his temperament and concluded it was ideal.

So I went on a limb and asked Jane Clark, who'd been the USEF's biggest supporter for many years and had owned horses in several disciplines in every Olympic Games for as long as I can remember, to buy him for me. I'd known her casually for a long time and thought it may be something she'd be interested in. She said, Competing in able-bodied then Para in two consecutive Games? I don't think that's been done. Sounds like fun. So she bought Buddy, I changed his show name to Make Lemonade and got back into show mode.

But Buddy wasn't a Roxy. He had the training of a dressage horse but not the heart of a therapy horse and he quickly learned to take advantage of me. He insisted on walking very slowly and knew I wouldn't get after him for fear of instigating the bucking that was his reaction when Koryn did. So he'd completely ignore me, even learned he didn't have to go where I said. I decided not to go to the Selection Trials because not only did I know I wouldn't make the team, I questioned if I'd be safe. Jane donated him to a college and I learned that a well-trained dressage horse with a quiet temperament doesn't necessarily make a Para horse.

So I missed 2012. I was saddened but I knew I was very lucky to have even had a chance when I decided so late to try and I immediately set my sights on the 2014 WEGs. The answer to my quandary about finding a suitable Para horse, not just a quiet horse with a nice walk, miraculously appeared without any action from me at all. The owner of a mare who'd competed at Grade 1a in the 2008 Paralympic Games read about the Buddy saga on my blog, emailed me and said I could lease her for as long as I wanted. This was perfect, a proven Para horse. I couldn't believe my good fortune. But mid-way through the Florida season Rosie went lame.

As the weeks passed, I realized I was more upset about not being able to teach Koryn on Rosie than not being able to ride. Then it struck me. I'd assumed I wanted to ride because riding had always been my passion, but as I've said before, what I love about dressage is the constant ability to progress, and I get much more satisfaction from helping Koryn along than fighting with my belligerent body. There are some things it just can't do.

Koryn originally contacted me in the fall of 2009 asking if I'd take a working student. I said no, I can offer no riding but I'm hiring a groom if you want that position, fully expecting her to decline. To my surprise, she said great and joined me that winter in Florida, worked the whole season without placing her butt in the saddle. The only reason she started riding is because when my accident happened, there were too many horses for just Jennifer to ride. When I finally started teaching her in the summer, I found an exceptional student, absorbing everything I told her and making it her own.

I didn't realize it right away, but as she progressed it became clear: she's the only person I've taught whose body feels like an extension of my own. I tell her what to do and can feel her body do it exactly as mine would. I suppose in a way I'm riding vicariously through her, but more than that, I want to be her Lendon. She said she took the job simply because she knew she wanted to work *for me*. Perhaps like my gut insisting I go to Lendon allowed my future to be exceptional, her gut was leading her down the right path too because the opportunities she's gaining are nearly as incredible as the ones I got.

Alex wanted to sell Tomtom to buy me a Para horse, but when I told her my dream had changed, that developing Koryn was my passion, she said she'd buy a horse for Koryn instead. Francine breeds horses on the side and sent Koryn a fantastic young one. Then she decided to give us her own extremely nice nearly Grand Prix horse. Kim gave me a Grandioso baby and although that one's too young, she said she'd sell her and when the right one for Koryn comes along, she'll send that one. Debbie, Scott, Lendon, Steffen and many others have taught her and refused to charge. The people in my life astound me. They're making a group effort to help actualize my dream. Does the world ever stop giving to me?

I've come to accept that full recovery simply isn't going to happen no matter how hard I try, and like a five-foot-ten inch girl struggling to become a gymnast or a hundred-thirty pound man wanting to be a sumo wrestler, yearning to reach the Grand Prix ring again would be filling my life with pointless agony. So I've simply changed my dreams to be consistent with my abilities. I'll never drive again, run, dress or shower standing up, or spend a day and night alone. I still can't walk unassisted by either a cane or a person or speak properly, but I know I couldn't have tried any harder, so I can move forward with no regrets and just enjoy the immense amount of joys my life still holds.

I still put a great amount of effort into improving what I can, still do physical and occupational therapies, but I've decided to not sacrifice enjoying what I can in my current condition in a constant effort to become what I once was.

Although bringing Koryn along is my passion, I get a great amount of satisfaction teaching people in general, and being part of the Emerging Dressage Athletes Program provides me with a special joy as I hope to be able to help kids like me—those who have the painful yearning but not the opportunity to exercise it—fulfill their dreams. Finding and developing the youth who will become America's next generation of international riders is something I'd eventually have done anyway, I just happen to have gotten there sooner.

Beyond finding fulfillment in teaching, the influence of Riders4Helmets provides me with a sense of my life achieving a purpose. Countless lives have been saved because of the attention to safety it's provoked, and beyond the individuals it reaches, this attention to safety has instigated many rule changes both nationally and internationally. In 2011, the USEF passed a rule requiring all riders at a dressage show younger than eighteen years of age, as well as those of all ages showing at the national levels (levels below Prix St. Georges) or on non-competing horses, to wear approved protective headgear. Dressage Canada also made helmets mandatory for the national levels in 2011 and in 2012, it modified the rule to include the FEI Levels which are Prix St. Georges to Grand Prix. British Dressage also made a rule requiring helmets for the national levels in 2012. In 2013, the USEF expanded their rule requiring helmets at the national levels to include the FEI levels and the FEI itself, which is our international governing body, mandated that all dressage riders anywhere in the world who are competing in international, or CDI, classes wear a helmet when not in the show ring or in a final warm-up with no break before showing. They also require helmets to be worn by any rider on a horse below seven years of age. Many rule changes have been implemented in other disciplines as well since the creation of Riders4Helmets including eventing, competitive trail riding, hunters and jumpers.

Although Riders4Helmets and hence my accident aren't directly responsible for these changes, they enflamed the attention to safety enough to make it become a serious worldwide concern.

◆ ◆ ◆

I wrote this book because the public has shown me they're interested in my story and has been telling me for years I should write an autobiography. My response was always *I don't have time*, but the brain injury has not only made the story more interesting, it's allowed me to have the time. Time which would otherwise have terrified me.

Journal
2/18/99
My worry is that one day I'm gonna get all my shit done and have nothing to do. When I'm forty, I'll have a day off and realize I have absolutely nothing to do, nothing to get done, nothing to accomplish.

There are many days I'm left at home alone when Jason has to work, and the book has provided me with a task to accomplish. As only my left index finger was capable of typing, the book probably took much longer to complete, but that was fine with me.

As it neared completion, I was filled with anxiety of how I'd fill my days. So I started painting again. Lefty's taken over and this is his latest effort:

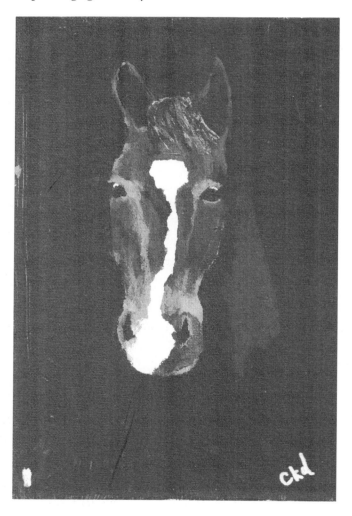

Harmony's Mythilus

I also signed up for a creative writing course because, although I can write about things that happened, I don't have an iota of imaginative creativity. I asked Daniel Wallace, the author of Big Fish, how he does it and he said, *Like anything, it takes practice.* Writing this book showed me how much I enjoy writing so I decided to start practicing.

And then something occurred which completely eliminates my fear: I'm pregnant! A little girl due February 24, 2014. My family may not grow every two years as Judith planned as I'm now thirty-six, but if we have as much luck as we had this time, Jason and I may get our intended four.

Blog
When Jason and I were trying, anxiety tainted my desire. I feared feeling like an incomplete mother: I'm not going to be able to dress the baby, do her hair, change her diapers, hold her, ever even be alone with her. What made me try is simply the realization that regret at not having a child at all would cause more sadness than would be created by my inability to be able to be completely involved.

But as soon as I knew I was pregnant, all anxiety disappeared. It's done, I'm pregnant, we'll make it work because there's no choice! Pure happiness is my only companion.

In many speeches I've announced that of course I wouldn't do it again but I'm extremely happy with the results my accident instigated. But I changed my mind. I *would* do it again. A great many good things have happened because of it and although my life is certainly different from what I imagined, it's no less fulfilling. I can't imagine being happier.

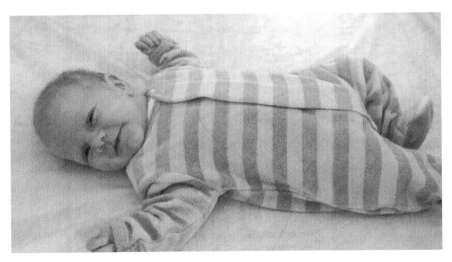

River Madison Dye, five days old

Acknowledgements

I have a great many people to thank:. My opinion-reader, Margaret A. Watson Ed. D., who gave me great insights and told me where feeling was lacking. The many people who read bits and pieces to check their accuracy including Rick Mitchell, Steffen Peters, Debbie McDonald, Jim Wolf and Joann Benjamin. Lendon Gray who gave me sound advice on my many small quandaries. Bernadette Szost who guided me through the whole publishing process and whose company designed the gorgeous cover. Richard Kelley whose professional expertise was both well-thought-out and understanding of my particular situation and desires. My initial proofreader, Jennifer Hippensteel, who read this book several times to check for mistakes and Margaret Freeman, my final proofreader, whose professionalism allowed me to feel comfortable that this book was fit to publish. The many photographers—Sue Stickle, Mary Phelps, Terri Miller, Sara Lieser, Sharon Packer, Stacie Lynch and Judy Bosco—who permitted me to use their wonderful photos which helped add life to the story. Beth Baumert, the person I unfairly hired initially to be my ghostwriter, who's been incredibly understanding and supportive. Daniel Wallace also has my eternal gratitude as he's advised me and given me feedback every step of the way, answered all my annoying emails, shared his professional wisdom and taken time out of his busy schedule to read my work.

The deepest gratitude I need to express is to the public as they've given me a reason to document details of every stage in my life. When I was young, I kept personal journals to express my angst, and of course the angst stopped when I got married—the last entry is six days before my wedding—so without the public, recording the details of my life would have stopped. They gave me a reason to write about my thoughts, feelings and experiences at Young Riders, Schumacher's, the two World Cups, the Olympics and through my efforts going for the Paralympics. And their constant caring convinced me to keep my blog which I still do today nearly four years after my accident. Without these records, many in-the-moment feelings and details would have disappeared from my memory and this book would never have existed. So thank you.

About the Author

Courtney King Dye began riding horses at nine years old and went on to represent the United States at the 2007 and 2008 World Cups aboard Idocus and at the 2008 Beijing Olympics aboard Harmony's Mythilus.

In 2010, she sustained a traumatic brain injury when a horse she was riding tripped and fell, and her accident provoked world-wide attention to helmet use as well as instigating many rule changes requiring approved headgear in several equestrian disciplines.

She continues to teach dressage lessons and has become an active supporter of the next generation of international riders. She lives with her husband and daughter in New Milford, Connecticut.

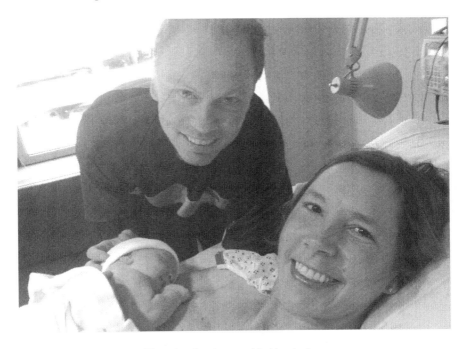

First family photo on birthing bed